CW01333067

THE SLOW COOKER COOKBOOK

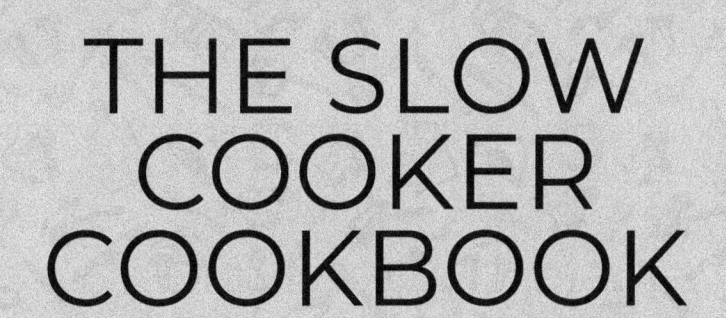

600 FLAVORFUL RECIPES. PREP FAST AND COOK SLOW YOUR HEALTHY DAILY MEALS, FROM BREAKFAST TO DESSERT

Vivian Bayne

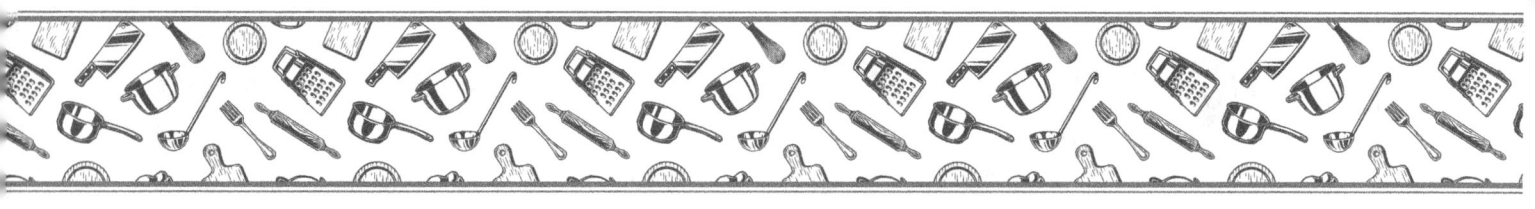

Copyright - 2020 -

All rights reserved.

The content contained within this book may not be reproduced, duplicated or transmitted without direct written permission from the author or the publisher.

Under no circumstances will any blame or legal responsibility be held against the publisher, or author, for any damages, reparation, or monetary loss due to the information contained within this book. Either directly or indirectly.

Legal Notice:

This book is copyright protected. This book is only for personal use. You cannot amend, distribute, sell, use, quote or paraphrase any part, or the content within this book, without the consent of the author or publisher.

Disclaimer Notice:

Please note the information contained within this document is for educational and entertainment purposes only. All effort has been executed to present accurate, up to date, and reliable, complete information. No warranties of any kind are declared or implied. Readers acknowledge that the author is not engaging in the rendering of legal, financial, medical or professional advice. The content within this book has been derived from various sources. Please consult a licensed professional before attempting any techniques outlined in this book.

By reading this document, the reader agrees that under no circumstances is the author responsible for any losses, direct or indirect, which are incurred as a result of the use of information contained within this document, including, but not limited to, - errors, omissions, or inaccuracies.

TABLE OF CONTENTS

INTRODUCTION   4

CHAPTER 1. HOW TO USE THE SLOW COOKER, TIPS AND TRICKS   6

CHAPTER 2. BREAKFAST   9

CHAPTER 3. SNACKS & APPETIZERS   40

CHAPTER 4. RICE, GRAINS & BEANS   68

CHAPTER 5. SIDE DISHES   97

CHAPTER 6. POULTRY   124

CHAPTER 7. MEAT   154

CHAPTER 8. FISH AND SEAFOOD   184

CHAPTER 9. VEGETABLES AND VEGETARIAN   212

CHAPTER 10. BEVERAGES   241

CHAPTER 11. SOUPS STEWS AND CHILIES   249

CHAPTER 12. SWEETS AND DESSERTS   272

CONCLUSION   304

INDEX OF RECIPES AT THE END OF THE BOOK

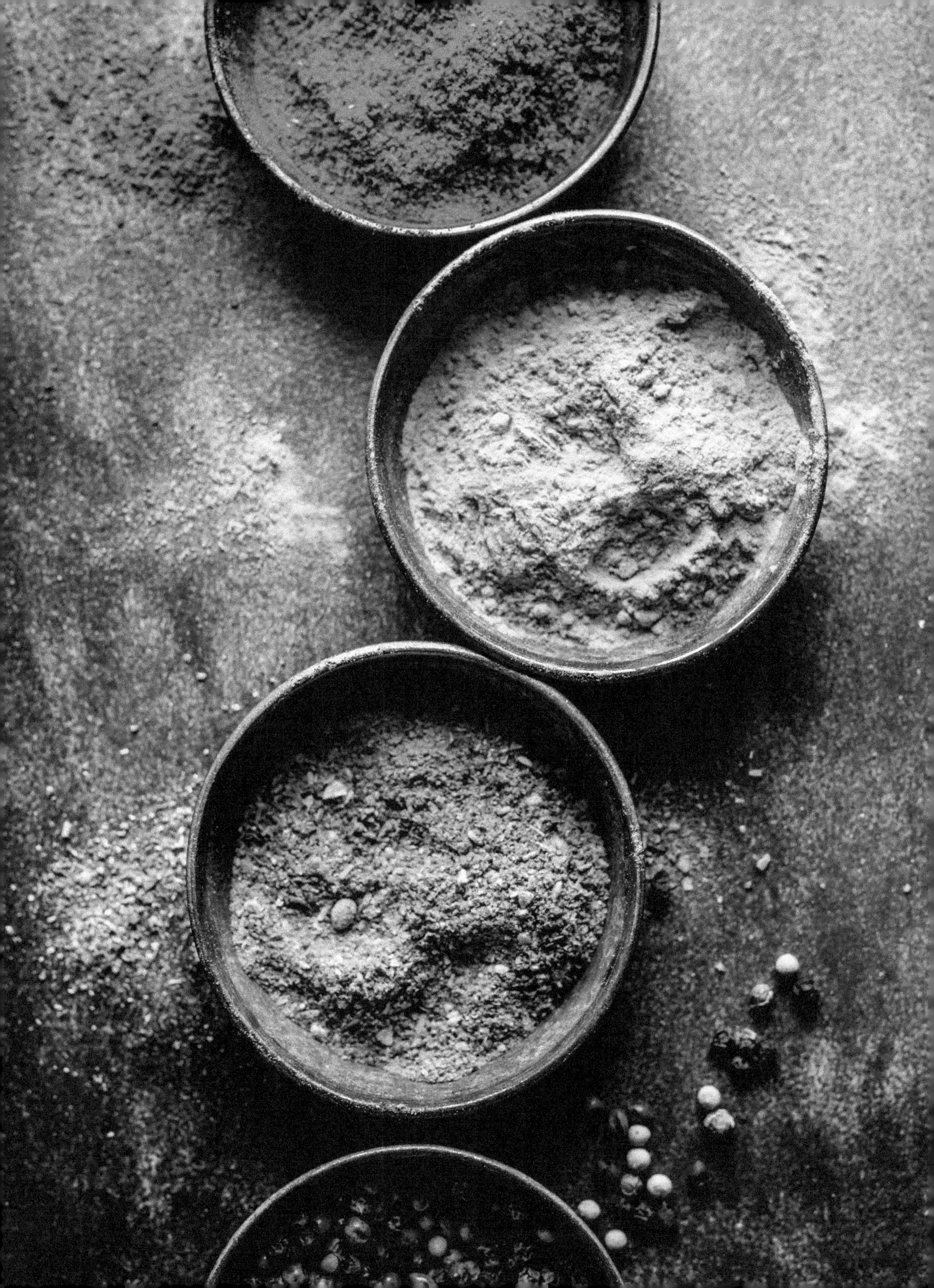

INTRODUCTION

The idea of slow cooking has been there since the beginning of human history. Even before slow cookers were invented, people in every part of the world were aware of this method of preparing food.

There are many benefits of slow cooking, which is why it is still popular to date. So how did this technique come into use? It started primarily in Germany in the 16th century. At that time, the kitchens did not have any heating device. Therefore the food was cooked on top of wood, coal, or charcoal, just like preparing our meals at night. To prepare meals for the next day early in the morning, people brought in heavy vessels.

Modern slow cookers were invented in the late 19th century as a countertop heating device for cooking. They were designed to cook food longer and also to enhance it with more flavor. Slow cookers started to gain popularity in the US in the 1940s, as women who started working outside their home could not spend the whole day cooking and saw the advantages of setting the meal up in the morning, letting it cook throughout the day. In 1971 the slow cooker continued to gain popularity after it was introduced under the Crock-Pot name. It had a heating element in the body along with a container in which people could put ingredients. He put the idea into the public domain and made people aware of slow cooking. Crock-Pot's word was actually a mispronunciation of the word crock, which means a large, heavy cooking pot. The inventors explained that the device was light on the countertop as it had a one-way vent. In 1990, it was changed completely, and the word Crock-Pot was made popular.

Slow cookers have been changing overtime for the past 40 years. It is now more energy efficient as it uses 25%-30% less energy than conventional cooking methods. It is cheaper than other ways as it is more economical. The slow cooker dish is not time-consuming as it doesn't require a lot of preparation time.

Nowadays, slow cookers have become a popular appliance because of some other unique advantages. There are many slow cookers in the market, and all come with a digital timer, which helps count the cooking time, an automatic warning device to deactivate on low steaming and electrical shock. They also have a dual button, which can be used to switch between high and low power settings and a feature to keep the lid closed and sealed when cooking.

WHY SLOW COOKING?

The main reason for slow cooking is to cook food for a longer time. It is a health factor that helps in maintaining the freshness of the food. It keeps the food tender and can be cooked in larger quantities. The food tastes different after cooking for a long time. It keeps all flavors intact and makes the food grains and fats to be melt-in-mouth. The slow cooker has an advantage when cooking ready meals and several dishes such as pizza, casseroles, soups, etc.

The benefits include the fact that by cooking food at a slower speed longer, the moisture loss is less. It also prevents over-cooking. The slow cooker is more economical than other cooking methods. It will cook food on a lower heat for a long time for the same power. Slow cookers are suitable for people who are not that confident with cooking, but can also be a wonderful kitchen gadget for expert chefs. You can use the slow cooker for preparing dinner ahead of time and enjoy the benefits of slow cooking. A slow cooker will take the responsibility of a whole cooked dinner.

Due to its versatility, it has become a favorite for many people, including the author of this book. Simply put, in a slow cooker, you simply have to add ingredients and then let them cook. You can use it for cooking breakfast foods, soups, stews, and starchy foods.

There are 600 different slow cooker recipes available in this cookbook, which are tried and tested. We will be starting with breakfast and brunch, to end on a sweet note with desserts. My goal here is to help the readers understand the main advantages and techniques of slow cooking and learn how to appreciate this kitchen wonder's versatility. I truly hope that reading this book will open up a whole new world for you, as discovering slow-cooking did for me many years ago. This book is a one-stop solution for all the slow cooker recipes. It will make your life easier and your food tastier. So, with all that said, happy slow cooking!

BENEFITS OF SLOW COOKING

When I first started using a slow cooker to prepare my daily meals, I was mainly attracted by this kitchen appliance's flexibility. At the time, I had a very busy life, leaving very little time to cook for my family and me. I soon discovered that besides its versatility, the slow cooker allowed me to bring out the flavors hidden in many of the ingredients that I used for my meals. That's when I decided to start writing down my recipes, leading to the creation fo this book many years later.

Here below, I'm listing some of the main features/benefits of slow cooking. You'll find many more listed throughout the book and in the recipes.

- Slow cooking is one of the healthiest ways to cook meat. When we cook the meat over high heat, the meat's fats and protein interact with harmful compounds. This doesn't happen with a slow cooker.

- Slow cooker brings out flavors in foods, and you can cook a wide variety of foods. Veggies prepared in slow cookers can deliver disease-fighting nutrients.

- The slow cooker is ideal for cooking cheaper cuts like pork shoulder, chicken thighs, lamb shoulder and beef brisket.

- The slow cooker helps to make the meat soften and tender. When cooked properly, the meat will literally fall off the bone.

- The slow cooker was designed to cook a lot of food at once, so you can make big recipes or double batches for dinner and tomorrow's lunch.

- As you'll see in the recipes, the slow cooker can make just about everything. That simplifies the whole "healthy cooking" process, and just makes life way easier. You're a busy person with deadlines and commitments, and you don't want to have to use a bunch of different devices for cooking different meals. With the slow cooker, you can make everything from eggs to cakes.

- Complimentary spices and herbs are best to add near the end of cooking. In addition, thickeners such as corn starch and tomato paste are used to give the dish's texture.

- Ingredients can be taken directly from the refrigerator and placed in a slow cooker. This will cause extended cooking times, but it's super convenient when trying to prep a meal in a hurry. General rule: Always thaw ingredients, but if for some reason you have to use frozen beef (small pieces), add at least 1 cup of warm liquid to the cooker prior to adding the beef to help prevent sudden temperature changes and longer cooking times.

- The slow cooker is also ideal for cooking dried beans. You just need to add some water and beans and forget it for 8 to 9 hours. Using this, we can avoid canned beans.

- Vegetables cooked in a slow cooker can absorb spices and stock, giving a fuller flavor.

CHAPTER 1.
HOW TO USE THE SLOW COOKER, TIPS AND TRICKS

Slow cookers have changed a lot over the years. These days you can purchase models that range from very simple models all the way to ones that look like they should be on a space station. When buying the right model for your needs, you have to consider what you are cooking, how many portions, and if you will be home during the cooking process. All these factors are important when deciding on your slow cooker's size, shape, and features.

SIZE AND SHAPE

Slow cookers come in a multitude of sizes and shapes, so it is important to consider your needs and what will work best for the type of food prepared. There are models that range from ½-quart to large 8-quart models and everything in-between.

The small slow cookers (½-quart to 2-quart) are usually used for dips or sauces, as well as recipes designed for one person. Medium-sized slow cookers (3-quart to 4-quart) are great for baking or for meals that create food for two to three people. The slow cooker recommended for most of the recipes in this book is the 5-quart to 6-quart model because it is perfect for the large cuts of meat and can prepare food for four people, including leftovers. The enormous 7-quart to 8-quart appliance is meant for very large meals. If you have money in your budget, owning both a 3-quart and 6-quart model would be the best of both worlds.

When it comes to shapes, you will have to decide between round, oval, and rectangular. Round slow cookers are fine for stews and chili but do not work well for large pieces of meat. These should probably not be your choice. Oval and rectangular slow cookers both allow for the ingredients you will use regularly that are large, like roasts, ribs, and chops, and have the added advantage of fitting loaf pans, ramekins, and casserole dishes, as well. Some desserts and breads are best cooked in another container placed in the slow cooker, and you will see several recipes in this book that use that technique.

FEATURES

Now that you know the recommended slow cooker's size and shape, it is time to consider what you want this appliance to do for you. Depending on your budget, at a minimum you want a slow cooker with temperature controls that cover warm, low, and high, as well as a removable insert. These are the primary features of the bare-bones models that will get the job done. However, if you want to truly experience a set-it-and-forget-it appliance that creates the best meals possible in this cooking environment, you might want to consider the following features:

Digital programmable controls: You can program temperature, when the slow cooker starts, how long it cooks, and when the slow cooker switches to warm.

Glass lid: These are heavier and allow you to look into the slow cooker without removing them, so there is little heat loss. Opt for a lid with clamps, and you can transport your cooked meal easily to parties and gatherings if needed.

Temperature probe: Once you have a slow cooker with this feature, you will wonder how you cooked previously without it. The temperature probe allows you to cook your meat, poultry, and egg dishes to an exact temperature and then switches to warm when completed.

Precooking feature: Some models have a precooking feature that allows you to brown your meat and poultry right in the insert. You will still have to take the time to do this step, but you won't have a skillet to clean afterward.

TAKING CARE OF YOUR SLOW COOKER

- Thaw frozen poultry and meat in the refrigerator before cooking in the slow cooker. Do not put frozen meat in a slow cooker.

- Vegetables cook slower in the slow cooker compared to meat and poultry. Place the vegetables first and second, put the meat over it and at last top it with broth, sauce or water.

- Always put your slow cooker on high for the first hour then turn the setting high to low until you finish cooking.

- To prevent curdling, add cheese, cream and milk during the last hour

- Soft vegetables such as zucchini, tomatoes, and mushrooms are added when 45 minutes of cooking remaining

- Fill the slow cooker no less than half full and not more than 2/3 full. Too much and too little food in a slow cooker affects cooking safety, cooking time and cooking quality.

- For easily clean the slow cooker use spray or oil, spray the slow cooker inside with nonstick cooking spray.

- Slow Cooker vs. Pressure Cooker

- Time: When a pressure cooker cooks food in 50 minutes, a slow cooker takes 8 hours

- Texture: Carrots cooked in a pressure cooker come out mushy and soft whereas a slow cooker maintains their shape and texture

- Taste: Gravy cooked about 8 hours in the slow cooker is richer and tastier than gravy made in a pressure cooker

TIPS FOR SLOW-COOKING SUCCESS

Slow cookers are simple to use, but you can increase your success with a few tips and techniques. Some tips are suggestions in the following list, and some should be considered more seriously for safety or health reasons. The intent is to provide the best information possible so that your meals are delicious and easy.

ALWAYS

Read the user manual and any other literature. You will find an assortment of instructions included in the slow-cooker box, so take the time to sit down and read everything completely before using a new device. You might think you know how everything works, but each model is a little different, and it is best to be informed about all of the things your slow cooker can do.

Grease the insert of the slow cooker before cooking. Cleaning a slow cooker insert can be a challenge, so grease the insert, even for soups and stews. You don't want to scrub the insert with abrasive brushes or scraping bits of cooked-on food off, because you will wreck its nonstick surface.

Add dairy and herbs at the end of the cooking process. As stated earlier in this book, dairy and fresh herbs do not hold up well during long cooking times. Dairy splits and creates a grainy, unpleasant texture, and herbs lose their flavor, color, and texture. Always add these ingredients at the end.

Always cut your ingredients into similar-sized pieces. Slow cookers are not meant to be used for staggered cooking recipes such as stir-fries, where the more delicate ingredients are added last to avoid overcooking. Evenly sized pieces mean your ingredients will be ready at the same time, and your meals will be cooked evenly.

Adjust your seasonings. Slow cookers can have an unexpected effect on herbs and spices so it is important to taste and adjust at the end of the process. Some spices, such as curry or cayenne, can get more intense, while the long cooking time can reduce the impact of dried herbs. It is best to hold off on too much salt until the very end as well, because it will get stronger.

NEVER

Use frozen meats or poultry. The ingredients in slow cookers need to reach 140°F within 4 hours for food safety, so large cuts of meat or poultry should be fully thawed. You can add small frozen items like meatballs to a slow cooker because these can come to temperature within this time range.

Place your insert right from the refrigerator into the slow cooker. When you remove your previously prepared meal from the refrigerator, let the insert sit out at room temperature for 30 minutes or so to avoid cracking it with extreme temperature changes. Also, never remove the hot insert from your slow cooker and place it on a cold surface.

Resume cooking after a power outage of over two hours. Power outages can happen in any season, and for food-safety reasons, you have to err on the side of caution. If an outage lasts for more than two hours, especially during the first few hours of cooking, you need to discard the food because the amount of time spent in the food danger zone (40°F to 140°F) will have been too long. If the outage is less than two hours and it occurs after your food has been cooking for at least four hours, then you can resume cooking until the end of the original time or transfer the food to a pot or casserole dish and finish it on the stove or in the oven. When in doubt, throw the food out.

Use the recommended cooking times in high altitudes. As with most other cooking methods, slow cookers need more cooking time if you live above an altitude of 3,000 feet. The liquid in the slow cooker will simmer at a lower temperature, so high-heat settings are recommended, or if you can program the slow cooker, then set it to maintain the food at 200°F or higher. You can also use a temperature probe set to 165°F internal temperature if your slow cooker has this feature.

CHAPTER 1.
BREAKFAST

1. ZUCCHINI & SPINACH WITH BACON

PREPARATION: 10 MIN   **COOKING:** 6 H   **SERVINGS:** 4

INGREDIENTS

- 8 slices bacon
- 1 tablespoon olive oil
- 4 medium zucchinis, cubed
- 2 cups baby spinach
- 1 red onion, diced
- 6 garlic cloves, sliced thin
- 1 cup chicken broth
- salt and pepper to taste

DIRECTIONS

1. Warm-up olive oil in a pan, brown the bacon for 5 minutes. Break it into pieces in the pan. Place remaining ingredients in the slow cooker, pour the bacon and fat from the pan over the fixing inside the slow cooker. Cover, cook on low for 6 hours.

Nutrition: *Calories: 290 Carbs: 16g Fat: 20g Protein: 12g*

2. PEPPERONI PIZZA WITH MEAT CRUST

PREPARATION: 10 MIN   **COOKING:** 6 H   **SERVINGS:** 4

INGREDIENTS

- 2.2. pounds lean ground beef
- 2 garlic cloves, minced
- 1 tablespoon dry, fried onions
- salt and pepper to taste
- 2 cups shredded mozzarella
- 1 ¾ cup sugarless ready-made pizza sauce
- 2 cups shredded yellow cheese, cheddar
- ½ cup sliced pepperoni

DIRECTIONS

1. Brown the beef with the seasoning in a pan. Mix the beef with the cheese. Butter the slow cooker and spread the crust out evenly over the bottom.
2. Pour the pizza sauce over the crust and spread evenly. Top with the cheese and arrange the pepperoni slices. Cover, cook on low for 4 hours. Serve.

Nutrition: *Calories: 320 Carbs: 31g Fat: 16g Protein: 15g*

3. SPINACH & SAUSAGE PIZZA

PREPARATION: 5 MIN   **COOKING:** 6 H   **SERVINGS:** 4

INGREDIENTS

- 1 tablespoon olive oil
- 1 cup lean ground beef
- 2 cups spicy pork sausage
- 2 garlic cloves, minced
- 1 tablespoon dry, fried onions
- salt and pepper to taste
- 1 ¾ cups sugarless ready-made pizza sauce
- 3 cups fresh spinach
- ½ cup sliced pepperoni
- ¼ cup pitted black olives, sliced
- ¼ cup sun-dried tomatoes, chopped
- ½ cup spring onions, chopped
- 3 cups shredded mozzarella

DIRECTIONS

1. In a pan, heat the olive oil. Brown the beef, then the pork. Drain the oil off the meat, then mix. Pour the meat into the slow cooker.
2. Spread evenly and press down. Alternate in layers the pizza sauce, toppings, and cheese. Cover and cook on low within 4-6 hours. Serve.

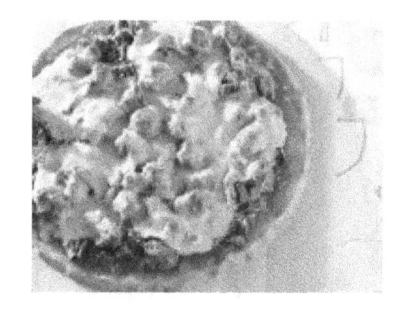

Nutrition: *Calories: 314 Carbs: 34g Fat: 12g Protein: 17g*

---

4. GREEK-STYLE FRITTATA WITH SPINACH AND FETA CHEESE

PREPARATION: 10 MIN   **COOKING:** 4 H   **SERVINGS:** 4

INGREDIENTS

- 2 cups spinach, fresh or frozen
- 8 eggs, lightly beaten
- 1 cup plain yogurt
- 1 small onion, cut into small pieces
- 2 red roasted peppers, peeled
- 1 garlic clove, crushed
- 1 cup feta cheese, crumbled
- 2 tablespoons softened butter
- 2 tablespoons olive oil
- salt and pepper to taste
- 1 teaspoon dried oregano

DIRECTIONS

1. Sauté the onion and garlic for 5 minutes. Add the spinach, heat for an additional 2 minutes. Let the mixture cool down.
2. Roast the red peppers in a dry pan or under the broiler. Peel them and cut them into small pieces.
3. Beat the eggs, yogurt, and seasoning in a separate bowl. Combine well. Add the peppers and the onion mixture. Mix again.
4. Crumble the feta cheese using a fork, add it to the frittata. Grease the bottom and sides of the slow cooker with butter. Pour the mixture into it. Cover, cook on low for 4 hours.

Nutrition: *Calories: 206 Carbs: 13g Fat: 13g Protein: 11g*

5. NUT & ZUCCHINI BREAD

PREPARATION: 10 MIN   **COOKING:** 3 H   **SERVINGS:** 4

INGREDIENTS

- 2 cups shredded zucchini
- ½ cup ground walnuts
- 1 cup ground almonds
- 1/3 cup coconut flakes
- 2 teaspoons cinnamon
- ½ teaspoon baking soda
- 1 ½ teaspoons baking powder
- ½ teaspoon salt
- 3 large eggs
- 1/3 cup softened coconut oil
- 1 cup sweetener, Swerve (or a suitable substitute)
- 2 teaspoons vanilla

DIRECTIONS

1. Shred the zucchini and ground the walnuts. In a bowl, beat the eggs, oil, sweetener, and vanilla together.
2. Add the dry ingredients to the wet mixture. Fold in the zucchini and walnuts. Pour the batter into your bread pan, which fits inside the slow cooker.
3. Crumble aluminum foil into four balls, place on the bottom of the slow cooker, and set the pan in the slow cooker with a paper towel on top to absorb the water—cook on high for 3 hours. Cool, wrap in foil, and refrigerate. Serve cold with tea or coffee.

Nutrition: *Calories: 90 Carbs: 12g Fat: 4g Protein: 1g*

---

6. CHEESE & CAULIFLOWER BAKE

PREPARATION: 5 MIN   **COOKING:** 4 H   **SERVINGS:** 4

INGREDIENTS

- 1 head cauliflower, cut into florets
- ½ cup cream cheese
- ¼ cup whipping cream
- 2 tablespoons lard or butter
- 1 tablespoon lard or butter to grease the slow cooker
- 1 teaspoon salt
- ½ teaspoon fresh ground black pepper
- ½ cup yellow cheese, cheddar, shredded
- 6 slices of bacon, crisped and crumbled

DIRECTIONS

1. Grease the slow cooker. Add all the fixing, except the cheese and the bacon. Cook on low for 3 hours. Open the lid and add cheese. Re-cover, cook for an additional hour. Top with the bacon and serve.

Tip: Good for brunch with a couple of cherry tomatoes and avocado slices.

Nutrition: *Calories: 178 Carbs: 8g Fat: 11g Protein: 5g*

7. HAM & CHEESE BROCCOLI BRUNCH BOWL

PREPARATION: 5 MIN **COOKING:** 8 H **SERVINGS:** 4

INGREDIENTS

- 1 medium head of broccoli, chopped small
- 4 cups vegetable broth
- 2 tablespoons olive oil
- 1 teaspoon mustard seeds, ground
- 3 garlic cloves, minced
- salt and pepper to taste
- 2 cups cheddar cheese, shredded
- 2 cups ham, cubed
- pinch of paprika

DIRECTIONS

1. Add all ingredients to the 6-quart slow cooker in order of the list. Cover, cook on low for 8 hours.

Nutrition: *Calories: 320 Carbs: 28g Fat: 17g Protein: 14g*

8. EGGPLANT & SAUSAGE BAKE

PREPARATION: 10 MIN **COOKING:** 4 H **SERVINGS:** 4

INGREDIENTS

- 2 cups eggplant, cubed, salted, and drained
- 1 tablespoon olive oil
- 2 pounds spicy pork sausage
- 1 tablespoon Worcestershire sauce
- 1 tablespoon mustard
- 2 regular cans Italian diced tomatoes
- 1 jar tomato passata
- 2 cups mozzarella cheese, shredded

DIRECTIONS

1. Grease the slow cooker with olive oil. Mix the sausage, Worcestershire sauce, and mustard. Pour the mixture into the slow cooker.
2. Top the meat mixture with eggplant. Pour the tomatoes over the batter, sprinkle with grated cheese. Cover, cook on low for 4 hours. Enjoy for brunch.

Nutrition: *Calories: 345 Carbs: 34g Fat: 15g Protein: 21g*

9. THREE-CHEESE ARTICHOKE HEARTS BAKE

PREPARATION: 5 MIN **COOKING:** 2 H **SERVINGS:** 4

INGREDIENTS

- 1 cup cheddar cheese, grated
- ½ cup dry parmesan cheese
- 1 cup cream cheese
- 1 cup spinach, chopped
- 1 clove of garlic, crushed
- 1 jar artichoke hearts, chopped
- salt and pepper to taste

DIRECTIONS

1. Place all the ingredients in the 6-quart slow cooker. Mix lightly. Cover, cook on high for 2 hours. Serve.

Nutrition: *Calories: 40 Carbs: 7g Fat: 0g Protein: 2g*

10. SWEET HAM MAPLE BREAKFAST

PREPARATION: 15 MIN **COOKING:** 3-4 H **SERVINGS:** 4

INGREDIENTS

- 3-pound fully-cooked boneless ham
- ½ cup of maple syrup
- ½ cup of Honey Dijon Mustard
- ½ cup of packed brown sugar

DIRECTIONS

1. Make cross-shaped diagonal patterns on the ham with a knife and place them into a slow cooker. In a large bowl, whisk together the rest of the ingredients and pour over the ham.
2. Cover and cook on low within 3-4 hours. Take the ham out and cover with foil for 10 minutes. Slice and serve.

Nutrition: *Calories: 430 Fat: 24g Protein: 32g Carbs: 13g*

11. SAUSAGE CASSEROLE BREAKFAST

PREPARATION: 15 MIN **COOKING:** 4-5 H **SERVINGS:** 4

INGREDIENTS

- 8 large eggs
- 1 ½ cups of low-fat milk
- 1 pound of cooked bulk sausage, drained
- 1 seeded and chopped jalapeño
- 1 chopped red bell pepper
- ¾ cup sliced green onions
- 2 cups of low-fat Mexican blend cheese
- 9 corn tortillas
- ½ cup of salsa

DIRECTIONS

1. Mix the eggs, jalapeño, and milk in a large bowl. In another large bowl, combine the cheese, green onions, sausage, and red bell pepper.
2. Arrange 3 tortillas on the base of a greased slow cooker. Spread a layer of the sausage mixture over the tortillas.
3. Repeat the layering, and then pour the egg mixture over the top. Cover and cook on low within 4-5 hours. Divide onto plates and serve with the salsa.

Nutrition: *Calories: 386 Fat: 24g Fiber: 2.6g Protein: 24.7g*

12. MUSHROOM BACON BREAKFAST

PREPARATION: 15 MIN **COOKING:** 4-6 H **SERVINGS:** 4

INGREDIENTS

- 2 cups of ground sausage, cooked
- ½ cup of chopped onion
- 1 tablespoon of dried parsley
- 1 teaspoon of garlic powder
- 1 teaspoon of thyme
- 6 slices of bacon, cooked and crumbled
- 2 cups of organic chicken broth
- 1 red bell pepper, chopped
- ½ cup of parmesan cheese
- 1 cup of heavy cream
- 2 cups of sliced mushrooms
- Salt and black pepper

DIRECTIONS

1. Place all of the fixings into a large slow cooker. Cook within 4-6 hours on a low setting.
2. Ensure that you don't overcook the ingredients or cook the food at too high heat. It will cause the cream to separate. When the food is cooked, divide onto plates and serve hot.

Nutrition: *Calories: 166 Carbs: 2.1g Fat: 15.5g Fiber: 0.3g Protein: 6.7g*

13. ZUCCHINI CINNAMON NUT BREAD

PREPARATION: 15 MIN   **COOKING:** 3 H   **SERVINGS:** 4

INGREDIENTS

- 2 cups of zucchini, shredded
- ½ cup of ground walnuts
- 1 cup of ground almonds
- 1/3 cup of coconut flakes
- 2 teaspoons of cinnamon
- ½ teaspoon of baking soda
- 1 ½ teaspoon of baking powder
- ½ teaspoon of salt
- 3 large eggs
- 1/3 cup of softened coconut oil
- 1 cup of sweetener of your choice
- 2 teaspoons of vanilla

DIRECTIONS

1. In a large bowl, beat the vanilla, sweetener, oil, and eggs and whisk them together thoroughly. Add all of the dry fixings to the egg mixture. Add the walnuts and the zucchini.
2. You will need a bread pan that is small enough to fit into the slow cooker. Pour the batter into it. Roll up aluminum foil into four balls and set them on the base of the slow cooker.
3. Put the pan into your slow cooker and place a paper towel over the top to absorb condensation. Cook on high for 3 hours.
4. Allow the bread to cool down, wrap it in foil and place it in the fridge. Serve cold with coffee or tea.

Nutrition: *Calories: 210 Carbs: 4g Protein: 5g Fat: 18g*

---

14. HAM AND SPINACH FRITTATA

PREPARATION: 15 MIN   **COOKING:** 2 H   **SERVINGS:** 4

INGREDIENTS

- 10 large eggs
- ½ diced green bell pepper, diced
- 1 cup of ham, diced
- 2 handfuls of fresh spinach
- Salt and pepper

DIRECTIONS

1. Put a parchment liner in your slow cooker and grease it with non-stick cooking spray. Put the peppers, spinach, and ham into the slow cooker.
2. Whisk the eggs into your large bowl. Add salt and pepper, and then pour the eggs into the slow cooker.
3. Cook the ingredients on high for 1 ½ to 2 hours. Slice the frittata, divide onto plates, and serve.

Nutrition: *Calories: 109 Fat: 6.9g Carbs: 1.8g Protein: 5.6g*

15. CHEESE GRITS

PREPARATION: 5 MIN   **COOKING:** 5-7 H   **SERVINGS:** 4

INGREDIENTS

- 1/2 cup stone-ground grits
- 5-6 cups of water
- 2 tsp salt
- 1/2 cup Cheddar cheese (shredded)
- 6 tbsp butter
- Black pepper (optionally)

DIRECTIONS

1. Preheat slow cooker on low, spray the dish with cooking spray, or cover with butter. In a wide bowl, mix grits and water, add salt. Cook on low temperatures for 5-7 hours; you can leave it overnight.
2. Remove the dish from the slow cooker, cover butter on top. Stir with the whisk to an even consistency and fully melted butter.
3. To serve, sprinkle more cheese on top and black pepper to your taste. Serve warm.

Nutrition: *Calories: 173 Fat: 7g Carbs: 4g Protein: 6g*

16. PINEAPPLE CAKE WITH PECANS

PREPARATION: 10 MIN   **COOKING:** 4 H   **SERVINGS:** 4

INGREDIENTS

- 2 cups of sugar
- 2 cups plain flour
- 2 eggs
- 4 tbsp vegetable oil
- 1 can pineapple with juice (crushed)
- 1 tsp baking soda
- 1 tsp vanilla extract
- Salt

For icing:
- 1 cup of sugar
- 1/2 cup butter
- 6 tbsp evaporated milk
- 3 tbsp shredded coconut
- 1/2 cup chopped pecans (toasted)

DIRECTIONS

1. Preheat your slow cooker to 180-200°F. Take a medium bowl and combine all cake ingredients.
2. Mix the dough until evenly combined and then pour into slow cooker dish. Bake for 3 hours on high; check if it is ready with a wooden toothpick.
3. When the cake is ready, make the icing: in a medium saucepan, combine sugar, evaporated milk, butter, and salt. Bring to boil, and then simmer with a lower heat for 10 minutes.
4. Add the coconut to the icing. Put the icing over the hot cake, then sprinkle with nuts. To serve, let the cake cool, then cut it and serve with your favorite drinks.

Nutrition: *Calories: 291 Fat: 7g Carbs: 6g Protein: 5g*

17. POTATO CASSEROLE FOR BREAKFAST

PREPARATION: 5 MIN   **COOKING:** 4 H   **SERVINGS:** 4

INGREDIENTS

- 4 big potatoes
- 5-6 sausages
- 1/2 cup cheddar cheese (shredded)
- 1/2 cup mozzarella cheese
- 5-6 green onions
- 10 chicken eggs
- 1/2 cup milk
- Salt
- Black pepper

DIRECTIONS

1. Preheat slow cooker on low; spray its dish with non-stick cooking spray. Rub the potatoes into small pieces and put them into the dish.
2. Cover the potatoes with rubbed sausages. Add both mozzarella, cheddar cheeses, and green onions. Continue the layers until all space in the dish is full.
3. Mix the wet ingredients (milk, eggs) in a medium bowl. Pour it into the main dish, then put salt and pepper. Leave to cook on low for 5 hours or until the eggs are set. Serve with guacamole or green onions.

Nutrition: *Calories: 190 Fat: 10g Carbs: 5g Protein: 10g*

18. CINNAMON ROLLS

PREPARATION: 15   **COOKING:** 2 H   **SERVINGS:** 10-12

INGREDIENTS

- 2 cups warm water
- 1 tbsp active yeast (dry)
- 2 tbsp wild honey
- 3 cups plain flour
- 1 tsp salt
- 4 tbsp butter
- 4 tbsp brown sugar
- 1 tsp cinnamon

DIRECTIONS

1. In a bowl, mix up water, yeast, and honey. Stir with a mixer and after the dough is homogenous, let it rest for several minutes; mixture will rise.
2. Sift flour and add salt. Mix on low to let the ingredients come together, then increase the mixing speed to medium. Remove dough and allow to rise on a floured table.
3. Roll dough into medium rectangles. You can use a pizza cutter to make the sides even. Spread the butter over the dough. Sprinkle it with sugar and cinnamon.
4. Roll the dough rectangles into a long log, and then cut it into 10-12 pieces. Cover your slow cooker inside with foil, place the rolls over it and cook on high for 2-3 hours. To serve, use fresh berries or mint leaves.

Nutrition: *Calories: 190 Fat: 5g Carbs: 7g Protein: 8g*

19. QUINOA PIE

PREPARATION: 10 MIN **COOKING:** 4 H **SERVINGS:** 4

INGREDIENTS

- 2 tbsp almond butter
- 2 tbsp maple syrup
- 1 cup vanilla almond milk
- 1 tsp salt
- 1/2 cup quinoa
- 2 chicken eggs
- Cinnamon
- 1/2 cup raisins
- 5 tbsp roasted almonds (chopped)
- 1/2 cup dried apples

DIRECTIONS

1. Spray the slow cooker dish with no-stick spray or cover it with foil or parchment paper. In another bowl, mix the almond butter and maple syrup. Melt in a microwave until creamy, about a minute.
2. Add almond milk, salt, and cinnamon, then whisk the mass until it is entirely even. Add the eggs and remaining products, mix well. Preheat your slow cooker to 100-110°F.
3. Put the dough into the dish, then place it into the slow cooker. Cook for 3-4 hours on high. To serve, remove the pie out of the dish with a knife. Cool in the refrigerator.

Nutrition: *Calories: 174 Fat: 8g Carbs: 20g Protein: 6g*

20. QUINOA MUFFINS WITH PEANUT BUTTER

PREPARATION: 10 MIN **COOKING:** 4 H **SERVINGS:** 8

INGREDIENTS

- 1 cup strawberries
- 1/2 cup almond vanilla milk
- 1 tsp salt
- 5-6 tbsp raw quinoa
- 2 tbsp peanut butter (better natural)
- 3 tbsp honey
- 4 egg whites
- 2 tbsp peanuts (roasted)

DIRECTIONS

1. Preheat your slow cooker to 190°F. Line the cooking dish bottom with parchment paper; additionally, spray it with cooking spray. Dice the strawberries and place them over the dish.
2. Sprinkle with honey and place the dish into the slow cooker for 10-15 minutes for releasing juices. In another pot, mix up the almond milk and salt. Boil with quinoa until ready.
3. Combine egg whites and almond butter in a separate bowl. Put the quinoa and wait until milk is absorbed.
4. Fill the muffin forms with quinoa mixture; place the strawberries on the top. Bake in the slow cooker on low until quinoa is set for about 4 hours. To serve, cool the muffins and decorate them with whole strawberries.

Nutrition: *Calories: 190 Fat: 6g Carbs: 8g Protein: 6g*

21. VEGGIE OMELETS

PREPARATION: 5 MIN　　**COOKING:** 2 H　　**SERVINGS:** 8

INGREDIENTS

- 6 chicken eggs
- 1/2 cup milk
- salt
- garlic powder
- white pepper
- red pepper
- small onion
- garlic clove
- parsley
- 5 small tomatoes

DIRECTIONS

1. Grease the slow cooker dish with butter or special cooking spray. In a separate bowl, mix up eggs and milk. Add pepper and garlic.
2. Whisk the mixture well and salt. Add to the mixture broccoli florets, onions, pepper, and garlic. Stir in the eggs.
3. Place the mixture into the slow cooker dish. Cook on high temperatures at 180-200°F for 2 hours. Cover with cheese and let it melt. To serve, cut the omelet into 8 pieces and garnish the plates with parsley and tomatoes.

Nutrition: *Calories: 210 Fat: 7g Carbs: 5g Protein: 8g*

22. APPLE PIE WITH OATMEAL

PREPARATION: 10 MIN　　**COOKING:** 4-6 H　　**SERVINGS:** 4

INGREDIENTS

- 1 cup oats
- 2 large apples
- 2 cups almond milk
- 2 cups warm water
- 2 tsp cinnamon
- Pinch nutmeg
- Salt
- 2 tbsp coconut oil
- 1 tsp vanilla extract
- 2 tbsp flaxseeds
- 2 tbsp maple syrup
- Raisins

DIRECTIONS

1. Grease your slow cooker. Rub a couple of spoons of coconut or olive oil. Peel the apples. Core and chop them into medium size pieces.
2. Starting with the apples, add all the ingredients into the slow cooker. Stir and leave to bake for 6 hours on low. When ready, stir the oatmeal well.
3. Serve the oatmeal into small cups. You can also garnish it with any berries or toppings you like.

Nutrition: *Calories: 159 Fat: 12g Carbs: 9g Protein: 28g*

23. VANILLA FRENCH TOAST

PREPARATION: 15 MIN   **COOKING:** 8 H   **SERVINGS:** 4

INGREDIENTS

- 1 loaf bread (better day-old)
- 2 cups cream
- 2 cups milk, whole
- 8 eggs
- almond extract
- 1 vanilla bean
- 5 tsp sugar
- Cinnamon
- Salt

DIRECTIONS

1. Coat the slow cooker dish with the cooking spray. Slice bread into small pieces (1-2 inches). Place them into the dish overlapping each other. In another dish, combine the remaining ingredients until perfectly blended.
2. Pour the wet mixture over the bread to cover it completely. Place the dish into a slow cooker and cook on low at 100-120°F for 7-8 hours. To serve, slightly cool and cut the French toast.

Nutrition: *Calories: 200 Fat: 6g Carbs: 4g Protein: 8g*

24. GREEK EGGS CASSEROLE

PREPARATION: 15 MIN   **COOKING:** 6 H   **SERVINGS:** 4

INGREDIENTS

- 10 chicken eggs
- 1/2 cup milk
- Salt
- 1 tsp black pepper
- 1 tbsp red onion
- 1/2 cup dried tomatoes
- 1 cup champignons
- 2cups spinach
- 1/2 cup feta

DIRECTIONS

1. Set your slow cooker to 120-150°F. In a separate wide bowl, combine and whisk the eggs. Add salt and pepper. Mix in garlic and red onion. Whisk again.
2. Wash and dice the mushrooms. Put them into the wet mixture. At last, and add dried tomatoes. Pour the mixture into the slow cooker.
3. Top the meal with the feta cheese and cook on low for 5-6 hours. Serve with milk or vegetables.

Nutrition: *Calories: 180 Fat: 8g Carbs: 4g Protein: 8g*

25. BANANA BREAD

PREPARATION: 15 MIN   **COOKING:** 4 H   **SERVINGS:** 3

INGREDIENTS

- 2 chicken eggs
- 1/2 cup softened butter
- 1 cup of sugar
- 2 cups plain flour
- 1/2 teaspoon baking soda
- Salt
- 3 medium bananas

DIRECTIONS

1. First, cover with cooking spray and preheat your slow cooker. Combine eggs with sugar and butter. Stir well. Mix in baking soda and baking powder.
2. Peel and mash bananas, mix them with flour, and combine with eggs. Pour the dough into the cooking dish and place it into the slow cooker. Cook on low for 3-4 hours.
3. When ready, remove the bread with a knife and enjoy your breakfast! To serve, use fresh bananas, apples, or berries to your taste.

Nutrition: *Calories: 130 Fat: 8g Carbs: 5g Protein: 7g*

26. TREACLE SPONGE WITH HONEY

PREPARATION: 15 MIN   **COOKING:** 3 H   **SERVINGS:** 4

INGREDIENTS

- 1 cup unsalted butter
- 3 tbsp. honey
- 1 tbsp. white breadcrumbs (fresh)
- 1 cup of sugar
- 1 lemon zest
- 3 large chicken eggs
- 2 cup flour
- 2 tbsp. milk
- Clotted cream (to serve)
- Little brandy splash (optional)

DIRECTIONS

1. Grease your slow cooker dish heavily and preheat it. Mix the breadcrumbs with the honey in a medium bowl. Melt butter and beat it with lemon zest and sugar until fluffy and light. Sift in the flour slowly.
2. Add the milk and stir well. Spoon the mixture into the slow cooker dish. Cook for 3 hours on low mode. Serve with honey or clotted cream.

Nutrition: *Calories: 200 Fat: 10g Carbs: 20g Protein: 10g*

27. STICKY PECAN BUNS WITH MAPLE

PREPARATION: 15 MIN   **COOKING:** 5 H   **SERVINGS:** 12

INGREDIENTS

- 6 tbsp. milk (nonfat)
- 4 tbsp. maple syrup
- 1/2 tbsp. melted butter
- 1 tsp. vanilla extract
- Salt
- 2 tbsp. yeast
- 2 cup flour (whole wheat)
- Chopped pecans
- Ground cinnamon

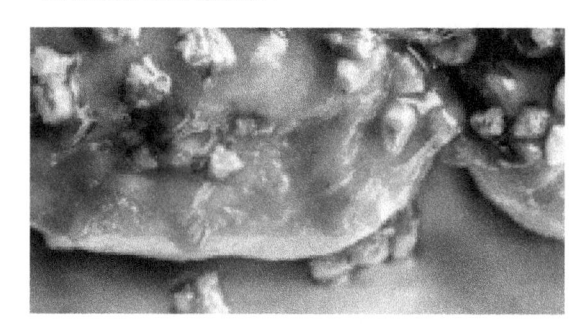

DIRECTIONS

1. Coat the inside of your slow cooker using a non-stick cooking spray. For the dough, combine milk, vanilla butter, and maple syrup. Mix well.
2. Microwave the mixture until warm and add the yeast. Let sit for 15 minutes. Sift in the flour and mix until the dough is no stickier.
3. For the filling, mix the maple syrup and cinnamon. Roll out the dough and brush it with the maple filling. Roll up, then slice into 10-12 parts. Place the small rolls into the slow cooker.
4. For the caramel sauce, combine milk, butter, and syrup. Pour the sauce into the slow cooker. Cook for 2 hours on high or 5 hours on low. Serve.

Nutrition: *Calories: 230 Fat: 5g Carbs: 29g Protein: 42g*

28. VEGETARIAN POT PIE

PREPARATION: 15 MIN   **COOKING:** 9H + 15   **SERVINGS:** 4

INGREDIENTS

- 6 cups chopped vegetables (peas, potatoes, tomatoes, carrots, brussels sprouts)
- 1-2 cups diced mushrooms
- 2 onions
- 1/2 cup flour
- 4 cloves garlic
- 2 tbsp. garlic
- Thyme (fresh)
- Cornstarch
- 2 cups chicken broth

DIRECTIONS

1. Wash and chop vegetables or by frozen packed. Toss with flour to cover vegetables well.
2. Mix with the broth slowly, when well combined with flour. Preheat the slow cooker and place the vegetables into it.
3. Cook on low for 8-9 hours, or on high for 6-7 hours. Mix up cornstarch with the water and pour into the vegetable mix. Place it back in the slow cooker for 15 minutes. Serve hot with fresh vegetables.

Nutrition: *Calories: 267 Fat: 7g Carbs: 29g Protein: 7g*

29. BLUEBERRY PORRIDGE

PREPARATION: 5 MIN **COOKING:** 5-6 H **SERVINGS:** 4

INGREDIENTS

- 1 cup jumbo oats
- 4 cups of milk
- 1/2 cup dried fruits
- Brown sugar or honey
- Cinnamon
- Blueberries

DIRECTIONS

1. Heat the slow cooker before the start. Put the oats into the slow cooker dish, add some salt.
2. Pour over the milk, then place the dish into the slow cooker and cook on low for 7-8 hours (overnight). Stir the porridge in the morning.
3. For serving, ladle into the serving bowls and decorate with your favorite yogurt or syrup. Add blueberries.

Nutrition: *Calories: 210 Fat: 4g Carbs: 5g Protein: 8g*

30. CAULIFLOWER AND EGGS BOWLS

PREPARATION: 15 MIN **COOKING:** 7 H **SERVINGS:** 2

INGREDIENTS

- Cooking spray
- 4 eggs, whisked
- A pinch of salt and black pepper
- ¼ teaspoon thyme, dried
- ½ teaspoon turmeric powder
- 1 cup cauliflower florets
- ½ small yellow onion, chopped
- 3 oz. breakfast sausages, sliced
- ½ cup cheddar cheese, shredded

DIRECTIONS

1. Oiled your slow cooker with cooking spray and spread the cauliflower florets on the bottom of the pot. Add the eggs mixed with salt, pepper, and the other ingredients and toss. Put the lid on, cook on low for 7 hours, divide between plates, and serve for breakfast.

Nutrition: *Calories: 261 Fat: 6g Carbs: 22g Protein: 6g*

31. MILK OATMEAL

PREPARATION: 10 MIN **COOKING:** 2 H **SERVINGS:** 4

INGREDIENTS

- 2 cups oatmeal
- 1 cup of water
- 1 cup milk
- 1 tablespoon liquid honey
- 1 teaspoon vanilla extract
- 1 tablespoon coconut oil
- ¼ teaspoon ground cinnamon

DIRECTIONS

1. Put all ingredients except liquid honey in the slow cooker and mix. Cook the meal on high for hours.
2. Then stir the cooked oatmeal and transfer to the serving bowls. Top the meal with a small amount of liquid honey.

Nutrition: *Calories: 234 Protein: 7.4g Carbs: 35.3g Fat: 7.3g*

32. ASPARAGUS EGG CASSEROLE

PREPARATION: 15 MIN **COOKING:** 2H+30MIN **SERVINGS:** 4

INGREDIENTS

- 7 eggs, beaten
- 4 oz asparagus, chopped, boiled
- 1 oz Parmesan, grated
- 1 teaspoon sesame oil
- 1 teaspoon dried dill

DIRECTIONS

1. Pour the sesame oil into the slow cooker. Then mix dried dill with parmesan, asparagus, and eggs. Pour the egg batter into your slow cooker and close the lid. Cook the casserole on high for 2 hours and 30 minutes. Serve.

Nutrition: *Calories: 149 Protein: 12.6g Carbs: 2.1g Fat: 10.3g*

33. VANILLA MAPLE OATS

PREPARATION: 15 MIN **COOKING:** 8 H **SERVINGS:** 4

INGREDIENTS

- 1 cup steel-cut oats
- 2 tsp vanilla extract
- 2 cups vanilla almond milk
- 2 tbsp maple syrup
- 2 tsp cinnamon powder
- 2 cups of water
- 2 tsp flaxseed
- Cooking spray
- 2 tbsp blackberries

DIRECTIONS

1. Coat the base of your slow cooker with cooking spray. Stir in oats, almond milk, vanilla extract, cinnamon, maple syrup, flaxseeds, and water.
2. Put the cooker's lid on and set the cooking time to 8 hours on low. Stir well and serve with blackberries on top. Devour.

Nutrition: *Calories: 200 Fat: 3g Carbs: 9g Protein: 3g*

34. RASPBERRY OATMEAL

PREPARATION: 15 MIN **COOKING:** 8 H **SERVINGS:** 4

INGREDIENTS

- 2 cups of water
- 1 tablespoon coconut oil
- 1 cup steel-cut oats
- 1 tablespoon sugar
- 1 cup milk
- ½ teaspoon vanilla extract
- 1 cup raspberries
- 4 tablespoons walnuts, chopped

DIRECTIONS

1. In your slow cooker, mix oil with water, oats, sugar, milk, vanilla, and raspberries, cover, and cook on low for 8 hours. Stir oatmeal, divide into bowls, sprinkle walnuts on top, and serve for breakfast.

Nutrition: *Calories: 200 Fat: 10g Carbs: 20g Protein: 4g*

35. PORK AND EGGPLANT CASSEROLE

PREPARATION: 15 MIN   **COOKING:** 6 H   **SERVINGS:** 2

INGREDIENTS

- 1 red onion, chopped
- 1 eggplant, cubed
- ½ pound pork stew meat, ground
- 3 eggs, whisked
- ½ teaspoon chili powder
- ½ teaspoon garam masala
- 1 tablespoon sweet paprika
- 1 teaspoon olive oil

DIRECTIONS

1. Mix the eggs with the meat, onion, eggplant, and the other ingredients in the bowl except for the oil. Grease your slow cooker with oil, add the pork and eggplant mix, spread into the pot, cook on low for 6 hours. Divide the mixture between plates and serve for breakfast.

Nutrition: *Calories: 261 Fat: 7g Carbs: 16g Protein: 7g*

36. BABY SPINACH RICE MIX

PREPARATION: 15 MIN   **COOKING:** 6 H   **SERVINGS:** 4

INGREDIENTS

- ¼ cup mozzarella, shredded
- ½ cup baby spinach
- ½ cup wild rice
- 1 and ½ cups chicken stock
- ½ teaspoon turmeric powder
- ½ teaspoon oregano, dried
- A pinch of salt and black pepper
- 3 scallions, minced
- ¾ cup goat cheese, crumbled

DIRECTIONS

1. In your slow cooker, mix the rice with the stock, turmeric, and the other ingredients, toss, cook on low for 6 hours. Divide the mix into bowls and serve for breakfast.

Nutrition: *Calories: 165 Fat: 1.2g. Carbs: 32.6g Protein: 7.6g*

37. BABY CARROTS IN SYRUP

PREPARATION: 15 MIN   **COOKING:** 7 H   **SERVINGS:** 4

INGREDIENTS

- 3 cups baby carrots
- 1 cup apple juice
- 2 tablespoons brown sugar
- 1 teaspoon vanilla extract

DIRECTIONS

1. Mix apple juice, brown sugar, and vanilla extract. Pour the liquid into the slow cooker. Add baby carrots and close the lid. Cook the meal on low for 7 hours.

Nutrition: *Calories: 81 Protein: 0g Carbs: 18.8g Fat: 0.1g*

---

38. GREEN MUFFINS

PREPARATION: 15 MIN   **COOKING:** 2H 30 MIN   **SERVINGS:** 8

INGREDIENTS

- 1 cup spinach, washed
- 5 tbsp butter
- 1 cup flour
- 1 tsp salt
- ½ tsp baking soda
- 1 tbsp lemon juice
- 1 tbsp sugar
- 3 eggs

DIRECTIONS

1. Add the spinach leaves to a blender jug and blend until smooth. Whisk the eggs in a bowl and add the spinach mixture.
2. Stir in baking soda, salt, sugar, flour, and lemon juice. Mix well to form a smooth spinach batter. Divide the dough into a muffin tray lined with muffin cups.
3. Place this muffin tray in the slow cooker. Put the cooker's lid on and set the cooking time to 2 hours 30 minutes on high. Serve.

Nutrition: *Calories: 172 Fat: 6.1g Carbs: 9.23g Protein: 20g*

39. SCALLIONS AND BACON OMELET

PREPARATION: 15 MIN   **COOKING:** 2 H   **SERVINGS:** 4

INGREDIENTS

- 5 eggs, beaten
- 2 oz bacon, chopped, cooked
- 1 oz scallions, chopped
- 1 teaspoon olive oil
- ½ teaspoon ground black pepper
- ¼ teaspoon cayenne pepper

DIRECTIONS

1. Brush the slow cooker bowl bottom with olive oil. After this, mix eggs with bacon, scallions, ground black pepper, and cayenne pepper in the bowl. Pour the liquid into your slow cooker and close the lid. Cook the meal on high for 2 hours. Serve.

Nutrition: *Calories: 169 Protein: 12.3g Carbs: 1.4g Fat: 12.6g*

40. COWBOY BREAKFAST CASSEROLE

PREPARATION: 15 MIN   **COOKING:** 3 H   **SERVINGS:** 4

INGREDIENTS

- 1-pound ground beef
- 5 eggs, beaten
- 1 cup grass-fed Monterey Jack cheese, shredded
- Salt and pepper to taste
- 1 avocado, peeled and diced
- A handful of cilantros, chopped
- A dash of hot sauce

DIRECTIONS

1. In a skillet over medium flame, sauté the beef for three minutes until slightly golden. Pour into the slow cooker and pour in eggs.
2. Sprinkle with cheese on top and season with salt and pepper to taste. Close the lid and cook on high for hours or on low for 6 hours. Serve with avocado, cilantro, and hot sauce.

Nutrition: *Calories: 439 Carbs: 4.5g Protein: 32.7g Fat: 31.9g*

41. MAPLE BANANA OATMEAL

PREPARATION: 15 MIN   **COOKING:** 6 H   **SERVINGS:** 2

INGREDIENTS

- 1/2 cup old fashioned oats
- 1 banana, mashed
- ½ teaspoon cinnamon powder
- 2 tablespoons maple syrup
- 2 cups almond milk
- Cooking spray

DIRECTIONS

1. Grease your slow cooker with the cooking spray, add the oats, banana, and the other ingredients, stir, cook on low for 6 hours. Divide into bowls and serve for breakfast.

Nutrition: *Calories: 815 Fat: 60.3g Carbs: 67g Protein: 11.1g*

42. POTATO MUFFINS

PREPARATION: 15 MIN   **COOKING:** 2 H   **SERVINGS:** 4

INGREDIENTS

- 4 teaspoons flax meal
- 1 bell pepper, diced
- 1 cup potato, cooked, mashed
- 2 eggs, beaten
- 1 teaspoon ground paprika
- 2 oz Mozzarella, shredded

DIRECTIONS

1. Mix flax meal with potato and eggs. Then add ground paprika and bell pepper. Stir the mixture with the help of the spoon until homogenous.
2. Transfer the potato mixture to the muffin molds. Top the muffins with mozzarella and transfer them to the slow cooker. Close the lid and cook the muffins on high for 2 hours. Serve.

Nutrition: *Calories: 107 Protein: 8g Carbs: 7.2g Fat: 5.7g*

43. EGGS AND SWEET POTATO MIX

PREPARATION: 15 MIN   **COOKING:** 6 H   **SERVINGS:** 2

INGREDIENTS

- ½ red onion, chopped
- ½ green bell pepper, chopped
- 2 sweet potatoes, peeled and grated
- ½ red bell pepper, chopped
- 1 garlic clove, minced
- ½ teaspoon olive oil
- 4 eggs, whisked
- 1 tablespoon chives, chopped
- A pinch of red pepper, crushed
- A pinch of salt and black pepper

DIRECTIONS

1. Mix the eggs with the onion, bell peppers, and the other ingredients in a bowl except for the oil.
2. Grease your slow cooker with the oil, add the eggs and potato mix, spread, cook on low within 6 hours. Divide everything between plates and serve.

Nutrition: *Calories: 261 Fat: 6g Carbs: 16g Protein: 4g*

---

44. VEGGIE HASH BROWN MIX

PREPARATION: 15 MIN   **COOKING:** 6H 5 MIN   **SERVINGS:** 2

INGREDIENTS

- 1 tablespoon olive oil
- ½ cup white mushrooms, chopped
- ½ yellow onion, chopped
- ¼ teaspoon garlic powder
- ¼ teaspoon onion powder
- ¼ cup sour cream
- 10 oz. hash browns
- ¼ cup cheddar cheese, shredded
- Salt and black pepper to the taste
- ½ tablespoon parsley, chopped

DIRECTIONS

1. Heat-up a pan with the oil over medium heat, add the onion and mushrooms, stir and cook for 5 minutes.
2. Transfer this to the slow cooker, add hash browns and the other ingredients, toss, cook on low within 6 hours. Divide between plates and for breakfast.

Nutrition: *Calories: 571 Fat: 35.6g Carbs: 54.9g Protein: 9.7g*

45. COCONUT CRANBERRY QUINOA

PREPARATION: 5 MIN **COOKING:** 2 H **SERVINGS:** 4

INGREDIENTS

- 3 cups of coconut water
- 1 cup quinoa, uncooked and rinsed
- 3 teaspoons honey
- ¼ cup cranberries
- ½ cup coconut flakes

DIRECTIONS

1. Place all ingredients in the slow cooker. Add a dash of vanilla or cinnamon if desired. Give a good stir. Cook on low within 2 hours. Serve.

Nutrition: *Calories: 246 Carbs: 42g Protein: 8g Fat: 5g*

46. SCRAMBLED EGGS IN RAMEKINS

PREPARATION: 5 MIN **COOKING:** 2 H **SERVINGS:** 4

INGREDIENTS

- 2 eggs, beaten
- ¼ cup milk
- Salt and pepper
- ¼ cup cheddar cheese, grated
- ½ cup of salsa

DIRECTIONS

1. Mix the eggs and milk in a mixing bowl. Season with salt and pepper to taste. Place egg mixture in two ramekins. Sprinkle with cheddar cheese on top.
2. Put the ramekins in the slow cooker, then pour water around it. Cook on low within 4 hours. Serve with salsa.

Nutrition: *Calories: 243 Carbs: 9.3g Protein: 15.3g Fat: 164g*

47. ENCHILADA BREAKFAST CASSEROLE

PREPARATION: 5 MIN **COOKING:** 10 H **SERVINGS:** 4

INGREDIENTS

- 6 eggs, beaten
- 1-pound ground beef
- 2 cans enchilada sauce
- 1 can condensed cream of onion soup
- 3 cups sharp cheddar cheese, grated

DIRECTIONS

1. Beat the eggs, then season with salt plus pepper in a mixing bowl. Set aside. In a skillet, brown the beef for at least 5 minutes.
2. Pour the beef into the slow cooker and stir in the enchilada sauce and cream of onion soup. Stir in the eggs and place cheese on top. Cook on low within 10 hours. Serve.

Nutrition: *Calories: 320 Carbs: 9.4g Protein: 24.6g Fat: 20.1g*

48. WHITE CHOCOLATE OATMEAL

PREPARATION: 5 MIN **COOKING:** 4H **SERVINGS:** 4

INGREDIENTS

- 1 tablespoon white chocolate chips
- 1 cup of water
- ½ cup oatmeal
- 1 tablespoon brown sugar
- 1 teaspoon cinnamon

DIRECTIONS

1. Stir in all fixing in the slow cooker. Cook on low within 4 hours. Top with your favorite topping.

Nutrition: *Calories: 31 Carbs: 5.4g Protein: 0.5g Fat: 0.9g*

49. BACON-WRAPPED HOTDOGS

PREPARATION: 8 MIN   **COOKING:** 4 H   **SERVINGS:** 4

INGREDIENTS

- 8 small hotdogs
- 8 bacon
- ½ cup brown sugar
- 4 tablespoons water
- Salt and pepper to taste

DIRECTIONS

1. Wrap the individual hotdogs with bacon strips. Secure with a toothpick, then place inside the slow cooker.
2. Mix the sugar, water, salt, and pepper in a small mixing bowl. Pour over the hotdogs. Cook on low within 8 hours. Serve.

Nutrition: *Calories: 120 Carbs: 11.8g Protein: 3.1g Fat: 6.9g*

50. APPLE GRANOLA CRUMBLE

PREPARATION: 15 MIN   **COOKING:** 3 H   **SERVINGS:** 4

INGREDIENTS

- 2 Granny Smith apples, cored and sliced
- 1 cup granola cereal
- 1/8 cup maple syrup
- ¼ cup apple juice
- 1 teaspoon cinnamon

DIRECTIONS

1. Place all ingredients in the slow cooker. Give a good stir. Cook on low within 3 hours. Once cooked, serve with a tablespoon of butter.

Nutrition: *Calories: 369 Carbs: 56g Protein: 5g Fat:15g*

51. BANANA AND COCONUT MILK STEEL-CUT OATS

PREPARATION: 15 MIN   **COOKING:** 3 H   **SERVINGS:** 4

INGREDIENTS

- 2 medium ripe bananas, sliced
- 2 cans coconut milk, unsweetened
- 1 cup steel-cut oats
- 2 tablespoons brown sugar
- ½ teaspoon cinnamon

DIRECTIONS

1. Place all ingredients in the slow cooker. Add a dash of salt if needed. Give a good stir. Cook on low within 3 hours. Once cooked, serve with a tablespoon of melted butter.

Nutrition: *Calories:101 Carbs: 15.3g Protein: 2.6g Fat: 5.9g*

---

52. SPINACH AND MOZZARELLA FRITTATA

PREPARATION: 10 MIN   **COOKING:** 4 H   **SERVINGS:** 4

INGREDIENTS

- 6 eggs, beaten
- 2 tablespoons milk
- 1 cup baby spinach
- 1 cup mozzarella cheese
- 1 Roma tomatoes, diced

DIRECTIONS

1. Mix the eggs and milk in a mixing bowl. Season with salt and pepper to taste. Put the egg batter into the slow cooker and add the baby spinach, cheese, and tomatoes. Cook on low within 4 hours.

Nutrition: *Calories: 139 Carbs: 4g Protein: 12g Fat: 8g*

53. QUINOA ENERGY BARS

PREPARATION: 15 MIN **COOKING:** 8 H **SERVINGS:** 4

INGREDIENTS

- 2 cups quinoa flakes, rinsed
- ½ cup nuts of your choice
- ½ cup dried fruits of your choice
- ¼ cup butter, melted
- 1/3 cup maple syrup

DIRECTIONS

1. In a mixing bowl, combine all ingredients. Compress the fixing in a parchment-lined slow cooker. Cook on low within 8 hours.

Nutrition: *Calories: 306 Carbs: 39.9g Protein: 7.3g Fat: 13.9g*

54. OVERNIGHT APPLE OATMEAL

PREPARATION: 15 MIN **COOKING:** 8 H **SERVINGS:** 4

INGREDIENTS

- 4 apples, peeled and diced
- ¾ cup brown sugar
- 2 cups old-fashioned oats
- 4 cups evaporated milk
- 1 tablespoon cinnamon

DIRECTIONS

1. Stir in all fixing in the slow cooker. Cook on low within 8 hours. Add in butter if desired.

Nutrition: *Calories: 521 Carbs: 109.5g Protein: 16.4g Fat: 11.6g*

55. APPLE WALNUT STRATA

PREPARATION: 15 MIN **COOKING:** 2 H **SERVINGS:** 4

INGREDIENTS

- ¼ cup light cream
- ¼ cup of orange juice
- 3 eggs, beaten
- 3 tablespoons sugar
- ½ teaspoon cinnamon
- 1 teaspoon vanilla
- 4 cups cubed French bread
- 1 cup granola
- ½ cup chopped toasted walnuts
- 2 Granny Smith apples, peeled and cubed

DIRECTIONS

1. Oiled 3 or 4-quart slow cooker using a nonstick cooking spray. In a medium bowl, combine cream, orange juice, eggs, sugar, cinnamon, and vanilla and blend well with a whisk. Set aside.
2. Place the bread in the prepared slow cooker's bottom and sprinkle it with the granola, walnuts, and apples—repeat layers. Pour egg mixture overall. Cover and cook on high within 1½ to 2 hours or until just set. Serve.

Nutrition: *Calories: 357.67 Fat: 16.56g Protein: 11.97 g Carbs: 0g*

56. NUTTY OATMEAL

PREPARATION: 15 MIN   **COOKING:** 9 H   **SERVINGS:** 4

INGREDIENTS

- Slow cooker size: 3 1/2-quart
- 1½ cups steel-cut oatmeal
- 2 tablespoons butter
- 1 cup chopped walnuts
- 6 cups of water
- ½ cup brown sugar
- 1 teaspoon salt
- 1 teaspoon cinnamon
- 1 teaspoon nutmeg

DIRECTIONS

1. Put the oatmeal in a large skillet over medium-high heat. Toast, continually stirring, for 8–9 minutes or until oatmeal is fragrant and begins to brown around the edges. Remove to 3½-quart slow cooker.
2. Dissolve butter and add chopped walnuts in the same pan. Toast over medium heat, continually stirring, until nuts are toasted.
3. Combine with all remaining ingredients except spices in 3– the 4-quart slow cooker. Cover and cook on low for 7–9 hours, until oatmeal is tender.
4. Stir in spices, cover, and let stand for 10 minutes. Serve topped with a bit of butter, maple syrup, brown sugar, and more chopped nuts.

Nutrition: *Calories: 388 Carbs: 32g Fat: 26g Protein: 13g*

57. BACON AND WAFFLE STRATA

PREPARATION: 15 MIN   **COOKING:** 5 H   **SERVINGS:** 4

INGREDIENTS

- 4 slices bacon
- 5 frozen waffles, toasted
- 1 cup shredded Colby cheese
- ¼ cup chopped green onions
- 1 (5-ounce) can evaporate milk
- ½ package cream cheese softened
- 4 eggs
- ½ teaspoon dry mustard

DIRECTIONS

1. Cook bacon until crisp in your large skillet. Drain on paper towels, crumble, and set aside. Cut toasted waffles into cubes. Layer bacon and waffle cubes with cheese and green onions in a 3½-quart slow cooker.
2. Drain skillet, discarding bacon fat; do not wipe out. Put the milk plus cream cheese in skillet; cook over low heat, stirring frequently.
3. Remove, then beat in eggs, one at a time, until smooth. Stir in dry mustard, then pour into a slow cooker. Cover and cook on low within 4–5 hours, until eggs are set. Serve with warmed maple syrup, if desired.

Nutrition: *Calories: 382 Carbs: 25g Fat: 22g Protein: 21g*

58. HONEY APPLE BREAD PUDDING

PREPARATION: 15 MIN   **COOKING:** 4H 35 MIN   **SERVINGS:** 4

INGREDIENTS

- 2 apples, chopped
- ¼ cup apple juice
- cup brown sugar
- ¼ cup honey
- 2 tablespoons butter, melted
- 4 eggs, beaten
- cup whole milk
- 1 teaspoon vanilla
- ½ teaspoon cinnamon
- 8 slices raisin swirl bread
- ½ cup raisins

DIRECTIONS

1. In a medium saucepan, combine apples with apple juice. Bring to a simmer; simmer for 5 minutes, stirring frequently. Remove, then set aside within 10 minutes. Drain apples, reserving juice.
2. Mix brown sugar, honey, and butter in a small bowl; set aside. In a large bowl, combine reserved apple juice, eggs, milk, vanilla, and cinnamon; beat well and set aside.
3. Cut bread slices into cubes. In the slow cooker, layer the bread cubes, raisins, apples, and the brown sugar mixture. Repeat layers. Pour egg mixture overall.
4. Cover and cook on high within 3 to 4 hours and 30 minutes, until pudding is set. Let cool within 30 minutes, then serve.

Nutrition: *Calories: 312 Carbs: 41g Fat: 15g Protein: 7g*

59. SAUSAGE ROLLS

PREPARATION: 15 MIN   **COOKING:** 9 H 6 MIN   **SERVINGS:** 4

INGREDIENTS

- ¾ cup soft bread crumbs
- 1 egg, beaten
- ¼ cup brown sugar
- ¼ cup applesauce
- ½ teaspoon salt
- 1 teaspoon pepper
- ½ teaspoon dried marjoram leaves
- 1½-pounds mild bulk pork sausage
- 2 tablespoons butter
- ¼ cup honey
- ¼ cup chicken broth

Nutrition: *Calories: 102 Carbs: 7g Fat: 0g Protein: 7g*

DIRECTIONS

1. In a large bowl, combine crumbs, egg, brown sugar, applesauce, salt, pepper, and marjoram. Mix well. Stir in sausage.
2. Shape into rolls 3" × 1". Dissolve the butter over medium heat in a large skillet. Add sausage rolls, about 8 at a time, and cook until browned on all sides, about 5–6 minutes.
3. As rolls cook, drain on paper towels, then place into the 3-quart slow cooker. In a small bowl, combine honey and chicken broth and mix well. Pour over sausage rolls in a slow cooker.
4. Cook on low within 8–9 hours or until sausage rolls are thoroughly cooked, to 165°F on a meat thermometer. Remove from slow cooker with a slotted spoon to serve.

60. BREAKFAST PITAS

PREPARATION: 15 MIN   **COOKING:** 7-8H   **SERVINGS:** 4

INGREDIENTS

- 2 tablespoons butter
- 1 onion, chopped
- 2 cloves garlic, chopped
- 8 eggs, beaten
- ½ teaspoon salt
- 1 teaspoon pepper
- ½ cup of salsa
- 1 cup shredded pepper jack cheese
- 4 pita bread
- 2 tablespoons chopped parsley

DIRECTIONS

1. Oiled 2-quart slow cooker with nonstick cooking spray. In a small skillet, melt butter over medium heat. Put the onion plus garlic; cook and stir until tender, about 5 minutes. Remove from heat.
2. Mix eggs, salt, and pepper and beat well in a large bowl. Stir in onion mixture, salsa, and cheese. Pour into the slow cooker. Cover and cook on low within 7–8 hours.
3. In the morning, stir the mixture in a slow cooker. Split pita bread and fill with egg mixture; top with parsley and serve immediately.

Nutrition: *Calories: 200 Carbs: 14g Fat: 1g Protein: 6g*

CHAPTER 3.
SNACKS & APPETIZERS

61. OREGANO SALSA

PREPARATION: 10 MIN **COOKING:** 7 H **SERVINGS:** 4

INGREDIENTS

- 3 cups eggplant, cubed
- 4 garlic cloves, minced
- 6 oz. green olives, pitted and sliced
- 1 and ½ cups tomatoes, chopped
- 2 teaspoons balsamic vinegar
- 1 tablespoon oregano, chopped
- Black pepper to the taste

DIRECTIONS

1. In your slow cooker, mix tomatoes with eggplant, green olives, garlic, vinegar, oregano, and pepper, toss, cover, cook on low for 7 hours, divide into small bowls and serve as an appetizer.

Nutrition: *Calories: 78 Fat: 3.6g Carbs: 11.2g Protein: 2g*

62. SMOKED PAPRIKA CAULIFLOWER SPREAD

PREPARATION: 10 MIN **COOKING:** 7 H **SERVINGS:** 4

INGREDIENTS

- 2 cups cauliflower florets
- 1 cup of coconut milk
- 1/3 cup cashews, chopped
- 2 and ½ cups of water
- 1 cup turnips, chopped
- 1 teaspoon garlic powder
- ¼ teaspoon smoked paprika
- ¼ teaspoon mustard powder

DIRECTIONS

1. In your slow cooker, mix cauliflower with cashews, turnips, and water, stir, cover, cook on low for 7 hours, drain, transfer to a blender, add milk, garlic powder, paprika, and mustard powder, blend well, and serve.

Nutrition: *Calories: 228 Fat: 19.7g Carbs: 12.4g Protein: 4.6g*

63. FRENCH STYLE SALAD

PREPARATION: 10 MIN **COOKING:** 9 H **SERVINGS:** 4

INGREDIENTS

- 6 oz. canned tomato paste, no-salt-added
- 2 tomatoes, cut into medium wedges
- 2 yellow onions, chopped
- 1 eggplant, sliced
- 4 zucchinis, sliced
- 2 green bell peppers, cut into medium strips
- 2 garlic cloves, minced
- 2 tablespoons parsley, chopped
- 3 tablespoons olive oil
- 1 teaspoon oregano, dried
- 1 tablespoon basil, chopped
- A pinch of black pepper

DIRECTIONS

1. In your slow cooker, mix oil with onions, eggplant, zucchinis, garlic, bell peppers, tomato paste, tomatoes, basil, oregano, and pepper, cover, and cook on low for 9 hours. Add parsley, toss, divide into small bowls and serve warm as an appetizer.

Nutrition: *Calories: 161 Fat: 7.8g Carbs: 22.8g Protein: 4.9g*

---

64. STEVIA AND BULGUR SALAD

PREPARATION: 10 MIN **COOKING:** 12 H **SERVINGS:** 4

INGREDIENTS

- 2 cups white mushrooms, sliced
- 14 oz. canned kidney beans, no-salt-added, drained
- 14 oz. canned pinto beans, no-salt-added, drained
- 2 cups yellow onion, chopped
- 1 cup low sodium veggie stock
- 1 cup strong coffee
- ¾ cup bulgur, soaked and drained
- ½ cup red bell pepper, chopped
- 2 garlic cloves, minced
- 2 tablespoons stevia
- 2 tablespoons chili powder
- 1 tablespoon cocoa powder
- 1 teaspoon oregano, dried
- 2 teaspoons cumin, ground
- Black pepper to the taste

DIRECTIONS

1. In your slow cooker, mix mushrooms with bulgur, onion, bell pepper, stock, garlic, coffee, kidney and pinto beans, stevia, chili powder, cocoa, oregano, cumin, and pepper, stir gently, cover, and cook on low for 12 hours. Divide the mix into small bowls and serve cold as an appetizer.

Nutrition: *Calories: 837 Fat: 4.2g Carbs: 162g Protein: 49.9g*

65. PARMESAN STUFFED MUSHROOMS

PREPARATION: 10 MIN   **COOKING:** 5 H   **SERVINGS:** 4

INGREDIENTS

- 20 mushrooms, stems removed
- 2 cups basil, chopped
- 1 cup tomato sauce, no-salt-added
- 2 tablespoons parsley, chopped
- ¼ cup low-fat parmesan, grated
- 1 and ½ cups whole wheat breadcrumbs
- 1 tablespoon garlic, minced
- ¼ cup low-fat butter, melted
- 2 teaspoons lemon juice
- 1 tablespoon olive oil

DIRECTIONS

1. In a bowl, mix butter with breadcrumbs and parsley, stir well, and leave aside. In your blender, mix basil with oil, parmesan, garlic, and lemon juice and pulse well.
2. Stuff mushrooms with this mix, pour the tomato sauce on top, sprinkle breadcrumbs mix at the end, and cook in the slow cooker on low for 5 hours. Arrange mushrooms on a platter and serve.

Nutrition: *Calories: 51 Fat: 1.1g Carbs: 9g Protein: 2.2g*

---

66. GARLIC AND TOMATO APPETIZER

PREPARATION: 10 MIN   **COOKING:** 2H   **SERVINGS:** 4

INGREDIENTS

- 2 teaspoons olive oil
- 8 tomatoes, chopped
- 1 garlic clove, minced
- ¼ cup basil, chopped
- 4 Italian whole wheat bread slices, toasted
- 3 tablespoons low-sodium veggie stock
- Black pepper to the taste

DIRECTIONS

1. In your slow cooker, mix tomatoes with basil, garlic, oil, veggie stock, and black pepper, stir, cover, cook on high within 2 hours and then leave aside to cool down. Divide this mix on the toasted bread and serve as an appetizer.

Nutrition: *Calories: 158 Fat: 4.1g Carbs: 26.3g Protein: 5.9g*

67. TAHINI DIP

PREPARATION: 10 MIN **COOKING:** 3 H **SERVINGS:** 4

INGREDIENTS

- ½ pound cauliflower florets
- 1 teaspoon avocado oil
- 1 tablespoon ginger, grated
- 1 cup coconut cream
- 3 garlic cloves, minced
- Black pepper to the taste
- 1 tablespoon basil, chopped
- 1 tablespoon tahini paste
- 1 tablespoon lime juice

DIRECTIONS

1. In your slow cooker, combine the cauliflower with the oil, ginger, and the other ingredients, cook on low within 3 hours. Transfer to your blender, pulse well, divide into bowls and serve.

Nutrition: *Calories: 217 Fat: 18.1g Carbs: 13.3g Protein: 3.7g*

68. LIME JUICE SNACK

PREPARATION: 10 MIN **COOKING:** 2 H **SERVINGS:** 4

INGREDIENTS

- 1 pineapple, peeled and cut into medium sticks
- 2 tablespoons stevia
- 1 tablespoon olive oil
- 1 tablespoon lime juice
- 1 tablespoon lime zest, grated
- 1 teaspoon cinnamon powder
- ¼ teaspoon cloves, ground

DIRECTIONS

1. In a bowl, mix lime juice with stevia, oil, cinnamon, and cloves and whisk well. Add the pineapple sticks to your slow cooker, add lime mix, toss, cover, and cook on high for 2 hours. Serve the pineapple sticks as a snack with lime zest sprinkled on top.

Nutrition: *Calories: 26 Fat: 1.8g Carbs: 6.1g Protein: 0.1g*

69. CUMIN HUMMUS

PREPARATION: 10 MIN **COOKING:** 5 H **SERVINGS:** 4

INGREDIENTS

- 1 cup chickpeas, soaked overnight and drained
- 2 garlic cloves
- ¾ cup green onions, chopped
- 1 tablespoon olive oil
- 2 tablespoons sherry vinegar
- 3 cups of water
- 1 teaspoon cumin, ground

DIRECTIONS

1. Put the water in your slow cooker, add chickpeas and garlic, cover, and cook on low for 5 hours. Drain chickpeas, transfer them to your blender, add ½ cup of the cooking liquid, green onions, vinegar, oil, cilantro, and cumin, blend well, divide into bowls and serve.

Nutrition: *Calories: 150 Fat: 4.5g Carbs: 22.3g Protein: 6.8g*

70. PEPPERCORNS ASPARAGUS

PREPARATION: 10 MIN **COOKING:** 2H **SERVINGS:** 4

INGREDIENTS

- 3 cups asparagus spears, halved
- 3 garlic cloves, sliced
- 1 tablespoon dill
- ¼ cup white wine vinegar
- ¼ cup apple cider vinegar
- 2 cloves
- 1 cup of water
- ¼ teaspoon red pepper flakes
- 8 black peppercorns
- 1 teaspoon coriander seeds

DIRECTIONS

1. In your slow cooker, mix the asparagus with the cider vinegar, white vinegar, dill, cloves, water, garlic, pepper flakes, peppercorns, and coriander, cover, and cook on high for 2 hours. Drain asparagus, transfer it to bowls, and serve as a snack.

Nutrition: *Calories: 20 Fat: 0.1g Carbs: 3.6g Protein: 1.7g*

71. LIGHT SHRIMP SALAD

PREPARATION: 10 MIN   **COOKING:** 5 H 30 MIN   **SERVINGS:** 4

INGREDIENTS

- 1 cup tomato, chopped
- ¼ pound shrimp, peeled, deveined, and chopped
- 1 cup canned black beans, no-salt-added, drained and rinsed
- 1 cup cucumber, chopped
- 2 teaspoons cumin, ground
- 2 tablespoons olive oil
- ½ cup red onion, chopped
- Zest and juice of 2 limes
- Zest and juice of 2 lemons
- 2 tablespoons garlic, minced
- ¼ cup cilantro, chopped

DIRECTIONS

1. In a bowl, mix lime juice and lemon juice with shrimp and toss. Grease the slow cooker with the oil, add black beans, tomato, onion, garlic, and cumin, cover, and cook on low within 5 hours.
2. Add shrimp, cover, cook on low for 30 minutes, more, transfer everything to a bowl, add cucumber and cilantro, toss, leave aside to cool down, divide between small bowls and serve as an appetizer.

Nutrition: Calories: 153 Fat: 4.4g Carbs: 21.4g Protein: 9.3g

72. MUSHROOM SALSA WITH PUMPKIN SEEDS

PREPARATION: 10 MIN   **COOKING:** 3 H   **SERVINGS:** 4

INGREDIENTS

- 1-pound white mushrooms, sliced
- 1 cup cherry tomatoes, halved
- 1 cup black olives, pitted and sliced
- 1 tablespoon olive oil
- Juice of 1 lime
- 2 tablespoons parsley, chopped
- 2 tablespoons pumpkin seeds
- 1 tablespoon basil, chopped
- 1 tablespoon balsamic vinegar

DIRECTIONS

1. In a slow cooker, combine the mushrooms with the tomatoes, olives, and the other ingredients, cook on low within 3 hours. Divide the salsa into bowls and serve as an appetizer.

Nutrition: *Calories: 129 Fat: 9.5g Carbs: 9.4g Protein: 5.4g*

73. ONION CHICKPEAS DIP

PREPARATION: 10 MIN   **COOKING:** 2H   **SERVINGS:** 4

INGREDIENTS

- 2 cups canned chickpeas, no-salt-added, drained and rinsed
- 1 cup red bell pepper, sliced
- 1 teaspoon onion powder
- 1 tablespoon lemon juice
- 1 teaspoon garlic powder
- 1 tablespoon olive oil
- 2 tablespoons white sesame seeds
- A pinch of cayenne pepper
- 1 and ¼ teaspoons cumin, ground

DIRECTIONS

1. In your slow cooker, mix red bell pepper with oil, sesame seeds, chickpeas, lemon juice, garlic and onion powder, cayenne pepper, cumin, cover, and cook on high for 2 hours. Transfer this mix to your blender, pulse well, divide into serving bowls and serve cold.

Nutrition: *Calories: 143 Fat: 3.8g Carbs: 21.6g Protein: 6.8g*

74. GARLIC AND BEANS SPREAD

PREPARATION: 10 MIN **COOKING:** 6 H **SERVINGS:** 4

INGREDIENTS

- 15 oz. canned white beans, no-salt-added, drained and rinsed
- 8 garlic cloves, roasted
- 1 cup low-sodium veggie stock
- 2 tablespoons lemon juice
- 2 tablespoons olive oil

DIRECTIONS

1. In your blender, mix beans with oil, stock, garlic, and lemon juice, cover the slow cooker, cook on low for 6 hours, transfer to your blender, pulse well, divide into bowls and serve as a snack.

Nutrition: *Calories: 214 Fat: 4g Carbs: 33.2g Protein: 12.9g*

75. SOUR CREAM DIP

PREPARATION: 20 MIN **COOKING:** 2H **SERVINGS:** 4

INGREDIENTS

- 1 bunch spinach leaves, roughly chopped
- ¾ cup low-fat sour cream
- 1 scallion, sliced
- 2 tablespoons mint leaves, chopped
- Black pepper to the taste

DIRECTIONS

1. In your slow cooker, mix the spinach with the scallion, mint, cream, and black pepper, cover, cook on high within 2 hours, stir well, divide into bowls and serve.

Nutrition: *Calories: 121 Fat: 9.7g Carbs: 6.3g Protein: 4g*

76. SIMPLE MEATBALLS

PREPARATION: 10 MIN **COOKING:** 8 H **SERVINGS:** 16

INGREDIENTS

- 1 and ½ pounds beef, ground
- 1 egg, whisked
- 16 oz. canned tomatoes, crushed
- 14 oz. canned tomato puree
- ¼ cup parsley, chopped
- 2 garlic cloves, minced
- 1 yellow onion, chopped
- Black pepper to the taste

DIRECTIONS

1. In a bowl, mix beef with egg, parsley, garlic, black pepper, and onion and stir well.
2. Shape 16 meatballs, place them in your slow cooker, add tomato puree and crushed tomatoes on top, cover, and cook on low within 8 hours. Arrange them on a platter and serve. Enjoy!

Nutrition: *Calories: 160 Fat: 5g Carbs: 10g Protein: 7g*

77. TASTY CHICKEN WINGS

PREPARATION: 10 MIN   **COOKING:** 3 H   **SERVINGS:** 6

INGREDIENTS

- 2 tablespoons garlic, minced
- 2 and ¼ cups pineapple juice
- 3 tablespoons coconut aminos
- 2 tablespoons tapioca flour
- 1 tablespoon ginger, minced
- 1 teaspoon sesame oil
- A pinch of sea salt
- 3 pounds of chicken wings
- A few red pepper flakes, crushed
- 2 tablespoons 5 spice powder
- Sesame seeds, toasted for serving
- Chopped cilantro, for serving

DIRECTIONS

1. Put 2 cups pineapple juice in your slow cooker, add sesame oil, a pinch of salt, coconut aminos, ginger, and garlic, and whisk well.
2. In a bowl, mix tapioca flour with the rest of the pineapple juice, whisk, and add to your slow cooker. Whisk everything and then add chicken wings.
3. Season them with pepper flakes and 5 spice, toss everything, cover and cook on high for 3 hours. Transfer chicken wings to a platter and sprinkle cilantro and sesame seeds on top.
4. Transfer sauce from the slow cooker to a pot and heat it for 2 minutes over medium-high heat. Whisk well, pour into small bowls, and serve your wings with it. Enjoy!

Nutrition: *Calories: 200 Fat: 4g Carbs: 9g Protein: 20g*

78. CHICKEN SPREAD

PREPARATION: 10 MIN   **COOKING:** 2 H   **SERVINGS:** 4

INGREDIENTS

- 12 oz. chicken breasts, skinless, boneless, cooked and shredded
- 10 oz. coconut cream
- 1 cup of coconut milk
- 1 cup hot sauce
- A pinch of salt and black pepper
- ½ teaspoon garlic powder
- ¼ cup scallions, chopped
- ½ teaspoon onion powder

DIRECTIONS

1. Mix the chicken with the cream, coconut milk, hot sauce, salt, pepper, garlic powder, scallions, and onion powder in your slow cooker, toss, cover, cook on low for 2 hours, stir again, divide into bowls and serve as a spread. Enjoy!

Nutrition: *Calories: 214 Fat: 4g Carbs: 16g Protein: 17g*

79. DIFFERENT CHICKEN DIP

PREPARATION: 10 MIN   **COOKING:** 3 H 30 MIN   **SERVINGS:** 4

INGREDIENTS

- 1 yellow onion, chopped
- 2 teaspoons olive oil
- 1 red bell pepper, chopped
- 3 cups rotisserie chicken, cooked and shredded
- 12 oz. coconut cream
- ½ cup chili sauce
- 2 tablespoons chives, chopped

DIRECTIONS

1. Heat-up a pan with the oil over medium-high heat, add the onion, stir, cook for 5 minutes and transfer to your slow cooker.
2. Add bell pepper, cream, chicken, chili sauce, chives, toss, cover, cook on low for 3 hours and 30 minutes, divide into bowls and serve as a party dip. Enjoy!

Nutrition: *Calories: 251 Fat: 5g Carbs: 17g Protein: 18g*

80. CARROT DIP

PREPARATION: 10 MIN   **COOKING:** 5 H   **SERVINGS:** 4

INGREDIENTS

- 2-pound carrots, peeled and chopped
- ¼ cup olive oil
- 2 teaspoons cumin, ground
- A pinch of salt and black pepper
- 4 garlic cloves, minced
- ½ cup veggie stock

DIRECTIONS

1. Grease your slow cooker with half of the oil, add carrots, cumin, salt, pepper, garlic, and stock, toss, cover, cook on low for 5 hours, transfer to your blender, add the rest of the oil, pulse well, divide into bowls and serve. Enjoy!

Nutrition: *Calories: 211 Fat: 6g Carbs: 13g Protein: 7g*

81. PEPPERONI DIP

PREPARATION: 10 MIN **COOKING:** 1 H **SERVINGS:** 4

INGREDIENTS

- 13 oz. coconut cream
- 8 oz. pepperoni, sliced
- A pinch of black pepper

DIRECTIONS

1. In your slow cooker, combine the cream with the pepperoni and black pepper, cover, cook on low for 1 hour, stir, divide into bowls and serve. Enjoy!

Nutrition: *Calories: 231 Fat: 4g Carbs: 16g Protein: 11g*

82. EGGPLANT SPREAD

PREPARATION: 10 MIN **COOKING:** 1 H 30 MIN **SERVINGS:** 4

INGREDIENTS

- 2 pounds eggplants, peeled and cubed
- 1 tablespoon sesame paste
- 3 tablespoons lemon juice
- 1 garlic clove, minced
- ¼ teaspoon liquid smoke
- ½ teaspoon olive oil
- Handful parsley, chopped

DIRECTIONS

1. In your slow cooker, combine the eggplants with the sesame paste, lemon juice, garlic, liquid smoke, oil, parsley, toss, cover, cook on high for 1 hour and 30 minutes, pulse using an immersion blender, and serve. Enjoy!

Nutrition: *Calories: 211 Fat: 4g Carbs: 15g Protein: 7g*

83. JALAPENO POPPERS

PREPARATION: 10 MIN   **COOKING:** 3 MIN   **SERVINGS:** 4

INGREDIENTS

- ½ pound chorizo, chopped
- 10 jalapenos, tops cut off and deseeded
- 1 small white onion, chopped
- ½ pound beef, ground
- ¼ teaspoon garlic powder
- 1 tablespoon maple syrup
- 1 tablespoon mustard
- 1/3 cup water

DIRECTIONS

1. Mix the beef with chorizo, garlic powder, and onion in a bowl. Stuff your jalapenos with the mix and put them in your slow cooker.
2. Put the water, cover, and cook on high within 3 hours. Move the jalapeno poppers to a lined baking sheet. In a bowl, mix maple syrup with mustard and whisk well.
3. Brush poppers with this mix, introduce in the preheated broiler and cook for 10 minutes. Arrange on a platter and serve. Enjoy!

Nutrition: *Calories: 200 Fat: 2g Carbs: 8g Protein: 3g*

84. FISH STICKS

PREPARATION: 10 MIN   **COOKING:** 2 H   **SERVINGS:** 4

INGREDIENTS

- 2 eggs, whisked
- 1-pound cod fillets, cut into medium strips
- 1 and ½ cups almond flour
- A pinch of sea salt
- Black pepper to the taste
- ½ cup tapioca flour
- ¼ teaspoon paprika
- Cooking spray

DIRECTIONS

1. In a bowl, mix almond flour, salt, pepper, tapioca, and paprika and stir. Put the eggs in another bowl. Dip fish sticks in the eggs and then dredge in the flour mix.
2. Spray your slow cooker with cooking spray and arrange fish sticks in it—cover and cook on high within 2 hours. Arrange on a platter and serve. Enjoy!

Nutrition: *Calories: 200 Fat: 2g Carbs: 7g Protein: 12g*

85. SPICY PECANS

PREPARATION: 10 MIN **COOKING:** 2 H 15 MIN **SERVINGS:** 4

INGREDIENTS

- 1-pound pecans halved
- 2 tablespoons olive oil
- 1 teaspoon basil, dried
- 1 tablespoon chili powder
- 1 teaspoon oregano, dried
- ¼ teaspoon garlic powder
- 1 teaspoon thyme, dried
- ½ teaspoon onion powder
- A pinch of cayenne pepper

DIRECTIONS

1. In your slow cooker, mix pecans with oil, basil, chili powder, oregano, garlic powder, onion powder, thyme, and cayenne and toss to coat.
2. Cover and cook on high within 15 minutes. Switch slow cooker to low and cook for 2 hours. Serve as a snack. Enjoy!

Nutrition: *Calories: 78 Fat: 3g Carbs: 9g Protein: 2g*

86. SAUSAGE APPETIZER

PREPARATION: 10 MIN **COOKING:** 2 H **SERVINGS:** 15

INGREDIENTS

- 2 pounds sausages, sliced
- 18 oz. unsweetened apple jelly
- 9 oz. Dijon mustard

DIRECTIONS

1. Place sausage slices in your slow cooker, add apple jelly and mustard and toss to coat well. Cover and cook on low within 2 hours, stirring every 20 minutes. Arrange sausage slices on a platter and serve as an appetizer. Enjoy!

Nutrition: *Calories: 140 Fat: 3g Carbs: 9g Protein: 10g*

87. ASPARAGUS SPREAD

PREPARATION: 10 MIN **COOKING:** 2H 30 MIN **SERVINGS:** 4

INGREDIENTS

- 1 bunch asparagus, roughly chopped
- 4 garlic cloves, minced
- 5 oz. coconut cream
- ½ teaspoon garlic powder
- ½ teaspoon red pepper flakes
- ¼ teaspoon onion powder
- ¼ teaspoon paprika
- 6 oz. baby spinach
- 2 teaspoons olive oil
- ½ cup veggie stock

DIRECTIONS

1. In your slow cooker, combine the asparagus with the garlic, cream, garlic powder, pepper flakes, onion powder, paprika, spinach, stock, and oil, toss, cover, cook on low for 2 hours and 30 minutes, pulse using an immersion blender and serve. Enjoy!

Nutrition: *Calories: 221 Fat: 4g Carbs: 16g Protein: 8g*

88. BROCCOLI DIP

PREPARATION: 10 MIN **COOKING:** 2 H **SERVINGS:** 4

INGREDIENTS

- 1 yellow onion, chopped
- 6 bacon slices, cooked and chopped
- 2 garlic cloves, minced
- ¼ teaspoon red pepper flakes, crushed
- 4 cups broccoli florets, chopped
- 8 oz. coconut cream
- 1 tablespoon scallions, chopped
- ½ cup avocado mayonnaise
- ½ cup of coconut milk
- A pinch of salt and black pepper

DIRECTIONS

1. In your slow cooker, combine the onion with the bacon, garlic, pepper flakes, broccoli, cream, scallions, mayo, milk, salt and pepper, stir, cover, cook on low for 2 hours, stir again really well, divide into bowls and serve. Enjoy!

Nutrition: *Calories: 261 Fat: 11g Carbs: 8g Protein: 12g*

89. CRAB AND ONION DIP

PREPARATION: 10 MIN **COOKING:** 4 H **SERVINGS:** 4

INGREDIENTS

- 24 oz. coconut cream
- 12 oz. canned crabmeat, drained
- ¼ cup of coconut milk
- 4 green onions, chopped
- 2 teaspoons horseradish, prepared
- A pinch of salt and black pepper

DIRECTIONS

1. In your slow cooker, combine the cream with the crabmeat, milk, onions, salt, pepper, and horseradish, stir, cover, cook on low for 4 hours, divide into bowls and serve. Enjoy!

Nutrition: *Calories: 167 Fat: 8g Carbs: 2g Protein: 7g*

90. SPINACH AND BACON DIP

PREPARATION: 10 MIN   **COOKING:** 2 H   **SERVINGS:** 4

INGREDIENTS

- 16 oz. coconut cream
- 1 cup of coconut milk
- 15 oz. canned artichokes, drained and chopped
- 10 oz. spinach, chopped
- 2 tomatoes, chopped
- ½ cup bacon, cooked and crumbled
- 4 green onions, chopped

DIRECTIONS

1. In your slow cooker, combine the cream with coconut milk, spinach, artichokes, tomatoes, and green onions, stir, cover, cook on low for 2 hours, divide into bowls, sprinkle bacon on top, and serve. Enjoy!

Nutrition: *Calories: 200 Fat: 6g Carbs: 9g Protein: 6g*

91. BEAN PESTO DIP

PREPARATION: 10 MIN   **COOKING:** 6 H   **SERVINGS:** 4

INGREDIENTS

- 10 oz. refried beans
- 1 tbsp pesto sauce
- 1 tsp salt
- 7 oz. Cheddar cheese, shredded
- 1 tsp paprika
- 1 cup of salsa
- 4 tbsp sour cream
- 2-oz. cream cheese
- 1 tsp dried dill

DIRECTIONS

1. Mix pesto with salt, salsa, sour cream, dill, beans, cheese, paprika, and cream cheese in the slow cooker.
2. Put the cooker's lid on and set the cooking time to 6 hours on low. Blend the mixture using a hand blender. Serve fresh.

Nutrition: *Calories: 102 Fat: 6.3g Carbs: 7.43g Protein: 5g*

92. CHEESY CHILI PEPPER DIP

PREPARATION: 10 MIN   **COOKING:** 9 H   **SERVINGS:** 4

INGREDIENTS

- 4 chili pepper, sliced and deseeded
- 7 oz. Monterey cheese
- 3 tbsp cream cheese
- 1 tbsp onion powder
- 3 tbsp dried dill
- 3 oz. butter
- 1 tbsp cornstarch
- 1 tbsp flour
- ¼ tsp salt

DIRECTIONS

1. Add chili peppers to a blender and add salt, butter, onion powder, and dill. Blend the chili peppers well, then transfer to the slow cooker.
2. Stir in flour, cornstarch, cream cheese, and Monterey cheese. Put the cooker's lid on and set the cooking time to 6 hours on low. Serve.

Nutrition: *Calories: 212 Fat: 18.2g Carbs: 6.06g Protein: 8g*

93. CREAMY MUSHROOM SPREAD

PREPARATION: 15 MIN   **COOKING:** 4 H   **SERVINGS:** 2

INGREDIENTS

- 1-pound mushrooms, sliced
- 3 garlic cloves, minced
- 1 cup heavy cream
- 2 teaspoons smoked paprika
- Salt and black pepper to the taste
- 2 tablespoons parsley, chopped

DIRECTIONS

1. In your slow cooker, mix the mushrooms with the garlic and the other ingredients, whisk, cook on low within 4 hours. Whisk, divide into bowls, and serve as a party spread.

Nutrition: *Calories: 300 Fat: 6g Carbs: 16g Protein: 6g*

94. PORK TOSTADAS

PREPARATION: 15 MIN   **COOKING:** 4 H   **SERVINGS:** 4

INGREDIENTS

- 4 lbs. pork shoulder, boneless and cubed
- Salt and black pepper to the taste
- 2 cups coca cola
- 1/3 cup brown sugar
- ½ cup hot sauce
- 2 tsp chili powder
- 2 tbsp tomato paste
- ¼ tsp cumin, ground
- 1 cup enchilada sauce
- Corn tortillas, toasted for a few minutes in the oven
- Mexican cheese, shredded for serving
- 4 shredded lettuce leaves, for serving
- Salsa
- Guacamole for serving

DIRECTIONS

1. Add cup coke, salsa, sugar, chili powder, cumin, pork, hot sauce, and tomato paste to the slow cooker. Put the cooker's lid on and set the cooking time to 4 hours on low.
2. Drain the cooked pork and shred it finely. Mix well the shredded pork with enchilada sauce and remaining coke.
3. Divide the pork into the tortillas and top it with lettuce leaves, guacamole, and Mexican cheese. Serve.

Nutrition: *Calories: 162 Fat: 3g Carbs: 12g Protein: 5g*

95. BBQ CHICKEN DIP

PREPARATION: 15 MIN   **COOKING:** 1 H 30 MIN   **SERVINGS:** 4

INGREDIENTS

- 1 and ½ cups BBQ sauce
- 1 small red onion, chopped
- 24 oz. cream cheese, cubed
- 2 cups rotisserie chicken, shredded
- 3 bacon slices, cooked and crumbled
- 1 plum tomato, chopped
- ½ cup cheddar cheese, shredded
- 1 tablespoon green onions, chopped

DIRECTIONS

1. In your slow cooker, mix BBQ sauce with onion, cream cheese, rotisserie chicken, bacon, tomato, cheddar, and green onions, stir, cover, and cook on low for 1 hour and 30 minutes. Divide into bowls and serve.

Nutrition: *Calories: 251 Fat: 4g Carbs: 10g Protein: 4g*

96. LEMON SHRIMP DIP

PREPARATION: 15 MIN **COOKING:** 2 H **SERVINGS:** 2

INGREDIENTS

- 3 oz. cream cheese, soft
- ½ cup heavy cream
- 1-pound shrimp, peeled, deveined, and chopped
- ½ tablespoon balsamic vinegar
- 2 tablespoons mayonnaise
- ½ tablespoon lemon juice
- A pinch of salt and black pepper
- 2 oz. mozzarella, shredded
- 1 tablespoon parsley, chopped

DIRECTIONS

1. In your slow cooker, mix the cream cheese with the shrimp, heavy cream, and the other ingredients, whisk, put the lid on and cook on low for 2 hours. Divide into bowls and serve.

Nutrition: *Calories: 342 Fat: 4g Carbs: 7g Protein: 10g*

97. ZUCCHINI STICKS

PREPARATION: 15 MIN **COOKING:** 2 H **SERVINGS:** 13 STICKS

INGREDIENTS

- 9 oz. green zucchini, cut into thick sticks
- 4 oz. Parmesan, grated
- 1 egg
- 1 tsp salt
- 1 tsp ground white pepper
- 1 tsp olive oil
- 2 tbsp milk

Nutrition: *Calories: 51 Fat: 1.7g Carbs: 4.62g Protein: 5g*

DIRECTIONS

1. Grease the base of your slow cooker with olive oil. Whisk egg with milk, white pepper, and salt in a bowl.
2. Dip the prepared zucchini sticks in the egg mixture, then place them in the slow cooker. Put the cooker's lid on and set the cooking time to 2 hours on high.
3. Spread the cheese over the zucchini sticks evenly. Put the cooker's lid on and set the cooking time to 2 hours on high. Serve.

98. CHICKEN CORDON BLEU DIP

PREPARATION: 15 MIN **COOKING:** 1 H 30 MIN **SERVINGS:** 4

INGREDIENTS

- 16 oz. cream cheese
- 2 chicken breasts, baked and shredded
- 1 cup cheddar cheese, shredded
- 1 cup Swiss cheese, shredded
- 3 garlic cloves, minced
- 6 oz. ham, chopped
- 2 tablespoons green onions
- Salt and black pepper to the taste

Nutrition: *Calories: 243 Fat: 5g Carbs: 15g Protein: 3g*

DIRECTIONS

1. In your slow cooker, mix cream cheese with chicken, cheddar cheese, Swiss cheese, garlic, ham, green onions, salt, and pepper, stir, cover, and cook on low for 1 hour and 30 minutes. Serve.

99. EGGPLANT ZUCCHINI DIP

PREPARATION: 15 MIN **COOKING:** 4 H 5 MIN **SERVINGS:** 15

INGREDIENTS

- 1 eggplant
- 1 zucchini, chopped
- 2 tbsp olive oil
- 2 tbsp balsamic vinegar
- 1 tbsp parsley, chopped
- 1 yellow onion, chopped
- 1 celery stick, chopped
- 1 tomato, chopped
- 2 tbsp tomato paste
- 1 and ½ tsp garlic, minced
- A pinch of sea salt
- Black pepper to the taste

DIRECTIONS

1. Rub the eggplant with cooking oil and grill it for 5 minutes per side on a preheated grill. Chop the grilled eggplant and transfer it to the slow cooker.
2. Add tomato, parsley, and all other ingredients to the cooker. Put the cooker's lid on and set the cooking time to 4 hours on high. Serve.

Nutrition: *Calories: 110. Fat: 1g Carbs: 7g Protein: 5g*

100. CALAMARI RINGS BOWLS

PREPARATION: 15 MIN **COOKING:** 6 H **SERVINGS:** 2

INGREDIENTS

- ½ pound calamari rings
- 1 tablespoon balsamic vinegar
- ½ tablespoon soy sauce
- 1 tablespoon sugar
- 1 cup veggie stock
- ½ teaspoon turmeric powder
- ½ teaspoon sweet paprika
- ½ cup chicken stock

DIRECTIONS

1. In your slow cooker, mix the calamari rings with the vinegar, soy sauce, and the other fixing, toss, put the lid on and cook on high for 6 hours. Divide into bowls and serve right away as an appetizer.

Nutrition: *Calories: 230 Fat: 2g Carbs: 7g Protein: 5g*

101. CHICKEN BITES

PREPARATION: 15 MIN   **COOKING:** 7 H   **SERVINGS:** 4

INGREDIENTS

- 1-pound chicken thighs, boneless and skinless
- 1 tbsp ginger, grated
- 1 yellow onion, sliced
- 1 tbsp garlic, minced
- 2 tsp cumin, ground
- 1 tsp cinnamon powder
- 2 tbsp sweet paprika
- 1 & ½ cups chicken stock
- 2 tbsp lemon juice
- ½ cup green olives pitted and roughly chopped
- Salt
- 3 tbsp olive oil
- 5 pita bread, cut in quarters and warmed in the oven

DIRECTIONS

1. Heat-up a pan with the olive oil over medium-high heat, put onions, garlic, ginger, salt, and pepper, stir and cook for 2 minutes. Put the cumin and cinnamon, mix well, and take off the heat.
2. Put chicken pieces in your slow cooker, then the onions mix, lemon juice, olives plus stock, stir, cover and cook on low within 7 hours. Shred meat, stir the whole mixture again, divide it on pita chips, and serve as a snack.

Nutrition: *Calories: 265 Fat: 7g Carbs: 14g Protein: 6g*

102. MAPLE GLAZED TURKEY STRIPS

PREPARATION: 15 MIN   **COOKING:** 3 H 30 MIN   **SERVINGS:** 4

INGREDIENTS

- 15 oz. turkey fillets, cut into strips
- 2 tbsp honey
- 1 tbsp maple syrup
- 1 tsp cayenne pepper
- 1 tbsp butter
- 1 tsp paprika
- 1 tsp oregano
- 1 tsp dried dill
- 2 tbsp mayo

DIRECTIONS

1. Place the turkey strips in the slow cooker. Add all other spices, herbs, and mayo on top of the turkey.
2. Put the cooker's lid on and set the cooking time to 3 hours on high. During this time, mix honey with maple syrup and melted butter in a bowl.
3. Pour this honey glaze over the turkey evenly. Put the cooker's lid on and set the cooking time to 30 minutes on high. Serve warm.

Nutrition: *Calories: 295 Fat: 25.2g Carbs: 6.82g Protein: 10g*

103. LENTILS ROLLS

PREPARATION: 15 MIN **COOKING:** 8 H **SERVINGS:** 4

INGREDIENTS

- 1 cup brown lentils, cooked
- 1 green cabbage head, leaves separated
- ½ cup onion, chopped
- 1 cup brown rice, already cooked
- 2 oz. white mushrooms, chopped
- ¼ cup pine nuts, toasted
- ¼ cup raisins
- 2 garlic cloves, minced
- 2 tablespoons dill, chopped
- 1 tablespoon olive oil
- 25 oz. marinara sauce
- A pinch of salt and black pepper
- ¼ cup of water

DIRECTIONS

1. In a bowl, mix lentils with onion, rice, mushrooms, pine nuts, raisins, garlic, dill, salt, and pepper, and whisk well.
2. Arrange cabbage leaves on a working surface, divide lentils mix and wrap them well. Add marinara sauce and water to your slow cooker and stir.
3. Add cabbage rolls, cover, and cook on low for 8 hours. Arrange cabbage rolls on a platter and serve.

Nutrition: *Calories: 281 Fat: 6g Carbs: 12g Protein: 3g*

104. CAULIFLOWER BITES

PREPARATION: 15 MIN **COOKING:** 4 H **SERVINGS:** 2

INGREDIENTS

- 2 cups cauliflower florets
- 1 tablespoon Italian seasoning
- 1 tablespoon sweet paprika
- 2 tablespoons tomato sauce
- 1 teaspoon sweet paprika
- 1 tablespoon olive oil
- ¼ cup veggie stock

DIRECTIONS

1. In your slow cooker, mix the cauliflower florets with the Italian seasoning and the other fixing, toss, cook on low within 4 hours. Serve.

Nutrition: *Calories: 251 Fat: 4g Carbs: 7g Protein: 3g*

105. LEMON PEEL SNACK

PREPARATION: 15 MIN **COOKING:** 4 H **SERVINGS:** 4

INGREDIENTS

- 5 big lemons, sliced halves, pulp removed and peel cut into strips
- 2 and ¼ cups white sugar
- 5 cups of water

DIRECTIONS

1. Put strips in your slow cooker, add water and sugar, stir cover and cook on low for 4 hours. Drain lemon peel and keep in jars until serving.

Nutrition: *Calories: 7 Fat: 1g Carbs: 2g Protein: 1g*

106. CANDIED PECANS

PREPARATION: 10 MIN **COOKING:** 3 H **SERVINGS:** 4

INGREDIENTS

- 1 cup white sugar
- 1 and ½ tablespoons cinnamon powder
- ½ cup brown sugar
- 1 egg white, whisked
- 4 cups pecans
- 2 teaspoons vanilla extract
- ¼ cup of water

DIRECTIONS

1. In a bowl, mix white sugar with cinnamon, brown sugar, and vanilla and stir. Dip pecans in egg white, then in the sugar mix, put them in your slow cooker, add the water, and cook on low for 3 hours. Serve.

Nutrition: Calories: 152 Fat: 4g Carbs: 16g Protein: 6g

107. DILL POTATO SALAD

PREPARATION: 10 MIN **COOKING:** 8 H **SERVINGS:** 2

INGREDIENTS

- 1 red onion, sliced
- 1-pound gold potatoes, peeled and roughly cubed
- 2 tablespoons balsamic vinegar
- ½ cup heavy cream
- 1 tablespoons mustard
- A pinch of salt and black pepper
- 1 tablespoon dill, chopped
- ½ cup celery, chopped

DIRECTIONS

1. In your slow cooker, mix the potatoes with the cream, mustard, and the other, toss, cook on low within 8 hours. Divide salad into bowls, and serve as an appetizer.

Nutrition: Calories: 251 Fat: 6g Carbs: 8g Protein: 7g

108. STUFFED PEPPERS PLATTER

PREPARATION: 10 MIN **COOKING:** 4 H **SERVINGS:** 2

INGREDIENTS

- 1 red onion, chopped
- 1 teaspoon olive oil
- ½ teaspoon sweet paprika
- ½ tablespoon chili powder
- 1 garlic clove, minced
- 1 cup white rice, cooked
- ½ cup of corn
- A pinch of salt and black pepper
- 2 colored bell peppers, tops, and insides scooped out
- ½ cup tomato sauce

DIRECTIONS

1. In a bowl, mix the onion with the oil, paprika, and the other ingredients except for the peppers and tomato sauce, stir well and stuff the peppers with this mix.
2. Put the peppers in the slow cooker, add the sauce, put the lid on, and cook on low for 4 hours. Move the peppers to a platter and serve as an appetizer.

Nutrition: *Calories: 253 Fat: 5g Carbs: 12g Protein: 3g*

109. PEANUT SNACK

PREPARATION: 10 MIN **COOKING:** 1 H 30 MIN **SERVINGS:** 4

INGREDIENTS

- 1 cup peanuts
- 1 cup chocolate peanut butter
- 12 oz. dark chocolate chips
- 12 oz. white chocolate chips

DIRECTIONS

1. In your slow cooker, mix peanuts with peanut butter, dark and white chocolate chips, cook on low within 1 hour and 30 minutes. Divide this mix into small muffin cups, leave aside to cool down, and serve as a snack.

Nutrition: *Calories: 200 Fat: 4g Carbs: 10g Protein: 5g*

110. CORN DIP

PREPARATION: 10 MIN **COOKING:** 2 H **SERVINGS:** 2

INGREDIENTS

- 1 cup of corn
- 1 tablespoon chives, chopped
- ½ cup heavy cream
- 2 oz. cream cheese, cubed
- ¼ teaspoon chili powder

DIRECTIONS

1. In your slow cooker, mix the corn with the chives and the other ingredients, whisk, cook on low within 2 hours. Divide into bowls and serve.

Nutrition: *Calories: 272 Fat: 5g Carbs: 12g Protein: 4g*

111. APPLE DIP

PREPARATION: 10 MIN **COOKING:** 1 H 30 MIN **SERVINGS:** 4

INGREDIENTS

- 5 apples, peeled and chopped
- ½ teaspoon cinnamon powder
- 12 oz. jarred caramel sauce
- A pinch of nutmeg, ground

DIRECTIONS

1. In your slow cooker, mix apples with cinnamon, caramel sauce, and nutmeg stir, cook on high within 1 hour and 30 minutes. Divide into bowls and serve.

Nutrition: *Calories: 200 Fat: 3g Carbs: 10g Protein: 5g*

112. BEEF AND CHIPOTLE DIP

PREPARATION: 10 MIN   **COOKING:** 2 H   **SERVINGS:** 4

INGREDIENTS

- 8 oz. cream cheese, soft
- 2 tablespoons yellow onion, chopped
- 2 tablespoons mayonnaise
- 2 oz. hot pepper Monterey Jack cheese, shredded
- ¼ teaspoon garlic powder
- 2 chipotle chilies in adobo sauce, chopped
- 2 oz. dried beef, chopped
- ¼ cup pecans, chopped

DIRECTIONS

1. In your slow cooker, mix cream cheese with onion, mayo, Monterey Jack cheese, garlic powder, chilies, and dried beef, stir, cover, and cook on low for 2 hours. Add pecans, stir, divide into bowls and serve.

Nutrition: *Calories: 130 Fat: 11g Carbs: 3g Protein: 4g*

113. PINEAPPLE AND TOFU SALSA

PREPARATION: 10 MIN   **COOKING:** 6 H   **SERVINGS:** 2

INGREDIENTS

- ½ cup firm tofu, cubed
- 1 cup pineapple, peeled and cubed
- 1 cup cherry tomatoes, halved
- ½ tablespoons sesame oil
- 1 tablespoon soy sauce
- ½ cup pineapple juice
- ½ tablespoon ginger, grated
- 1 garlic clove, minced

DIRECTIONS

1. In your slow cooker, mix the tofu with the pineapple and the other ingredients, toss, put the lid on and cook on low within 6 hours. Divide into bowls and serve as an appetizer.

Nutrition: *Calories: 201 Fat: 5g Carbs: 15g Protein: 4g*

114. BUFFALO MEATBALLS

PREPARATION: 10 MIN   **COOKING:** 3 H 10 MIN   **SERVINGS:** 36

INGREDIENTS

- 1 cup breadcrumbs
- 2 pounds chicken, ground
- 2 eggs
- ¾ cup buffalo wings sauce
- ½ cup yellow onion, chopped
- 3 garlic cloves, minced
- Salt and black pepper to the taste
- 2 tablespoons olive oil
- ¼ cup butter, melted
- 1 cup blue cheese dressing

DIRECTIONS

1. Mix the chicken, breadcrumbs, eggs, onion, garlic, salt, pepper in a bowl, and stir and shape small meatballs out of this mix.
2. Heat-up a pan with the oil over medium-high heat, plus meatballs, brown them within a few minutes on each side, and move them to your slow cooker.
3. Put the melted butter plus buffalo wings sauce, cover, and cook on low for 3 hours. Serve with the blue cheese dressing.

Nutrition: *Calories: 100 Fat: 7g Carbs: 4g Protein: 4g*

---

115. GLAZED SAUSAGES

PREPARATION: 10 MIN   **COOKING:** 4 H   **SERVINGS:** 24

INGREDIENTS

- 10 oz. jarred red pepper jelly
- 1/3 cup BBQ sauce
- ½ cup brown sugar
- 16 oz. pineapple chunks and juice
- 24 oz. cocktail-size sausages
- 1 tablespoons cornstarch
- 2 tablespoons water
- Cooking spray

DIRECTIONS

1. Oiled your slow cooker with cooking spray, add pepper jelly, BBQ sauce, brown sugar, pineapple plus sausages, stir, cover, and cook on low within 3 hours.
2. Put the cornstarch mixed with the water, whisk everything, and cook on high for 1 more hour. Serve.

Nutrition: *Calories: 170 Fat: 10g Carbs: 17g Protein: 4g*

116. BULGUR AND BEANS SALSA

PREPARATION: 10 MIN **COOKING:** 8 H **SERVINGS:** 2

INGREDIENTS

- 1 cup veggie stock
- ½ cup bulgur
- 1 small yellow onion, chopped
- 1 red bell pepper, chopped
- 1 garlic clove, minced
- 5 oz. canned kidney beans, drained
- ½ cup of salsa
- 1 tablespoon chili powder
- ¼ teaspoon oregano, dried
- Salt and black pepper to the taste

DIRECTIONS

1. In your slow cooker, mix the bulgur with the stock and the other fixing, toss, put the lid on and cook on low within 8 hours. Divide into bowls and serve cold as an appetizer.

Nutrition: *Calories: 351 Fat: 4g Carbs: 12g Protein: 4g*

---

117. CHEESY MIX

PREPARATION: 10 MIN **COOKING:** 2 H **SERVINGS:** 4

INGREDIENTS

- 2 cups small pretzels
- 2 cups of wheat cereal
- 3 cups of rice cereal
- 3 cups of corn cereal
- 2 cups small cheese crackers
- 1/3 cup parmesan, grated
- 1/3 cup bacon flavor chips
- ½ cup melted butter
- 1/3 cup canola oil
- 1-ounce ranch dressing

DIRECTIONS

1. Mix the pretzels with wheat cereal, rice cereal, corn cereal, crackers, chips, and parmesan in your slow cooker, cover, and cook on high within 2 hours, stirring every 20 minutes.
2. Mix the butter with oil and ranch dressing in a bowl and whisk well. Serve with the ranch dressing.

Nutrition: *Calories: 182 Fat: 2g Carbs: 12g Protein: 4g*

---

118. BEETS SALAD

PREPARATION: 10 MIN **COOKING:** 6 H **SERVINGS:** 2

INGREDIENTS

- 2 cups beets, cubed
- ¼ cup carrots, grated
- 2 oz. tempeh, rinsed and cubed
- 1 cup cherry tomatoes, halved
- ¼ cup veggie stock
- 3 oz. canned black beans, drained
- Salt and black pepper to the taste
- ½ teaspoon nutmeg, ground
- ½ teaspoon sweet paprika
- ½ cup parsley, chopped

DIRECTIONS

1. In your slow cooker, mix the beets with the carrots, tempeh, and the other, toss, cook on low within 6 hours. Divide into bowls and serve cold as an appetizer.

Nutrition: *Calories: 300 Fat: 6g Carbs: 16g Protein: 6g*

119. LENTILS SALSA

PREPARATION: 10 MIN **COOKING:** 3 H **SERVINGS:** 2

INGREDIENTS

- 1 cup canned lentils, drained
- 1 cup mild salsa
- 3 oz. tomato paste
- 2 tablespoons balsamic vinegar
- 1 small sweet onion, chopped
- 1 garlic clove, minced
- ½ tablespoon sugar
- A pinch of red pepper flakes
- A bit of salt and black pepper
- 1 tablespoon chives, chopped

DIRECTIONS

1. In your slow cooker, mix the lentils with the salsa and the other ingredients, toss, cook on high within 3 hours. Divide into bowls and serve.

Nutrition: *Calories: 260 Fat: 3g Carbs: 6g Protein: 7g*

120. TACOS

PREPARATION: 10 MIN **COOKING:** 4H **SERVINGS:** 2

INGREDIENTS

- 13 oz. canned pinto beans, drained
- ¼ cup chili sauce
- 2 oz. chipotle pepper in adobo sauce, chopped
- ½ tablespoon cocoa powder
- ¼ teaspoon cinnamon powder
- 4 taco shells

DIRECTIONS

1. In your slow cooker, mix the beans with the chili sauce and the other ingredients except for the taco shells, toss, put the lid on and cook on low for 4 hours. Divide the mix into the taco shells and serve them as an appetizer.

Nutrition: *Calories: 352 Fat: 3g Carbs: 12g Protein: 10g*

CHAPTER 4.
RICE, GRAINS & BEANS

121. THREE BEAN MEDITERRANEAN CHILI

PREPARATION: 10 MIN   **COOKING:** 12 H   **SERVINGS:** 4

INGREDIENTS

- 1 1/3 pounds ground turkey breast 99% lean
- 28 oz. diced tomatoes, drained
- 1 onion, small, chopped
- 16 oz tomato sauce
- 4 ½ oz chopped chilies in the can
- 15 ½ oz black beans drained
- 15 oz chickpeas drained
- 15 ½ oz small red beans, drained
- 2 tbsp chili powder
- 1 tsp cumin

For the topping:
- ½ cup chopped fresh cilantro for topping
- ½ cup red onion, chopped
- ¼ cup shredded cheddar
- ¼ cup sour cream
- ¼ cup avocado pieces

DIRECTIONS

1. Put turkey and onion into a medium-size skillet on medium-high heat. Continue cooking until the turkey becomes brown on all sides.
2. Now, take a slow cooker and transfer the turkey and onion into it. Add beans, tomatoes, chickpeas, chilies, tomato sauce, cumin, and chili powder into the cooker and combine.
3. Slow cook it for 12 hours. Top it with onions, cilantro, avocado pieces, shredded cheddar, and sour cream while serving. Serve it hot.

Nutrition: *Calories: 231 Carbs: 27.5g Protein: 19.5g Fat: 5g*

122. BEANS AND BARLEY STEW

PREPARATION: 10 MIN   **COOKING:** 8H 10 MIN   **SERVINGS:** 4

INGREDIENTS

- 1-pound dried bean mix, rinsed, kidney, navy, pinto
- 8 oz. dried barley
- 8 cups chicken broth
- 1 yellow onion, chopped
- 3 celery stalks, diced
- ½ pound barley
- 2 carrots, diced
- 2 cloves garlic, minced
- 1 bay leaf
- few springs fresh thyme
- 8 oz. baby spinach
- 2 teaspoons kosher salt
- 2 cups of water

DIRECTIONS

1. In the slow cooker, combine bean mix, pepper, carrots, celery, garlic, thyme, onions, bay leaf, and salt. Pour the broth and also 2 cups of water and stir thoroughly.
2. Cover the cooker and slow cook for 7 hours. Now add barely. If the stew consistency is too thick, add some more water. Cover again and cook for 1 more hour. Before serving, add spinach and stir. Serve hot.

Nutrition: *Calories: 262 Fat: 1.1g Carbs: 48.8g Protein: 15.6g*

123. MEDITERRANEAN LENTILS AND RICE

PREPARATION: 15 MIN **COOKING:** 8 H **SERVINGS:** 4

INGREDIENTS

- 1 cup brown lentils
- 1 onion, chopped
- ½ cup of rice
- ¾ teaspoon salt
- ½ teaspoon cinnamon
- 1 tablespoon ground cumin
- 4½ teaspoons olive oil
- 6 cups water or homemade vegetable stock or chicken stock

DIRECTIONS

1. Pour olive oil into the slow cooker. Set the slow cooker on high heat. Put onion into it and sauté. After 10-15 minutes, put all the remaining ingredients into the slow cooker, including water.
2. Cover the slow cooker and cook for 8 hours. You may stir the dish in between to check whether the food is dry or moisturized. Add water if required. Serve hot.

Nutrition: *Calories: 98 Fat: 3.8g Carbs: 14.7 Protein: 1.5g*

124. ITALIAN-MEDITERRANEAN MULTI-BEAN SOUP

PREPARATION: 10 MIN **COOKING:** 10 H **SERVINGS:** 4

INGREDIENTS

- 8 ¾ cups chicken broth
- 14 ½ oz. organic tomato, diced
- 16 oz. dried bean soup
- 4 medium carrots, chopped
- 1 large onion, chopped
- 3 medium stalks celery, chopped
- 2 tablespoons tomato paste
- ½ teaspoon pepper
- 1 teaspoon Italian seasoning
- 1 teaspoon salt

DIRECTIONS

1. Mix all the fixing in a slow cooker, except tomatoes. Cover the slow cooker, and set low cooking for 10 hours. Add tomatoes and mix them well.
2. Switch from low heat to high heat. Cover the cooker and cook further 15 more minutes or until it becomes hot. Serve hot.

Nutrition: *Calories: 180 Carbs: 30g Protein: 13g Fat: 1g*

125. SLOW COOKED GREEN BEANS

PREPARATION: 15 MIN **COOKING:** 3 H 30 MIN **SERVINGS:** 4

INGREDIENTS

- 6 slices bacon sliced crosswise into ½ inch pieces
- 3 cloves garlic, minced
- 1 onion, sliced lengthwise
- 2 pounds fresh green beans, trimmed
- 3 cups chicken broth
- ¼ cup tomato sauce
- 1 pinch cayenne pepper
- ¼ teaspoon salt
- ¼ teaspoon black pepper ground

DIRECTIONS

1. Heat a saucepan on medium heat. Add sliced bacon into the hot pan. Stir and cook it for about 6 minutes until it becomes brown and crispy.
2. Now, add onion into the pan and cook it for about 5 minutes until the onion becomes mushy and golden brown. Let the brown chunks of food at the bottom get dissolved with the onion's juices.
3. Add tomato sauce and minced garlic into the pan and mix it well. Cook for about 1 more minute until the garlic becomes soft.
4. Take a skillet and add green beans into it and add chicken broth into it. Heat the skillet on high heat and add black pepper, cayenne pepper, and salt into the skillet. Cook the beans until it becomes soft.
5. Now, switch the cooker from high heat to slow cooking mode for 3 hours. Keep stirring the mixture intermittently. If the mixture appears to be dry, pour more water or broth into it.
6. Check the salt and pepper. If required, adjust its taste as needed. After adding salt and pepper, cook it further for about 30 minutes. Serve it hot along with its juice.

Nutrition: *Calories: 124 Carbs: 16g Protein: 7.3g Fat: 4.3g*

---

126. SPANISH RICE

PREPARATION: 10 MIN **COOKING:** 4 H 10 MIN **SERVINGS:** 4

INGREDIENTS

- 2 tbsp olive oil, + extra for greasing
- 2 cups whole grain rice
- 14½ oz. diced tomatoes in the can
- 1 medium yellow onion, chopped
- 3 cloves garlic, minced
- 2 cups broth or stock, or water
- ½ red bell pepper, medium cut size
- ½ yellow bell pepper, medium dice
- 1 ½ teaspoon ground cumin
- 2 teaspoons chili powder
- 1½ teaspoons kosher salt
- 2 tablespoons fresh cilantro leaves, for garnishing

DIRECTIONS

1. Put the olive oil into a large skillet and bring it to medium heat. Add rice into the skillet and combine well so that the grains get olive oil coating.
2. Now put the onion into the skillet and sauté for about 5 minutes, until the rice becomes pale golden brown. Slightly grease the inside of the slow cooker with olive oil.
3. Transfer the browned rice to the slow cooker. Add broth, bell peppers, tomatoes, garlic, cumin, chili powder, salt and combine thoroughly.
4. Cook on low within 4 hours. Check if the liquid is being absorbed by the rice well after 2 hours.
5. Continue cooking until the rice becomes soft, and all the moisture gets absorbed. Top it with cilantro leaves and serve hot.

Nutrition: *Calories: 55 Carbs: 5.36g Protein: 1.01g Fat: 3.78g*

127. WHOLE WHEAT LASAGNA

PREPARATION: 10 MIN   **COOKING:** 5 H   **SERVINGS:** 4

INGREDIENTS

- 2 pounds extra lean ground turkey
- 8 uncooked, whole wheat lasagna noodles
- 28 oz. spaghetti sauce
- 4 oz. sliced mushrooms
- 1 teaspoon Italian seasoning
- 2 cups shredded skim milk mozzarella cheese
- 1/3 cup water
- 15 oz. ricotta cheese, fat-free

DIRECTIONS

1. Clean, rinse, and drain the mushrooms. Keep them ready. Before starting the cooking, add a little olive oil to the slow cooker. Put the 4 lasagna noodles in the bottom of the slow cooker.
2. In a non-stick pan, sauté the ground turkey until it becomes brown. Add Italian seasoning and mix well. Place half of the browned turkey over the noodles in the slow cooker and spread it well.
3. Spread a layer of ½ of the sauce over the turkey. Now, add another layer of ½ of the mushrooms over it.
4. Similarly, add a layer of ½ of the ricotta and then half of the mozzarella over it. Repeat the layering. Cook on low for 5 hours.

Nutrition: *Calories: 469 Carbs: 31.3g Protein: 36.7g Fat: 21g*

128. HOMINY CHILI

PREPARATION: 5 MIN   **COOKING:** 8 H   **SERVINGS:** 4

INGREDIENTS

- 2 cans of diced tomatoes
- 1 can of hominy
- 1 can of kidney beans
- ¼ cup of sour cream
- ¼ cup of cheddar
- 4 squares of dark chocolate
- 2 tablespoons of chili powder
- 2 tablespoons of cilantro
- 1 teaspoon of cumin
- salt and pepper

DIRECTIONS

1. 1. Mix all the ingredients in the slow cooker. Cook on a low for 8 hours. Serve.

Nutrition: *Calories: 217 Carbs: 13g Fat: 2g Protein: 0g*

129. SANTA FE BLACK BEANS

PREPARATION: 5 MIN   **COOKING:** 8 H   **SERVINGS:** 4

INGREDIENTS

- 1 lb. of dry black beans
- 3 cups of vegetable bouillon
- 2 cups of diced onion
- 1 cup of queso fresco
- 1 chopped chipotle chili
- ½ cup of fresh cilantro, chopped
- 2 tablespoons of minced garlic
- 1 tablespoon of lime juice
- salt and pepper

DIRECTIONS

1. Mix all the ingredients except for the queso fresco in a slow cooker. Cook on low pressure for 8 hours. Add the queso fresco and pour on top. Serve.

Nutrition: *Calories: 165 Carbs: 23g Fat: 4g Protein: 10g*

130. CHICKEN AND CHICKPEA TAGINE

PREPARATION: 15 MIN   **COOKING:** 8 H   **SERVINGS:** 4

INGREDIENTS

- 8 chicken thighs
- 2 1/2 cups of chopped red onion
- 2 cans of chickpeas
- 1 cup of chicken stock
- spicy Moroccan herb mix
- 2 tablespoons of honey
- salt and pepper

DIRECTIONS

1. Mix all ingredients in the slow cooker. Cook on a low for 8 hours. Serve.

Nutrition: *Calories: 349 Carbs: 35g Fat: 9g Protein: 34g*

131. WHITE BEAN AND SMOKED HAM SOUP

PREPARATION: 5 MIN   COOKING: 8 H   SERVINGS: 4

INGREDIENTS

- 2 lbs. of smoked ham, diced
- 1 lb. of dried white beans
- 4 cups of chicken stock
- 1 cup of chopped onion
- 1 cup of chopped celery
- 1 cup of chopped carrot
- 3 tablespoons of minced garlic
- Herb mix
- salt and pepper

DIRECTIONS

1. Mix all ingredients in a slow cooker. Cook on a low for 8 hours. Serve.

Nutrition: *Calories: 210 Carbs: 26g Fat: 7g Protein: 11g*

132. CINCINNATI CHILI

PREPARATION: 5 MIN   COOKING: 8 H   SERVINGS: 4

INGREDIENTS

- 2 1/2 lbs. of meat, mince
- 3 cans of red kidney beans
- 2 cans of chopped tomatoes
- 2 tablespoons of eastern spice mix
- 1 tablespoon of warm spice mix, including cinnamon and nutmeg
- 1 tablespoon of minced garlic
- salt and pepper

DIRECTIONS

1. Mix all the ingredients in the slow cooker. Cook on a low for 8 hours. Serve.

Nutrition: *Calories: 100 Carbs: 5g Fat: 4g Protein: 12g*

133. BLACK BEAN AND SWEET POTATO CHILI

PREPARATION: 5 MIN   **COOKING:** 8 H   **SERVINGS:** 4

INGREDIENTS

- 3 cans of black beans
- 1 can of chopped tomato
- 1 cup of diced sweet potato
- 1 cup of diced onion
- ¼ cup fresh cilantro, chopped
- ¼ cup of sour cream or alternative
- 1 tablespoon of chili paste
- 1 tablespoon of minced garlic
- 1 tablespoon of cumin
- salt and pepper

DIRECTIONS

1. Mix all ingredients in a slow cooker. Cook on low for 8 hours. Serve

Nutrition: *Calories: 422 Carbs: 35g Fat: 16g Protein: 36g*

134. WHITE LIME TOFU CHILI

PREPARATION: 5 MIN   **COOKING:** 8 H   **SERVINGS:** 4

INGREDIENTS

- 1 ½ lbs. of firm silken tofu, cubed and fried
- 2 cans of white beans
- 2 cups of bouillon
- 1 ½ cup of chopped onion
- ½ cup of yogurt or alternative
- 3 tablespoon of lime juice
- 2 tablespoons of Tabasco sauce
- 2 tablespoons of minced garlic
- salt and pepper

DIRECTIONS

1. Mix all the ingredients in the slow cooker. Cook on a low for 8 hours. Serve.

Nutrition: *Calories: 120 Carbs: 7g Fat: 6g Protein: 9g*

135. BAKED BEANS

PREPARATION: 10 MIN   **COOKING:** 8 H   **SERVINGS:** 4

INGREDIENTS

- 3 cups dried navy beans, soaked in water overnight & drained
- 4 cups chicken broth
- 1/4 cup molasses
- 3/4 cup brown sugar
- 15 oz can tomato sauce
- 1/4 tsp cayenne pepper
- 1 tsp black pepper
- 1 tbsp ground mustard
- 1 bell pepper, diced
- 1 onion, diced
- 1 lb. bacon, cut into 1-inch pieces
- 1 tbsp kosher salt

DIRECTIONS

1. Add bacon, bell pepper, and onion into the slow cooker. Sauté until onion softens. Add remaining ingredients into it and stir well. Cook on low for 8 hours. Stir and serve.

Nutrition: *Calories: 561 Fat: 20.9g Carbs: 60.5g Protein: 33.8g*

136. BBQ BEANS

PREPARATION: 10 MIN **COOKING:** 6 H **SERVINGS:** 4

INGREDIENTS

- 15 oz can kidney beans, drained & rinsed
- 30 oz can great northern beans, drained & rinsed
- 30 oz can black beans, drained & rinsed
- 2 lbs. kielbasa, cut into bite-size pieces
- 1/2 lb. bacon, cooked & chopped
- 14 oz chicken broth
- 1/4 cup molasses
- 1/2 cup maple syrup
- 1 tbsp apple cider vinegar
- 1 tsp chili powder
- 1 tbsp mustard
- 1 tbsp Worcestershire sauce
- 3/4 cup ketchup
- 1/2 cup BBQ sauce
- 1 onion, diced

DIRECTIONS

1. Add all ingredients except kielbasa into the slow cooker and stir well. Top with kielbasa and stir gently. Cook on low for 6 hours. Stir and serve.

Nutrition: *Calories: 412 Fat: 16.9g Carbs: 44.5g Protein: 21.8g*

137. SWEET & TANGY COWBOY BEANS

PREPARATION: 10 MIN **COOKING:** 4 H **SERVINGS:** 4

INGREDIENTS

- 1 lb. ground beef
- 15 oz can pork and beans
- 15 oz can white beans
- 15 oz of kidney beans
- 2 tbsp bacon drippings
- 1 lb. bacon, cooked and chopped
- 2 1/2 tbsp yellow mustard
- 1/4 cup molasses
- 1 cup ketchup
- 3/4 cup brown sugar
- 1 large onion, diced

DIRECTIONS

1. Add ground beef and onion into the slow cooker and sauté until meat is no longer pink. Add remaining fixing into the slow cooker and stir well. Cook on high for 4 hours. Stir and serve.

Nutrition: *Calories: 279 Fat: 11.8g Carbs: 24.6g Protein: 19.7g*

138. JALAPENO PINTO BEANS

PREPARATION: 10 MIN   **COOKING:** 8 H   **SERVINGS:** 4

INGREDIENTS

- 1 lb. pinto beans, soak in water for overnight & drain
- 14 oz beef broth
- 32 oz vegetable broth
- 6 bacon sliced, cooked & chopped
- 2 jalapeno peppers, seeded & chopped
- 15 oz can tomato, diced & drained
- 1 tsp garlic powder
- 1 tsp cumin
- 1 tsp black pepper
- 1 tbsp garlic, minced
- 1 onion, sliced

DIRECTIONS

1. Add all fixing into the slow cooker and stir well. Cook on high for 8 hours. Stir and serve.

Nutrition: *Calories: 441 Fat: 5.4g Carbs: 55g Protein: 30.8g*

---

139. HAWAIIAN BEANS

PREPARATION: 10 MIN   **COOKING:** 8 H   **SERVINGS:** 4

INGREDIENTS

- 15 oz kidney beans, rinsed & drained
- 15 oz white beans, rinsed & drained
- 28 oz pinto beans, rinsed & drained
- 1 tbsp Cajun seasoning
- 6 oz pineapple juice
- 1 tbsp Worcestershire sauce
- 2 tbsp Dijon mustard
- 2 tbsp vinegar
- 1/3 cup molasses
- 1/3 cup brown sugar
- 1/2 cup ketchup
- 1 tbsp garlic, minced
- 1/2 onion, diced

DIRECTIONS

1. Add all fixing into the slow cooker and stir well. Cook on low for 8 hours. Stir and serve.

Nutrition: *Calories: 187 Fat: 0.9g Carbs: 39.1g Protein: 8.2g*

140. HEALTHY WILD RICE

PREPARATION: 10 MIN   **COOKING:** 6 H   **SERVINGS:** 4

INGREDIENTS

- 12 oz wild rice
- 8 oz mushrooms, sliced
- 21 oz vegetable broth
- 1/4 cup pecans, chopped
- 1/8 tsp black pepper
- 1/2 tsp dried tarragon
- 1/2 tsp dried marjoram
- 1/3 cup onion, diced
- 3 tbsp soy sauce
- 1 tbsp butter
- 1/2 cup carrot, chopped
- 1 tsp sea salt

DIRECTIONS

1. Add all ingredients except pecans into the slow cooker and stir well. Cook on low for 6 hours. Add pecans and mix well and let it sit for 10 minutes. Stir and serve.

Nutrition: *Calories: 434 Fat: 10.2g Carbs: 70.5g Protein: 19.2g*

---

141. HERBED BROWN RICE

PREPARATION: 10 MIN   **COOKING:** 3 H   **SERVINGS:** 4

INGREDIENTS

- 2 cups brown rice
- 1/2 tsp dried oregano
- 1/2 tsp dried thyme
- 4 cups chicken broth
- 8 oz mushrooms, sliced
- 2 tbsp butter
- Pepper
- salt

DIRECTIONS

1. Add butter into the slow cooker and set on sauté mode. Once butter is melted, add brown rice into the slow cooker and sauté for 2-4 minutes.
2. Add the rest of the fixing into the slow cooker and stir well—cook on high for 3 hours. Stir well and serve.

Nutrition: *Calories: 446 Fat: 9.9g Carbs: 75.4g Protein: 13.9g*

142. RED BEANS & RICE

PREPARATION: 10 MIN   **COOKING:** 8 H   **SERVINGS:** 4

INGREDIENTS

- 2 cups dried red beans, soaked & drained
- 4 cups of water
- 1/2 lb. smoked sausage, cut into small pieces
- 2 garlic cloves, minced
- 1/2 cup onion, chopped
- Pepper
- Salt

DIRECTIONS

1. Add all fixing into the slow cooker and stir well. Cook on low for 7 hours and 30 minutes. Remove 1/4 cup beans from the slow cooker and mash well. Return mashed beans into the slow cooker and cook for 30 minutes more. Stir and serve.

Nutrition: *Calories: 340 Fat: 11.4g Carbs: 38.8g Protein: 21.3g*

143. PUMPKIN RISOTTO

PREPARATION: 10 MIN   **COOKING:** 1 H 30 MIN   **SERVINGS:** 4

INGREDIENTS

- 1 1/2 cup Arborio rice
- 2 cups roasted pumpkin
- 1 tsp black pepper
- 4 cups vegetable broth
- 1/2 cup onion, chopped
- 1 tbsp garlic, crushed
- 2 tsp dried sage
- 2 tbsp olive oil
- 2 tsp salt

DIRECTIONS

1. Add oil into the slow cooker and set on sauté mode. Add onion, garlic, and sage into the slow cooker and sauté until onion is softened.
2. Add remaining fixing into the slow cooker and stir well. Cook on high for 1 hour and 30 minutes. Stir well and serve.

Nutrition: *Calories: 509 Fat: 15g Carbs: 77.4g Protein: 15.9g*

144. PARMESAN RISOTTO

PREPARATION: 10 MIN **COOKING:** 2 H **SERVINGS:** 6

INGREDIENTS

- 1 1/4 cups Arborio rice
- 3/4 cup parmesan cheese, shredded
- 1 tbsp garlic powder
- 1 tbsp dried onion flakes
- 1/4 cup white wine
- 1/4 cup olive oil
- 4 cups vegetable broth
- 1/2 tsp black pepper
- 1 tsp kosher salt

DIRECTIONS

1. Add all ingredients except parmesan cheese into the slow cooker and stir well. Cook on high for 2 hours. Add parmesan cheese and mix well. Serve and enjoy.

Nutrition: *Calories: 351 Fat: 15.8g Carbs: 35.2g Protein: 15.6g*

145. MEXICAN RICE

PREPARATION: 10 MIN **COOKING:** 5 H **SERVINGS:** 4

INGREDIENTS

- 1 cup white rice
- 1/2 tsp dried oregano
- 1/2 tsp chili powder
- 1 tsp cumin
- 1/4 tsp black pepper
- 1/2 jalapeno, chopped
- 4 oz can green chilies, diced
- 1/2 cup can tomato, diced
- 1 cup tomato sauce
- 1 cup chicken stock
- 1/2 tsp salt

DIRECTIONS

1. Add all fixing into the slow cooker and stir well. Cook on low for 5 hours. Stir well and serve.

Nutrition: *Calories: 203 Fat: 0.9g Carbs: 44g Protein: 4.9g*

146. MEXICAN QUINOA

PREPARATION: 10 MIN **COOKING:** 2 H **SERVINGS:** 4

INGREDIENTS

- 3/4 cup quinoa, rinsed
- 14 oz black beans, rinsed & drained
- 1/2 tsp garlic, minced
- 1 tsp cumin
- 1 bay leaf
- 3/4 cup salsa
- 1 1/2 cups water
- 1 tsp salt

Nutrition: Calories: 150 Fat: 1.7g Carbs: 27.7g Protein: 7.1g

DIRECTIONS

1. Add all fixing into the slow cooker and stir well. Cook on high for 2 hours. Fluff quinoa with fork and discard bay leaf. Stir well and serve.

147. APPLE CINNAMON QUINOA

PREPARATION: 10 MIN **COOKING:** 2 H **SERVINGS:** 4

INGREDIENTS

- 1 cup quinoa, rinsed
- 1 tsp vanilla
- 1/4 tsp nutmeg
- 2 tsp cinnamon
- 1 apple, peel & dice
- 1/4 cup pepitas
- 4 dates, chopped
- 3 cups almond milk
- 1/4 tsp salt

DIRECTIONS

1. Add all fixing into the slow cooker and stir well. Cook on high for 2 hours. Stir well and serve.

Nutrition: *Calories: 504 Fat: 37.2g Carbs: 42.1g Protein: 8.8g*

148. SPINACH BARLEY RISOTTO

PREPARATION: 10 MIN **COOKING:** 6 H **SERVINGS:** 4

INGREDIENTS

- 1 cup pearl barley
- 1/2 cup halloumi, cut into small pieces
- 2 1/2 cups fresh spinach, chopped
- 2 1/2 cups vegetable stock
- 2 garlic cloves, chopped
- 1 onion, chopped

DIRECTIONS

1. Add barley, stock, garlic, and onion into the slow cooker and stir well. Cook on low for 6 hours. Put the spinach and stir until spinach is wilted. Top with halloumi and serve.

Nutrition: *Calories: 237 Fat: 3.9g Carbs: 43.6g Protein: 8.8g*

149. CUBAN BLACK BEANS

PREPARATION: 10 MIN **COOKING:** 8 H **SERVINGS:** 4

INGREDIENTS

- 16 oz dry black beans, soak in water for overnight & drained
- 1 bay leaf
- 1 tomato, chopped
- 1 tsp balsamic vinegar
- 1/2 cup onion, diced
- 1/2 cup bell pepper, chopped
- 2 tbsp olive oil
- 2 garlic cloves, minced
- 1 tsp dry oregano
- 4 cups of water
- 1 tbsp salt

DIRECTIONS

1. Add oil into the slow cooker and set on sauté mode. Add onion, bell pepper, and garlic and sauté until onion is softened. Add remaining fixing into the slow cooker and stir well. Cook on low for 8 hours. Stir well and serve.

Nutrition: *Calories: 232 Fat: 4.4g Carbs: 37.3g Protein: 12.6 g*

150. TOMATILLO RICE

PREPARATION: 15 MIN   **COOKING:** 6 H   **SERVINGS:** 4

INGREDIENTS

- 2 tbsps. olive oil
- ½ red onion, diced
- ½ red bell pepper, diced
- 2 cloves garlic, minced
- Juice of 1 lime
- 1 cup tomatillo salsa
- 1 cup of water
- 1 tsp. salt
- 1 cup long-grain white rice
- ½ cup cilantro, chopped

DIRECTIONS

1. Heat oil in the slow cooker, then put the bell pepper, onion, and garlic and cook for 5 minutes. Add the rest of the fixing, except for the cilantro. Cover and cook on low within 6 hours. Stir in cilantro and serve.

Nutrition: *Calories: 268 Carbs: 47g Fat: 7g Protein: 5g*

151. VEGETABLE FRIED RICE

PREPARATION: 15 MIN   **COOKING:** 4 H 30 MIN   **SERVINGS:** 4

INGREDIENTS

- 1 tbsp. butter
- 2 cups white rice, uncooked
- 3 garlic cloves, minced
- 2 cups of water
- 2 cups vegetable broth
- 2 ½ tsp soy sauce
- 1 tsp. brown sugar
- ½ tsp. Sriracha sauce
- 1 tsp. lime juice
- 1 cup carrots, diced
- 1 cup broccoli, chopped
- 1 egg, lightly beaten

DIRECTIONS

1. Grease the slow cooker with the butter. Add the rest of the fixing except for the egg. Cover and cook within 4 hours on low. Open and add the egg and cook for 30 minutes more.

Nutrition: *Calories: 390 Carbs: 70g Fat: 3.6g Protein: 9g*

152. PAELLA

PREPARATION: 15 MIN **COOKING:** 4 H 30 MIN **SERVINGS:** 4

INGREDIENTS

- 1 tbsp. butter
- ½ onion, diced
- 1 cup diced tomato
- ½ tsp. turmeric
- 1 tsp. salt
- 2 tbsp. fresh parsley
- 1 cup long-grain white rice
- 1 cup frozen peas
- 2 cups of water
- 1 (12-ounce) package vegan chorizo, crumbled

DIRECTIONS

1. Melt the butter in a slow cooker. Add onion and cook for 3 minutes. Add tomato, turmeric, salt, and parsley and mix. Add the rice, peas, and water.
2. Cover and cook on low within 4 hours. Pour the crumbled chorizo on top. Cover and cook for 30 minutes more. Serve.

Nutrition: Calories: 421 Carbs: 32g Fat: 24g Protein: 17g

153. PORTOBELLO BARLEY

PREPARATION: 15 MIN **COOKING:** 8 H **SERVINGS:** 4

INGREDIENTS

- 1 tsp. olive oil
- 2 shallots, minced
- 2 cloves garlic, minced
- 3 portobello mushroom caps, sliced
- 1 cup pearl barley
- 3¼ cups water
- ¼ tsp. salt
- ½ tsp. freshly ground black pepper
- 1 tsp. crushed rosemary
- 1 tsp. dried chervil
- ¼ cup grated parmesan

DIRECTIONS

1. Heat oil on the slow cooker. Cook shallots, garlic, and mushrooms for 4 minutes. Add everything except for the parmesan. Cover and cook on low within 8 hours. Open and sprinkle with parmesan. Serve.

Nutrition: Calories: 130 Carbs: 25g Fat: 1.5g Protein: 5g

154. WILD RICE WITH MIXED VEGETABLES

PREPARATION: 15 MIN **COOKING:** 4 H 30 MIN **SERVINGS:** 4

INGREDIENTS

- 2½ cups water
- 1 cup wild rice
- 3 cloves garlic, minced
- 1 medium onion, diced
- 1 carrot, diced
- 1 stalk celery, diced

DIRECTIONS

1. Place all the fixings in the slow cooker and mix. Cover and cook on low for 4 hours. Then check if the kernels are open and tender. If not, then cover and cook for 15 to 30 minutes more. Serve.

Nutrition: *Calories: 90 Carbs: 18g Fat: 0g Protein: 3g*

---

155. SAFFRON RICE

PREPARATION: 10 MIN **COOKING:** 2H **SERVINGS:** 4

INGREDIENTS

- 2 cups white rice, uncooked
- 2 tbsps. margarine
- 2 cups of water
- 2 cups vegetarian stock
- ¾ tsp. saffron threads
- 1 tsp. salt

DIRECTIONS

1. Add everything to the slow cooker. Cook on low for 4 hours. Check if the rice is tender. If not, then cook for 30 minutes more. Serve.

Nutrition: *Calories: 420 Carbs: 82g Fat: 7g Protein: 9g*

156. BULGUR WITH BROCCOLI AND CARROT

PREPARATION: 15 MIN   **COOKING:** 7 H   **SERVINGS:** 4

INGREDIENTS

- 2 cups bulgur, uncooked
- 2 tbsps. butter
- 1 cup carrots, diced
- 1 cup broccoli, chopped
- 2 cups vegetable broth
- 1 tsp. salt

DIRECTIONS

1. Add everything to the slow cooker and cover. Cook on low for 6 hours. Check if it is tender; if not, cook for 1 hour more. Serve.

Nutrition: Calories: 360 Carbs: 13g Fat: 6g Protein: 9g

---

157. RED BEANS AND RICE

PREPARATION: 15 MIN   **COOKING:** 7 H   **SERVINGS:** 4

INGREDIENTS

- 3 cups of water
- 3½ cups vegetarian stock
- 2 tbsps. butter
- 1 can kidney beans, drained
- 2 cups white rice, uncooked
- 1 onion, chopped
- 1 green bell pepper, chopped
- 1 cup celery, chopped
- 1 tsp thyme
- 1 tsp paprika
- 1 tsp Cajun seasoning
- ½ tsp red pepper flakes
- 1 tsp salt
- ¼ tsp black pepper

DIRECTIONS

1. Add everything to the slow cooker. Cover and cook on low within 6 hours. Check the rice and cook 1 hour more if necessary. Serve.

Nutrition: *Calories: 340 Carbs: 52g Fat: 7g Protein: 11g*

---

158. SPINACH RICE

PREPARATION: 15 MIN   **COOKING:** 5 H   **SERVINGS:** 4

INGREDIENTS

- 2 cups spinach
- 2 cups white rice, uncooked
- 2 tbsps. butter
- 2 cups of water
- 2 cups vegetable broth
- 1 onion, diced
- 1 green bell pepper, diced
- 1 cup canned tomatoes, diced
- 1/8 cup pickled jalapenos, diced
- 1 tsp. chili powder
- ½ tsp. garlic powder
- 1 tsp. salt
- ¼ tsp. black pepper

DIRECTIONS

1. Add everything to the slow cooker. Cover and cook on low within 5 hours. Open and add the spinach. Cover and cook on Sauté for 5 minutes. Serve.

Nutrition: Calories: 230 Carbs: 45g Fat: 3g Protein: 4g

159. BROWN RICE AND VEGETABLES

PREPARATION: 15 MIN   **COOKING:** 5 H   **SERVINGS:** 4

INGREDIENTS

- 2 cups brown rice, uncooked
- 2 tbsps. butter
- 3 cups vegetable broth
- 2 cups of water
- ½ cup yellow squash, chopped
- ½ cup zucchini, chopped
- ½ onion, chopped
- ½ cup button mushrooms, sliced
- ½ cup red bell pepper, chopped
- 1 tsp. salt
- ¼ tsp. black pepper

DIRECTIONS

1. Add everything to the slow cooker. Cover and cook on low within 5 hours. Serve.

Nutrition: *Calories: 225 Carbs: 42gFat: 4g Protein: 4.6g*

160. CURRIED RICE

PREPARATION: 15 MIN   **COOKING:** 4 H 30 MIN   **SERVINGS:** 4

INGREDIENTS

- 2 cups white rice, uncooked
- 2 tbsp olive oil
- 2 cups of water
- 2 cups vegetable broth
- 2 tbsp curry powder
- 1 tsp salt
- ¼ tsp black pepper
- 1 tbsp lime juice
- ¼ cup cilantro, chopped

DIRECTIONS

1. Add all the fixings to the slow cooker except the lime juice and cilantro. Cover and cook on low within 4 hours. Stir in lime juice and cilantro and cook for 30 minutes more. Serve.

Nutrition: *Calories: 387 Carbs: 85g Fat: 1g Protein: 7.6g*

161. CHIPOTLE BLACK BEAN SALAD

PREPARATION: 15 MIN **COOKING:** 5 H **SERVINGS:** 4

INGREDIENTS

- 1 (16-ounce) bag dried black beans, soaked overnight and boiled for 10 minutes
- Enough water to cover beans by 1-inch
- 2 tsp salt
- 1 tbs. chipotle powder
- 2 tsp thyme
- 2 fresh tomatoes, diced
- 1 red onion, diced
- ¼ cup cilantro, chopped

DIRECTIONS

1. Put the black beans, water, plus salt in the slow cooker. Cover and cook on medium heat within 5 hours. Check the beans after 5 hours and cook 1 hour more if necessary. Drain the beans and cool. Mix in the remaining ingredients and serve.

Nutrition: *Calories: 198 Carbs: 37g Fat: 1g Protein: 10g*

162. MEDITERRANEAN CHICKPEAS

PREPARATION: 15 MIN **COOKING:** 2H **SERVINGS:** 4

INGREDIENTS

- 2 (15-ounce) cans chickpeas, drained
- 1 cup of water
- 4 tsp salt
- ¼ cup extra-virgin olive oil
- 1 tsp. black pepper
- 1 cup fresh basil, chopped
- 5 cloves garlic, minced
- 2 tomatoes, diced
- ½ cup kalamata olives, sliced

DIRECTIONS

1. Add everything in the slow cooker. Cover and cook on low within 2 hours. Serve.

Nutrition: *Calories: 243 Carbs: 37g Fat: 8g Protein: 7g*

163. CURRIED LENTILS

PREPARATION: 15 MIN   **COOKING:** 3 H   **SERVINGS:** 4

INGREDIENTS

- 2 tsp butter
- 1 large onion, thinly sliced
- 2 cloves garlic, minced
- 2 jalapenos, diced
- ½ tsp red pepper flakes
- ½ tsp ground cumin
- 1-pound yellow lentils
- 6 cups of water
- ½ tsp. salt
- ½ tsp. ground turmeric
- 4 cups chopped fresh spinach

DIRECTIONS

1. Melt the butter in a slow cooker. Cook the onions within 8 minutes or until brown. Add the garlic, jalapenos, red pepper flakes, and cumin. Cook for 3 minutes.
2. Add the lentils and stir in water, salt, and turmeric. Cover and cook on high within 2 hours and 30 minutes. Add spinach and mix. Cook on high for 15 minutes more. Serve.

Nutrition: *Calories: 280 Carbs: 49g Fat: 2g Protein: 21g*

---

164. BOURBON BAKED BEANS

PREPARATION: 15 MIN   **COOKING:** 6 H   **SERVINGS:** 4

INGREDIENTS

- 1 large sweet onion, peeled and diced
- 3 (15-ounce) cans cannellini beans
- 1 (15-ounce) can diced tomatoes
- ¼ cup maple syrup
- 3 tbsp apple cider vinegar
- 1 tsp liquid smoke
- 4 cloves garlic, peeled and minced
- 2 tbsp dry mustard
- 1½ tsp ground black pepper
- ½ tsp ground ginger
- ¼ tsp dried red pepper flakes
- 2 tbsp bourbon
- Salt, to taste

DIRECTIONS

1. Add all the fixings to the slow cooker and mix. Cover and cook on low within 6 hours. Serve.

Nutrition: *Calories: 290 Carbs: 48g Fat: 2g Protein: 15g*

165. ITALIAN CHICKPEAS

PREPARATION: 10 MIN **COOKING:** 4-6 H **SERVINGS:** 4

INGREDIENTS

- 1-pound dry chickpeas, soaked overnight
- 1 (28-ounce) can no-salt-added diced tomatoes
- 1 onion, chopped
- 1 bell pepper, seeded and chopped
- 3 garlic cloves, minced
- 1 teaspoon salt
- ½ teaspoon freshly ground black pepper
- ½ teaspoon paprika
- ½ teaspoon dried basil
- ½ teaspoon dried oregano
- ½ teaspoon dried parsley
- ¼ teaspoon red pepper flakes

DIRECTIONS

1. Mix the chickpeas, tomatoes and their juices, onion, bell pepper, garlic, salt, pepper, paprika, basil, oregano, parsley, and red pepper flakes in the slow cooker. Stir to mix well.
2. Cook on low within 4 to 6 hours, or until the chickpeas are tender, and serve.

Nutrition: *Calories: 289 Fat: 5g Carbs: 49g Protein: 15g*

166. SWEET AND SPICY CHICKPEAS

PREPARATION: 15 MIN **COOKING:** 4-6 H **SERVINGS:** 4

INGREDIENTS

- 2 pounds dry chickpeas, soaked overnight
- 2 bell peppers, seeded and chopped
- 1 onion, chopped
- 1-pound potatoes, peeled and chopped
- ¾ cup honey
- 1/3 cup sriracha sauce
- 2 tablespoons low-sodium soy sauce or tamari
- 2 garlic cloves, minced
- 1 teaspoon dried basil

DIRECTIONS

1. In the slow cooker, combine the chickpeas, bell peppers, onion, and potatoes.
2. In a medium bowl, mix the honey, sriracha, soy sauce, garlic, and basil. Put the sauce into the slow cooker, then stir to combine well. Cook on low for 4 to 6 hours and serve.

Nutrition: *Calories: 570 Fat: 7g Carbs: 109g Protein: 24g*

167. MEDITERRANEAN CHICKPEAS AND BROWN RICE

PREPARATION: 15 MIN   **COOKING:** 4-6 H   **SERVINGS:** 4

INGREDIENTS

- Nonstick cooking spray
- 1 (15-ounce) can chickpeas, drained and rinsed
- 1 cup uncooked brown rice
- 2½ cups low-sodium vegetable broth
- 3 garlic cloves, minced
- Juice of 1 lemon
- 1 tablespoon extra-virgin olive oil
- 1 teaspoon dried oregano
- 1 teaspoon paprika
- 1 teaspoon ground coriander
- 1 teaspoon ground cumin
- 1 teaspoon curry powder
- 1 teaspoon chili powder
- ½ teaspoon salt
- ¼ teaspoon freshly ground black pepper

DIRECTIONS

1. Oiled slow cooker generously with nonstick cooking spray. In the slow cooker, combine the chickpeas, rice, broth, garlic, lemon juice, olive oil, oregano, paprika, coriander, cumin, curry powder, chili powder, salt, and pepper.
2. Stir to mix well. Cook on low within 4 to 6 hours, or until the rice is tender, and serve.

Nutrition: *Calories: 372 Fat: 8g Carbs: 62g Protein: 14g*

168. RICE PILAF

PREPARATION: 15 MIN   **COOKING:** 4-6 H   **SERVINGS:** 4

INGREDIENTS

- Nonstick cooking spray
- 1 cup uncooked long-grain brown rice
- 2¼ cups low-sodium vegetable broth
- 1 teaspoon extra-virgin olive oil
- ½ teaspoon salt
- 1/8 teaspoon freshly ground black pepper

DIRECTIONS

1. Oiled slow cooker generously with nonstick cooking spray. In the slow cooker, combine the rice, broth, olive oil, salt, and pepper. Stir to mix well. Cook on low within 4 to 6 hours and serve.

Nutrition: *Calories: 203 Fat: 3g Carbs: 37g Protein: 6g*

169. WILD RICE AND MUSHROOM CASSEROLE

PREPARATION: 15 MIN **COOKING:** 5-7 H **SERVINGS:** 4

INGREDIENTS

- Nonstick cooking spray
- 1-pound mushrooms, sliced
- ¾ cup uncooked wild rice
- 1½ cups low-sodium chicken broth
- 1 onion, finely chopped
- ¼ teaspoon dried thyme
- ¼ teaspoon dried basil
- ½ teaspoon salt
- ½ teaspoon freshly ground black pepper
- 2 tablespoons chopped fresh parsley

DIRECTIONS

1. Oiled slow cooker generously with nonstick cooking spray. In the slow cooker, combine the mushrooms, rice, broth, onion, thyme, basil, salt, and pepper. Stir to mix well.
2. Cook on low within 5 to 7 hours, or until the rice is tender. Top with fresh parsley and serve.

Nutrition: *Calories: 154 Fat: 1g Carbs: 29g Protein: 10g*

170. RICE WITH CHICKEN AND ASPARAGUS

PREPARATION: 15 MIN **COOKING:** 5-7 H **SERVINGS:** 4

INGREDIENTS

- Nonstick cooking spray
- 1-pound boneless, skinless chicken breasts or thighs
- 1 cup uncooked brown rice
- 2½ cups water
- 1-pound asparagus, cut into 1-inch pieces
- 2 garlic cloves, minced
- Juice of 2 limes
- 1 teaspoon ground cumin
- ½ teaspoon salt
- ½ teaspoon freshly ground black pepper

DIRECTIONS

1. Oiled slow cooker generously with nonstick cooking spray. Mix the chicken, rice, water, asparagus, garlic, lime juice, cumin, salt, and pepper in the slow cooker. Stir to mix well. Cook on low within 5 to 7 hours, or until the rice is tender, and serve.

Nutrition: *Calories: 321 Fat: 3g Carbs: 41g Protein: 32g*

171. CILANTRO-LIME CHICKEN AND RICE

PREPARATION: 15 MIN   **COOKING:** 5-7 H   **SERVINGS:** 4

INGREDIENTS

- Nonstick cooking spray
- 1-pound boneless, skinless chicken breasts or thighs
- 2 cups uncooked brown rice
- 4 cups of water
- 1 can no-salt-added diced tomatoes
- 1 can black beans, drained and rinsed
- 1 can corn, drained and rinsed
- 2 garlic cloves, minced
- Juice of 2 limes
- 1 teaspoon ground cumin
- 1 teaspoon salt
- ½ teaspoon freshly ground black pepper
- ½ teaspoon dried oregano
- ½ cup chopped fresh cilantro

DIRECTIONS

1. Oiled slow cooker generously with nonstick cooking spray. Mix the chicken, rice, water, tomatoes, beans, corn, garlic, lime juice, cumin, salt, pepper, and oregano in the slow cooker.
2. Stir to mix well. Cook on low within 5 to 7 hours, or until the rice is tender. Sprinkle with fresh cilantro before serving.

Nutrition: *Calories: 432 Fat: 3g Carbs: 72g Protein: 29g*

172. INDIAN SPICED BROWN RICE WITH GROUND LAMB

PREPARATION: 15 MIN   **COOKING:** 4-6 H   **SERVINGS:** 4

INGREDIENTS

- 1 cup uncooked brown rice
- 2 cups low-sodium chicken broth
- 1 cup Marinara Sauce
- 1 onion, chopped
- 3 garlic cloves, minced
- 2 teaspoons curry powder or garam masala
- 2 teaspoons ground cumin
- 2 teaspoons ground ginger
- 2 teaspoons ground turmeric
- 1 teaspoon ground coriander
- ½ teaspoon ground cayenne pepper
- 1-pound ground lamb, cooked

DIRECTIONS

1. In the slow cooker, combine the rice, broth, marinara sauce, onion, garlic, curry powder, cumin, ginger, turmeric, coriander, and cayenne pepper. Stir to mix well. Cook on low within 4 to 6 hours. Stir in the ground lamb and serve.

Nutrition: *Calories: 325 Fat: 13g Carbs: 33g Protein: 18g*

173. BARLEY AND CHICKPEA RISOTTO

PREPARATION: 15 MIN   **COOKING:** 4-6 H   **SERVINGS:** 4

INGREDIENTS

- Nonstick cooking spray
- 1½ cups uncooked barley, rinsed
- 1 (15-ounce) can chickpeas, drained and rinsed
- 3 cups of water
- 2 garlic cloves, minced
- 1 onion, minced
- 1 teaspoon salt
- ½ teaspoon dried rosemary
- ½ teaspoon freshly ground black pepper
- ¼ cup grated Parmesan cheese
- ¼ cup chopped fresh parsley

DIRECTIONS

1. Oiled slow cooker generously with nonstick cooking spray. In the slow cooker, combine the barley, chickpeas, water, garlic, onion, salt, rosemary, pepper, and cheese. Stir to mix well. Cook on low within 4 to 6 hours. Top with fresh parsley before serving.

Tip: For more flavor, use low-sodium broth instead of water or a combo of the two.

Nutrition: *Calories: 445 Fat: 5g Carbs: 83g Protein: 17g*

---

174. COCONUT QUINOA CURRY

PREPARATION: 15 MIN   **COOKING:** 4-6 H   **SERVINGS:** 8

INGREDIENTS

- 1 can full-fat coconut milk
- 1 cup Coconut-Curry Sauce
- 1 can no-salt-added diced tomatoes
- 1 cup uncooked quinoa, rinsed
- 1 small onion, chopped
- 2 garlic cloves, minced
- 1 tablespoon soy sauce
- 2 teaspoons curry powder
- 1 teaspoon ground ginger
- ½ teaspoon salt
- ½ teaspoon freshly ground black pepper
- ¼ teaspoon red pepper flakes

DIRECTIONS

1. In the slow cooker, combine the coconut milk, curry sauce, tomatoes, and their juices, quinoa, onion, garlic, soy sauce, curry powder, ginger, salt, pepper, and red pepper flakes. Stir to mix well. Cook on low within 6 to 8 hours and serve.

Nutrition: *Calories: 445 Fat: 32g Carbs: 28g Protein: 9g*

175. SWEET AND SOUR BEANS

PREPARATION: 15 MIN **COOKING:** 7-8 H **SERVINGS:** 4

INGREDIENTS

- 1-pound white beans, soaked overnight
- 4 cups Vegetable Broth
- 1 can no-salt-added tomato paste
- 1 cup of water
- 3 carrots, diced
- 1 sweet onion, diced
- 2 bell peppers (red, orange, yellow, or green), diced
- ¼ cup Ketchup
- ¼ cup dry cooking sherry
- ¼ cup low-sodium tamari
- ¼ cup cider vinegar
- 2 tablespoons sugar
- 1 tablespoon dried marjoram
- 1 tablespoon dried thyme
- 2 teaspoons freshly ground black pepper
- 1 tablespoon cornstarch or arrowroot

Nutrition: *Calories: 263 Fat: 0g Carbs: 49g Protein: 16g*

DIRECTIONS

1. Drain and rinse the beans. Put them in a 6-quart slow cooker along with the broth, tomato paste, water, carrots, onion, bell peppers, ketchup, sherry, tamari, vinegar, sugar, marjoram, thyme, and pepper.
2. Cover and cook on low within 7 to 8 hours. With 15 minutes left before serving, stir in the cornstarch. Cook again within 15 minutes until the broth thickens. Serve warm.

176. NAVY BEAN SOUP WITH HAM

PREPARATION: 10 MIN **COOKING:** 8-10 H **SERVINGS:** 4

INGREDIENTS

- 1-pound dried navy beans, drained & rinsed
- 2 cups Chicken Stock
- 1 can no-salt-added diced tomatoes
- 8 oz. 98% fat-free, reduced-sodium ham, finely diced
- 3 celery ribs, diced
- 3 carrots, diced
- 1 onion, diced
- 3 garlic cloves, minced
- 1½ teaspoons onion powder
- 1 teaspoon dried parsley
- 1 teaspoon dried sage
- 1 teaspoon garlic powder
- 1 bay leaf
- ½ teaspoon freshly ground black pepper
- ½ teaspoon salt

DIRECTIONS

1. Soak or dip the beans overnight at room temperature in a large bowl with 2 quarts of water. Put the beans in a 4- to 6-quart slow cooker.
2. Cover the beans with about 1 inch of water and add the rest of the ingredients. Stir well. Cover and cook on low within 8 to 10 hours.
3. Use the back of a spoon to mash some of the beans against the slow cooker's sides, then mix them back into the soup, creating a creamier texture. Serve hot.

Nutrition: *Calories: 256 Fat: 0g Carbs: 44g Protein: 21g*

177. COCONUT RED BEANS AND RICE

PREPARATION: 15 MIN **COOKING:** 7-8 H **SERVINGS:** 4

INGREDIENTS

- 1 cup dried red beans, soaked overnight
- 4 cups Chicken Stock
- 1 can light coconut milk
- 1½ cups long-grain basmati white rice
- 1 large onion, finely diced
- 2 garlic cloves, minced
- 1 teaspoon red pepper flakes
- ½ teaspoon coconut extract (optional)
- 1-2 tablespoons squeezed lime juice
- 2 limes, cut into wedges, for serving

DIRECTIONS

1. Drain and rinse the soaked beans. Add the beans to a 6-quart slow cooker along with the stock, coconut milk, rice, onion, garlic, red pepper flakes, and coconut extract (if using). Stir well.
2. Cover and cook for 7 to 8 hours on low. Stir in the lime juice and taste to adjust seasonings. Serve warm, with the lime wedges on the side.

Nutrition: *Calories: 262 Fat: 2g Carbs: 65g Protein: 16g*

178. RANCH STYLE PINTO BEANS

PREPARATION: 10 MIN **COOKING:** 7-8 H **SERVINGS:** 4

INGREDIENTS

- 1-pound dried pinto beans, soaked overnight
- 5 cups Beef Stock
- 1 cup low-sodium tomato sauce
- 1 medium white onion, diced
- 1 jalapeño pepper, seeded and finely diced
- 4 garlic cloves, minced
- 1 tablespoon ancho chili powder
- 1 teaspoon chili powder
- 1 teaspoon apple cider vinegar
- 1 teaspoon ground cumin
- 1 packed teaspoon brown sugar
- 1 teaspoon smoked paprika
- ½ teaspoon dried oregano
- Freshly ground black pepper

DIRECTIONS

1. Drain and rinse the soaked beans. Put them in a 6-quart slow cooker along with the stock, tomato sauce, onion, jalapeño, garlic, ancho chili powder, chili powder, vinegar, cumin, sugar, paprika, and oregano.
2. Cover and cook on low within 7 to 8 hours, until the beans are tender and the liquid has thickened slightly—taste and season with the pepper. Serve warm.

Nutrition: *Calories: 222 Fat: 0g Carbs: 40g Protein: 14g*

179. GARLIC VEGGIE LENTILS

PREPARATION: 15 MIN **COOKING:** 7-8 H **SERVINGS:** 4

INGREDIENTS

- 3 cups dried lentils
- 5 cups Vegetable Broth
- 1 can no-salt-added diced tomatoes
- 1 large onion, chopped
- 2 leeks, chopped
- 8 garlic cloves, minced
- 2 large carrots, chopped
- 2 bay leaves
- 1 teaspoon dried thyme
- Freshly ground black pepper

DIRECTIONS

1. Sort the lentils, discarding any stones or impurities. Rinse under cold water in a fine-mesh strainer. Combine all of the ingredients in a 6-quart slow cooker and stir.
2. Cover and cook on low within 7 to 8 hours until the lentils are tender and the sauce has thickened. Remove and discard the bay leaf. Serve warm.

Nutrition: *Calories: 185 Fat: 0g Carbs: 34g Protein: 11g*

180. VEGETARIAN CALICO BEANS

PREPARATION: 15 MIN **COOKING:** 7-8 H **SERVINGS:** 4

INGREDIENTS

- 6 cups Vegetable Broth
- 1 can lima beans, drained and rinsed
- 1 can fire-roasted tomatoes
- 1 cup dried kidney beans, soaked overnight
- 1 cup dried pinto beans, soaked overnight
- 1 large sweet onion, chopped
- 1 medium red bell pepper, chopped
- ½ cup Ketchup
- 1/3 cup loosely packed brown sugar
- 1 tablespoon Dijon mustard
- 1 tablespoon apple cider vinegar
- Freshly ground black pepper

DIRECTIONS

1. Combine the ingredients in a 6-quart slow cooker. Cover and cook on low within 7 to 8 hours, until the beans are tender. Serve warm.

Nutrition: *Calories: 246 Fat: 0g Carbs: 47g Protein: 13g*

CHAPTER 5.
SIDE DISHES

181. SUMMER SQUASH MIX

PREPARATION: 15 MIN **COOKING:** 2 H **SERVINGS:** 4

INGREDIENTS

- ¼ cup olive oil
- 2 tablespoons basil, chopped
- 2 tablespoons balsamic vinegar
- 2 garlic cloves, minced
- 2 teaspoons mustard
- Salt and black pepper to the taste
- 3 summer squash, sliced
- 2 zucchinis, sliced

DIRECTIONS

1. In your slow cooker, mix squash with zucchinis, salt, pepper, mustard, garlic, vinegar, basil, and oil, toss a bit, cook on high within 2 hours. Divide between plates and serve as a side dish.

Nutrition: Calories: 179 Fat: 13g Carbs: 10g Protein: 4g

---

182. HOT ZUCCHINI MIX

PREPARATION: 5 MIN **COOKING:** 2 H **SERVINGS:** 2

INGREDIENTS

- ¼ cup carrots, grated
- 1-pound zucchinis, roughly cubed
- 1 teaspoon hot paprika
- ½ teaspoon chili powder
- 2 spring onions, chopped
- ½ tablespoon olive oil
- ½ teaspoon curry powder
- 1 garlic clove, minced
- ½ teaspoon ginger powder
- A pinch of salt and black pepper
- 1 tablespoon cilantro, chopped

DIRECTIONS

1. In your slow cooker, mix the carrots with the zucchinis, paprika, and the rest of the fixing, toss, cook on low for 2 hours. Divide between plates and serve as a side dish.

Nutrition: Calories: 200 Fat: 5g Carbs: 28g Protein: 4g

---

183. CREAMY BUTTER PARSNIPS

PREPARATION: 15 MIN **COOKING:** 7-8 H **SERVINGS:** 4

INGREDIENTS

- 1 cup cream
- 2 tsp butter
- 1 lb. parsnip, peeled and chopped
- 1 carrot, chopped
- 1 yellow onion, chopped
- 1 tbsp chives, chopped
- 1 tsp salt
- 1 tsp ground white pepper
- ½ tsp paprika
- 1 tbsp salt
- ¼ tsp sugar

DIRECTIONS

1. Add parsnips, carrots, and the rest of the ingredients to the slow cooker. Put the cooker's lid on and set the cooking time to 7 hours on low. Serve warm.

Nutrition: Calories: 190 Fat: 11.2g Carbs: 22g Protein: 3g

184. BUTTERNUT SQUASH AND EGGPLANT MIX

PREPARATION: 15 MIN   **COOKING:** 4 H   **SERVINGS:** 2

INGREDIENTS

- 1 butternut squash, peeled and roughly cubed
- 1 eggplant, roughly cubed
- 1 red onion, chopped
- Cooking spray
- ½ cup veggie stock
- ¼ cup tomato paste
- ½ tablespoon parsley, chopped
- Salt and black pepper to the taste
- 2 garlic cloves, minced

DIRECTIONS

1. Grease the slow cooker with the cooking spray and mix the squash with the eggplant, onion, and the other ingredients inside.
2. Cook on low within 4 hours. Divide between plates and serve as a side dish. it

Nutrition: *Calories: 114 Fat: 4g Carbs: 18g Protein: 4g*

185. CLASSIC VEGGIES MIX

PREPARATION: 15 MIN   **COOKING:** 3H   **SERVINGS:** 4

INGREDIENTS

- 1 and ½ cups red onion, cut into medium chunks
- 1 cup cherry tomatoes, halved
- 2 and ½ cups zucchini, sliced
- 2 cups yellow bell pepper, chopped
- 1 cup mushrooms, sliced
- 2 tablespoons basil, chopped
- 1 tablespoon thyme, chopped
- ½ cup olive oil
- ½ cup balsamic vinegar

DIRECTIONS

1. In your slow cooker, mix onion pieces with tomatoes, zucchini, bell pepper, mushrooms, basil, thyme, oil, and vinegar, toss to coat everything, cover, and cook on high for 3 hours. Divide between plates and serve as a side dish.

Nutrition: *Calories: 150 Fat: 2g Carbs: 6g Protein: 5g*

186. SPINACH AND SQUASH SIDE SALAD

PREPARATION: 15 MIN   **COOKING:** 4 H   **SERVINGS:** 4

INGREDIENTS

- 3 pounds butternut squash, peeled and cubed
- 1 yellow onion, chopped
- 2 teaspoons thyme, chopped
- 3 garlic cloves, minced
- A pinch of salt and black pepper
- 10 oz. veggie stock
- 6 oz. baby spinach

DIRECTIONS

1. In your slow cooker, mix squash cubes with onion, thyme, salt, pepper, and stock, stir, cover, and cook on low for 4 hours. Transfer squash mixture to a bowl, add spinach, toss, divide between plates and serve as a side dish.

Nutrition: *Calories: 100 Fat: 1g Carbs: 18g Protein: 4g*

187. CHEDDAR POTATOES MIX

PREPARATION: 15 MIN   **COOKING:** 3 H   **SERVINGS:** 4

INGREDIENTS

- ½ pound gold potatoes, cut into wedges
- 2 oz. heavy cream
- ½ teaspoon turmeric powder
- ½ teaspoon rosemary, dried
- ¼ cup cheddar cheese, shredded
- 1 tablespoon butter, melted
- Cooking spray
- A pinch of salt and black pepper

DIRECTIONS

1. Grease your slow cooker with the cooking spray, add the potatoes, cream, turmeric, and the rest of the fixing, toss, put the lid on and cook on high for 3 hours. Divide between plates and serve as a side dish.

Nutrition: *Calories: 300 Fat: 14g Carbs: 22g Protein: 6g*

188. OKRA AND CORN

PREPARATION: 15 MIN   **COOKING:** 8 H   **SERVINGS:** 4

INGREDIENTS

- 3 garlic cloves, minced
- 1 small green bell pepper, chopped
- 1 small yellow onion, chopped
- 1 cup of water
- 16 oz. okra, sliced
- 2 cups corn
- 1 and ½ teaspoon smoked paprika
- 28 oz. canned tomatoes, crushed
- 1 teaspoon oregano, dried
- 1 teaspoon thyme, dried
- 1 teaspoon marjoram, dried
- A pinch of cayenne pepper
- Salt and black pepper to the taste

DIRECTIONS

1. In your slow cooker, mix garlic with bell pepper, onion, water, okra, corn, paprika, tomatoes, oregano, thyme, marjoram, cayenne, salt and pepper, cover, cook on low for 8 hours, divide between plates and serve as a side dish.

Nutrition: *Calories: 182 Fat: 3g Carbs: 8g Protein: 5g*

189. ROASTED BEETS

PREPARATION: 15 MIN   **COOKING:** 4 H   **SERVINGS:** 4

INGREDIENTS

- 10 small beets
- 5 teaspoons olive oil
- A pinch of salt and black pepper

DIRECTIONS

1. Divide each beet on a tin foil piece, drizzle oil, season them with salt and pepper, rub well, wrap beets, place them in your slow cooker, cover and cook on high for 4 hours. Unwrap beets, cool them down a bit, peel, slice and serve them as a side dish.

Nutrition: *Calories: 100 Fat: 2g Carbs: 4g Protein: 5g*

190. CAULIFLOWER PILAF

PREPARATION: 15 MIN **COOKING:** 3 H **SERVINGS:** 4

INGREDIENTS

- 1 cup cauliflower rice
- 6 green onions, chopped
- 3 tablespoons ghee, melted
- 2 garlic cloves, minced
- ½ pound Portobello mushrooms, sliced
- 2 cups warm water
- Salt and black pepper to the taste

DIRECTIONS

1. In your slow cooker, mix cauliflower rice with green onions, melted ghee, garlic, mushrooms, water, salt, and pepper, stir well, cover, and cook on low for 3 hours. Divide between plates and serve as a side dish.

Nutrition: *Calories: 200 Fat: 5g Carbs: 14g Protein: 4g*

191. MARJORAM RICE MIX

PREPARATION: 15 MIN **COOKING:** 6 H **SERVINGS:** 2

INGREDIENTS

- 1 cup wild rice
- 2 cups chicken stock
- 1 carrot, peeled and grated
- 2 tablespoons marjoram, chopped
- 1 tablespoon olive oil
- A pinch of salt and black pepper
- 1 tablespoon green onions, chopped

DIRECTIONS

1. In your slow cooker, mix the rice with the stock and the rest of the fixing, toss, cook on low within 6 hours. Divide between plates and serve.

Nutrition: *Calories: 200 Fat: 2g Carbs: 7g Protein: 5g*

192. CINNAMON SQUASH

PREPARATION: 15 MIN **COOKING:** 4 H **SERVINGS:** 2

INGREDIENTS

- 1 acorn squash, peeled and cut into medium wedges
- 1 cup coconut cream
- A pinch of cinnamon powder
- A bit of salt and black pepper

DIRECTIONS

1. In your slow cooker, mix the squash with the cream and the rest of the fixing, toss, cook on low within 4 hours. Divide between plates and serve as a side dish.

Nutrition: *Calories: 230 Fat: 3g Carbs: 10g Protein: 2g*

193. BROCCOLI FILLING

PREPARATION: 15 MIN **COOKING:** 5 H **SERVINGS:** 4

INGREDIENTS

- 10 oz. broccoli, chopped
- 7 oz. Cheddar cheese, shredded
- 4 eggs
- ½ cup onion, chopped
- 1 cup heavy cream
- 3 tbsp mayo sauce
- 3 tbsp butter
- ½ cup bread crumbs

DIRECTIONS

1. Spread broccoli in the insert of the slow cooker and top it with ½ cup cream. Put the cooker's lid on and set the cooking time to 3 hours on high.
2. Beat eggs with onion, mayo sauce, butter, and remaining cream in a bowl. Mash the cooked broccoli and stir in the mayo-eggs mixture.
3. Spread the breadcrumbs over the broccoli mixture. Put the cooker's lid on and set the cooking time to 2 hours on high. Serve warm.

Nutrition: *Calories: 289 Fat: 22.9g Carbs: 9.07g Protein: 13g*

---

194. THYME BEETS

PREPARATION: 5 MIN **COOKING:** 6 H **SERVINGS:** 4

INGREDIENTS

- 12 small beets, peeled and sliced
- ¼ cup of water
- 4 garlic cloves, minced
- 2 tablespoons olive oil
- 1 teaspoon thyme, dried
- Salt and black pepper to the taste
- 1 tablespoon fresh thyme, chopped

DIRECTIONS

1. In your slow cooker, mix beets with water, garlic, oil, dried thyme, salt, pepper, cover, and cook on low for 6 hours. Divide beets on plates, sprinkle fresh thyme all over, and serve as a side dish.

Nutrition: *Calories: 66 Fat: 4g Carbs: 8g Protein: 1g*

---

195. KALE AND HAM MIX

PREPARATION: 15 MIN **COOKING:** 6 H **SERVINGS:** 4

INGREDIENTS

- 8 oz. ham hock slices
- 1 and ½ cups of water
- 1 cup chicken stock
- 12 cups kale leaves, torn
- A pinch of salt and cayenne pepper
- 2 tablespoons olive oil
- 1 yellow onion, chopped
- 2 tablespoons apple cider vinegar
- Cooking spray

DIRECTIONS

1. Put ham in a heatproof bowl, add the water and the stock, cover, and microwave for 3 minutes. Heat-up a pan with the oil over medium-high heat, add onion, stir and cook for 5 minutes.
2. Drain ham and add it to your slow cooker, add onions, kale, salt, cayenne, vinegar, toss, cover, and cook on low within 6 hours. Divide between plates and serve as a side dish.

Nutrition: *Calories: 200 Fat: 4g Carbs: 10g Protein: 3g*

196. BALSAMIC CAULIFLOWER

PREPARATION: 10 MIN **COOKING:** 5 H **SERVINGS:** 2

INGREDIENTS

- 2 cups cauliflower florets
- ½ cup veggie stock
- 1 tablespoon balsamic vinegar
- 1 tablespoon lemon zest, grated
- 2 spring onions, chopped
- ¼ teaspoon sweet paprika
- Salt and black pepper to the taste
- 1 tablespoon dill, chopped

DIRECTIONS

1. In your slow cooker, mix the cauliflower with the stock, vinegar, and the rest of the fixing, toss, cook on low within 5 hours. Divide the cauliflower mix between plates and serve.

Nutrition: *Calories: 162 Fat: 11g Carbs: 11g Protein: 5g*

197. BLACK BEANS MIX

PREPARATION: 10 MIN **COOKING:** 5 H **SERVINGS:** 2

INGREDIENTS

- 2 tablespoons tomato paste
- Cooking spray
- 2 cups black beans
- ¼ cup veggie stock
- 1 red onion, sliced
- Cooking spray
- 1 teaspoon Italian seasoning
- ½ celery rib, chopped
- ½ red bell pepper, chopped
- ½ sweet red pepper, chopped
- ¼ teaspoon mustard seeds
- Salt and black pepper to the taste
- 2 oz. canned corn, drained
- 1 tablespoon cilantro, chopped

DIRECTIONS

1. Grease the slow cooker with the cooking spray, and mix the beans with the stock, onion, and the other ingredients. Put the lid on, cook on low for 5 hours, divide between plates, and serve.

Nutrition: *Calories: 255 Fat: 6g Carbs: 38g Protein: 7g*

198. BUTTER GREEN BEANS

PREPARATION: 10 MIN　　**COOKING:** 2 H　　**SERVINGS:** 2

INGREDIENTS

- 1-pound green beans, trimmed and halved
- 2 tablespoons butter, melted
- ½ cup veggie stock
- 1 teaspoon rosemary, dried
- 1 tablespoon chives, chopped
- Salt and black pepper to the taste
- ¼ teaspoon soy sauce

DIRECTIONS

1. In your slow cooker, combine the green beans with the melted butter, stock, and the rest of the fixing, toss, cook on low within 2 hours. Divide between plates and serve as a side dish.

Nutrition: *Calories: 236 Fat: 6g Carbs: 10g Protein: 6g*

199. CORN SAUTÉ

PREPARATION: 10 MIN　　**COOKING:** 2H　　**SERVINGS:** 2

INGREDIENTS

- 3 cups corn
- 2 tablespoon whipping cream
- 1 carrot, peeled and grated
- 1 tablespoon chives, chopped
- 2 tablespoons butter, melted
- Salt and black pepper to the taste
- 2 bacon strips, cooked and crumbled
- 1 tablespoon green onions, chopped

DIRECTIONS

1. In your slow cooker, combine the corn with the cream, carrot, and the other ingredients, toss, cook on low within 2 hours. Divide between plates, and serve.

Nutrition: *Calories: 261 Fat: 11g Carbs: 17g Protein: 6g*

200. SAGE PEAS

PREPARATION: 10 MIN　　**COOKING:** 2 H　　**SERVINGS:** 4

INGREDIENTS

- 1-pound peas
- 1 red onion, sliced
- ½ cup veggie stock
- ½ cup tomato sauce
- 2 garlic cloves, minced
- ¼ teaspoon sage, dried
- Salt and black pepper to the taste
- 1 tablespoon dill, chopped

DIRECTIONS

1. In your slow cooker, combine the peas with the onion, stock, and the other ingredients, toss, cook on low within 2 hours. Divide between plates and serve as a side dish.

Nutrition: *Calories: 100 Fat: 4g Carbs: 15g Protein: 4g*

201. TOMATO AND CORN

PREPARATION: 10 MIN **COOKING:** 4 H 10 MIN **SERVINGS:** 2

INGREDIENTS

- 1 red onion, sliced
- 2 spring onions, chopped
- 1 cup of corn
- 1 cup tomatoes, cubed
- 1 tablespoon olive oil
- ½ red bell pepper, chopped
- ½ cup tomato sauce
- ¼ teaspoon sweet paprika
- ½ teaspoon cumin, ground
- 1 tablespoon chives, chopped
- Salt and black pepper to the taste

DIRECTIONS

1. Heat-up a pan with the oil over medium-high heat, add the onion, spring onions, and bell pepper, and cook for 10 minutes.
2. Move the mix to the slow cooker, add the corn and the rest of the fixing, toss, cook on low within 4 hours. Divide the mixture between plates and serve as a side dish.

Nutrition: *Calories: 312 Fat: 4g Carbs: 12g Protein: 6g*

202. DILL MUSHROOM SAUTÉ

PREPARATION: 10 MIN **COOKING:** 3 H **SERVINGS:** 3

INGREDIENTS

- 1-pound white mushrooms halved
- 1 tablespoon olive oil
- 1 red onion, sliced
- 1 carrot, peeled and grated
- 2 green onions, chopped
- 1 garlic clove, minced
- 1 cup beef stock
- ½ cup tomato sauce
- 1 tablespoon dill, chopped

DIRECTIONS

1. Grease the slow cooker with the oil and mix the mushrooms with the onion, carrot, and the other ingredients. Put the lid on, cook on low for 3 hours, divide between plates, and serve as a side dish.

Nutrition: *Calories: 200 Fat: 6g Carbs: 28g Protein: 5g*

203. CARROTS AND SPINACH MIX

PREPARATION: 10 MIN **COOKING:** 2 H **SERVINGS:** 2

INGREDIENTS

- 2 carrots, sliced
- 1 small yellow onion, chopped
- Salt and black pepper to the taste
- ¼ teaspoon oregano, dried
- ½ teaspoon sweet paprika
- 2 oz. baby spinach
- 1 cup veggie stock
- 1 tablespoon lemon juice
- 2 tablespoons pistachios, chopped

DIRECTIONS

1. In your slow cooker, mix the spinach with the carrots, onion, and the other ingredients, toss, cook on low within 2 hours. Divide everything between plates and serve.

Nutrition: *Calories: 219 Fat: 8g Carbs: 15g Protein: 17g*

204. COCONUT POTATOES

PREPARATION: 10 MIN **COOKING:** 4 H **SERVINGS:** 4

INGREDIENTS

- ½ pound gold potatoes, halved and sliced
- 2 scallions, chopped
- 1 tablespoon avocado oil
- 2 oz. of coconut milk
- ¼ cup veggie stock
- Salt and black pepper to the taste
- 1 tablespoons parsley, chopped

DIRECTIONS

1. In your slow cooker, mix the potatoes with the scallions and the other ingredients, toss, cook on high within 4 hours. Divide the mix between plates and serve.

Nutrition: *Calories: 306 Fat: 14g Carbs: 15g Protein: 12g*

205. SAGE SWEET POTATOES

PREPARATION: 10 MIN **COOKING:** 3 H **SERVINGS:** 2

INGREDIENTS

- ½ pound sweet potatoes, thinly sliced
- 1 tablespoon sage, chopped
- 2 tablespoons orange juice
- A pinch of salt and black pepper
- ½ cup veggie stock
- ½ tablespoon olive oil

DIRECTIONS

1. In your slow cooker, mix the potatoes with the sage and the other ingredients, toss, cook on high within 3 hours. Divide between plates and serve as a side dish.

Nutrition: *Calories: 189 Fat: 4g Carbs: 17g Protein: 4g*

206. CAULIFLOWER AND ALMONDS

PREPARATION: 10 MIN **COOKING:** 3 H **SERVINGS:** 2

INGREDIENTS

- 2 cups cauliflower florets
- 2 oz. tomato paste
- 1 small yellow onion, chopped
- 1 tablespoon chives, chopped
- Salt and black pepper to the taste
- 1 tablespoon almonds, sliced

DIRECTIONS

1. In your slow cooker, mix the cauliflower with the tomato paste and the other ingredients, toss, cook on high within 3 hours. Divide between plates and serve as a side dish.

Nutrition: *Calories: 177 Fat: 12g Carbs: 20g Protein: 7g*

207. ROSEMARY LEEKS

PREPARATION: 10 MIN **COOKING:** 3 H **SERVINGS:** 2

INGREDIENTS

- ½ tablespoon olive oil
- ½ leeks, sliced
- ½ cup tomato sauce
- 2 garlic cloves, minced
- Salt and black pepper to the taste
- ¼ tablespoon rosemary, chopped

DIRECTIONS

1. In your slow cooker, mix the leeks with the oil, sauce, and the other ingredients, toss, put the lid on, cook on high for 3 hours, divide between plates and serve as a side dish.

Nutrition: *Calories: 202 Fat: 2g Carbs: 18g Protein: 8g*

208. SPICY BRUSSELS SPROUTS

PREPARATION: 10 MIN **COOKING:** 3 H **SERVINGS:** 2

INGREDIENTS

- ½ pounds Brussels sprouts, trimmed and halved
- A pinch of salt and black pepper
- 2 tablespoons mustard
- ½ cup veggie stock
- 1 tablespoon olive oil
- 2 tablespoons maple syrup
- 1 tablespoon thyme, chopped

DIRECTIONS

1. In your slow cooker, mix the sprouts with the mustard and the rest of the fixing, toss, cook on low within 3 hours. Divide between plates and serve as a side dish.

Nutrition: *Calories: 170 Fat: 4g Carbs: 14g Protein: 6g*

209. POTATOES AND LEEKS MIX

PREPARATION: 10 MIN **COOKING:** 4 H **SERVINGS:** 2

INGREDIENTS

- 2 leeks, sliced
- ½ pound sweet potatoes, cut into medium wedges
- ½ cup veggie stock
- ½ tablespoon balsamic vinegar
- 1 tablespoon chives, chopped
- ½ teaspoon pumpkin pie spice

DIRECTIONS

1. In your slow cooker, mix the leeks with the potatoes and the rest of the fixing, toss, cook on high within 4 hours. Divide between plates and serve as a side dish.

Nutrition: *Calories: 351 Fat: 8g Carbs: 48g Protein: 7g*

210. ORANGE CARROTS MIX

PREPARATION: 10 MIN **COOKING:** 6 H **SERVINGS:** 2

INGREDIENTS

- ½ pound carrots, sliced
- A pinch of salt and black pepper
- ½ tablespoon olive oil
- ½ cup of orange juice
- ½ teaspoon orange rind, grated

DIRECTIONS

1. In your slow cooker, mix the carrots with the oil and the rest of the fixing, toss, cook on low within 6 hours. Divide between plates and serve as a side dish.

Nutrition: *Calories: 140 Fat: 2g Carbs: 7g Protein: 6g*

211. BAKED APPLES

PREPARATION: 15 MIN **COOKING:** 6 H **SERVINGS:** 4

INGREDIENTS

- Slow cooker size: 6-quart
- 1/2 cup granulated sugar
- 3 pounds apples granny smith or fuji
- 1/2 cup brown sugar
- 1/2 teaspoon ground nutmeg
- 1 teaspoon ground cinnamon
- 2 tablespoons butter cut into slices

DIRECTIONS

1. Wash, slice, core, and peel the apples and add to the bottom of a 6-quart slow cooker the apple slices. To coat the slices, whisk in the sugar, brown sugar, nutmeg, cinnamon, and butter. Cover for 6 hours on low. At least once halfway during the cooking process, stirring. Serve.

Nutrition: *Calories: 310 Fat: 5g Carbs: 71g Protein: 1g*

212. BAKED POTATOES

PREPARATION: 15 MIN **COOKING:** 6-8 H **SERVINGS:** 4

INGREDIENTS

- 6 whole potatoes, medium-sized
- salt (optional)

DIRECTIONS

1. On an aluminum foil sheet, put each potato and sprinkle with a little pinch of salt (optional). Roll each potato into foil and put in a slow cooker at the bottom.
2. Cook within 6-8 hours on low or 3 to 4 hours on high. Top and enjoy baked potatoes with your favorite toppings!

Nutrition: *Calories: 164 Fat: 0.2g Carbs: 37g Protein: 4g*

213. PUMPKIN PUREE

PREPARATION: 15 MIN   **COOKING:** 8 H   **SERVINGS:** 4

INGREDIENTS

- 1 medium fresh pie pumpkin

DIRECTIONS

1. Carefully cut the pumpkin in half using a sharp knife and scoop out the seeds and pulp using a large spoon from each half of the pumpkin.
2. Cut each half of the pumpkin into 4 to 6 wedges, cut each wedge off the pumpkin's skin, and then cut it into pieces. In a 6-quart or larger slow cooker, put chunks of pumpkin.
3. Cook and cover for 6 to 8 hours on low or until the pumpkin chunks are tender and smooth. Puree the pumpkin using a hand-held immersion blender, food processor, or blender. Serve.

Nutrition: *Calories: 26 Fat: 0.1g Carbs: 7g Protein: 1g*

214. GARLIC PARSLEY POTATOES

PREPARATION: 15 MIN   **COOKING:** 4-6 H   **SERVINGS:** 4

INGREDIENTS

- 1 1/2 pounds new potatoes washed
- 3-4 cloves garlic minced
- 1/4 cup extra virgin olive oil
- salt and pepper to taste
- 3 tbsp dried parsley or fresh parsley, finely minced

DIRECTIONS

1. Peel away a strip of potato peel around the center of each new potato with a vegetable peeler and put a 4-quart slow cooker on the bottom.
2. Drizzle the olive oil with the potatoes and sprinkle with the garlic and parsley. Mix to brush each potato with oil with a spoon and spread the garlic and parsley evenly.
3. Cover and cook within 4 to 6 hours on LOW or until the potatoes are tender with a fork.

Nutrition: *Calories: 219 Carbs: 31g Fat: 9g Protein: 4g*

215. CRANBERRY-ORANGE CHUTNEY

PREPARATION: 15 MIN **COOKING:** 4 H **SERVINGS:** 4

INGREDIENTS

- Slow cooker size: 3-quart
- 12 oz. cranberries fresh
- 1 whole orange navel, zested and juiced
- 2 apples, peeled and diced
- 1 cup golden raisins
- 1 teaspoon ground cinnamon
- 3/4 cup brown sugar light
- 1/2 teaspoon ground nutmeg
- 1 cup walnuts chopped (optional)
- 1/4 teaspoon ground cloves

DIRECTIONS

1. In a 3-quart slow-cooker, add all ingredients except walnuts. Stir to blend. Cover and cook within 4 hours or until all is cooked through and saucy on low heat. If used, add chopped walnuts. Serve

Nutrition: *Calories: 290 Fat: 13g Carbs: 43g Protein: 4g*

216. CREAMY CORN

PREPARATION: 15 MIN **COOKING:** 2 H **SERVINGS:** 4

INGREDIENTS

- 1 cup whole milk
- 16 oz. frozen corn kernels
- 2 tablespoons granulated sugar
- 1/4 cup all-purpose flour
- 2 large eggs beaten
- 1/2 teaspoon kosher salt
- 2 tablespoons unsalted butter

DIRECTIONS

1. In a 3 to 5-quart slow cooker, add all ingredients and mix to blend. Cover and cook for 1 to 2 hours on high or until the corn is smooth and thickened. Serve.

Nutrition: *Calories: 296 Carbs: 45g Fat: 11g Protein: 10g*

217. SWEET POTATOES WITH MARSHMALLOWS

PREPARATION: 15 MIN **COOKING:** 7 H 30 MIN **SERVINGS:** 4

INGREDIENTS

- 3/4 cup brown sugar
- 5 large sweet potatoes, cut into a 1-inch cube
- 1/4 cup butter melted
- 1 teaspoon ground nutmeg
- 1 teaspoon ground cinnamon
- 1/2 teaspoon kosher salt
- 3 cups miniature marshmallows
- 1/2 cup orange juice

DIRECTIONS

1. In a 4 to 6-quart slow cooker, put the sweet potatoes, brown sugar, butter, cinnamon, nutmeg, and salt on the bottom.
2. Cover and cook within 6 to 7 hours on low or 3 to 4 hours on high. Mash the sweet potatoes using your potato masher. Add orange juice to the mix.
3. Cover the top with marshmallows, cover with mashed sweet potatoes, and cook for an additional 20 to 30 minutes. Serve.

Nutrition: *Calories: 531 Fat: 6g Carbs: 117g Protein: 5g*

218. GREEN BEANS AND BACON

PREPARATION: 15 MIN **COOKING:** 8 H **SERVINGS:** 4

INGREDIENTS

- 29 oz. canned green beans
- 12 oz. center-cut bacon
- 1/2 cup real maple syrup
- 1 medium yellow onion chopped
- 1/4 cup brown sugar

DIRECTIONS

1. Just heat the bacon and onion in a saucepan until the bacon is cooked. Drain and empty the green beans into a 5-quart or larger slow cooker.
2. On top of the green beans, add the bacon, onion, and drippings. Put the brown sugar and maple syrup in the mixture and combine well—cover and cook within 6 to 8 hours on low or within 4 to 5 hours on high. Serve.

Nutrition: *Calories: 185 Fat: 9g Carbs: 17g Protein: 12g*

219. CHUNKY APPLESAUCE

PREPARATION: 15 MIN **COOKING:** 6 H **SERVINGS:** 4

INGREDIENTS

- 1 cup granulated sugar
- 3 pounds apples peeled, slice into large chunks
- 1 teaspoon ground cloves
- 2 teaspoons ground cinnamon
- 1 cup of water

DIRECTIONS

1. Put all the ingredients and mix to combine in a 6-quart or larger slow cooker. Cover and cook for 2 hours on high, then turn down to low and cook 4 to 6 hours or until tender. Mash the apples using a potato masher.
2. Stir in more sugar or honey, if necessary, while the applesauce is still warm. Add in tiny amounts until you achieve the perfect sweetness. Serve hot or refrigerate for up to 1 week.

Nutrition: *Calories: 139 Fat: 0.3g Carbs: 36g Protein: 0.3g*

220. PARMESAN GARLIC POTATOES

PREPARATION: 15 MIN **COOKING:** 5 H **SERVINGS:** 4

INGREDIENTS

- 3 tablespoons unsalted butter melted
- 3 pounds baby potatoes washed and halved
- 1/2 teaspoon dried oregano
- 2 tablespoons olive oil
- 4 cloves garlic minced
- 1/2 teaspoon dried basil
- 1/4 teaspoon kosher salt
- 1/4 teaspoon freshly ground black pepper
- 1/2 teaspoon dried dill
- 1/2 cup parmesan cheese grated

DIRECTIONS

1. In a dish, toss the melted butter, olive oil, and minced garlic with the halved potatoes. Attach a 5-quart or larger slow cooker to the potatoes.
2. Mix dry seasoning (oregano, basil, dill, salt, and pepper) in another tub. Sprinkle the seasoning with the potatoes and toss gently.
3. Cook within 4 to 5 hours on low or 2 to 3 hours on high. Until serving, remove the potatoes from the slow cooker and sprinkle them with parmesan cheese.

Nutrition: *Calories: 191 Fat: 16g Carbs: 3g Protein: 8g*

221. COCONUT-PECAN SWEET POTATOES

PREPARATION: 15 MIN   **COOKING:** 5 H   **SERVINGS:** 4

INGREDIENTS

- 1/2 cup chopped pecans
- 4 pounds sweet potatoes, diced
- 1/2 cup butter melted
- 1/3 cup granulated sugar
- 1/2 cup unsweetened flaked coconut
- 1/3 cup brown sugar packed
- 1/4 teaspoon kosher salt
- 1/2 teaspoon pure vanilla extract

DIRECTIONS

1. Put the sweet potatoes in a slow cooker of 5 quarts or greater. Mix the pecans, coconut, melted butter sugar, vanilla extract, and salt in a dish.
2. Put the pecan mixture and toss it with the sweet potatoes in the slow cooker—cover and cook within 4 to 5 hours on low.

Nutrition: *Calories: 307 Fat: 16g Carbs: 42g Protein: 3g*

222. SUGAR CARROTS WITH GINGER

PREPARATION: 15 MIN   **COOKING:** 6 H   **SERVINGS:** 4

INGREDIENTS

- 7 whole carrots sliced into 1/4-inch slices
- 1/4 cup brown sugar
- 3 tablespoons fresh ginger, minced
- 1/4 cup butter
- 1/4 cup orange juice

DIRECTIONS

1. Clean and remove the carrots and slice them into 1/4-inch pieces. Add carrots, ginger, orange juice, brown sugar, and butter to a 4-quart slow cooker.
2. Cover and cook for 1 hour. To ensure no clumps of brown sugar, remove the lid from the slow cooker and whisk in the carrot mixture.
3. Cover the slow cooker, adjust the temperature to low, and cook for an extra 4 to 5 hours or until the carrots hit the perfect tenderness amount. Serve.

Nutrition: *Calories: 221 Fat: 12g Carbs: 29g Protein: 1g*

223. SWEET ACORN SQUASH

PREPARATION: 15 MIN **COOKING:** 3 H **SERVINGS:** 4

INGREDIENTS

- 2 tablespoons Butter
- 1 medium Acorn Squash, cut in half
- 2 tablespoons Brown Sugar

DIRECTIONS

1. By cutting each of them in half and scooping out the seeds and pulp, prepare your acorn squashes. Place a 4 quart or larger slow cooker with acorn squash halves skin-side down.
2. Score the inside of the squash all over the flesh with a sharp kitchen knife, being careful not to pierce the skin. Divide the butter and brown sugar equally between the two halves of the squash.
3. Cover and cook on high within 3 hours or until the squash's flesh is soft and tender. Serve.

Nutrition: *Calories: 124 Fat: 6g Protein: 1g Carbs: 18g*

224. SWEET POTATOES WITH ORANGE

PREPARATION: 15 MIN **COOKING:** 6 H **SERVINGS:** 4

INGREDIENTS

- Slow cooker size: 6-quart
- 4 medium sweet potatoes
- 2 tablespoons orange zest
- 1/4 cup water or orange juice
- salt & pepper to taste
- 1/2 cup butter or dairy-free margarine

DIRECTIONS

1. Break the sweet potatoes lengthwise into quarters and then into large chunks. In a 6-quart slow cooker, add the sweet potatoes, water, and orange zest.
2. Cover and cook within 2 to 3 hours on high or 4 to 6 hours on low or until the sweet potatoes are easily fork-pierced.
3. Use a potato masher right in the slow cooker to mix up the sweet potatoes; add butter, salt, and pepper to taste. Serve.

Nutrition: Calories: 237 Fat: 16g Carbs: 23g Protein: 2g

225. VEGGIE AND GARBANZO MIX

PREPARATION: 10 MIN **COOKING:** 6 H **SERVINGS:** 4

INGREDIENTS

- 15 oz. canned garbanzo beans, drained
- 3 cups cauliflower florets
- 1 cup green beans
- 1 cup carrot, sliced
- 14 oz. veggie stock
- ½ cup onion, chopped
- 2 teaspoons curry powder
- ¼ cup basil, chopped
- 14 oz. of coconut milk

DIRECTIONS

1. In your slow cooker, mix beans with cauliflower, green beans, carrot, onion, stock, curry powder, basil, and milk, stir, cover, and cook on low for 6 hours. Stir veggie mix again, divide between plates and serve as a side dish.

Nutrition: Calories: 219 Fat: 5g Carbs: 32g Protein: 7g

226. MUSHROOMS AND SAUSAGE MIX

PREPARATION: 10 MIN **COOKING:** 2 H 30 MIN **SERVINGS:** 4

INGREDIENTS

- ½ cup butter, melted
- 1-pound pork sausage, ground
- ½ pound mushrooms, sliced
- 6 celery ribs, chopped
- 2 yellow onions, chopped
- 2 garlic cloves, minced
- 1 tablespoon sage, chopped
- 1 cup cranberries, dried
- ½ cup cauliflower florets, chopped
- ½ cup veggie stock

DIRECTIONS

1. Heat-up a pan with the butter over medium-high heat, add sausage, stir, cook for a couple of minutes and transfer to your slow cooker.
2. Add mushrooms, celery, onion, garlic, sage, cranberries, cauliflower, stock, stir, cover, and cook on high for 2 hours and 30 minutes. Divide between plates and serve as a side dish.

Nutrition: *Calories: 200 Fat: 3g Carbs: 9g Protein: 4g*

227. GLAZED BABY CARROTS

PREPARATION: 10 MIN **COOKING:** 6 H **SERVINGS:** 4

INGREDIENTS

- ½ cup peach preserves
- ½ cup butter, melted
- 2 pounds baby carrots
- 2 tablespoon sugar
- 1 teaspoon vanilla extract
- A pinch of salt and black pepper
- A bit of nutmeg, ground
- ½ teaspoon cinnamon powder
- 2 tablespoons water

DIRECTIONS

1. Put baby carrots in your slow cooker, add butter, peach preserves, sugar, vanilla, salt, pepper, nutmeg, cinnamon, and water, toss well, cover, and cook on low for 6 hours. Divide between plates and serve as a side dish.

Nutrition: *Calories: 283 Fat: 14g Carbs: 28g Protein: 3g*

228. BUTTERY MUSHROOMS

PREPARATION: 10 MIN **COOKING:** 4 H **SERVINGS:** 4

INGREDIENTS

- 1 yellow onion, chopped
- 1 pound's mushrooms, halved
- ½ cup butter, melted
- 1 teaspoon Italian seasoning
- Salt and black pepper to the taste
- 1 teaspoon sweet paprika

DIRECTIONS

1. In your slow cooker, mix mushrooms with onion, butter, Italian seasoning, salt, pepper, and paprika, toss, cover, and cook on low within 4 hours. Divide between plates and serve as a side dish.

Nutrition: *Calories: 120 Fat: 6g Carbs: 8g Protein: 4g*

229. CAULIFLOWER RICE AND SPINACH

PREPARATION: 10 MIN **COOKING:** 3 H **SERVINGS:** 4

INGREDIENTS

- 2 garlic cloves, minced
- 2 tablespoons butter, melted
- 1 yellow onion, chopped
- ¼ teaspoon thyme, dried
- 3 cups veggie stock
- 20 oz. spinach, chopped
- 6 oz. coconut cream
- Salt and black pepper to the taste
- 2 cups cauliflower rice

DIRECTIONS

1. Heat-up a pan with the butter over medium heat, add onion, stir and cook for 4 minutes. Add garlic, thyme, and stock, stir, cook for 1 minute more, and transfer to your slow cooker.
2. Add spinach, coconut cream, cauliflower rice, salt, and pepper, stir a bit, cover and cook on high for 3 hours. Divide between plates and serve as a side dish.

Nutrition: *Calories: 200 Fat: 4g Carbs: 8g Protein: 2g*

230. MAPLE SWEET POTATOES

PREPARATION: 10 MIN   **COOKING:** 5 H   **SERVINGS:** 4

INGREDIENTS

- 4 sweet potatoes, halved and sliced
- 1 cup walnuts, chopped
- ½ cup cherries, dried and chopped
- ½ cup maple syrup
- ¼ cup apple juice
- A pinch of salt

DIRECTIONS

1. Arrange sweet potatoes in your slow cooker, add walnuts, dried cherries, maple syrup, apple juice, and a pinch of salt, toss a bit, cover, and cook on low for 5 hours. Divide between plates and serve as a side dish.

Nutrition: *Calories: 271 Fat: 6g Carbs: 26g Protein: 6g*

231. SWEET POTATO MASH

PREPARATION: 10 MIN   **COOKING:** 5 H   **SERVINGS:** 4

INGREDIENTS

- 2 pounds sweet potatoes, peeled and sliced
- 1 tablespoon cinnamon powder
- 1 cup apple juice
- 1 teaspoon nutmeg, ground
- ¼ teaspoon cloves, ground
- ½ teaspoon allspice
- 1 tablespoon butter, melted

DIRECTIONS

1. In your slow cooker, mix sweet potatoes with cinnamon, apple juice, nutmeg, cloves, and allspice, stir, cover, and cook on low within 5 hours. Mash using a potato masher, add butter, whisk well, divide between plates and serve as a side dish.

Nutrition: *Calories: 111 Fat: 2g Carbs: 16g Protein: 3g*

232. DILL CAULIFLOWER MASH

PREPARATION: 10 MIN   **COOKING:** 5 H   **SERVINGS:** 4

INGREDIENTS

- 1 cauliflower head, florets separated
- 1/3 cup dill, chopped
- 6 garlic cloves
- 2 tablespoons butter, melted
- A pinch of salt and black pepper

DIRECTIONS

1. Put cauliflower in your slow cooker, add dill, garlic, and water to cover cauliflower, cover, and cook on high for 5 hours.
2. Drain cauliflower and dill, add salt, pepper, and butter, mash using a potato masher, whisk well and serve as a side dish.

Nutrition: *Calories: 187 Fat: 4g Carbs: 12g Protein: 3g*

233. EGGPLANT AND KALE MIX

PREPARATION: 10 MIN   **COOKING:** 2H   **SERVINGS:** 4

INGREDIENTS

- 14 oz. canned roasted tomatoes and garlic
- 4 cups eggplant, cubed
- 1 yellow bell pepper, chopped
- 1 red onion, cut into medium wedges
- 4 cups kale leaves
- 2 tablespoons olive oil
- 1 teaspoon mustard
- 3 tablespoons red vinegar
- 1 garlic clove, minced
- Salt and black pepper to the taste
- ½ cup basil, chopped

DIRECTIONS

1. In your slow cooker, mix the eggplant with tomatoes, bell pepper, and onion, toss, cover, and cook on high for 2 hours.
2. Add kale, toss, cover slow cooker and leave aside for now. In a bowl, mix oil with vinegar, mustard, garlic, salt, and pepper and whisk well. Add this over eggplant mix, add basil, toss, divide between plates and serve as a side dish.

Nutrition: *Calories: 251 Fat: 9g Carbs: 34g Protein: 8g*

234. THAI SIDE SALAD

PREPARATION: 10 MIN   **COOKING:** 3 H   **SERVINGS:** 4

INGREDIENTS

- 8 oz. yellow summer squash, peeled and roughly chopped
- 12 oz. zucchini, halved and sliced
- 2 cups button mushrooms, quartered
- 1 red sweet potato, chopped
- 2 leeks, sliced
- 2 tablespoons veggie stock
- 2 garlic cloves, minced
- 2 tablespoon Thai red curry paste
- 1 tablespoon ginger, grated
- 1/3 cup coconut milk
- ¼ cup basil, chopped

DIRECTIONS

1. In your slow cooker, mix zucchini with summer squash, mushrooms, red pepper, leeks, garlic, stock, curry paste, ginger, coconut milk, and basil, toss, cover, and cook on low for 3 hours. Stir your Thai mix one more time, divide between plates and serve as a side dish.

Nutrition: *Calories: 69 Fat: 2g Carbs: 8g Protein: 2g*

235. MINT FARRO PILAF

PREPARATION: 10 MIN   **COOKING:** 4 H   **SERVINGS:** 2

INGREDIENTS

- ½ tablespoon balsamic vinegar
- ½ cup whole grain farro
- A pinch of salt and black pepper
- 1 cup chicken stock
- ½ tablespoon olive oil
- 1 tablespoon green onions, chopped
- 1 tablespoon mint, chopped

DIRECTIONS

1. In your slow cooker, mix the farro with the vinegar and the other ingredients, toss, cook on low within 4 hours. Divide between plates and serve.

Nutrition: *Calories: 162 Fat: 3g Carbs: 9g Protein: 4g*

236. PARMESAN RICE

PREPARATION: 10 MIN   **COOKING:** 2 H 30 MIN   **SERVINGS:** 2

INGREDIENTS

- 1 cup of rice
- 2 cups chicken stock
- 1 tablespoon olive oil
- 1 red onion, chopped
- 1 tablespoon lemon juice
- Salt and black pepper to the taste
- 1 tablespoon parmesan, grated

DIRECTIONS

1. In your slow cooker, mix the rice with the stock, oil, and the rest of the fixing, toss, cook on high for 2 hours and 30 minutes. Divide between plates and serve as a side dish.

Nutrition: *Calories: 162 Fat: 4g Carbs: 29g Protein: 6g*

237. LEMON ARTICHOKES

PREPARATION: 10 MIN **COOKING:** 3 H **SERVINGS:** 2

INGREDIENTS

- 1 cup veggie stock
- 2 medium artichokes, trimmed
- 1 tablespoon lemon juice
- 1 tablespoon lemon zest, grated
- Salt to the taste

DIRECTIONS

1. In your slow cooker, mix the artichokes with the stock and the rest of the fixing, toss, cook on low for 3 hours. Divide artichokes between plates and serve as a side dish.

Nutrition: Calories: 100 Fat: 2g Carbs: 10g Protein: 4g

238. ITALIAN EGGPLANT

PREPARATION: 10 MIN **COOKING:** 2 H **SERVINGS:** 2

INGREDIENTS

- 2 small eggplants, roughly cubed
- ½ cup heavy cream
- Salt and black pepper to the taste
- 1 tablespoon olive oil
- A pinch of hot pepper flakes
- 2 tablespoons oregano, chopped

DIRECTIONS

1. In your slow cooker, mix the eggplants, cream, and the rest of the fixing, toss, and cook on high within 2 hours. Divide between plates and serve as a side dish.

Nutrition: Calories: 132 Fat: 4g Carbs: 12g Protein: 3g

239. CABBAGE AND ONION MIX

PREPARATION: 10 MIN **COOKING:** 2 H **SERVINGS:** 2

INGREDIENTS

- 1 and ½ cups green cabbage, shredded
- 1 cup red cabbage, shredded
- 1 tablespoon olive oil
- 1 red onion, sliced
- 2 spring onions, chopped
- ½ cup tomato paste
- ¼ cup veggie stock
- 2 tomatoes, chopped
- 2 jalapenos, chopped
- 1 tablespoon chili powder
- 1 tablespoon chives, chopped
- A pinch of salt and black pepper

DIRECTIONS

1. Grease your slow cooker with the oil and mix the cabbage with the onion, spring onions, and the other ingredients inside. Toss, and cook on high within 2 hours. Divide between plates and serve as a side dish.

Nutrition: Calories: 211 Fat: 3g Carbs: 6g Protein: 8g

240. BALSAMIC OKRA MIX

PREPARATION: 10 MIN **COOKING:** 2 H **SERVINGS:** 4

INGREDIENTS

- 2 cups okra, sliced
- 1 cup cherry tomatoes, halved
- 1 tablespoon olive oil
- ½ teaspoon turmeric powder
- ½ cup canned tomatoes, crushed
- 2 tablespoons balsamic vinegar
- 2 tablespoons basil, chopped
- 1 tablespoon thyme, chopped

DIRECTIONS

1. In your slow cooker, mix the okra with the tomatoes, crushed tomatoes, and the rest of the fixing, toss, put the lid on and cook on high for 2 hours. Divide between plates and serve as a side dish.

Nutrition: *Calories: 233 Fat: 12g Carbs: 8g Protein: 4g*

CHAPTER 6.
POULTRY

241. CHICKEN CURRY

PREPARATION: 15 MIN   **COOKING:** 6 H   **SERVINGS:** 4

INGREDIENTS

- 2 pounds of chicken breasts/thighs
- 2 cups full fat coconut milk
- 6 cups, your choice, fresh vegetables
- 1 tablespoon cumin
- 1 cup tomato sauce
- 2 teaspoons ground ginger
- 2 teaspoons ground coriander
- 1 teaspoon cinnamon
- 2 teaspoons garlic powder
- 1 cup of water
- ½ teaspoon cayenne pepper
- pinch of salt and fresh ground pepper, each

DIRECTIONS

1. Rinse the chicken, pat dry. Dice the vegetables and chicken into chunks. Place all the fixings in your slow cooker.
2. Add the coconut milk, tomatoes, and spices. Add the cup of water. Cover and cook on low within 6 hours. Serve hot—side with rice or greens.

Nutrition: *Calories: 515 Fat: 29.3g Carb 23.2g Protein: 39.8g*

242. STUFFED CHICKEN BREASTS

PREPARATION: 15 MIN   **COOKING:** 6 H   **SERVINGS:** 2-4

INGREDIENTS

- 6 boneless chicken breasts
- 1/3 cup feta cheese, crumbled
- 1-2 teaspoons fresh oregano
- pinch of salt, fresh ground pepper, each
- 1 tablespoon olive oil
- ½ onion, diced
- 2 teaspoons minced garlic
- ¾ cup fresh spinach
- juice of 1 lemon
- 2 pepperoncini peppers
- ½ red pepper, diced
- 1 cup chicken stock
- ½ cup white wine

Nutrition: *Calories: 357 Fat: 15.2g Carbs: 5.2g Protein: 44.8g*

DIRECTIONS

1. Rinse the chicken, pat dry. Slice the chicken breasts ¾ open. Leave them attached. In a large bowl, combine feta cheese, oregano, salt, and pepper.
2. In a large skillet, heat the olive oil. Add the onion, cook 2 minutes, then put the garlic, cook 1 minute. Add the spinach. Heat until the spinach wilts.
3. Add the spinach batter to the bowl with feta cheese. Add the lemon juice, pepperoncini peppers, red pepper. Stir to combine.
4. Stuff the chicken breasts with the mixture. Place them in the slow cooker. Pour in chicken stock and wine—cover and cook on for 6 hours, then serve hot—side with salad.

243. CHICKEN HEARTS

PREPARATION: 15 MIN   **COOKING:** 8 H   **SERVINGS:** 2

INGREDIENTS

- 2 pounds of chicken hearts
- 1 onion, sliced
- 1-pound mushrooms, sliced
- 4 garlic cloves, minced
- 1 tablespoon Dijon mustard
- 1 teaspoon salt, fresh ground pepper, each
- ½ tablespoon paprika
- ½ tablespoon cayenne pepper
- 1 cup chicken stock
- ¼ cup of coconut milk
- 7 oz. Greek yogurt, full fat

DIRECTIONS

1. Rinse the chicken, pat dry. Place all the ingredients, up to the chicken stock, in a slow cooker. Cover and cook on low within 8 hours.
2. Once finished cooking, stir in the cream and yogurt, wait 10 minutes and serve—side with potatoes, greens.

Nutrition: *Calories: 241 Fat: 11.8g Carbs: 20.4g Protein: 14.8g*

244. HONEY CHICKEN DRUMSTICKS

PREPARATION: 15 MIN   **COOKING:** 6 H   **SERVINGS:** 2-4

INGREDIENTS

- 8 chicken drumsticks
- 1 tablespoon honey
- 3 apples, peeled and diced
- ½ teaspoon cinnamon
- 1 teaspoon salt
- Garnish: chopped parsley, sesame seeds

DIRECTIONS

1. Rinse the chicken, pat dry. Mix the honey and salt in a medium bowl. Pour mixture over the drumsticks.
2. Place the drumsticks in the slow cooker. Cover and cook on low within 6 hours, until chicken is tender. Serve hot. Garnish with parsley and sesame seeds.

Nutrition: *Calories: 259 Fat: 5.6g Carbs: 27.7g Protein: 25.8g*

245. ROSEMARY LEMON CHICKEN

PREPARATION: 15 MIN **COOKING:** 6 H **SERVINGS:** 4

INGREDIENTS

- 4 pounds of chicken thighs, bone & skin in
- 1 tablespoon olive oil
- Pinch of sea salt and ground black pepper, each
- ½ cup of preferred flour
- 3 medium yellow onions, sliced
- 8 carrots, sliced
- 6 garlic cloves, chopped
- 3 springs rosemary
- ½ cup lime juice
- ¾ cup chicken broth
- 1 tablespoon lemon zest
- 1 lemon sliced

DIRECTIONS

1. Rinse the chicken, pat dry. Place the chicken, salt, pepper, onions, carrots in your slow cooker. Sprinkle the flour over ingredients. Stir until they are coated.
2. Add garlic, rosemary, lime juice, broth, lemon zest, sliced lemon. Cover and cook on low within 6 hours, until chicken is tender. Serve hot.

Nutrition: *Calories: 510 Fat: 14g Carbs: 24.7g Protein: 63g*

---

246. ROTISSERIE CHICKEN

PREPARATION: 15 MIN **COOKING:** 6 H **SERVINGS:** 4

INGREDIENTS

- 5-pound fresh chicken
- 2 tablespoons olive oil
- 4-5 sweet potatoes, small size
- a couple pinches sea salt, fresh ground pepper, each

DIRECTIONS

1. Rinse the chicken, pat dry. Coat the chicken with oil. Season with salt and pepper. Coat the potatoes with oil, salt, plus pepper. Wrap in foil.
2. Place the potatoes along the bottom of the slow cooker. Place chicken over the potatoes. Cover and cook on low within 6 hours. Serve hot.

Nutrition: *Calories: 443 Fat: 15.3g Carbs: 17.4g Protein: 55.6g*

247. SALSA CHICKEN

PREPARATION: 15 MIN   **COOKING:** 6 H   **SERVINGS:** 4

INGREDIENTS

- 4 chicken thighs
- salad greens
- 1 pint of salsa
- shredded cheese

DIRECTIONS

1. Rinse the chicken, pat dry. Place the chicken, greens, and salsa in the slow cooker. Cook on low for 6 hours. Garnish with cheese.

Nutrition: Calories: 310 Fat: 10.9g Carbs: 7.1g Protein: 44.6g

248. TURMERIC CHICKEN

PREPARATION: 15 MIN   **COOKING:** 5 H   **SERVINGS:** 4

INGREDIENTS

- 5 pounds of chicken, organic
- 1 teaspoon turmeric
- ½ cup coconut milk, full fat
- 4 garlic cloves, finely grated
- 2-3-inch fresh ginger, grated
- Pinch of salt and fresh ground pepper, each
- Garnish: Scallions

DIRECTIONS

1. In the slow cooker, combine the turmeric, ginger, and garlic. Stir in the coconut milk. Season chicken with salt and pepper. Place in the slow cooker. Cook on low within 5 hours, until chicken cooked. Shred with 2 forks.

Nutrition: *Calories: 359 Fat: 7.7g Carbs: 2.1g Protein: 66g*

249. MARINARA CHICKEN

PREPARATION: 15 MIN **COOKING:** 4 H **SERVINGS:** 4

INGREDIENTS

- 4 pounds of chicken
- 1 jar marinara sauce
- 1 onion, diced
- 2 garlic cloves, diced
- ½ green pepper, diced
- 2 zucchinis, diced
- ¼ cup basil
- Pinch of salt and fresh ground pepper, each
- Garnish: Parmigiano Reggiano, grated

DIRECTIONS

1. Rinse the chicken, pat dry. Season the chicken with salt and pepper. Place in the slow cooker. Add the onions, garlic, green pepper, and zucchini.
2. Pour the marinara sauce over the ingredients. Cover and cook on medium within 4 hours, until cooked through.
3. Shred the chicken with 2 forks. Serve warm over favorite pasta. Top with Parmigiano Reggiano.

Nutrition: *Calories: 319 Fat: 6.1g Carbs: 8.9g Protein: 54.5g*

250. CHOCOLATE CHICKEN

PREPARATION: 15 MIN **COOKING:** 6 H **SERVINGS:** 4-6

INGREDIENTS

- 2 pounds chicken breasts, bone-in
- Pinch of sea salt, fresh ground pepper, each
- 2 tablespoons ghee
- 1 medium onion, diced
- 4 garlic cloves, minced
- 7 medium tomatoes, peeled and chopped
- 2 1/2 oz. of dark chocolate, crumbled
- 5 dried chili peppers, finely chopped
- 1 teaspoon cumin powder
- ¼ cup Almond Butter
- ½ teaspoon cinnamon powder
- 1/2 teaspoon guajillo chili powder
- Garnish: diced Avocado, chopped cilantro, and diced jalapeno pepper, seeds out

DIRECTIONS

1. Rinse the chicken, pat dry. Place all the other fixings in the slow cooker. Cover and cook on low within 6 hours. Serve warm. Garnish with avocado chunks, cilantro, and diced jalapeno.

Nutrition: *Calories: 477 Fat: 20.6g Carbs: 19.6g Protein: 53.4g*

251. COCONUT CURRIED CHICKEN

PREPARATION: 15 MIN   **COOKING:** 5 H   **SERVINGS:** 4

INGREDIENTS

- 3 pounds of chicken breasts/thighs
- 1 large onion, chopped
- 2 small carrots, chopped
- 2 garlic cloves, minced
- 1 tablespoon curry powder
- 1 tablespoon mustard condiment
- ½ cup coconut cream
- ½ cup chicken stock
- 2 tablespoons ghee
- Pinch of salt
- 2 Yukon gold potatoes, peeled, chopped
- Garnish: chopped parsley

DIRECTIONS

1. Rinse the chicken, pat dry. Place all the fixings, except the potatoes, in the slow cooker. Stir well. After 3 hours of cooking, add the potatoes. Cover and cook on low within 4-5 hours, until chicken and potatoes are tender. Serve warm.

Nutrition: Calories: 377 Fat: 25g Carbs: 6.3g Protein: 30.4g

252. BUFFALO CHICKEN

PREPARATION: 15 MIN   **COOKING:** 6H   **SERVINGS:** 4

INGREDIENTS

- ½ pound chicken breast, boneless, skinless
- ½ pound chicken thighs, boneless, skinless
- 1/3 cup hot sauce
- 1 tablespoon coconut aminos
- 2 tablespoons ghee
- ¼ teaspoon cayenne
- ½ teaspoon garlic powder
- 4 small sweet potatoes, chopped
- ¼ - ½ cup of water
- Garnish: ranch dressing, chives

DIRECTIONS

1. Rinse the chicken, pat dry. In a skillet, combine the ghee, garlic powder, hot sauce, cayenne, and coconut aminos. Simmer for 5 minutes.
2. Coat the chicken with the mixture—place in the slow cooker. Add the potatoes, then pour in ¼ cup of water.
3. Cover and cook on low within 5-6 hours, until chicken cooked. Serve warm. Garnish with ranch dressing, chives.

Nutrition: Calories: 423 Fat: 11.4g Carbs: 56.4g Protein: 24.1g

253. TERIYAKI CHICKEN

PREPARATION: 15 MIN   **COOKING:** 6 H   **SERVINGS:** 4

INGREDIENTS

- 2 pounds chicken thighs, boneless, skinless
- 3 tablespoons honey
- ½ cup coconut aminos
- 1 ½ teaspoons minced ginger
- 4 garlic cloves, minced
- 1 tablespoon sesame seeds, toasted
- 1 teaspoon of sea salt

DIRECTIONS

1. Rinse the chicken, pat dry. Place all the fixings, except sesame seeds, in the slow cooker. Cook on low within 5-6 hours, until chicken cooked through.
2. Cut the chicken into bite-size pieces. Garnish with sesame seeds. Serve warm on a bed of rice.

Nutrition: Calories: 341 Fat: 12g Carbs: 11.7g Protein: 44.2g

254. PULLED BBQ CHICKEN

PREPARATION: 15 MIN   **COOKING:** 4 H   **SERVINGS:** 2-4 H

INGREDIENTS

- 3 pounds of chicken breasts
- 2 cups tomatoes, diced
- 3-4 pitted dates
- 3 garlic cloves, minced
- ½ large yellow onion, diced
- 3 tablespoons apple cider vinegar
- 2 teaspoons sea salt
- 1 tablespoon smoked paprika
- 6 oz. tomato paste
- 1 ½ tablespoon avocado oil

DIRECTIONS

1. Rinse the chicken, pat dry. Drizzle the chicken with avocado oil. Place in the slow cooker. Blend the rest of the ingredients in a food processor. Pour over chicken. Cook on low for 4 hours. Shred with 2 forks. Serve hot.

Nutrition: *Calories: 217 Fat: 6.3g Carbs: 19.6g Protein: 22.1g*

255. LEMON THYME CHICKEN

PREPARATION: 15 MIN   **COOKING:** 4 H   **SERVINGS:** 4

INGREDIENTS

- 4-pound chicken
- ¼ cup lemon juice
- 1 teaspoon dried thyme
- 2-3 bay leaves
- 5 garlic cloves, diced
- 1 teaspoon of sea salt
- ¼ teaspoon black pepper
- ¼ cup of water

DIRECTIONS

1. Rinse the chicken, pat dry. Place in the slow cooker. Pour lemon juice over the chicken. Season with thyme, salt, and pepper. Add bay leaves, garlic.
2. Put the water in the bottom of the slow cooker. Cover and cook for 4 hours, until chicken is cooked through. Serve hot.

Nutrition: *Calories: 276 Fat: 5.6g Carbs: 0.3g Protein: 52.7g*

256. CHICKEN AND GRAVY

PREPARATION: 10 MIN **COOKING:** 8 H **SERVINGS:** 4

INGREDIENTS

- 2 lbs. chicken breasts, skinless, boneless, and cut into pieces
- 3 cups chicken stock
- 1 oz brown gravy mix
- 1 oz onion soup mix

DIRECTIONS

1. Add chicken stock, brown gravy mix, and onion soup mix into the slow cooker and stir well. Add chicken into the slow cooker. Cover and cook on low within 8 hours. Stir well and serve.

Nutrition: *Calories: 323 Fat: 12g Carbs: 6.2g Protein: 44.9g*

257. CILANTRO LIME CHICKEN

PREPARATION: 10 MIN **COOKING:** 6 H **SERVINGS:** 4

INGREDIENTS

- 6 chicken breasts, boneless
- 2 jalapeno peppers, chopped
- 1 1/4 oz taco seasoning
- 1/4 cup fresh cilantro, chopped
- 1 lime juice
- 24 oz salsa

DIRECTIONS

1. Add all fixings except chicken into the slow cooker and mix well. Add chicken into the slow cooker. Cover and cook on low within 6 hours. Shred chicken using a fork and serve.

Nutrition: *Calories: 162 Fat: 5.9 g Carbs: 4.5 g Protein: 22.4 g*

258. GARLIC CHICKEN

PREPARATION: 10 MIN   **COOKING:** 6 H   **SERVINGS:** 4

INGREDIENTS

- 4 lbs. whole chicken
- 1 tsp dried oregano
- 1 tsp dried basil leaves
- 1 1/2 tsp dried thyme leaves
- 1 tbsp garlic, chopped
- 1 large onion, sliced
- 1/2 tsp pepper
- 1 tsp salt

DIRECTIONS

1. Place sliced onion into the slow cooker. Mix garlic, thyme, basil, oregano, pepper, and salt in a small bowl.
2. Rub garlic mixture all over chicken and place into the slow cooker. Cover and cook on low within 6 hours. Sliced and serve.

Nutrition: *Calories: 589 Fat: 22.5g Carbs: 3.2g Protein: 87.9g*

259. CARIBBEAN JERK CHICKEN

PREPARATION: 10 MIN   **COOKING:** 6 H   **SERVINGS:** 4

INGREDIENTS

- 4 lbs. whole chicken
- 1/3 cup fresh lime juice
- 1/2 tsp cayenne pepper
- 1 tsp cinnamon
- 1 tbsp allspice
- 2 tsp kosher salt

DIRECTIONS

1. Mix allspice, cinnamon, cayenne pepper, and kosher salt in a small bowl. Rub spice mixture all over the chicken.
2. Place chicken into the slow cooker. Pour lime juice over the chicken. Cover and cook on low within 6 hours. Slice and serve.

Nutrition: *Calories: 437 Fat: 16.9g Carbs: 1.1g Protein: 65.7g*

260. BALSAMIC CHICKEN

PREPARATION: 10 MIN **COOKING:** 4 H **SERVINGS:** 4

INGREDIENTS

- 2 1/2 lb. chicken thighs, skinless and boneless
- 1/4 cup fresh basil leaves, chopped
- 1/2 cup grape tomatoes, quartered
- 1 tsp garlic, chopped
- 1 1/4 cups balsamic vinaigrette dressing

DIRECTIONS

1. Spray slow cooker from inside with cooking spray. Place chicken into the slow cooker. Pour balsamic vinaigrette dressing and garlic over the chicken.
2. Cover and cook on low within 4 hours. Remove chicken from slow cooker and place on a serving dish. Top with basil and grape tomatoes. Serve and enjoy.

Nutrition: *Calories: 375 Fat: 15g Carbs: 1.2g Protein: 54.9g*

261. CAESAR CHICKEN

PREPARATION: 10 MIN **COOKING:** 8 H **SERVINGS:** 4

INGREDIENTS

- 4 chicken breasts, skinless and boneless
- 1/2 tsp dried parsley
- 1/4 cup fresh basil, chopped
- 3/4 cup creamy Caesar dressing
- 1/8 tsp black pepper
- 1/8 tsp salt

DIRECTIONS

1. Place chicken into the slow cooker. Add parsley, Caesar dressing, black pepper, and salt into the slow cooker. Cover and cook on low within 8 hours. Shred the chicken using a fork. Garnish with basil and serve.

Nutrition: *Calories: 366, Fat: 21.9 g, Carbs: 4.6 g, Protein: 32.9 g*

262. CHEESY CHEDDAR CHICKEN

PREPARATION: 10 MIN **COOKING:** 6 H **SERVINGS:** 4

INGREDIENTS

- 1 1/2 lbs. chicken tenderloins, boneless
- 1 cup cheddar cheese, shredded
- 1 oz ranch dressing
- 10 3/4 oz cream of chicken soup

Nutrition: *Calories: 349 Fat: 18.7 g Carbs: 4.4 g Protein: 38.8 g*

DIRECTIONS

1. Place chicken into the slow cooker and sprinkle with ranch dressing. Pour chicken soup over the chicken. Cover and cook on low within 6 hours.
2. Sprinkle with shredded cheddar cheese and cover until cheese is melted. Serve and enjoy.

---

263. LEMON BUTTER CHICKEN

PREPARATION: 10 MIN **COOKING:** 4 H **SERVINGS:** 4

INGREDIENTS

- 4 chicken breasts, skinless and boneless
- 2 lemon juice
- 1 oz Italian salad dressing mix
- 2 tbsp butter

DIRECTIONS

1. Place chicken into the slow cooker. Top with lemon juice and butter. Sprinkle Italian salad dressing over the chicken. Cover and cook on low within 4 hours. Serve and enjoy.

Nutrition: *Calories: 355 Fat: 17 g Carbs: 5 g Protein: 42.7 g*

---

264. TAHINI CHICKEN

PREPARATION: 10 MIN **COOKING:** 8 H **SERVINGS:** 4

INGREDIENTS

- 1 1/2 lbs. chicken thighs, skinless and boneless
- 1 tbsp shallot, grated
- 2 garlic cloves, minced
- 2 tbsp lemon juice
- 2 tsp lemon zest
- 3 tbsp water
- 3 tbsp olive oil
- 1/4 cup tahini
- 1/2 tsp salt

DIRECTIONS

1. Place chicken into the slow cooker. Pour remaining ingredients over the chicken. Cover and cook on low within 8 hours. Shred the chicken using a fork and serve.

Nutrition: *Calories: 255 Fat: 15.6 g Carbs: 2.2 g Protein: 26g*

265. SHREDDED MEXICAN CHICKEN

PREPARATION: 10 MIN   **COOKING:** 6 H   **SERVINGS:** 4

INGREDIENTS

- 4 lbs. chicken breasts, skinless and boneless
- 2 tbsp chili powder
- 1/4 tsp pepper
- 2 tsp coriander
- 2 tsp cumin
- 2 tsp garlic, minced
- 2 tbsp dried onion flakes
- 1 cup of water
- 15 oz can tomato sauce
- 1/4 tsp pepper
- 1/2 tsp salt

DIRECTIONS

1. Place chicken into the bottom of the slow cooker. Mix all remaining ingredients and pour over chicken. Cover and cook on low within 6 hours.
2. Remove chicken from slow cooker and shred the chicken using a fork, then return into the slow cooker and stir well. Serve and enjoy.

Nutrition: *Calories: 457 Fat: 17.4 g Carbs: 5.4 g Protein: 66.8 g*

266. PARMESAN CHICKEN DRUMSTICKS

PREPARATION: 10 MIN   **COOKING:** 4 H   **SERVINGS:** 4

INGREDIENTS

- 5 lbs. chicken drumsticks
- 1 tbsp parsley, chopped
- 1/4 cup parmesan cheese, grated
- 1 tbsp garlic, minced
- 1 tbsp lemon juice
- 1/2 cup butter, melted
- 1 cup chicken broth
- 2 tsp onion powder
- 2 tsp garlic powder
- 2 tbsp olive oil
- 1/2 tsp pepper
- 1 tsp salt

DIRECTIONS

1. Coat chicken drumsticks with olive oil. In a small bowl, mix onion powder, garlic powder, pepper, and salt.
2. Sprinkle onion powder mixture over the chicken drumsticks. Place chicken drumsticks into the slow cooker.
3. Pour chicken broth into the slow cooker—cover and cook on high within 4 hours. Mix remaining ingredients and pour over chicken. Serve and enjoy.

Nutrition: *Calories: 465, Fat: 23.9 g Carbs: 1.1 g Protein: 56.7 g*

267. MEDITERRANEAN CHICKEN

PREPARATION: 10 MIN **COOKING:** 4 H **SERVINGS:** 4

INGREDIENTS

- 4 chicken breasts, skinless and boneless
- 2 tbsp capers
- 1 small onion, chopped
- 1 tbsp garlic, minced
- 2 tbsp fresh lemon juice
- 1 cup roasted red peppers, chopped
- 1 cup olives
- 3 tsp Italian seasoning
- Pepper
- Salt

DIRECTIONS

1. Season chicken with pepper and salt. Cook the chicken in a pan over medium-high heat 2 minutes on each side until browned.
2. Transfer chicken into the slow cooker. Pour remaining ingredients over the chicken. Cover and cook on low within 4 hours. Serve and enjoy.

Nutrition: *Calories: 352 Fat: 15.7 g Carbs: 8 g Protein: 43.4 g*

268. LEMON GARLIC CHICKEN

PREPARATION: 10 MIN **COOKING:** 5 H **SERVINGS:** 4

INGREDIENTS

- 2 lbs. chicken breasts, skinless and boneless
- 3 tbsp fresh lemon juice
- 1/4 cup water
- 2 tbsp butter
- 1 tsp dried oregano
- 1 tbsp fresh parsley, chopped
- 1 tsp chicken bouillon granules
- 2 garlic cloves, minced
- 1/4 tsp black pepper
- 1/2 tsp salt

DIRECTIONS

1. Mix garlic, oregano, pepper, and salt in a small bowl. Rub garlic mixture all over chicken breasts.
2. Dissolve the butter in a large pan over medium heat—brown chicken in hot butter and place in the slow cooker's bottom.
3. Pour remaining ingredients over chicken. Cover and cook on low within 5 hours. Serve and enjoy.

Nutrition: *Calories: 326 Fat: 15.1 g Carbs: 0.8 g Protein: 44 g*

269. SWEET & SMOKY PULLED CHICKEN

PREPARATION: 5 MIN   **COOKING:** 7 H 5 MIN   **SERVINGS:** 4

INGREDIENTS

- 1-pound pasture-raised chicken breasts, skinless
- 13 1/2 fluid ounce tomato passata, unsweetened
- 1 teaspoon garlic powder
- 1 teaspoon of sea salt
- 1 teaspoon ground black pepper
- ½ cup apple cider vinegar
- 3 tablespoon Swerve sweeteners
- 1/4 tsp cayenne pepper
- 1 tablespoon smoked paprika
- 3 tablespoons coconut aminos
- ½ cup avocado oil
- 1 cup sour cream for serving

DIRECTIONS

1. Put the chicken breast in your slow cooker. Whisk together remaining ingredients except for sour cream and pour over chicken.
2. Shut with lid and cook for 6 to 7 hours at low heat setting or 2 to 4 hours at high heat setting or until cooked. When done, transfer chicken to a cutting board and shred with two forks.
3. Transfer sauce in the slow cooker to a saucepan and simmer for 3 minutes or more.
4. Spoon this sauce over chicken, stir until chicken is coated with sauce. Add a little more oil, toss until combined, then top with sour cream and serve straightaway.

Nutrition: *Calories: 234 Fat: 12g Protein: 27.5g Carbs: 4g*

---

270. MEXICAN CHICKEN FAJITA SOUP

PREPARATION: 5 MIN   **COOKING:** 6 H   **SERVINGS:** 4

INGREDIENTS

- 2 pasture-raised chicken breasts, skinless
- 2 tablespoons cashew butter
- 1 medium red bell pepper, diced
- 1/2 small white onion, diced
- 1 teaspoon minced garlic
- 10-ounce tomatoes & chilies
- 1 tablespoon taco seasoning
- 1 cup chicken broth
- 2/3 cup and 1 tablespoon cream cheese
- 1/2 cup heavy whipping cream
- 4 tablespoons sour cream for topping

DIRECTIONS

1. Put a large skillet pan on medium heat, add butter and when it melts, add pepper, onion, garlic, taco seasoning and cook for 3 minutes or until fragrant and onion are slightly tender.
2. Spoon this mixture in a 6-quart slow cooker, add chicken, tomato, chilies, and broth, and shut with lid. Plugin the slow cooker and cook chicken for 4 to 6 hours at a low heat setting or until chicken is tender.
3. When done, stir in cream cheese and heavy cream until creamy, then top with sour cream and serve.

Nutrition: *Calories: 476 Fat: 35.9g Protein: 31.8g Carbs: 10.8g*

271. CREAMY TUSCAN GARLIC CHICKEN

PREPARATION: 15 MIN **COOKING:** 8 H 10 MIN **SERVINGS:** 4

INGREDIENTS

- 4 large pasture-raised chicken breast, each about 6 oz.
- 1/2 cup sun-dried tomatoes, chopped
- 2 cup spinach, chopped
- 3 teaspoons minced garlic
- 1 ½ teaspoon sea salt
- 1 teaspoon ground black pepper
- 1 tablespoon Italian seasoning
- 1 tablespoon avocado oil
- 1 cup heavy cream
- 1/3 cup chicken broth
- 3/4 cup grated parmesan cheese

DIRECTIONS

1. Put oil in your saucepan on medium heat, then put garlic and cook for 1 minute or until fragrant.
2. Whisk in cream and broth, bring the mixture to simmer, reduce heat to a low level, and simmer more for 10 minutes or until sauce thickens enough to coat the spoon's back.
3. In the meantime, place the chicken in a 6-quarts slow cooker. When the sauce is ready, stir in cheese until smooth, and then pour it over the chicken.
4. Cook within 6 to 8 hours at low heat setting or 3 to 4 hours at high heat setting or until cooked. When done, transfer chicken to a serving plate and set aside.
5. Add spinach to the sauce in the slow cooker and cook for 3 to 5 minutes or until spinach leaves wilt. Spoon sauce over chicken, then top with tomatoes and serve.

Nutrition: *Calories: 531 Fat: 35g Protein: 45g Carbs: 9g*

---

272. CHICKEN STEW

PREPARATION: 5 MIN **COOKING:** 2 H 10 MIN **SERVINGS:** 4

INGREDIENTS

- 28 oz. skinless pasture-raised chicken thighs, diced into 1-inch pieces
- ½ cup chopped white onion
- 1 cup fresh spinach
- 2 sticks of celery, diced
- 1 ½ teaspoon minced garlic
- 1 teaspoon salt
- ½ teaspoon ground black pepper
- ½ teaspoon dried rosemary
- ¼ teaspoon dried thyme
- ½ teaspoon dried oregano
- 2 cups chicken stock
- ½ cup heavy cream

DIRECTIONS

1. Place all the ingredients except for spinach and cream in a 6-quart slow cooker and shut with a lid. Cook for 4 hours at a low heat setting or 2 hours at a high heat setting or until cooked.
2. Then stir in spinach and cream and cook for 5 to 10 minutes at a high heat setting or until spinach leaves wilt. Serve straight away.

Nutrition: *Calories: 356 Fat: 24g Protein: 31g Carbs: 6g*

273. CURRIED CHICKEN TACOS

PREPARATION: 5 MIN   **COOKING:** 8 H   **SERVINGS:** 4

INGREDIENTS

For Curried Chicken:
- 2 pounds skinless pasture-raised chicken breasts
- 15-ounce diced tomatoes
- 3 chilis de Arbol, chopped
- 1/2 of medium white onion, chopped
- 2 teaspoon grated ginger
- 2 teaspoons minced garlic
- 1 teaspoon salt
- 1 1/2 teaspoons ground turmeric
- 2 teaspoons ground cumin
- 1 tablespoon ground coriander
- 1/4 teaspoon cinnamon
- 1/4 teaspoon ground cardamom
- 2-star anise
- 1/2 cup chicken stock

For Avocado Cream:
- 1 large avocado, pitted
- 1/3 cup chopped cilantro
- 2 teaspoons onion powder
- 1/2 teaspoon salt
- 1 1/2 teaspoons red chili powder
- 5 tablespoons yogurt, high-fat
- 1 1/2 tablespoons lemon juice

For Taco:
- 1/2 of small red cabbage, sliced
- 8 large leaves of collard greens
- 1 large red pepper, sliced
- 2 cups sour cream

Nutrition: *Calories: 371.25 Fat: 19g Protein: 41g Carbs: 9g*

DIRECTIONS

1. Place all the ingredients, except for star anise, and stock in a 6-quart slow cooker and toss until just mixed. Then pour in chicken stock, add star anise, and shut with lid.
2. Cook within 7 to 8 hours at low heat setting or 4 to5 hours at high heat setting.
3. For the avocado cream, place the ingredients for avocado cream in a food processor and pulse for 1 to 2 minutes or until smooth; set aside until required.
4. Trim the tough stem from collard greens, rinse well, pat dry, and set aside until required. When chicken is cooked, shred with two forks and toss until coated with sauce.
5. Arrange collard greens in a clean working space, then top with chicken, cabbage, pepper, avocado cream, and sour cream in the end. Serve straight away.

274. RANCH CHICKEN

PREPARATION: 5 MIN   **COOKING:** 7 H   **SERVINGS:** 4

INGREDIENTS

- 2 pounds skinless pasture-raised chicken breast
- 3 tablespoons dried ranch dressing
- 3 tablespoons butter, chopped
- 4-ounce cream cheese, chopped

DIRECTIONS

1. Place chicken in a 6-quart slow cooker, scatter with butter and cream cheese, and sprinkle with ranch dressing.
2. Shut with lid, then plug in the slow cooker and cook for 4 hours at high heat setting or 5 to 7 hours at low heat setting or until cooked. Shred chicken with two forks and stirs until evenly coated and serve straightaway.

Nutrition: *Calories: 251.3 Fat: 12.9g Protein: 33g Carbs: 0.8g*

275. CHICKEN AND SAUSAGE

PREPARATION: 5 MIN **COOKING:** 6 H **SERVINGS:** 4

INGREDIENTS

- 1 1/2-pound skinless pasture-raised chicken breasts
- 13-ounce smoked sausage
- 1 small white onion, diced
- 1 ½ teaspoon minced garlic
- 1/2 teaspoon salt
- 2 tablespoons mustard paste, sugar-free
- 1/2 cup white wine
- 8-ounce cream cheese softened
- 1 cup chicken stock
- Scallions for garnish

DIRECTIONS

1. Place chicken and sausage in a 6-quart slow cooker and top with onion. Whisk together garlic, salt, mustard, white wine, cream cheese, and chicken stock until smooth and pour this mixture all over the chicken.
2. Plugin the slow cooker, and cook for 5 to 6 hours or 4 hours at a high heat setting. Garnish with scallion and serve straight away.

Nutrition: *Calories: 561 Fat: 37.4g Protein: 50.5g Carbs: 5.6g*

276. CRACK CHICKEN

PREPARATION: 5 MIN **COOKING:** 8 H **SERVINGS:** 4

INGREDIENTS

- 2 pounds pasture-raised chicken breasts
- 8 slices of bacon, cooked and crumbled
- 2 tablespoons Ranch seasoning
- 1/2 cup chicken broth
- 8-ounce block of Cream cheese, cubed
- 1/2 cup shredded cheddar cheese

DIRECTIONS

1. Pour broth in a 6-quart slow cooker, stir in ranch dressing and then add chicken. Plugin the slow cooker, shut with lid, and cook for 4 hours at a high heat setting or 8 hours at low heat or until cooked.
2. When done, shred chicken with two forks, then add bacon, cream cheese, and cheddar cheese and stir until well combined.
3. Continue cooking for 5 to 10 minutes at a high heat setting or until cheese melts. Serve straight away.

Nutrition: *Calories: 331 Fat: 23g Protein: 30g Carbs: 1g*

277. CHEESY ADOBO CHICKEN

PREPARATION: 5 MIN **COOKING:** 8 H 5 MIN **SERVINGS:** 4

INGREDIENTS

- 1-pound pasture-raised chicken breasts, skin on
- 2 tablespoons adobo sauce
- 1/2 cup salsa, sugar-free

For Cheese Sauce:
- 1 tablespoon arrowroot powder
- 1 tablespoon unsalted butter
- 1/2 cup coconut milk, unsweetened and full-fat
- 6 tablespoons grated cheddar cheese
- 6 tablespoons grated Monterey jack cheese

DIRECTIONS

1. Place adobo sauce and salsa in a 6-quart slow cooker, whisk together until combined, and then add chicken.
2. Plugin the slow cooker, shut with lid and cook for 6 to 8 hours at low heat setting or 3 to 4 hours at high heat setting or until cooked. Shred chicken with two forks and tosses until mixed with the sauce.
3. Prepare cheese sauce and for this, place a medium saucepan over medium-high heat, add butter and when it melts, whisk in arrowroot powder and simmer for 1 minute.
4. Then slowly whisk in milk until smooth and cook for 4 minutes or until sauce thickens slightly. Remove saucepan from heat, add cheese and stir well until cheese melts and the smooth sauce comes together. Pour cheese over chicken and serve.

Nutrition: *Calories: 313 Fat: 21g Protein: 26g Carbs: 5g*

278. GREEN BEANS & CHICKEN THIGHS

PREPARATION: 5 MIN **COOKING:** 8 H **SERVINGS:** 4

INGREDIENTS

- 4 skin-on pasture-raised chicken thighs
- 1-pound green beans, trimmed
- 2 large tomatoes, diced
- 1 medium white onion, peeled and diced
- 1 teaspoon minced garlic
- 2 teaspoons salt and more for seasoning chicken
- 1 teaspoon ground black pepper and more for seasoning chicken
- 1/4 cup fresh chopped dill
- 6 tablespoons avocado oil, divided
- 1 lemon, juiced
- 1 cup chicken broth
- 1 cup sour cream

DIRECTIONS

1. Place green beans in a 6-quarts slow cooker, add remaining ingredients except for 3 tablespoons oil, chicken, and sour cream and stir until mixed.
2. Plugin slow cooker, top green beans with chicken, drizzle with oil, season with salt and black pepper, and shut with lid.
3. Cook for 8 hours at a low heat setting or 4 hours at a high heat setting or until chicken is cooked through. Serve with sour cream.

Nutrition: *Calories: 622 Fat: 46.3g Protein: 35.7g Carbs: 15.5g*

279. PIZZA CHICKEN

PREPARATION: 5 MIN **COOKING:** 3 H 30 MIN **SERVINGS:** 4

INGREDIENTS

- 4 skinless pasture-raised chicken breasts
- 20 slices of pepperoni
- 1 ½ teaspoon salt
- 1 teaspoon ground black pepper
- 2 cups marinara sauce, sugar-free
- 1 cup grated parmesan cheese

DIRECTIONS

1. Spread marinara sauce into a 6-quart slow cooker, then add chicken and season with salt and black pepper. Plugin the slow cooker, top chicken with pepperoni slices, and shut with lid.
2. Cook chicken for 3 hours at a low heat setting, then add cheese and continue cooking for 15 to 30 minutes. Serve straight away.

Nutrition: *Calories: 418 Fat: 20g Protein: 49g Carbs: 10.5g*

280. CHICKEN WITH BACON GRAVY

PREPARATION: 5 MIN **COOKING:** 3 H 30 MIN **SERVINGS:** 4

INGREDIENTS

- 1 ½ pound skinless pasture-raised chicken breasts
- 6 slices of bacon, cooked and crumbled
- 1 teaspoon minced garlic
- ¼ teaspoon ground black pepper
- 1 teaspoon dried thyme
- 3 ½ tablespoons dried chicken gravy mix
- 4 tablespoons oil
- 1¼ cup of water
- 1 cup heavy cream

DIRECTIONS

1. Place chicken in a 4-quart slow cooker, add bacon and sprinkle with garlic, black pepper, and garlic, and drizzle with oil.
2. Whisk together water and chicken gravy mix until smooth, and then pour this mixture over the chicken.
3. Plugin the slow cooker, shut with lid, and cook for 3 ½ hours at a high heat setting or until chicken is cooked.
4. When done, add cream, then shred chicken with 2 forks and stir until well combined. Serve straight away.

Nutrition: *Calories: 551 Fat: 38g Protein: 51g Carbs: 1.3g*

281. CHICKEN LO MEIN

PREPARATION: 15 MIN **COOKING:** 4 H 10 MIN **SERVINGS:** 4

INGREDIENTS

- 1 1/2 pounds boneless pasture-raised chicken thighs, sliced
- 12 oz. kelp noodles
- 1 bunch bok choy, sliced
- 1 teaspoon minced garlic
- 1 teaspoon grated ginger
- 1 ½ teaspoon salt
- ¾ teaspoon ground black pepper
- For Chicken Marinade:
- 1/2 teaspoon minced garlic
- 1 tablespoon coconut aminos
- 1/2 teaspoon avocado oil

For Sauce:
- 1/2 teaspoon xanthan gum
- 1 tablespoon swerve sweetener
- 1 teaspoon red pepper chili flakes
- 1/4 cup coconut aminos
- 2 teaspoon sesame oil
- 1 tablespoon apple cider vinegar
- 3/4 cup chicken broth

Nutrition: *Calories: 198 Fat: 10.1g Protein: 24.5g Carbs: 3.1g*

DIRECTIONS

1. Place all the ingredients for the marinade in a large bowl, whisk until combined, then add chicken, toss until well coated, and let marinate in the refrigerator for 30 minutes.
2. Then grease a 6-quart slow cooker with oil, add marinated chicken, and shut with lid. Cook within 2 hours at a low heat setting or for 1 hour at high heat.
3. Move the cooked chicken to a serving plate and add cabbage, ginger, garlic to the slow cooker, and top with chicken.
4. Whisk the sauce ingredients in a bowl, pour all over the chicken, and shut with lid—Cook for 1 hour to 2 hours on low or 30 minutes to 1 hour on high.
5. In the meantime, rinse kelp noodles and soak them in water. When cooking time is up, add kelp noodles to the slow cooker and stir with tongs until evenly coated with sauce.
6. Stir in xanthan gum and cook for 10 to 15 minutes on high. Serve straight away.

282. CHICKEN BACON CHOWDER

PREPARATION: 5 MIN **COOKING:** 9 H 5 MIN **SERVINGS:** 4

INGREDIENTS

- 1-pound pasture-raised chicken breast, skinless
- 1-pound bacon
- 6-ounce Cremini mushrooms
- 2 celery, diced
- 1 medium white onion, peeled and diced
- 2 teaspoons minced garlic
- 1 teaspoon garlic powder
- 1 teaspoon salt
- 1 teaspoon ground black pepper
- 1 teaspoon dried thyme
- 2 tablespoons avocado oil
- 2 tablespoons unsalted butter
- 2 cups chicken stock
- 8-ounce cream cheese, cubed
- 1 cup heavy cream

Nutrition: *Calories: 879.3 Fat: 66.4g Protein: 59.3g Carbs: 11g*

DIRECTIONS

1. Plug in a 6-quart slow cooker and let preheat at a low heat setting. Then add mushrooms, celery, onion, garlic, salt, black pepper, butter, and 1 cup stock and stir until mixed.
2. Shut with lid and cook for 1 hour at a low heat setting. Place a large skillet pan over medium-high heat, add oil and when hot, add oil and when hot, put the chicken and cook within 5 minutes or until seared on all sides.
3. Transfer seared chicken to a plate, deglaze the pan with remaining stock and stir well to remove browned bits stuck on the pan's bottom, and then add to slow cooker when vegetables are cooked.
4. Add remaining ingredients to cooked vegetables, stir well until cream cheese is mixed. Cut chicken into cubes, add to slow cooker along with bacon, and stir until mixed.
5. Shut with lid and cook for 6 to 8 hours at a low heat setting or until cooked. Serve.

283. SESAME GINGER CHICKEN

PREPARATION: 5 MIN **COOKING:** 6 H **SERVINGS:** 4

INGREDIENTS

- 1 ½ pound skinless pasture-raised chicken breasts
- 2 tablespoons chopped red bell pepper
- ¼ cup minced onion
- 1 teaspoon minced garlic
- ½ tablespoon grated fresh ginger
- ½ teaspoon crushed red pepper flakes
- 1 tablespoon swerve sweetener
- 2 tablespoons coconut aminos
- 3 tablespoons sesame seed oil
- ½ cup tomato puree
- 1/3 cup peach jam, sugar-free
- 1/3 cup chicken broth
- 2 teaspoons sesame seeds

DIRECTIONS

1. Place all the fixings in a 6-quart slow cooker, except for sesame seeds, chicken, and pepper, and stir until mixed.
2. Add chicken, turn to coat chicken with sauce and then top with red bell pepper. Plugin the slow cooker, shut with lid, and cook for 6 hours at low heat setting or 4 hours at high heat setting. Garnish with sesame seeds and serve.

Nutrition: *Calories: 180 Fat: 12.8g Protein: 37.8g Carbs: 2g*

284. COCO LOCO CHICKEN CURRY

PREPARATION: 15 MIN **COOKING:** 5 H **SERVINGS:** 4

INGREDIENTS

- 6 boneless chicken thighs
- 13½ oz. coconut milk
- 1 tbsp. curry powder
- 2 tbsps. coconut oil
- 1 tbsp. minced garlic
- 1 chopped jalapeno
- sea salt
- 2 tsp. almond flour
- 1 cup lime juice
- 20 fresh basil leaves

DIRECTIONS

1. Put the chicken in the slow cooker and pour the milk all over it. Cook the chicken on high for 4 hours.
2. Meanwhile, in a saucepan over medium-high heat, add in the coconut oil. Once it melts, toss in the garlic and jalapeno peppers. Sauté it for 2-3 minutes.
3. Add the curry powder, salt, and almond flour, then simmer for 2 minutes. Pour the curry mixture over the chicken.
4. Let it simmer for 45-60 minutes. Once cooked, add the basil and lime juice. You may opt to shred the chicken before serving.

Nutrition: *Calories: 351 Fat: 36.5g Carbs: 6.0g Protein: 17.1g*

285. RANCH CHICKEN WITH BROCCOLI

PREPARATION: 10 MIN **COOKING:** 5 H **SERVINGS:** 4

INGREDIENTS

Homemade ranch seasoning:
- ½ tsp garlic powder
- 1½ tsp Dill, dry
- 1 tbsp dried parsley
- 2 tsp dried chives
- ½ tsp. paprika
- sea salt
- black pepper

Chicken:
- 3 boneless chicken breasts
- 12 slices bacon
- 1 tbsp homemade seasoning
- 1½ tsp steak seasoning
- 6 cups broccoli florets
- ½ cup mayonnaise
- 3 tbsps. red wine vinegar
- ¼ tsp. sea salt
- Hot sauce

Nutrition: *Calories: 239 Fat: 21.3g Carbs: 7.8g Protein: 18.7g*

DIRECTIONS

1. Mix the ranch seasoning ingredients in a bowl. Transfer it to a small jar with a tight cap. Put the chicken in your slow cooker. Season it with ranch and steak seasonings. Cook it on low for 4 hours.
2. Toss the broccoli into the pot. Let it cook for another 30-60 minutes. Transfer chicken to a bowl once cooked, and shred it using 2 forks. Mix in the broccoli, mayo, vinegar, and hot sauce.

---

286. GARLIC PARMESAN CHICKEN WINGS

PREPARATION: 10 MIN **COOKING:** 2 H 50 MIN **SERVINGS:** 4

INGREDIENTS

- 8 tbsps. butter
- 2 minced garlic cloves
- 1 tbsp. Italian seasoning, dried
- ¼ cup parmesan cheese, grated
- Sea salt
- Black pepper
- 1 lb. chicken wings

DIRECTIONS

1. Set slow cooker to high. Line an aluminum foil on the baking sheet. Put the butter, garlic, Italian seasoning, and ¼ cup of parmesan cheese in the slow cooker, and season with pink salt and pepper. Dissolve the butter, and stir the ingredients until well mixed.
2. Add the chicken wings and stir until coated with the butter mixture. Cook for 2 hours and 45 minutes while the slow cooker is covered.
3. Preheat the broiler. Move the wings on your prepared baking sheet, sprinkle the remaining ½ cup of Parmesan cheese over the wings, and cook under the broiler until crispy, about 5 minutes. Serve hot.

Nutrition: *Calories: 738 Fat: 66g Carbs: 4g Protein: 39g*

287. LUAU CHICKEN

PREPARATION: 15 MIN   **COOKING:** 6 H   **SERVINGS:** 4

INGREDIENTS

- 6 bacon strips
- 6 boneless chicken thighs
- Salt
- Pepper
- ½ cup red onion
- 1 cup sliced pineapple

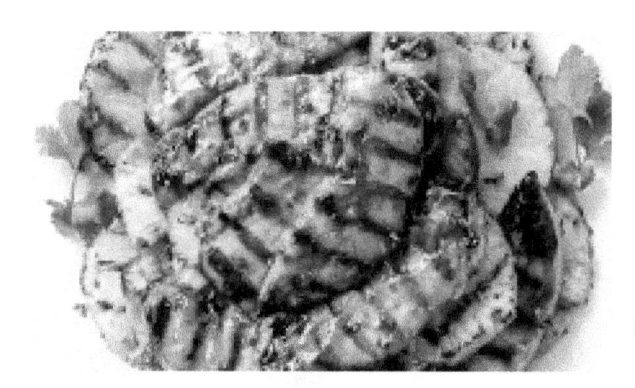

DIRECTIONS

1. Place half of the bacon strips in a skillet over medium flame and cook until crispy. Drain and set aside on a paper towel.
2. Season the chicken with salt and pepper. Place inside the slow cooker and top with half of the uncooked bacon. Top with onions and pineapples.
3. Cook within 6 hours or until the chicken is very tender. Top with crumbled crispy bacon before serving.

Nutrition: *Calories: 375 Carbs: 8g Protein: 39g Fat: 17g*

288. SOUTHWEST CHICKEN

PREPARATION: 10 MIN   **COOKING:** 5 H   **SERVINGS:** 4

INGREDIENTS

- 1 chopped zucchini
- 1 jar sugar-free salsa
- 4 boneless chicken breasts
- 1 cubed red bell pepper
- Salt
- Pepper

DIRECTIONS

1. Place half of the zucchini at the bottom of the slow cooker. Pour over half of the salsa. Then arrange the chicken breasts and bell peppers on top.
2. Continue to layer until all ingredients are inside the slow cooker—season with salt and pepper to taste. Cook within 5 hours on low or until chicken is tender.
3. Give a good stir to mix everything. Serve with cilantro, sour cream, or cheese.

Nutrition: *Calories: 234 Carbs: 13g Protein: 24g Fat: 10g*

289. CAROLINA-STYLE VINEGAR CHICKEN

PREPARATION: 10 MIN   **COOKING:** 6 H   **SERVINGS:** 4

INGREDIENTS

- 1 cup white vinegar
- ¼ cup yacon syrup
- 1 tbsp. low sodium chicken stock
- 1½ lb. boneless chicken breast
- Salt
- pepper

DIRECTIONS

1. Use a small bowl, mix the white vinegar, yacon syrup, and chicken stock. Place the chicken breasts skin-side up inside the slow cooker. Pour over the mixture.
2. Season with salt and pepper to taste. Cook for 6 hours on low or until the chicken is tender. Shred the chicken meat apart using a fork. Serve on top of lettuce leaves.

Nutrition: *Calories: 188 Carbs: 3g Protein: 26g Fat: 12g*

290. CHICKEN CACCIATORE WITH ZOODLES

PREPARATION: 15 MIN   **COOKING:** 6-7 H   **SERVINGS:** 4

INGREDIENTS

- 2 lbs. minced chicken
- 1 cup chicken stock
- 1 cup chopped tomatoes
- 2 tbsps. olive oil
- ½ cup sliced onions
- 3 minced garlic cloves
- 1 tsp. oregano, dry
- 1 tsp. thyme, dry
- 1 tsp. parsley, dry
- salt
- Parmesan cheese

For zoodles:
- 1 washed and trimmed zucchini
- 2 tsp coconut oil

DIRECTIONS

1. Using a spiralizer, create zucchini noodles (zoodles). Heat coconut oil in a non-stick pan. Place the zoodles into the pan. Cook briefly for 3–5 minutes, depending on how tender you prefer the zoodles.
2. Heat the oil in the slow cooker on high. Put the onions and cook until they are golden brown. Add the chicken mince and garlic and cook for another 3 minutes.
3. Mix the remaining fixings in a large mixing bowl and add them to the chicken. Cook on low for about 6–7 hours. Serve hot over zoodles, with some grated Parmesan cheese if desired.

Nutrition: *Calories: 347 Fat: 17g Carbs: 6g Protein: 28g*

291. BOK CHOY CHICKEN

PREPARATION: 15 MIN **COOKING:** 6 H 30 MIN **SERVINGS:** 4

INGREDIENTS

- 6 lbs. cubed boneless chicken
- 8 oz. sliced bok choy
- 2 chopped green onions
- 2 tbsps. olive oil
- 1 tbsp. chopped ginger
- 2 minced garlic cloves
- 1 tbsp. soy sauce
- black pepper
- 2 tsp. paprika
- salt
- ½ cup of water

DIRECTIONS

1. Combine the chicken, onion, oil, ginger, garlic, soy sauce, black pepper, paprika, salt, and water in a slow cooker. Cook on high for 6 hours. Add the bok choy and cook for extra 30 minutes. Serve hot.

Nutrition: *Calories: 278 Fat: 18g Carbs: 5g Protein: 30g*

292. CHICKEN TIKKA MASALA

PREPARATION: 15 MIN **COOKING:** 6 H **SERVINGS:** 4

INGREDIENTS

- 3 lbs. cubed chicken
- 1 cup diced tomatoes
- 2 tbsp olive oil
- 1 chopped onion
- 3 minced garlic cloves
- 1 tsp ground ginger
- 3 tbsp tomato paste
- 2 tsp smoked paprika
- 1 tsp cumin powder
- ¼ cup garam masala
- 1 cup heavy cream
- 1 cup of coconut milk
- 1 tsp salt
- Fresh coriander

DIRECTIONS

1. Add the oil, chicken, and all the dry spices to the slow cooker. Add the diced tomatoes, onion, ginger, garlic, tomato paste, salt, and coconut milk. Mix thoroughly.
2. Cook for 6 hours on low. Add in the heavy cream and mix. Garnish with some fresh coriander and cream.

Nutrition: *Calories: 219 Fat: 20g Carbs: 5g Protein: 41g*

293. CHILI LIME CHICKEN WINGS

PREPARATION: 15 MIN **COOKING:** 6 H 15 MIN **SERVINGS:** 4

INGREDIENTS

- 2 lbs. chicken wings
- ¼ cup fresh lime juice
- 4 minced garlic cloves
- 1 tbsp. chopped ginger
- 1 tbsp. chili sauce
- ¼ cup coconut aminos
- 1 tbsp. fish sauce
- ¼ cup coconut oil
- 1 tsp. oregano, dry
- black pepper
- salt
- Sliced lemon

DIRECTIONS

1. Preheat the slow cooker on high. Mix all the fixings until well combined in a large bowl. Transfer into the slow cooker. Cook for 6 hours on high.
2. Preheat the oven to 350°F. Transfer the wings onto a parchment-lined baking tray. Bake for 15 minutes until nicely golden brown. Serve hot with some lemon slices.

Nutrition: *Calories: 176 Fat: 9g Carbs: 4g Protein: 30g*

294. GARLIC CHICKEN & MUSHROOM CHOWDER

PREPARATION: 15 MIN **COOKING:** 9 H **SERVINGS:** 4

INGREDIENTS

- 6 oz. sliced Cremini mushrooms
- 1 lb. chicken breasts
- 4 minced garlic cloves
- 1 chopped shallot
- 1 sliced leek
- 2 diced celery ribs
- 1 sliced sweet onion
- 4 tbsps. Butter
- 2 cups chicken stock
- 8 oz. cream cheese
- 1 cup heavy cream
- 1 lb. crumbled bacon
- sea salt
- black pepper
- 1 tsp. garlic powder
- 1 tsp. thyme, dry

DIRECTIONS

1. Combine the leek, garlic, shallots, celery, onions, mushrooms, 1 cup chicken stock, salt, pepper, and 2 tablespoon butter in a slow cooker and cook covered for 1 hour on low.
2. Melt the remaining butter in a skillet and sear the chicken breasts in it. Chop into cubes. Remove the chicken and deglaze the skillet using the chicken stock.
3. Add the chicken along with the chicken stock to the slow cooker. Stir in the rest of the ingredients. Cook covered for 6-8 hours on low.

Nutrition: *Calories: 355 Fat: 28g Carbs: 6.4g Protein: 21 g*

295. SAUCY DUCK

PREPARATION: 10 MIN **COOKING:** 6 H **SERVINGS:** 4

INGREDIENTS

- 1 duck, cut into small chunks
- 4 garlic cloves, minced
- 4 tablespoons of swerves
- 2 green onions, roughly diced
- 4 tablespoon of soy sauce
- 4 tablespoon of sherry wine
- 1/4 cup of water
- 1-inch ginger root, sliced
- A pinch salt
- black pepper to taste

Nutrition: *Calories: 338 Fat: 3.8g Carbs: 8.3g Protein: 15.4g*

DIRECTIONS

1. Put all the fixings into the slow cooker and mix them well. Cover it and cook for 6 hours on low. Garnish as desired. Serve warm.

---

296. CHICKEN ROUX GUMBO

PREPARATION: 10 MIN **COOKING:** 6 H **SERVINGS:** 4

INGREDIENTS

- 1 lb. chicken thighs, cut into halves
- 1 tablespoon of vegetable oil
- 1 lb. smoky sausage, sliced, crispy, and crumbled.

Salt and black pepper- to taste
Aromatics:
- 1 bell pepper, diced
- 2 quarts' chicken stock
- 15 oz. canned tomatoes, diced
- 1 celery stalk, diced
- salt to taste
- 4 garlic cloves, minced
- 1/2 lbs. okra, sliced
- 1 yellow onion, diced
- a dash tabasco sauce

For the roux:
- 1/2 cup of almond flour
- 1/4 cup of vegetable oil
- 1 teaspoon of Cajun spice

Nutrition: *Calories: 604 Fat: 30.6g Carbs: 1.4g Protein: 54.6g*

DIRECTIONS

1. Start by throwing all the ingredients except okra and roux ingredients into the slow cooker. Cover it and cook for 5 hours on low.
2. Stir in okra and cook for another 1 hour on low heat. Mix all the roux ingredients and add them to the slow cooker. Stir cook on high until the sauce thickens. Serve warm.

297. CIDER-BRAISED CHICKEN

PREPARATION: 10 MIN **COOKING:** 5 H **SERVINGS:** 2

INGREDIENTS

- 4 chicken drumsticks
- 2 tablespoon of olive oil
- ½ cup of apple cider vinegar
- 1 tablespoon of balsamic vinegar
- 1 chili pepper, diced
- 1 yellow onion, minced
- Salt and black pepper- to taste

DIRECTIONS

1. Start by throwing all the ingredients into a bowl and mix them well. Marinate this chicken for 2 hours in the refrigerator.
2. Spread the chicken along with its marinade in the slow cooker. Cover it and cook for 5 hours on low. Serve warm.

Nutrition: *Calories: 311 Fat: 25.5g Carbs: 1.4g Protein: 18.4g*

---

298. CHUNKY CHICKEN SALSA

PREPARATION: 10 MIN **COOKING:** 6 H **SERVINGS:** 2

INGREDIENTS

- 1 lb. chicken breast, skinless and boneless
- 1 cup of chunky salsa
- 3/4 teaspoon of cumin
- A pinch oregano
- Salt and black pepper- to taste

DIRECTIONS

1. Put all the fixings into the slow cooker and mix them well. Cover it and cook for 6 hours on low. Serve warm.

Nutrition: *Calories: 541 Fat: 34g Carbs: 3.4g Protein: 20.3g*

299. DIJON CHICKEN

PREPARATION: 10 MIN **COOKING:** 6 H **SERVINGS:** 4

INGREDIENTS

- 2 lbs. chicken thighs, skinless and boneless
- 3/4 cup of chicken stock
- 1/4 cup of lemon juice
- 2 tablespoon of extra virgin olive oil
- 3 tablespoon of Dijon mustard
- 2 tablespoons of Italian seasoning
- Salt and black pepper- to taste

DIRECTIONS

1. Put all the fixings into the slow cooker and mix them well. Cover it and cook for 6 hours on low. Serve warm.

Nutrition: *Calories: 398 Fat: 13.8g Carbs: 3.6g Protein: 51.8g*

300. CHICKEN DIPPED IN TOMATILLO SAUCE

PREPARATION: 10 MIN **COOKING:** 6 H **SERVINGS:** 4

INGREDIENTS

- 1 lb. chicken thighs, skinless and boneless
- 2 tablespoon of extra virgin olive oil
- 1 yellow onion, sliced
- 1 garlic clove, crushed
- 4 oz. canned green chilies, diced
- 1 handful cilantro, diced
- 15 oz. cauliflower rice, already cooked
- 5 oz. tomatoes, diced
- 15 oz. cheddar cheese, grated
- 4 oz. black olives, pitted and diced
- Salt and black pepper- to taste
- 15 oz. canned tomatillos, diced

DIRECTIONS

1. 1. Put all the fixings into the slow cooker and mix them well. Cover it and cook for 5 6 hours on low. Shred the slow-cooked chicken and return to the slow cooker. Mix well and garnish as desired. Serve warm.

Nutrition: *Calories: 427 Fat: 31.1g Carbs: 9g Protein: 23.5g*

CHAPTER 7.
MEAT

301. MEDITERRANEAN BEEF BRISKET

PREPARATION: 20 MIN   **COOKING:** 5 H   **SERVINGS:** 4

INGREDIENTS

- 3 lb. beef brisket, fat trimmed
- 3 teaspoons dried Italian seasoning
- 2 fennel bulbs, cored and sliced into wedges
- 14 oz. canned diced tomatoes with herbs
- 1 cup reduced-sodium beef stock
- ½ cup olives pitted
- 1 teaspoon lemon zest
- Salt and pepper to taste
- ¼ cup cold water mixed with 2 tablespoons all-purpose flour

DIRECTIONS

1. Sprinkle all sides of the beef brisket with 2 teaspoons Italian seasoning. Add to your slow cooker. Put the fennel on top of the beef.
2. In a bowl, mix the remaining Italian seasoning with the rest of the ingredients except the flour mixture. Pour over the beef and fennel. Cover the pot—cook on high for 5 hours.
3. Take the beef out of the pot and slice. Put it with the vegetables on a serving platter. Transfer the cooking liquid to a pan but discard the fat.
4. Stir in the flour mixture. Cook until the sauce has thickened. Pour the sauce over the beef and vegetables. Serve.

Nutrition: *Calories: 254 Fat: 8g Carbs: 10g Protein: 35g*

302. SPANISH BEEF

PREPARATION: 10 MIN   **COOKING:** 4 H 10 MIN   **SERVINGS:** 4

INGREDIENTS

- 1 tablespoon olive oil
- 1 lb. beef stew meat
- salt and pepper to taste
- ½ cup onion, chopped
- 2 cloves garlic, crushed and minced
- 12 oz. sofrito
- ½ cup green olives, sliced in half
- 14 oz. canned diced tomatoes
- 2 cups potatoes, chopped

DIRECTIONS

1. Pour the oil into your pan over medium heat. Brown the beef in the pan. Season the beef with salt and pepper. Put the beef in your slow cooker.
2. Cook the onion and garlic in the beef drippings in the pan. Transfer to the slow cooker after 5 minutes. Stir in the rest of the ingredients. Cover the pot and set it to low—Cook for 4 hours.

Nutrition: *Calories: 560 Fat: 11.6g Carbs: 13.6g Protein: 19.6g*

303. BEEF WITH ARTICHOKES & OLIVES

PREPARATION: 10 MIN   **COOKING:** 7 H 10   **SERVINGS:** 4

INGREDIENTS

- 1 tablespoon olive oil
- 2 lb. beef stew meat
- 1 onion, diced
- 4 cloves garlic, chopped
- ½ cup Kalamata olives, chopped
- 14 oz artichoke hearts, drained and sliced in half.
- 14 oz canned diced tomatoes
- 15 oz canned tomato sauce
- 32 oz beef broth
- 1 bay leaf
- 1 teaspoon dried parsley
- 1 teaspoon dried oregano
- ½ teaspoon ground cumin
- 1 teaspoon dried basil

Nutrition: Calories: 416 Fat: 26.2g Carbs: 14.1g Protein: 29.9g

DIRECTIONS

1. Put the oil into a pan on medium heat. Cook the beef for 3 to 5 minutes per side. Transfer to your slow cooker. Stir in the rest of the ingredients. Cook on low for 7 hours. Discard the bay leaf before serving.

---

304. MEATBALLS & GREEN BEANS

PREPARATION: 20 MIN   **COOKING:** 8 H   **SERVINGS:** 4

INGREDIENTS

Green Beans:
- 1 lb. frozen green beans
- 1 onion, diced
- 2 cloves garlic, crushed and minced
- 15 oz. canned tomato sauce
- 30 oz. canned diced tomatoes
- ¼ teaspoon cayenne pepper
- 1 teaspoon cinnamon
- 1 teaspoon cumin
- Salt and pepper to taste

Meatballs:
- 1 lb. lean ground beef
- 1 tablespoon olive oil
- Salt and pepper to taste
- ¼ teaspoon cayenne pepper
- ½ teaspoon cinnamon
- ½ teaspoon allspice
- ½ teaspoon cumin
- ¼ cup plain breadcrumbs
- ¼ cup parsley, minced

DIRECTIONS

1. Mix all the green beans ingredients in your slow cooker. Mix all the fixings for the meatballs in a bowl.
2. Form meatballs from the ground beef mixture. Add the meatballs to the slow cooker. Coat with the sauce. Cook on low for 8 hours.

Nutrition: Calories: 103 Fat: 3.2g Carbs: 8.3g Protein: 11g

305. BEEF IN BALSAMIC VINEGAR

PREPARATION: 5 MIN   **COOKING:** 8 H   **SERVINGS:** 4

INGREDIENTS

- 1 tablespoon olive oil
- 8 oz. mushrooms, sliced
- 1 onion, diced
- 2 lb. beef chuck steak, cut into cubes
- 1 cup beef stock
- 1 cup black olives, sliced
- 1 tablespoon capers
- ½ cup tomato sauce
- 14 oz. diced tomatoes
- ¼ cup balsamic vinegar
- 2 tablespoons fresh parsley, chopped
- 2 tablespoons fresh rosemary, chopped
- Salt and pepper to taste

DIRECTIONS

1. Pour the oil into your pan over medium heat. Cook the mushrooms for 5 minutes. Add the onions and cook for 5 more minutes. Transfer to the cooker.
2. Brown the beef in the pan for 12 to 15 minutes, turning once or twice. Put the beef in the slow cooker.
3. Pour the beef stock into the pan to deglaze. Scrape the brown bits and add them to the slow cooker. Stir in the rest of the ingredients. Cook on low for 8 hours.

Nutrition: *Calories: 368 Fat: 14.7g Carbs: 9g Protein: 48.9g*

306. MEDITERRANEAN PORK TENDERLOIN

PREPARATION: 10 MIN   **COOKING:** 2 H   **SERVINGS:** 4

INGREDIENTS

- 4 cloves garlic, crushed and minced
- 1 cup chicken broth
- 1 tablespoon garam masala
- Salt and pepper to taste
- 16 oz. pork tenderloin, trimmed
- 1 cup couscous
- ½ cup raisins
- ½ cup almonds, sliced and toasted
- 2 tablespoons red wine vinegar
- ½ cup fresh parsley, minced
- ½ cup olive oil

DIRECTIONS

1. Add the garlic and broth to the slow cooker. In a bowl, mix the garam masala, salt, and pepper. Rub this mixture on both sides of the pork.
2. Add the pork to the slow cooker. Cook on low for 2 hours. Transfer the pork to a cutting board, then let rest for 2 minutes before slicing. Remove the fat off the cooking liquid in the pot.
3. Add the raisins and couscous and cook on high for 15 minutes. Add the almonds and mix well. In another bowl, combine the vinegar, oil, and parsley. Serve the pork with the couscous and vinaigrette.

Nutrition: *Calories: 682 Fat: 35.9g Carbs: 52.2g Protein: 39.9g*

307. MEDITERRANEAN PORK ROAST

PREPARATION: 15 MIN **COOKING:** 6 H **SERVINGS:** 4

INGREDIENTS

- 4 teaspoons Greek seasoning, divided
- 1 pork loin roast (boneless), fat trimmed
- 2 fennel bulbs, sliced
- 4 tomatoes, chopped
- ½ cup reduced-sodium chicken broth
- 2 tablespoons reduced-sodium chicken broth
- Salt and pepper to taste
- 2 teaspoons cornstarch
- 1 ½ teaspoon Worcestershire sauce
- ¼ cup black olives, chopped

DIRECTIONS

1. Sprinkle 1 teaspoon Greek seasoning on both sides of the pork. Add the fennel to the slow cooker. Put the pork on top.
2. Add the tomatoes around the pork. Pour ½ cup chicken broth into the slow cooker, then stir in the salt, pepper, and remaining Greek seasoning.
3. Set it to low and cook for 6 hours. Stir the remaining broth with the cornstarch and Worcestershire sauce. Put the sauce over the pork, then sprinkle with olives on top before serving.

Nutrition: *Calories: 213 Fat: 8.6g Carbs: 8.5g Protein: 24.9g*

---

308. PORK CHOPS & COUSCOUS

PREPARATION: 10 MIN **COOKING:** 8 H **SERVINGS:** 4

INGREDIENTS

- ¾ cup low-sodium chicken broth
- 2 tablespoons olive oil
- 2 ¼ teaspoons dried sage
- 1 teaspoon oregano
- 1 teaspoon basil
- ½ tablespoon garlic powder
- ½ tablespoon paprika
- ¼ teaspoon dried thyme
- ¼ teaspoon dried marjoram
- ¼ teaspoon dried rosemary
- 2 lb. pork chops, fat trimmed (boneless)
- 2 cups couscous, cooked

DIRECTIONS

1. Combine the chicken broth, olive oil, and spices in a bowl. Make slits on the pork chops. Pour the spice mixture into your slow cooker.
2. Put the pork and turn to coat evenly. Cook on low for 8 hours. Serve pork chops with couscous.

Nutrition: *Calories: 561 Fat: 32.1g Carbs: 34.5g Protein: 31.4g*

309. CREAMY PORK CHOPS WITH POTATOES

PREPARATION: 10 MIN   **COOKING:** 4 H   **SERVINGS:** 4

INGREDIENTS

- cooking spray
- 4 pork chops
- 6 potatoes, cubed
- 1 cup milk
- 1 packet dry ranch dressing mix
- garlic salt and pepper to taste
- 3 cups cream of onion soup

DIRECTIONS

1. Coat a slow cooker with oil. Arrange the potatoes inside the pot. Top with the pork chops. Mix the rest of the fixings in a bowl.
2. Pour this mixture over the pork chops and potatoes. Set it to high and cook for 4 hours. Pour the sauce over the pork chops and potatoes before serving.

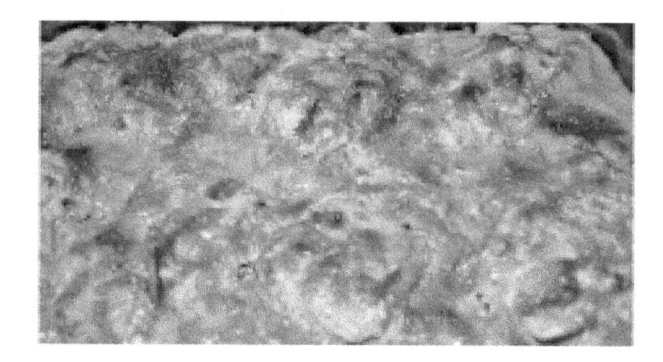

Nutrition: *Calories: 488 Fat: 11g Carbs: 57g Protein: 36g*

310. MEDITERRANEAN PORK CHOPS

PREPARATION: 15 MIN   **COOKING:** 6 H   **SERVINGS:** 4

INGREDIENTS

- 6 pork chops
- garlic salt and pepper to taste
- 2 teaspoons dried basil
- 1 teaspoon oregano
- 2 teaspoons paprika
- 3 tablespoons olive oil
- 4 tablespoons balsamic vinegar
- 8 oz. chicken broth
- 1 cup carrot, cubed
- 1 cups potato, cubed

DIRECTIONS

1. Coat the slow cooker with cooking spray. Sprinkle both sides of the pork chops with garlic salt, pepper, basil, oregano, and paprika.
2. Transfer to the slow cooker. Mix the balsamic vinegar and olive oil. Pour into the pot. Pour in the chicken broth. Stir in the carrots and potatoes. Cook on low for 6 hours. Serve.

Nutrition: Calories: 344 Fat: 27.2g Carbs: 4.8g Protein: 19.3g

311. GREEK SHREDDED BEEF

PREPARATION: 15 MIN   **COOKING:** 4 H   **SERVINGS:** 4

INGREDIENTS

- 2 lb. beef chuck roast, fat trimmed and cubed
- Salt to taste
- 1 cup onion, chopped
- ¾ cup red bell pepper, chopped
- ¾ cup carrots, chopped
- 14 oz. canned roasted tomatoes
- 2 tablespoons red wine vinegar
- 1 tablespoon garlic, crushed and minced
- 1 tablespoon Italian seasoning blend
- ½ tablespoon dried red pepper

DIRECTIONS

1. Season the beef chuck roast with salt. Put the beef cubes in the slow cooker. Sprinkle the onion, bell pepper, and carrots on top.
2. In a bowl, mix the rest of the ingredients and pour into the pot—cook on high for 4 hours. Shred with the beef. Serve with salad or whole wheat bread.

Nutrition: *Calories: 589 Fat: 42.1g Carbs: 8.6g Protein: 40.8g*

---

312. PORK WITH SWEET POTATOES & MUSHROOMS

PREPARATION: 15 MIN   **COOKING:** 5 H   **SERVINGS:** 2

INGREDIENTS

- 1 lb. pork tenderloin, diced
- 1 yellow bell pepper, sliced
- 1 zucchini, sliced into rounds
- 1 sweet potato, cubed
- 1 tablespoon olive oil
- 2 onions, sliced
- 1 clove garlic, minced
- ¼ cup tomato sauce
- 2 cups pork broth
- 1 teaspoon dried oregano
- Pepper to taste
- 1 cup mushrooms

DIRECTIONS

1. Put the pork, bell pepper, zucchini, and sweet potato into the slow cooker. Put the oil and cook the onion for 2 minutes in a pan over medium heat.
2. Stir in the garlic and cook for 2 minutes. Transfer the onion and garlic to the slow cooker. In the same pan, pour in the tomato sauce and broth.
3. Season with pepper and oregano. Boil and then move to the slow cooker. Mix everything. Cook on low for 3 hours. Stir in the mushrooms and cook on low for another 1 hour.

Nutrition: *Calories: 572 Fat: 17.1g Carbs: 34.6g Protein: 70g*

313. MOROCCAN LAMB

PREPARATION: 15 MIN   **COOKING:** 4 H 15 MIN   **SERVINGS:** 4

INGREDIENTS

- 1 onion, chopped
- 3 cloves garlic, chopped
- 6 potatoes, cubed
- 3 carrots, sliced into cubes
- 2 lb. lamb leg, cut into cubes
- ½ cup dried apricots
- 1 bay leaf
- 1 cinnamon stick
- ½ teaspoon ground ginger
- 1 teaspoon Moroccan spice blend
- 1 ½ teaspoon ground allspice
- 6 tomatoes from the can slice in half
- 3 cups reduced-sodium beef stock
- 15 oz. canned chickpeas

DIRECTIONS

1. Put the olive oil and cook the onion, garlic, potatoes, and carrots for 5 minutes in a pan over medium heat. Season with salt and pepper.
2. Transfer the vegetables to the slow cooker. Add the lamb and brown on both sides, then put the apricots, bay leaf, cinnamon stick, and spices.
3. Stir in the tomatoes. Bring to a boil for 5 minutes. Move it to the slow cooker—cook on high for 4 hours. Serve.

Nutrition: *Calories: 502 Fat: 9.7g Carbs: 65.4g Protein: 43.5g*

314. MEDITERRANEAN LAMB CHOPS

PREPARATION: 10 MIN   **COOKING:** 8 H   **SERVINGS:** 4

INGREDIENTS

- 4 lamb shoulder chops, fat trimmed
- 2 onions, sliced
- 4 cloves garlic, sliced
- 1 tablespoon paprika
- 2 cups canned tomatoes
- 1 tablespoon tomato paste
- 2 sprigs rosemary
- 1 pack frozen mixed vegetables

DIRECTIONS

1. Combine all the ingredients except vegetables in the slow cooker. Cook on low for 7 hours. Stir in the vegetables. Cook for another 1 hour. Pour the sauce over the lamb chops before serving.

Nutrition: *Calories: 307 Fat: 8.9g Carbs: 20.4g Protein: 35.8g*

315. GREEK LEG OF LAMB

PREPARATION: 20 MIN   **COOKING:** 4-6 H   **SERVINGS:** 4

INGREDIENTS

- 3 lb. leg of lamb
- Salt and pepper to taste
- 4 tablespoons olive oil, divided
- 12 cloves garlic
- 1 tablespoon freshly squeezed lemon juice
- ¾ teaspoons sweet paprika
- 2 teaspoons fresh thyme, chopped
- 1 teaspoon dried oregano
- 2 teaspoons dried rosemary
- 1 lb. onion, peeled
- ½ cup reduced-sodium beef broth
- 1 cup dry red wine
- Chopped parsley

DIRECTIONS

1. Flavor both sides of the lamb with salt plus pepper to taste. Pour half of the olive oil into a pan over medium heat.
2. Add the lamb and cook for 3 minutes per side. After cooking, make several slits on the lamb. Insert garlic clove in each slit.
3. In a bowl, mix the lemon juice, paprika, thyme, oregano, and rosemary. Rub mixture all over the lamb. Add the lamb to the slow cooker.
4. Top with the onion and pour in the broth and wine. Seal the pot and cook on high for 4 hours.

Nutrition: *Calories179 Fat: 12.9g Carbs: 13.2g Protein: 5.1g*

316. BEEF TENDERLOIN WITH ROSEMARY

PREPARATION: 15 MIN   **COOKING:** 8H   **SERVINGS:** 4

INGREDIENTS

- 1 tbsp of tallow
- 3 ½ lbs. beef tenderloin roast
- Salt and freshly ground pepper, to taste
- 3 cloves of garlic finely chopped
- 6 fresh rosemary sprigs chopped
- 1/4 cup of extra-virgin olive oil
- 1/4 cup of mustard
- 1 cup of white wine or water

DIRECTIONS

1. Coat your slow cooker with tallow. Season beef with salt and pepper, and place in a slow cooker.
2. Sprinkle the rosemary evenly over the meat. In a bowl, combine olive oil, mustard, wine, and salt and pepper. Pour the mixture over meat and toss to mix well.
3. Cook on high within 4 hours or low heat for 6 to 8 hours. Remove the beef on a working surface and allow it to cool for 10 minutes. Slice and serve.

Nutrition: *Calories: 477 Carbs: 3g Fat: 39g Protein: 28g*

317. BRAISED ROUND STEAK WITH ROSEMARY

PREPARATION: 15 MIN   **COOKING:** 8 H   **SERVINGS:** 4

INGREDIENTS

- 1 tbsp of beef tallow
- 2 lbs. of beef cheeks cut into slices
- 2 spring onions finely sliced
- 1/2 cup of fresh celery finely chopped
- 1 clove of garlic minced
- 2 bay leaves
- 1 tbsp of dried rosemary (or fresh)
- salt and ground black pepper to taste
- 2 to 3 cloves (whole)
- 1 cup of red wine
- 1 cup of water

DIRECTIONS

1. Add tallow in your slow cooker. Add the beef slices and all remaining ingredients (except red wine).
2. Pour red wine and water into a slow cooker and toss to combine well—cover and cook on high within 4 hours or low for 8 hours. Serve hot.

Nutrition: *Calories: 94 Carbs: 15g Fat: 2g Protein: 8g*

318. BRAISED BEEF TENDERLOIN WITH BROCCOLI AND SESAME

PREPARATION: 15 MIN   **COOKING:** 4 H 30 MIN   **SERVINGS:** 4

INGREDIENTS

- 2 lbs. of beef tenderloin sliced
- 1 cup of bone broth
- 1/4 cup of coconut aminos
- 2 tbsp of olive oil
- 1/4 cup of granulated stevia sweetener
- 3 cups of broccoli flowerets
- Salt and ground black pepper to taste
- 3 tbsp of sesame seeds

DIRECTIONS

1. Place the beef meat directly on the bottom of the slow cooker. Combine the coconut aminos, olive oil, and stevia sweetener.
2. Pour the mixture evenly over the beef. Cook on high within 3 to 4 hours. Open the lid and add broccoli florets—season with salt and pepper.
3. Cook on high for 30 minutes. Sprinkle with sesame seeds and serve hot.

Nutrition: *Calories: 360 Carbs: 27g Fat: 15g Protein: 28g*

319. OLD RANCH PORK CHOPS

PREPARATION: 15 MIN **COOKING:** 4 H 10 MIN **SERVINGS:** 4

INGREDIENTS

- 2 lbs. of pork chops
- 3/4 cup of beer
- 3/4 tsp of cumin
- 1/2 tsp of caraway
- 2 tbsp of olive oil
- salt and ground black pepper to taste
- 1 tbsp of lard softened

DIRECTIONS

1. In a bowl, stir bear, cumin, caraway, salt, pepper, and olive oil. Put the pork chops in a large container and pour the beer mixture; toss to combine well, and refrigerate for 3 hours.
2. Add softened lard to your slow cooker. Remove the chops from marinade and place in a slow cooker.
3. Pour a little marinade and cover. Cook on high heat for 4 hours. Baste with marinade occasionally. Serve hot.

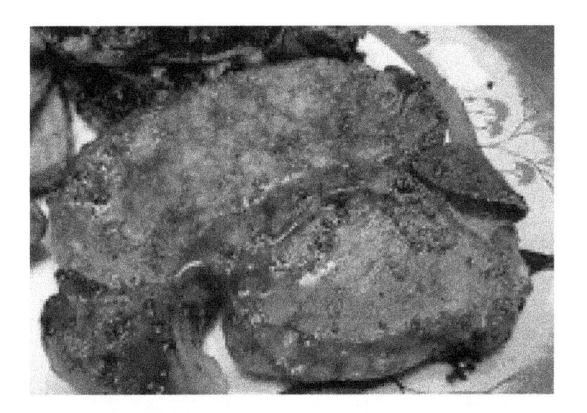

Nutrition: *Calories: 248 Carbs: 5g Fat: 12g Protein: 27g*

320. LAMB SHANKS WITH CELERY ROOT

PREPARATION: 15 MIN **COOKING:** 9 H **SERVINGS:** 4

INGREDIENTS

- 4 lamb shanks
- 16 oz sliced mushrooms
- 1 large carrot, diced
- 1 medium onion
- 1 large celery root
- 1 tbsp fresh chopped rosemary
- 2 tbsp extra virgin olive oil
- 1 cup dry red wine
- 3 tbsp Dijon mustard
- 1 tsp balsamic vinegar
- salt, black pepper
- 1 tbsp chopped parsley
- 4 large cloves garlic

DIRECTIONS

1. Place all ingredients in your slow cooker. Close and cook on low for 8 to 9 hours. Serve hot.

Nutrition: *Calories: 416 Carbs: 3g Fat: 30g Protein: 45g*

321. BACON OMELET

PREPARATION: 15MIN **COOKING:** 2 **SERVINGS:** 4

INGREDIENTS

- 20 mushrooms, stems removed
- 2 cups basil, chopped
- 1 cup tomato sauce, no-salt-added
- 2 tablespoons parsley, chopped
- ¼ cup low-fat parmesan, grated
- 1 and ½ cups whole wheat breadcrumbs
- 1 tablespoon garlic, minced
- ¼ cup low-fat butter, melted
- 2 teaspoons lemon juice
- 1 tablespoon olive oil

DIRECTIONS

1. In a bowl, mix butter with breadcrumbs and parsley, stir well, and leave aside. In your blender, mix basil with oil, parmesan, garlic, and lemon juice and pulse well.
2. Stuff mushrooms with this mix, pour the tomato sauce on top, sprinkle breadcrumbs mix at the end, and cook in the slow cooker on low for 5 hours. Arrange mushrooms on a platter and serve.

Nutrition: *Calories: 377 Carbs: 7g Fat: 31g Protein: 17g*

322. GREEK BEEF STEW WITH PAPRIKA

PREPARATION: 15 MIN **COOKING:** 4-5 H **SERVINGS:** 4

INGREDIENTS

- 1 tbsp of tallow
- 1 1/4 lb. of beef chunks, boneless cut into small pieces
- 2 green onions finely chopped
- 2 cloves of garlic
- Salt and ground pepper to taste
- 1 tbsp of Italian seasonings
- 1 tsp of sweet ground red pepper
- 2 tbsp of tomato paste
- 2 cups of bone broth
- 1 1/2 cups of water
- 2 Bay leaves
- 2 to 3 tbsp fresh chopped parsley

DIRECTIONS

1. Heat-up tallow in a large frying pan on medium-high heat. Sauté the beef, green onion, and garlic with a pinch of salt for 2 to 3 minutes.
2. Add all remaining ingredients and simmer for 2 minutes. Transfer the beef mixture to your slow cooker and stir—cover, and cook on high heat for 4 to 5 hours. Adjust the seasonings and serve hot.

Nutrition: *Calories: 320 Carbs: 25g Fat: 9g Protein: 38g*

323. CREAMY LAMB LEGS

PREPARATION: 15 MIN   **COOKING:** 5 H   **SERVINGS:** 4

INGREDIENTS

- 3 lbs. lamb legs cut into chunks
- 1/2 cup garlic-infused olive oil
- 1 lemon juice
- 1 tsp fresh chopped thyme
- 1/2 tsp fresh chopped parsley
- 1/4 cup water
- 2 cups of Greek yogurt
- 2 eggs from free-range chickens
- Salt and pepper to taste

DIRECTIONS

1. Wash the lamb, season with the salt, cover, and leave it in the fridge overnight. Pour the oil into your slow cooker and add the lamb chunks.
2. Sprinkle with thyme and parsley and pour the lemon juice and water—cover and cook on low for 3 hours. In a bowl, whisk eggs, Greek yogurt, and some salt and pepper.
3. Pour the egg mixture over the lamb in the slow cooker. Cover and cook on low within 2 hours. Serve hot.

Nutrition: *Calories: 210 Carbs: 0g Fat: 13g Protein: 22g*

324. GRILLED AROMATIC BEEF-PORK PATTIES

PREPARATION: 15 MIN   **COOKING:** 8 H   **SERVINGS:** 6

INGREDIENTS

- ·2 onions finely chopped
- ·1 lb. fresh kale, roughly chopped
- ·1 1/2 lbs. ground beef meat
- ·1/2 lb. ground pork meat
- ·1 large egg
- ·½ cup of olive oil
- ·3/4 tsp fresh tarragon, finely chopped
- ·1/2 tsp cilantro, finely chopped
- ·salt and ground pepper to taste

DIRECTIONS

1. Heat-up oil in a frying pan, and sauté onion and kale with a pinch of salt. Add the ground meat, egg, oil, tarragon, cilantro, salt, and pepper to taste.
2. Sauté for 2 minutes and remove from the heat; let it cool for 10 minutes. Knead the mixture until all ingredients are combined well.
3. Using your hands, shape 6 patties. Grease the bottom of your slow cooker and arrange patties—cover and cook on low for 7 to 8 hours. Serve hot.

Nutrition: *Calories: 219 Carbs: 10g Fat: 15g Protein: 12g*

325. MARINATED CURRY-SPICED GOAT

PREPARATION: 15 MIN **COOKING:** 8 H **SERVINGS:** 4

INGREDIENTS

- 1 lb. of goat or goat meat
- Juice of 1 lemon (fresh)
- 2 tbsp of curry powder
- 3 cloves of garlic, finely chopped
- 1 fresh ginger root, finely chopped
- 1 medium onion, finely chopped
- 2 tbsp of avocado oil
- 1 tbsp of flour
- 2 red onions, cut into rings
- 1 cup of cauliflower in flowerets
- 1 red chili pepper finely chopped
- 1 tbsp of curry powder
- 1 cup of grated tomatoes
- 1 1/4 cup of goat milk
- Salt and pepper to taste

DIRECTIONS

1. Rinse, dry and wrap the goat meat with kitchen paper, and place in a large container. Season generously with salt and pepper.
2. Sprinkle with lemon juice and curry powder, garlic, ginger, and chopped onion. Cover and marinate overnight in the refrigerator.
3. Pour oil into your slow cooker and add goat meat with marinade. Add the onion, cauliflower, red chili, curry powder, tomatoes, and goat milk. Adjust salt and pepper.
4. Close lid and cook on high within 5 hours, or on low 6 - 8 hours. Serve hot.

Nutrition: *Calories: 230 Carbs: 25g Fat: 8g Protein: 13g*

326. MUSTARD OLIVES WITH PORK LOIN

PREPARATION: 15 MIN **COOKING:** 8 H **SERVINGS:** 4

INGREDIENTS

- 1 tbsp of lard
- 1 1/2 lbs. of pork loin cut into small pieces
- 2 medium yellow onions, finely chopped
- 1 cup of olives, pitted and sliced
- 1 large red bell pepper finely chopped
- ½ cup of beef broth
- 1 cup of white wine
- 3 tbsp of olive oil
- 3 tbsp of mustard
- salt and ground black pepper to taste

DIRECTIONS

1. Coat your slow cooker with lard. Season pork loin with salt and pepper and add it into the slow cooker. Add the onions, bell pepper, and sliced olives.
2. In a bowl, combine the olive oil, mustard, and white wine and pour over meat and vegetables. Cover and cook on high within 4 hours or on low heat for 8 hours. Serve hot.

Nutrition: *Calories: 135 Carbs: 2g Fat: 4g Protein: 22g*

327. PORK FILLETS WITH MUSTARD -MUSHROOMS SAUCE

PREPARATION: 15 MIN   **COOKING:** 4 H   **SERVINGS:** 4

INGREDIENTS

- 1 lb. pork tenderloin
- 1 tbsp of flour
- 1 tsp rosemary, dried
- Sea salt
- ground black pepper
- ¼ cup of olive oil
- 1/2 lb. of white mushrooms, sliced
- 2 cloves garlic, finely chopped
- 1 1/4 cup vegetable broth
- Fresh mint leaves for servings

DIRECTIONS

1. Heat the oil in a deep-frying pan with a lid. Sauté the pork fillets with a pinch of salt for 5-6 minutes from both sides.
2. Add the onion, garlic, and mushrooms and sauté for 5 minutes; stir—transfer port fillets in your slow cooker.
3. Pour the wine, add salt, pepper, warm water, oregano, and basil, the mustard dissolved in 1/2 beef broth, and toss to combine well. Cover and cook on low within 4 to 5 hours. Serve hot.

Nutrition: *Calories: 393 Carbs: 23g Fat: 17g Protein: 42g*

328. PORK TENDERLOIN WITH CREAMY MUSHROOMS SAUCE

PREPARATION: 10 MIN   **COOKING:** 2H   **SERVINGS:** 4

INGREDIENTS

- 2 teaspoons olive oil
- 8 tomatoes, chopped
- 1 garlic clove, minced
- ¼ cup basil, chopped
- 4 Italian whole wheat bread slices, toasted
- 3 tablespoons low-sodium veggie stock
- Black pepper to the taste

DIRECTIONS

1. Cut the pork into slices. Put the flour and rosemary, add salt and pepper, and pork in a large plastic food bag.
2. Close the bag shake it until the meat is covered well. Pour the oil into your slow cooker and add the pork. Add the mushrooms, chopped garlic, and vegetable broth; stir well.
3. Cover and cook on high within 4 hours. Sprinkle with fresh mint leaves and serve.

Nutrition: *Calories: 450 Carbs: 31g Fat: 16g Protein: 35g*

329. SIRLOIN STEAK WITH BROCCOLI

PREPARATION: 15 MIN **COOKING:** 4 H 30 MIN **SERVINGS:** 4

INGREDIENTS

- 1 1/2 lb. sirloin steak, thinly sliced
- 1 1/2 cups of beef broth
- 2 tbsp of sesame oil
- 1 tbsp of chili sauce
- 2 of green onions, thinly sliced
- 2 cloves of garlic, minced
- 2 cup of broccoli flowerets
- 2 tbsp of flour
- Sesame seeds, for garnish

DIRECTIONS

1. Season the beef steak with salt and ground black pepper. Place the steak on the bottom of your slow cooker and pour the broth, sesame oil, chili sauce, garlic, and sliced green onions.
2. Cover and cook on low heat for 4 hours. Open the lid and spoon 1/2 cup of broth and stir the flour. Place the broccoli flowerets over the beef, and cover with the flour mixture.
3. Cover and cook on high within 20 to 30 minutes. Serve hot with sesame seeds.

Nutrition: *Calories: 250 Carbs: 12g Fat: 7g Protein: 37g*

330. SUCCULENT LAMB

PREPARATION: 18 MIN **COOKING:** 8 H **SERVINGS:** 2

INGREDIENTS

- 2/3 lb. leg of lamb
- 2 tbsp wholegrain mustard
- 1/3 tbsp maple syrup
- 1 sprig thyme
- 1/4 tsp dried rosemary

DIRECTIONS

1. Cut 3 slits across the top of the lamb. Put some garlic and rosemary in each slit. Add lamb to slow cooker and rub with olive oil, mustard, maple syrup, salt, and pepper. Cook for 7 hours on low, add a sprig of thyme, then cook for an additional 1 hour.

Nutrition: *Calories: 414 Fat: 35.2g Carbs: 0.3g Protein: 26.7g*

331. LAMB WITH MINT AND GREEN BEANS

PREPARATION: 10 MIN   **COOKING:** 6 H   **SERVINGS:** 2

INGREDIENTS

- 1/2 lamb leg (bone-in)
- 1 tbsp ghee, tallow, or lard
- 1/8 cup freshly chopped mint leaves
- 3 cups green beans, trimmed

DIRECTIONS

1. Pat the lamb, dry with paper towels, and season it with salt and pepper. Grease the slow cooker with ghee, tallow, or lard, then put the lamb inside.
2. Sprinkle with garlic and mint all over. If it makes you more comfortable, add up to half a cup of water. Cover and cook within 4 hours on high.
3. Transfer the lamb to a plate, then place the green beans on the bottom of the slow cooker. Add the lamb again inside—cover and cook for another 2 hours on high.
4.

Nutrition: *Calories: 525 Fat: 36.4g Carbs: 7.6g Protein: 37.3g*

332 BRAISED LAMB STEW

PREPARATION: 15 MIN   **COOKING:** 4 H   **SERVINGS:** 2

INGREDIENTS

- 1 lb. leg of lamb
- 1/2 cup bone broth
- 1/2 cup white wine
- 1 1/2 carrots, chopped
- 1 tbsp butter

DIRECTIONS

1. Rub lamb with salt, pepper, and oil. Brown it in a slow cooker set on high. Set it aside and throw in your veggies in the slow cooker, including onion and garlic to taste.
2. When the veggies have acquired the desired crispness, add in the bone broth and wine. Mix thoroughly. Submerge the lamb legs into the mixture. Cover and cook within 4 hours on high.

Tip: Add rosemary and thyme for extra flavor.

Nutrition: *Calories: 782 Fat: 45g Carbs: 7g Protein: 72g*

333. KERALA LAMB STEW

PREPARATION: 10 MIN **COOKING:** 6 H **SERVINGS:** 2

INGREDIENTS

- 1 1/3 tbsp coconut oil
- 4 1/2 oz coconut milk
- 1 1/3 bay leaves
- 10 curry leaves
- 4 3/4 oz boneless lamb

DIRECTIONS

1. Marinate the mutton with the salt, pepper, chili powder, and other spices desired. In a slow cooker, heat some coconut oil and fry the mutton, browning it on each side
2. Add bay leaves. Cover and cook on low within 5-6 hours. When simmering starts, add the curry leaves and coconut milk. Cook this for another hour.

Nutrition: *Calories: 284 Fat: 20g Carbs: 3g Protein: 22g*

334. FALL-OFF-THE-BONE LAMB SHANKS

PREPARATION: 10 MIN **COOKING:** 4-8 H **SERVINGS:** 2

INGREDIENTS

- 1 tsp smoked paprika
- 2 rosemary sprigs
- 2 lb. lamb shanks, seasoned and browned
- 1 tbsp extra virgin olive oil
- 2 organic chicken or beef stock

Nutrition: *Calories: 441 Fat: 27g Carbs: 4g Protein: 19g*

DIRECTIONS

1. Place lamb shanks in the slow cooker. Add the chicken stock; rosemary sprigs, smoked paprika, onions, salt, and pepper to taste into the slow cooker. The meat should be submerged. Cook on high within 4 hours, or low for 8 hours.

335. LAMB CHOPS

PREPARATION: 10 MIN **COOKING:** 6 H **SERVINGS:** 2

INGREDIENTS

- 4 lamb loin chops
- 1/2 tsp dried oregano
- 1/4 tsp dried thyme

Nutrition: *Calories: 201 Fat: 8g Carbs: 3g Protein: 26g*

DIRECTIONS

1. Prepare the seasonings: oregano and thyme with some garlic powder, salt, and pepper to taste. Rub it on the lamb chops.
2. Put the onion slices in a slow cooker and place chops over the onion slices. Top with garlic, too. Cover and cook within 6 hours on low.

336. GARLIC LAMB ROAST

PREPARATION: 10 MIN **COOKING:** 10 H **SERVINGS:** 2

INGREDIENTS

- 2 tbsp coconut vinegar
- 1 tsp rosemary
- 1 leg of lamb
- 2 tbsp Worcestershire sauce
- Desired veggies: chopped carrots, onions, and butternut squash

DIRECTIONS

1. Put all ingredients in a slow cooker. Add seasonings such as garlic, pepper, and salt to taste. Cook on low within 6-10 hours or until the lamb is tender.

Nutrition: *Calories: 435 Fat: 31g Carbs: 6g Protein: 44g*

337. LAMB SHANKS WITH TOMATOES

PREPARATION: 15 MIN **COOKING:** 8 H **SERVINGS:** 2

INGREDIENTS

- 1/3 tbsp tomato paste
- 1 x 400g tin diced tomatoes
- 1/3 tbsp sundried tomato pesto
- 1/3 cup beef stock
- 2 lb. lamb shanks

Nutrition: *Calories: 397 Fat: 34g Carbs: 5g Protein: 29g*

DIRECTIONS

1. Heat-up oil in a saucepan and cook onions until translucent. Add garlic and cook for 3 minutes. Add tomato paste and cook for another 2 minutes, stirring.
2. Add diced tomatoes, sundried tomato pesto, and beef stock, then boil. Put the lamb into the slow cooker and pour tomato sauce over—Cook for 8 hours on low.

338. LAMB CURRY

PREPARATION: 25 MIN **COOKING:** 8 H **SERVINGS:** 2

INGREDIENTS

- 1 lamb shoulder
- 1 tbsp curry powder
- 1 tbsp ground coriander powder
- 1/2 cup tomato paste
- 1 can coconut cream

DIRECTIONS

1. Place lamb shoulder, roughly diced onions, roughly chopped garlic, and 1/4 cup water in the slow cooker. Cover and cook on low for 6-8 hours.
2. Put the meat aside and add the onions and garlic from the slow cooker to a frying pan. Add curry powder and coriander powder. Cook until they are integrated.
3. Add tomato paste and cooked lamb meat—Cook for a further 5 minutes. Add coconut cream and simmer within 10 minutes on low heat.

Nutrition: *Calories: 554 Fat: 42g Carbs: 4g Protein: 28g*

339. LAMB STROGANOFF

PREPARATION: 5 MIN **COOKING:** 8 H 30 MIN **SERVINGS:** 2

INGREDIENTS

- 8 oz light sour cream
- 1/8 cup all-purpose flour
- 1/4 cup beef broth
- 1 cup sliced white mushrooms
- 3/4 lb. boneless lamb in 1-inch pieces, browned

DIRECTIONS

1. Combine the browned lamb, broth, mushrooms, onions, garlic, salt and pepper, and spices of choice (bay leaf, mustard, or parsley) in a slow cooker. Cover and cook within 6 to 8 hours on low.
2. In a bowl, whisk sour cream and flour until completely integrated. Pour mixture into the slow cooker. Cover and cook on for another 30 minutes on high.

Nutrition: *Calories: 373 Fat: 10g Carbs: 5g Protein: 31g*

340. GROUND LAMB CASSEROLE

PREPARATION: 5 MIN **COOKING:** 8 H **SERVINGS:** 2

INGREDIENTS

- 2 slices bacon, diced cooked crispy
- 1/2 lb. ground lamb
- 1/8 cup chopped green bell pepper
- 2 cups thinly sliced cabbage
- 1 cup tomato sauce

DIRECTIONS

1. Add the ground lamb, bacon, pepper, onion, and garlic to taste into the slow cooker. Cover and cook within 6 hours on low. Add the cabbage and tomato sauce to the pot, stir, then cook for another 2 hours.

Nutrition: *Calories: 295 Fat: 19g Carbs: 6g Protein: 22g*

341. LAMB HOTPOT

PREPARATION: 10 MIN **COOKING:** 4 H 7 MIN **SERVINGS:** 2

INGREDIENTS

- 1 cup lamb stock
- 2/3 lb. diced lamb leg
- 1 1/2 large potatoes in 3mm slices
- 1 large carrot in bitesize pieces

DIRECTIONS

1. In a slow cooker, add a little oil plus the onion and carrot. Cover and cook on a low for 5 minutes or until soft but not brown.
2. Change to high, then add the lamb. Cook for 2-3 minutes until browned. Add the lamb stock and a little salt and pepper.
3. Arrange the potato slices for them to overlap slightly. Cover and cook within 4 hours on high.

Nutrition: *Calories: 310 Fat: 8g Carbs: 7g Protein: 36g*

342. BALSAMIC BEEF POT ROAST

PREPARATION: 15 MIN **COOKING:** 3-4 H **SERVINGS:** 4

INGREDIENTS

- 1 boneless (3 lb.) chuck roast
- 1 tbsp Kosher salt
- 1 tbsp Black ground pepper
- 1 tbsp Garlic powder
- ¼ cup balsamic vinegar
- ½ cup chopped onion
- 2 cups of water
- ¼ tsp xanthan gum

For the Garnish:
- Fresh parsley

Nutrition: *Calories: 393 Carbs: 3g Protein: 30 g Fat: 28 g*

DIRECTIONS

1. Flavor the chuck roast with garlic powder, pepper, and salt over the entire surface. Use a large skillet to sear the roast until browned. Deglaze the bottom of the pot using balsamic vinegar. Cook 1 minute. Add to the slow cooker.
2. Mix in the onion, and add the water. Once it starts to boil, secure the lid, and continue cooking on low for 3 to 4 hours.
3. Take the meat out of the slow cooker, and place it in a large bowl where you will break it up carefully into large chunks.
4. Remove all fat and anything else that may not be healthy such as too much fat. Mix the xanthan gum into the broth, then add it back to the slow cooker. Serve!

343. BEEF BOURGUIGNON WITH CARROT NOODLES

PREPARATION: 15 MIN **COOKING:** 5 H **SERVINGS:** 4

INGREDIENTS

- 5 slices - thick-cut bacon
- 1 (3 lb.) chuck roast/round roast/your favorite
- 1 large yellow onion
- 3 diced celery stalks
- 1 bay leaf
- 3 large minced garlic cloves
- 4 sprigs of fresh thyme
- 1 lb. sliced white button mushrooms
- 1 tbsp. tomato paste
- 1 cup Beef/chicken broth (+) more as needed
- 1 cup Red wine
- 1 large carrot

For the Garnish:
- Chopped parsley
- Salt & Pepper
- Optional: Dash of red pepper flakes

DIRECTIONS

1. Prepare the bacon in a frying pan using the med-high setting on the stovetop. Place on a paper towel to drain the grease.
2. Flavor the beef cubes with pepper and salt to taste. Layer the meat in the skillet, and sear 1 to 3 minutes. Flip it over and sear another 2 to 3 minutes. Toss it in the slow cooker after all of the cubes are cooked.
3. Fold in the bacon, garlic, mushrooms, celery, and onion in the cooker. Push the thyme and bay leaves between the layers. Empty the broth and wine to cover the mixture approximately ¾ of the way up the cooker.
4. Close the top and cook for 4 hours on high. Shred the carrots to make 'noodles' using a peeler. Cover and cook for another hour or until the beef falls from the bone.
5. Trash the bay leaves when the meal is done and mix well. Serve with the parsley and pepper flakes.

Nutrition: *Calories: 548 Carbs: 6g Fat: 32g Protein: 50 g*

344. BEEF & BROCCOLI

PREPARATION: 15 MIN **COOKING:** 6 H **SERVINGS:** 4

INGREDIENTS

- 2/3 cup liquid aminos
- 2 lbs. flank steak
- 1 cup beef broth
- 1 tsp freshly grated ginger
- 3 tbsp. sweetener - your choice
- 3 minced garlic cloves
- ½ tsp salt
- ½ tsp red pepper flakes - to taste - more or less
- 1 red bell pepper
- 1 head broccoli
- 1 red bell pepper

DIRECTIONS

1. Set the slow cooker on low. Slice the steak into one to two-inch chunks. Pour in the beef broth, aminos, and steak - along with the ginger, sweetener, garlic cloves, salt, and red pepper flakes.
2. Cook 5 to 6 hours on the low setting. Slice the red pepper into one-inch pieces, and chop the broccoli into florets. After the steak is cooked, stir well.
3. Toss in the peppers and broccoli on top of everything in the slow cooker. Continue cooking for at least 1 more hour. Add everything together, and sprinkle with sesame seeds for the topping.

Nutrition: *Calories: 430 Carbs: 3 g Protein: 54 g Fat: 19 g*

345. BEEF CURRY

PREPARATION: 15 MIN **COOKING:** 5-8 H **SERVINGS:** 4

INGREDIENTS

- 2 ½ lb. chuck roast
- 6 tbsp. coconut milk powder
- 2 cups of water
- 3 tbsp. red curry paste
- 5 cracked cardamom pods
- 2 tbsp dried Thai chilis/fresh red chilis
- 2 tbsp Thai fish sauce
- 1/8 tsp ground cloves
- 1/8 tsp ground nutmeg
- 1 tbsp dried onion flakes
- 1 tbsp ground coriander
- 1 tbsp ground ginger
- 1 tbsp ground cumin
- 1 tbsp granulated sugar

To Serve:
- 2 tbsp coconut milk powder
- 2 tbsp granulated sugar substitute
- 1 tbsp. red curry paste
- ¼ cup chopped fresh cilantro
- ¼ cup chopped cashews
- optional: ¼ tsp xanthan gum

DIRECTIONS

1. Arrange the chuck roast in the cooker. Empty the milk, water, fish sauce, curry paste, ginger, cloves, nutmeg, coriander, cumin, your chosen sweetener, the onion flakes, chilis, and cardamom pods.
2. Use the low setting for 8 hours or high for 5 hours. Right before serving, arrange the meat on a plate. Whisk the sauce with two tablespoons of the milk powder, the xanthan gum, sugar substitute sweetener, and curry paste.
3. Tear the meat to shreds, and stir into the sauce. Garnish with some cilantro, and serve.

Nutrition: *Calories: 351 Protein: 26.0g Carbs: 5g Fat: 22g*

346. BEEF DIJON

PREPARATION: 15 MIN **COOKING:** 4 H **SERVINGS:** 4

INGREDIENTS

- 4 (6 oz.) small round steaks
- 2 tbsp steak seasoning - to taste
- 2 tbsp avocado oil
- 2 tbsp peanut oil
- 2 tbsp balsamic vinegar/dry sherry
- 4 tbsp. large chopped green onions/small chopped onions for the garnish - extra
- 1/4 cup whipping cream
- 1 cup fresh cremini mushrooms - sliced
- 1 tbsp. Dijon mustard

DIRECTIONS

1. Warm up the oils using the high heat setting on the stovetop. Flavor each of the steaks with pepper and arrange to a skillet. Cook 2 to 3 minutes per side until done.
2. Place into the slow cooker. Pour in the skillet drippings, half of the mushrooms, and the onions. Cook on the low setting for 4 hours. When the cooking time is done, scoop out the onions, mushrooms, and steaks to a serving platter.
3. In a separate dish, whisk together the mustard, balsamic vinegar, whipping cream, and the steak drippings from the slow cooker.
4. Empty the gravy into a gravy server and pour over the steaks. Enjoy with some brown rice, riced cauliflower, or potatoes.

Nutrition: *Calories: 535 Carbs: 5.0 g Fat: 40g Protein: 39 g*

347. BEEF RIBS

PREPARATION: 15 MIN **COOKING:** 6H **SERVINGS:** 4

INGREDIENTS

- 3 lb. beef back ribs
- 1 tbsp sesame oil
- 1 tbsp rice vinegar
- 1 tbsp hot sauce
- 1 tbsp honey
- 1 tbsp garlic powder
- 1 tbsp kosher salt
- ½ tsp black pepper
- 1 tbsp. potato starch/ cornstarch
- ¼ cup light soy sauce

DIRECTIONS

1. Arrange the ribs in your slow cooker. Whisk the rest of the ingredients together, but omit the cornstarch for now.
2. Pour the mixture over the ribs, making sure the sauce covers all sides. Use the low setting and cook for 6 hours. It will be fall off the bone tender.
3. Prepare the oven to 200°F. Move the ribs to a baking pan, and cover with foil to keep warm. Use a strainer to pour the liquid from the slow cooker into a saucepan.
4. Use the high setting and whisk in the cornstarch with a little bit of cold water.
5. Continue cooking - whisking often - just until the sauce has thickened into a glaze - usually about 5 to 10 minutes. Brush the glaze over the ribs and serve.

Nutrition: *Calories: 342 Carbs: 7 g Fat: 27g Protein: 23 g*

348. BEEF STROGANOFF

PREPARATION: 15MIN **COOKING:** 6 H **SERVINGS:** 4

INGREDIENTS

- 4 minced garlic cloves
- 1 cup white mushrooms (approx. 10)
- 1 large chopped onion
- 3 tbsp. chopped parsley
- 2 cup bone broth
- 2 lbs. beef roast into small strips
- Pepper & salt to taste
- For Serving:
- 1 cucumber – peeled into long wide strips
- ½ cup coconut milk/cream
- 3 tbsp. Dijon mustard
- Garnish with parsley
- Salt to taste

DIRECTIONS

1. Arrange the strips of roast in the slow cooker. Stir in the salt, pepper, beef broth, mushrooms, garlic, and onion. Cook for 6 to 8 hours using the low-temperature setting.
2. When done, stir in the coconut cream, mustard, and salt. Cover a serving bowl with the cucumber noodles. Top it off with the stroganoff. Garnish with the parsley if desired.

Nutrition: *Calories: 462 Carbs: 4.0g Fat: 36g Protein: 26.0g*

349. CABBAGE & CORNED BEEF

PREPARATION: 15 MIN **COOKING:** 8 H **SERVINGS:** 4

INGREDIENTS

- 6 lb. corned beef
- 1 large head of cabbage
- 4 cups of water
- 1 celery bunch
- 1 small onion
- 4 carrots
- ½ tsp ground mustard
- ½ tsp ground coriander
- ½ tsp ground marjoram
- ½ tsp black pepper
- ½ tsp salt
- ½ tsp ground thyme
- ½ tsp allspice

DIRECTIONS

1. Dice the carrots, onions, and celery and toss them into the cooker. Pour in the water. Combine the spices, rub the beef, and arrange in the cooker. Cook on low within 7 hours.
2. Remove the top layer of cabbage. Wash and cut it into quarters until ready to cook. When the beef is done, add the cabbage, and cook for 1 hour on the low setting. Serve and enjoy.

Nutrition: *Calories: 583 Carbs: 13g Fat: 40g Protein: 42g*

350. CHIPOTLE BARBACOA – MEXICAN BARBECUE

PREPARATION: 15 MIN **COOKING:** 4-10 H **SERVINGS:** 4

INGREDIENTS

- ½ cup beef/chicken broth
- 2 med. chilis in adobo (with the sauce, it's about 4 teaspoons)
- 3 lb. chuck roast/beef brisket
- 5 minced garlic cloves
- 2 tbsp lime juice
- 2 tbsp apple cider vinegar
- 2 tsp sea salt
- 2 tsp cumin
- 1 tbsp. dried oregano
- 1 tsp black pepper
- 2 whole bay leaves
- optional: ½ tsp ground cloves

DIRECTIONS

1. Mix the chilis in the sauce, and add the broth, garlic, ground cloves, pepper, cumin, salt, vinegar, and lime juice in a blender, mixing until smooth.
2. Chop the beef into two-inch chunks, and toss it in the slow cooker. Empty the puree on top. Toss in the two bay leaves.
3. Cook 4 to 6 hours on the high setting or 8 to 10 on low. Dispose of the bay leaves when the meat is done. Shred and stir into the juices to simmer for 5 to 10 minutes.

Nutrition: *Calories: 242 Carbs: 2g Fat: 11g Protein: 32 g*

351. CORNED BEEF CABBAGE ROLLS

PREPARATION: 15 MIN **COOKING:** 6 H **SERVINGS:** 4

INGREDIENTS

- 3 ½ lb. corned beef
- 15 large savoy cabbage leaves
- ¼ cup white wine
- ¼ cup coffee
- 1 large lemon
- 1 medium sliced onion
- 1 tbsp rendered bacon fat
- 1 tbsp sweetener
- 1 tbsp yellow mustard
- 2 tsp kosher salt
- 2 tsp Worcestershire sauce
- ¼ tsp cloves
- ¼ tsp allspice
- 1 large bay leaf
- 1 tsp mustard seeds
- 1 tsp whole peppercorns
- ½ tsp red pepper flakes

DIRECTIONS

1. 1. Add the liquids, spices, and corned beef into the cooker. Cook 6 hours on the low setting. Prepare a pot of boiling water.
2. 2. When the time is up, add the leaves and the sliced onion to the water for 2 to 3 minutes. Transfer the leaves to a cold-water bath - blanching them for 3 to 4 minutes. Continue boiling the onion.
3. 3. Use a paper towel to dry the leaves. Add the onions and beef, then roll up the cabbage leaves. Drizzle with freshly squeezed lemon juice.

Nutrition: *CCalories: 481.4 Carbs: 4.2g Protein: 34.87g Fat: 25.38g*

352. CUBE STEAK

PREPARATION: 15 MIN   **COOKING:** 8 H   **SERVINGS:** 4

INGREDIENTS

- 8 cubed steaks
- 1 ¾ tsp adobo seasoning/garlic salt
- 1 can tomato sauce
- 1 cup of water
- black pepper to taste
- ½ medium onion
- 1 small red pepper
- 1/3 cup green pitted olives (+) 2 tbsp. brine

DIRECTIONS

1. 1. Slice the peppers and onions into ¼-inch strips. Sprinkle the steaks with the pepper and garlic salt as needed and place them in the slow cooker.
2. 2. Fold in the peppers and onion and the water, sauce, and olives with the liquid/brine from the jar. Close the lid. Prepare using the low setting for 8 hours.

Nutrition: *Calories: 154 Carbs: 4g Protein: 23.5g Fat: 5.5g*

353. ITALIAN MEATBALLS & ZOODLES

PREPARATION: 15 MIN   **COOKING:** 6 H   **SERVINGS:** 4

INGREDIENTS

- 1 medium spiraled zucchini
- 32 oz. beef stock
- 1 small diced onion
- 2 chopped celery ribs
- 1 chopped carrot
- 1 medium diced tomato
- 6 minced garlic cloves
- 1 ½ lb. ground beef
- 1 ½ tsp garlic salt
- ½ cup shredded parmesan cheese
- 1 large egg
- ½ tsp black pepper
- 4 tbsp. freshly chopped parsley
- 1 ½ tsp Onion powder
- 1 ½ tsp Sea salt
- 1 tsp Italian seasoning
- 1 tsp dried oregano

DIRECTIONS

1. 1. Warm up the slow cooker with the low setting. Add the zucchini, beef stock, onion, celery, tomato, garlic salt, and carrot to the cooker. Cover with the lid.
2. 2. Combine the beef, egg, parmesan, parsley, Italian seasonings, pepper, sea salt, oregano, garlic, and onion powder in a mixing container. Mix and shape into 30 meatballs.
3. 3. Warm up the oil using med-high heat in a frying pan. When it's hot, add the meatballs. Brown and toss into the cooker. Cook with the lid on within 6 hours on low. Serve.

Nutrition: *Calories: 129 Carbs: 3g Fat.: 6g Protein.: 15g*

354. LONDON BROIL

PREPARATION: 15 MIN **COOKING:** 4-6 H **SERVINGS:** 4

INGREDIENTS

- 2 lb. London broil
- 1 tbsp. Dijon mustard
- 2 tbsp reduced sugar ketchup
- 2 tbsp coconut aminos or soy sauce
- ½ cup coffee
- ½ cup chicken broth
- ¼ cup white wine
- 2 tsp onion powder
- 2 tsp minced garlic

DIRECTIONS

1. Arrange the beef in the slow cooker. Cover both sides with the mustard, soy sauce, ketchup, and minced garlic.
2. Pour the liquids into the cooker and give it a sprinkle of the onion powder. Cook it for 4 to 6 hours. When it's ready, shred the meat. Combine with the juices. Serve and enjoy.

Nutrition: *Calories: 409 Carbs: 2.6g Fat: 18.3g Protein: 47.3g*

355. MACHACA - MEXICAN POT ROAST

PREPARATION: 15 MIN **COOKING:** 7 H **SERVINGS:** 4

INGREDIENTS

- 3 ½ lb. beef chuck roast
- 2 tsp granulated garlic
- ½ tsp ground coriander
- 1 tsp ground cumin
- 3 tbsp. bacon grease
- 1 tsp freshly ground black pepper
- Kosher salt
- 2 tbsp organic tomato paste
- 2 tbsp Worcestershire sauce
- 1 cup low-sodium beef/bone broth
- 2 cup fresh salsa

DIRECTIONS

1. Combine the garlic, cumin, salt, pepper, coriander, and cumin. Rub the beef all over. Melt the bacon grease in a heavy skillet using the med-high setting.
2. Brown the meat 2 minutes on each side. Arrange in the slow cooker and add the salsa, Worcestershire, tomato paste, and broth over the roast. Add the juices from the bacon and cover the slow cooker.
3. Cook 1 hour on the high setting. Lower the heat and cook until tender on the low power setting – about 6 to 8 hours.
4. When ready, shred, and remove any fat. Place the meat back into the juices of the slow cooker. Stir to coat and serve.

Nutrition: *Calories: 365 Carbs: 3g Fat: 26g Protein: 27g*

356. CRANBERRY PORK ROAST

PREPARATION: 15 MIN **COOKING:** 6 H **SERVINGS:** 4

INGREDIENTS

- 2 lb. pork shoulder, on the bone
- 1/4 cup dried minced onion
- 8 oz cranberry sauce, low-carb and sugar-free
- 1/4 cup raw honey

DIRECTIONS

1. Grease a 4-quart slow-cooker with a non-stick cooking spray and place the pork shoulder inside. Sprinkle with minced onion, then drizzle with honey, and top with the cranberry sauce.
2. Cover and seal the slow-cooker with its lid, then set the cooking timer for 5 to 6 hours. Allow to cook at a high heat setting, or until pork is cooked through and tender. Carve the meat and serve with the cooking juices alongside.

Nutrition: *Calories: 391.3 Carbs: 19.2g Fats: 25g Protein: 37g*

357. PULLED PORK

PREPARATION: 15 MIN **COOKING:** 6 H **SERVINGS:** 2

INGREDIENTS

- 1 small pork roast, quartered
- 1 white onion, peeled and chopped
- 1 green pepper, sliced and chopped
- 3 tablespoons dry Italian seasoning

DIRECTIONS

1. Grease a 4-quart slow-cooker with a non-stick cooking spray and place the pork roast inside it. Sprinkle with the Italian seasoning, then top with the onion and pepper.
2. Cover and seal the slow-cooker with its lid, then set the cooking timer for 5 to 6 hours. Allow to cook at a high heat setting, or until pork is cooked through and tender.
3. Shred the meat with forks and then serve between two roasted mushrooms caps with cream cheese.

Nutrition: *Calories: 214 Carbs: 4g Fats: 12g Protein: 21g*

358. BALSAMIC PORK TENDERLOIN

PREPARATION: 15 MIN **COOKING:** 6 H **SERVINGS:** 4

INGREDIENTS

- Slow cooker size: 4-quart
- 16 oz pork tenderloin
- 1/2 cup balsamic vinegar
- 2 tablespoon coconut aminos
- 1 tablespoon Worcestershire sauce
- 2 teaspoons minced garlic

DIRECTIONS

1. Grease a 4-quart slow-cooker with a non-stick cooking spray, place the pork inside, and sprinkle with the garlic.
2. Mix the remaining ingredients in a bowl, along with ½ teaspoon red pepper flakes. Pour this mixture over the pork, and seal the slow-cooker with its lid.
3. Set the cooking timer for 4 to 6 hours and cook at a low heat setting. Transfer the pork to a serving platter, drizzle with 1/2 cup of cooking liquid and carve to serve.

Nutrition: *Calories: 188 Carbs: 1.3g Fats: 5.8g Protein: 30.3g*

359. HONEY MUSTARD BARBECUE PORK RIBS

PREPARATION: 15 MIN **COOKING:** 4 H **SERVINGS:** 4

INGREDIENTS

- 1 ½ lb. pork ribs, boneless
- 2 teaspoons garlic-and-herb seasoning blend
- 2 oz Dijon mustard
- 2 oz soy sauce
- 4 oz raw honey

DIRECTIONS

1. Put a large skillet pan on medium heat, and grease with a dash of olive oil. Cook the ribs in batches until they are nicely browned on all sides.
2. Drain the grease and transfer the browned pork ribs to a 4-quart slow cooker. Mix the remaining ingredients in a bowl.
3. Pour this mixture over pork ribs, then cover and seal the slow cooker with its lid. Set the cooking timer for 4 to 5 hours and cook at a high heat setting.
4. Transfer the pork ribs to a serving platter, skim any fat from the sauce, and drizzle the sauce over the chops. Serve hot.

Nutrition: *Calories: 342 Carbs: 18.4g Fats: 20.2g Protein: 22.3g*

360. PORK CHOPS WITH BROCCOLI

PREPARATION: 15 MIN **COOKING:** 7 H 30 MIN **SERVINGS:** 4

INGREDIENTS

- 6 oz pork chops
- 1 medium-sized red onion, peeled and chopped
- 2 cups broccoli florets
- 4 tablespoons soy sauce
- 1 tablespoon sesame seeds

DIRECTIONS

1. 1. Grease a 4-quarts slow-cooker with a non-stick cooking spray and place the pork, onion, soy sauce, and 1/2 cup water inside.
2. 2.Cover and seal the slow cooker with its lid, and set the cooking timer for 7 hours, allowing it to cook at a high heat setting.
3. 3.Add the broccoli and continue cooking for 20 to 30 minutes or until the broccoli is tender. Serve the meat, garnished with sesame seeds, with the vegetables and the sauce alongside.

Nutrition: *Calories: 293.9 Carbs: 5.7g Carbs: 4.9g Fats: 15g Protein: 33.4g*

CHAPTER 8.
FISH AND SEAFOOD

361. POACHED SALMON

PREPARATION: 15 MIN **COOKING:** 2 H **SERVINGS:** 4

INGREDIENTS

- 4 salmon fillets
- 1 medium-sized white onion, peeled and sliced
- 1 lemon, sliced
- 1/2 cup chicken broth
- 1 cup of water

DIRECTIONS

1. Place the ingredients in a 4-quart slow-cooker, holding back 4 lemon slices to garnish. Cover and seal the slow cooker with its lid, then set the cooking timer for 2 hours on high. Serve hot, with the sauce alongside.

Nutrition: *Calories: 133 Carbs: 1.7g arbs: 0.96g Fats: 3.9g Protein: 22.9g*

362. APRICOT SALSA SALMON

PREPARATION: 15 MIN **COOKING:** 1H 30 MIN **SERVINGS:** 2

INGREDIENTS

- 8 oz wild salmon fillet
- 3 tablespoon apricot spread, sugar-free
- 1/4 cup Salsa Verde

DIRECTIONS

1. Grease a 4-quart slow-cooker with a non-stick cooking spray and place the salmon fillet into it. Stir the remaining ingredients together, and spread this mixture over the salmon.
2. Cover and seal the slow-cooker with its lid, and set the cooking timer for 1 to 1 1/2 hours. Allow to cook at a low heat setting or until salmon is cooked through. When done, flake the salmon fillet with forks and serve.

Nutrition: *Calories: 173.1 Carbs: 4.6g Carbs: 4.2g Fats: 6.3g Protein: 27.1g*

THE SLOW COOKER COOKBOOK

363. ORANGE FISH FILLETS

PREPARATION: 15 MIN **COOKING:** 2 H **SERVINGS:** 4

INGREDIENTS

- 4 salmon fillets
- 4 oranges, segmented
- 1 tablespoon Dijon Mustard
- 1 tablespoon orange juice and a large piece of orange rind, sugar-free
- 1/2 cup apple cider vinegar

DIRECTIONS

1. Mix the vinegar, mustard, orange juice, orange rind, salt, and ground black pepper. Cut out 4 aluminum foil pieces, big enough to wrap around each fish fillet, then place a salmon fillet on each aluminum foil piece.
2. Spread prepared vinegar mixture over the top and top with the orange segments. Gently fold aluminum foil over each fillet and form a parcel by crimping the edges.
3. Place these parcels into a 4-quart slow cooker, then cover and seal the slow cooker with its lid. Set the cooking timer for 2 hours, allowing it to cook at a high heat setting.
4. Remove the aluminum packets with a tong, uncover fillets, flake with forks, and serve.

Nutrition: *Calories: 120 Carbs: 2.7g Fats: 6.8g Protein: 19.1g*

364. FISH WITH TOMATOES

PREPARATION: 15 MIN **COOKING:** 1 H 30 MIN **SERVINGS:** 2

INGREDIENTS

- 6 oz cod
- 1 white onion, peeled and sliced
- 1 1/2 teaspoon minced garlic
- 1 can diced tomatoes
- 1/4 cup chicken broth

DIRECTIONS

1. Season the cod with a pinch of salt and pepper and red chili flakes. Mix the remaining ingredients, and place them into a 4-quart slow-cooker.
2. Gently place the seasoned cod on top, then cover and seal the slow-cooker with its lid, setting the cooking timer for 1 to 1 1/2 hours.
3. Allow to cook at a high heat setting or until fish is cooked through. Serve warm.

Nutrition: *Calories: 220 Carbs: 3.64g Fats: 6.7g Protein: 34.*

365. SHRIMP SCAMPI

PREPARATION: 15 MIN **COOKING:** 2 H 30 MIN **SERVINGS:** 4

INGREDIENTS

- 16 oz shrimps, peeled, deveined, and rinsed
- 1 tablespoon minced garlic
- 2 tablespoon melted unsalted butter or olive oil
- 1 tablespoon lemon juice
- 3/4 cup chicken broth

DIRECTIONS

1. Mix all of the ingredients, apart from the shrimps. Season with salt and black pepper, and place in a 4-quarts slow-cooker. Add shrimps, mixing the ingredients gently together.
2. Cover and seal the slow cooker with its lid, and set the cooking timer for 2 1/2 hours. Allow to cook at a low heat setting or until shrimps are cooked through. Garnish with cheese and serve immediately.

Nutrition: *Calories: 256 Carbs: 2.1g Fats: 14.7g Protein: 23.3g*

366. CLAM CHOWDER

PREPARATION: 15 MIN **COOKING:** 4-6 H **SERVINGS:** 4

INGREDIENTS

- 1 ¼ lb. baby clams, with juice
- 1 cup of chopped onion
- 1 cup chopped celery
- 1 teaspoon dried thyme
- 2 cups coconut cream, full-fat
- 2 cups chicken broth

DIRECTIONS

1. Grease a 4-quarts slow-cooker with a non-stick cooking spray and place all ingredients inside. Flavor it with a pinch of salt and ground black pepper.
2. Cover and seal the slow-cooker with its lid, and set the cooking timer for 4 to 6 hours. Allow cooking at a low heat setting or until cooked. Serve immediately.

Nutrition: *Calories: 391 Carbs: 5g Fats: 29g Protein: 27g*

367. LEMON PEPPER TILAPIA WITH ASPARAGUS

PREPARATION: 15 MIN **COOKING:** 3 H **SERVINGS:** 4

INGREDIENTS

- 6 Tilapia fillets
- 1 bundle of asparagus
- 4 teaspoons lemon-pepper seasoning
- 3 tablespoons unsalted butter
- 1/2 cup lemon juice

DIRECTIONS

1. Cut out 6 aluminum foil pieces, each big enough to wrap a tilapia fillet. Put each fillet on a piece of aluminum foil, then evenly sprinkle with lemon-pepper seasoning and lemon juice.
2. Top each fillet with a knob of butter, then place the asparagus spears on top. Gently fold the aluminum foil over each fillet, and form a parcel by crimping the edges.
3. Place these parcels into a 4-quart slow cooker, then cover and seal the slow cooker with its lid. Set the cooking timer for 3 hours, cook at a high heat setting or until fillets are cooked through.
4. Remove the parcels with a tong, unwrap the fillets, flake the fish with forks, and serve.

Nutrition: *Calories: 320 Carbs: 10g Fats: 24g Protein: 60g*

368. PESTO SALMON WITH VEGETABLES

PREPARATION: 15 MIN **COOKING:** 2-3 H **SERVINGS:** 2

INGREDIENTS

- 2 salmon fillets
- 8 oz fresh green beans, trimmed
- 4 teaspoons basil pesto
- 10 cherry tomatoes, quartered
- 3 lemons, juiced

DIRECTIONS

1. Grease a 4-quart slow cooker with a non-stick cooking spray and place the cherry tomatoes and green beans inside.
2. Rub the salmon fillets with salt and black pepper, and place on top of the vegetables. Mix the pesto and the lemon juice, then drizzle over the salmon fillets and vegetables.
3. Cover and seal the slow cooker with its lid, and set the cooking timer for 2 to 3 hours. Allow to cook at a low heat setting or until fillets are cooked through. Serve fish fillet and vegetables with cooked cauliflower rice.

Nutrition: *Calories: 435 Carbs: 5g Fats: 26g Protein: 33g*

369. MUSTARD GARLIC SHRIMPS

PREPARATION: 5 MIN   **COOKING:** 4 H   **SERVINGS:** 4

INGREDIENTS

- 1 teaspoon olive oil
- 3 tablespoons garlic, minced
- 1-pound shrimp, shelled and deveined
- 1 teaspoon Dijon mustards
- Salt and pepper to taste
- Parsley for garnish

DIRECTIONS

1. Heat-up olive oil in a skillet and sauté the garlic until fragrant and slightly browned. Transfer to the slow cooker and place the shrimps and Dijon mustard. Stir to combine.
2. Season with salt and pepper to taste. Close the lid and cook on low for 2 hours or high for 30 minutes. Once done, sprinkle with parsley.

Nutrition: *Calories: 138 Carbs: 3.2g Protein: 23.8g Fat: 2.7g*

370. MUSTARD CRUSTED SALMON

PREPARATION: 3 MIN   **COOKING:** 4 H   **SERVINGS:** 4

INGREDIENTS

- 4 pieces of salmon fillets
- salt and pepper to taste
- 2 teaspoons lemon juice
- 2 tablespoons stone-ground mustard
- ¼ cup full sour cream

DIRECTIONS

1. Flavor the salmon fillets with salt and pepper to taste. Sprinkle with lemon juice. Rub the stone-ground mustard all over the fillets.
2. Place inside the slow cooker and cook on high for 2 hours or on low for 4 hours. An hour before the cooking time, pour in the sour cream on top of the fish. Continue cooking until the fish becomes flaky.

Nutrition: *Calories: 74 Carbs: 4.2g Protein: 25.9g Fat:13.8g*

371. FIVE-SPICE TILAPIA

PREPARATION: 3 MIN   **COOKING:** 5 H   **SERVINGS:** 4

INGREDIENTS

- 12 large scallops, rinsed and patted dry
- Salt and pepper to taste
- 1 ¼ oz. prosciutto, cut into 12 long strips
- 1 tablespoon extra-virgin olive oil
- 1 tablespoon lemon juice

DIRECTIONS

1. Sprinkle individual scallops with salt and pepper to taste. Wrap prosciutto around the scallops. Set aside.
2. Add oil to the slow cooker and arrange on top the bacon-wrapped scallops. Pour over the lemon juice. Cook on low within 1 hour or on high for 3 hours.
3. Halfway through the cooking time, flip the scallops. Continue cooking until scallops are done.

Nutrition: *Calories: 153 Carbs: 0.9g Protein: 25.8g Fat: 5.6g*

---

372. PROSCIUTTO-WRAPPED SCALLOPS

PREPARATION: 3 MIN   **COOKING:** 3 H   **SERVINGS:** 4

INGREDIENTS

- 2 teaspoons olive oil
- 8 tomatoes, chopped
- 1 garlic clove, minced
- ¼ cup basil, chopped
- 4 Italian whole wheat bread slices, toasted
- 3 tablespoons low-sodium veggie stock
- Black pepper to the taste

DIRECTIONS

1. In your slow cooker, mix tomatoes with basil, garlic, oil, veggie stock, and black pepper, stir, cover, cook on high within 2 hours and then leave aside to cool down. Divide this mix on the toasted bread and serve as an appetizer.

Nutrition: *Calories: 113 Carbs: 5g Protein: 15.9g Fat: 8 g*

373. SHRIMPS AND SAUSAGE JAMBALAYA STEW

PREPARATION: 5 MIN   **COOKING:** 3 H   **SERVINGS:** 4

INGREDIENTS

- 1 teaspoon canola oil
- 8 oz. andouille sausage, cut into slices
- 1 bag frozen bell pepper plus onion mix
- 1 can chicken broth
- 8 oz. shrimps, shelled and deveined

DIRECTIONS

1. In a skillet, heat the oil and sauté the sausages until the sausages have rendered their fat. Set aside. Pour the vegetable mix into the slow cooker.
2. Add in the sausages and pour the chicken broth. Stir in the shrimps last. Cook on low within 1 hour or on low for 3 hours.

Nutrition: *Calories: 316 Carbs: 6.3 Protein: 32.1g Fat: 25.6g*

---

374. SPICY BASIL SHRIMP

PREPARATION: 3 MIN   **COOKING:** 2 H   **SERVINGS:** 4

INGREDIENTS

- 1-pound raw shrimp, shelled and deveined
- Salt and pepper to taste
- 1 tablespoon butter
- ¼ cup packed fresh basil leaves
- ¼ teaspoon cayenne pepper

DIRECTIONS

1. Add all ingredients to the slow cooker. Give a stir. Cook on high within 30 minutes or on low for 2 hours.

Nutrition: *Calories: 144 Carbs: 1.4g Protein: 23.4g Fat: 6.2g*

375. SCALLOPS WITH SOUR CREAM AND DILL

PREPARATION: 3 MIN   **COOKING:** 2 H   **SERVINGS:** 4

INGREDIENTS

- 1 ¼ pounds scallops
- Salt and pepper to taste
- 3 teaspoons butter
- ¼ cup sour cream
- 1 tablespoon fresh dill

DIRECTIONS

1. Add all ingredients into the slow cooker. Give a good stir to combine everything. Cook on high within 30 minutes or on low for 2 hours.

Nutrition: *Calories: 152 Carbs: 4.3g Protein: 18.2g Fat: 5.7g*

376. SALMON WITH LIME BUTTER

PREPARATION: 3 MIN   **COOKING:** 4 H   **SERVINGS:** 4

INGREDIENTS

- 1-pound salmon fillet cut into 4 portions
- 1 tablespoon butter, melted
- Salt and pepper to taste
- 2 tablespoons lime juice
- ½ teaspoon lime zest, grated

DIRECTIONS

1. Add all ingredients to the slow cooker. Close the lid. Cook on high within 2 hours and low for 4 hours.

Nutrition: *Calories: 206 Carbs: 1.8g Protein: 23.7 g Fat: 15.2g*

377. SPICY CURRIED SHRIMPS

PREPARATION: 3 MIN   **COOKING:** 2 H   **SERVINGS:** 4

INGREDIENTS

- 1 ½ pounds shrimp, shelled and deveined
- 1 tablespoon ghee or butter, melted
- 1 tablespoon curry powder
- 1 teaspoon cayenne pepper
- Salt and pepper to taste

DIRECTIONS

1. Place all ingredients in the slow cooker. Give a stir to incorporate everything. Cook on low within 2 hours or on high for 30 minutes.

Nutrition: *Calories: 207 Carbs: 2.2 g Protein: 35.2g Fat: 10.5g*

378. SMOKED TROUT

PREPARATION: 3 MIN **COOKING:** 2 H **SERVINGS:** 4

INGREDIENTS

- 2 tablespoons of liquid smoke
- 2 tablespoons olive oil
- 4 oz. smoked trout; skin removed then flaked
- Salt and pepper to taste
- 2 tablespoons mustard

DIRECTIONS

1. Place all ingredients in the slow cooker. Cook on high within 1 hour or low for 2 hours until the trout flakes have absorbed the sauce.

Nutrition: Calories: 116 Carbs: 1.5g Protein: 7.2g Fat: 9.2g

379. SALMON WITH GREEN PEPPERCORN SAUCE

PREPARATION: 5 MIN **COOKING:** 3 H **SERVINGS:** 4

INGREDIENTS

- 1 ¼ pounds salmon fillets, skin removed and cut into 4 portions
- Salt and pepper to taste
- 4 teaspoons unsalted butter
- ¼ cup lemon juice
- 1 teaspoon green peppercorns in vinegar

DIRECTIONS

1. Flavor the salmon fillets with salt plus pepper to taste. In a skillet, heat the butter and sear the salmon fillets for 2 minutes on each side.
2. Transfer in the slow cooker and pour the lemon juice and green peppercorns. Adjust the seasoning by adding in more salt or pepper depending on your taste. Cook on high within 1 hour or low for 3 hours.

Nutrition: Calories: 255 Carbs: 2.3g Protein: 37.4g Fat: 13.5g

380. COCONUT CURRY COD

PREPARATION: 3 MIN **COOKING:** 4 H **SERVINGS:** 4

INGREDIENTS

- 4 pieces of cod fillets
- Salt and pepper to taste
- 1 ½ cups coconut milk
- 2 teaspoons curry paste
- 2 teaspoons grated ginger

DIRECTIONS

1. Place all ingredients in the slow cooker. Give a good stir. Cook on high within 2 hours or on low for 4 hours. Garnish with chopped cilantro if desired.

Nutrition: Calories: 296 Carbs: 6.7g Protein: 20.1g Fat: 22.8g

381. ALMOND CRUSTED TILAPIA

PREPARATION: 5 MIN **COOKING:** 4 H **SERVINGS:** 4

INGREDIENTS

- 2 tablespoons olive oil
- 1 cup chopped almonds
- ¼ cup ground flaxseed
- 4 tilapia fillets
- Salt and pepper to taste

Nutrition: *Calories: 233 Carbs: 4.6g Protein: 25.5g Fat: 13.3g*

DIRECTIONS

1. Arrange the bottom of the slow cooker with a foil. Grease the foil with olive oil. In a mixing bowl, combine the almonds and flaxseed.
2. Season the tilapia with salt and pepper to taste. Dredge the tilapia fillets with the almond and flaxseed mixture.
3. Place neatly in the foil-lined slow cooker—cook on high within 2 hours and low for 4 hours.

382. BUTTERED BACON AND SCALLOPS

PREPARATION: 5 MIN **COOKING:** 2 H **SERVINGS:** 4

INGREDIENTS

- 1 tablespoon butter
- 2 cloves of garlic, chopped
- 24 scallops, rinsed and patted dry
- Salt and pepper to taste
- 1 cup bacon, chopped

Nutrition: *Calories: 261 Carbs:4.9 g Protein:24.7 g Fat:14.3 g*

DIRECTIONS

1. In a skillet, heat the butter and sauté the garlic until fragrant and lightly browned. Transfer to a slow cooker and add the scallops.
2. Season with salt and pepper to taste. Cook on high within 45 minutes or low for 2 hours.
3. Meanwhile, cook the bacon until the fat has rendered and crispy. Sprinkle the cooked scallops with crispy bacon.

383. LEMONY SHRIMPS IN HOISIN SAUCE

PREPARATION: 3 MIN **COOKING:** 2 H **SERVINGS:** 4

INGREDIENTS

- 1/3 cup hoisin sauce
- ½ cup lemon juice, freshly squeezed
- 1 ½ pounds shrimps, shelled and deveined
- Salt and pepper to taste
- 2 tablespoon cilantro leaves, chopped

Nutrition: *Calories: 228 Carbs: 6.3g Protein: 35.8g Fat: 3.2g*

DIRECTIONS

1. Into the slow cooker, place the hoisin sauce, lemon juice, and shrimps. Season with salt and pepper to taste.
2. Mix to incorporate all ingredients. Cook on high within 30 minutes or on low for 2 hours. Garnish with cilantro leaves.

384. GARLIC BUTTER TILAPIA

PREPARATION: 15 MIN   **COOKING:** 2 H   **SERVINGS:** 4

INGREDIENTS

- 2 tablespoons butter, at room temperature
- 2 garlic cloves, minced
- 2 teaspoons flat parsley, chopped
- 4 tilapia fillets
- 1 lemon, cut into wedges
- Salt and pepper to taste
- Cooking spray

DIRECTIONS

1. 1. Put a sheet of aluminum foil on a work surface. Place fillets in the middle. Place in a slow cooker. Season generously with salt and pepper.
2. 2. Mix butter with minced garlic and chopped parsley. Evenly spread mixture over each fillet. Wrap foil around fish, sealing all sides—cook on high for 2 hours. Serve with lemon wedges.

Nutrition: *Calories: 89 Fat: 9.8 g Carbs: 0.5 g Protein: 8.4g*

385. BUTTERY SALMON WITH ONIONS AND CARROTS

PREPARATION: 15 MIN   **COOKING:** 9 H   **SERVINGS:** 4

INGREDIENTS

- 4 salmon fillets
- 4 tablespoons butter
- 4 onions, chopped
- 16 oz. baby carrots
- 3 cloves garlic, minced
- Salt and pepper

DIRECTIONS

1. Dissolve the butter in the microwave, and pour into the slow cooker. Add onions, garlic, and baby carrots. Cover and cook for 6-7 hours on low, occasionally stirring until vegetables begin to caramelize.
2. Place fillet over vegetables in the slow cooker, and season with salt and pepper. Cover and cook on low for 1-2 hours until salmon flakes. Serve on a serving plate, and top with onion mixture.

Nutrition: *Calories: 367 Fat: 22 g Carbs: 12.2 g Protein: 39g*

386. CALLOPED POTATOES WITH SALMON

PREPARATION: 15 MIN   **COOKING:** 7-8 H   **SERVINGS:** 4

INGREDIENTS

- 3 tablespoons all-purpose flour
- 1 10¾-ounce can of cream of mushroom soup
- 5 medium-sized potatoes, peeled and sliced
- 1 16-ounce can of salmon, drained and flaked
- ½ cup chopped onions
- ¼ cup of water
- Salt and pepper
- Cooking spray

DIRECTIONS

1. Generously spray the slow cooker bottom and sides with cooking spray. Place half of the potatoes in a slow cooker. Sprinkle with half of the flour, then season with salt and pepper.
2. Cover with half the flaked salmon, then sprinkle with half the onions. Repeat layers. Combine soup and water.
3. Pour over top of potato and salmon mixture. Cover and cook on low within 7-8 hours or until potatoes are tender.

Nutrition: *Calories: 367 Fat: 22g Carbs: 5.2g Protein: 39g*

387. LEMON-HERB SALMON

PREPARATION: 15 MIN   **COOKING:** 3 H   **SERVINGS:** 4

INGREDIENTS

- 2 pounds skin-on salmon
- 2 cups of water
- 1 tablespoon crushed garlic
- 1 tablespoon lemon
- 1 cup onion
- 1 teaspoon black pepper
- 2 tablespoons dried parsley
- 3 tablespoons butter
- ¼ cup dill
- 1 teaspoon salt
- Fresh parsley, dill, and lemon slices for garnishing

DIRECTIONS

1. 1. Combine the water, garlic, lemon juice, onion, black pepper, parsley, butter, dill, and salt in the slow cooker and cook on high for 30 minutes.
2. 2. Place the salmon in the slow cooker and cook for about 2 hours and 30 minutes. Garnish with some fresh parsley, dill, and lemon slices.

Nutrition: *Calories: 418 Fat: 25.4 g Carbs: 2 g Protein: 46g*

388. ORANGE VINEGAR SALMON

PREPARATION: 15 MIN **COOKING:** 2 H **SERVINGS:** 2

INGREDIENTS

- 1 tablespoon Dijon mustard
- 3 tablespoons orange juice
- ¼ cup apple cider vinegar
- 4 salmon fillets
- Salt and pepper to taste
- 4 oranges, peeled and segmented

DIRECTIONS

1. 1. In a bowl, mix the mustard, orange juice, and apple cider vinegar. Layout 4 aluminum foil pieces big enough to wrap one fillet each.
2. 2. Place each fillet on a piece of aluminum foil, and season with salt and pepper. Top with some sauce and orange segments.
3. 3. Gently fold the aluminum foil over each fillet, and make a closed pack by crimping the edges. Place them in a slow cooker.
4. 4. Cook on high for 2 hours. Being mindful of the steam, open the foil packets. Flake the fish with forks, and serve.

Nutrition: *Calories: 123 Fat: 6.8g Carbs: 2.8g Protein: 19g*

389. COD STEW

PREPARATION: 15 MIN **COOKING:** 6-8 H **SERVINGS:** 2

INGREDIENTS

- 2 medium potatoes, finely chopped
- 1/3 cup corn kernels
- ¼ cup lima beans
- 1 small onion, chopped
- ½ stalk celery, sliced
- 1 small carrot, chopped
- 1 clove garlic, minced
- ½ bay leaf
- ¼ teaspoon crushed rosemary
- Salt and pepper to taste
- ¼ cup chicken broth
- 3 oz. condensed cream of celery soup
- ¼ cup white wine
- ½ pound cod fillets, cut in pieces, bones removed
- 4 oz. diced tomatoes, drained
- ½ cup evaporated milk

DIRECTIONS

1. 1. Combine the potatoes, corn, lima beans, onion, celery, carrot, garlic, bay leaf, rosemary, salt and pepper, chicken broth, celery soup, and white wine slow cooker. Mix well.
2. 2. Cover, and cook on low within 6–8 hours, until the potatoes are tender. Now, remove the bay leaf and add the cod, tomatoes, and milk. Mix well—cover and cook for 35 to 40 minutes. Serve.

Nutrition: *Calories: 168 Fat: 2g Carbs: 29g Protein: 14g*

390. FISH AND BEANS

PREPARATION: 7 MIN **COOKING:** 7 H 5 MIN **SERVINGS:** 4

INGREDIENTS

- 4 tablespoons olive oil
- 1 clove garlic, crushed
- 1-pound small white beans, soaked overnight, drained
- 6 cups of water
- 2 cups tomatoes, chopped
- 2 to 3 cans white tuna in water, drained, flaked
- 1½ teaspoons dried basil
- salt
- ground black pepper

DIRECTIONS

1. Sauté the garlic in oil for a minute over medium heat to flavor the oil. Pour the oil into the slow cooker and top with the beans and water.
2. Cook everything on high for 1 hour, and then on low for 4 to 7 hours. Mix in the rest of the ingredients and cook for another 5 minutes. Transfer everything to a bowl and serve.

Nutrition: *Calories: 250 Fat: 3 g Carbs: 15 g Protein: 10g*

391. ASIAN VEGETABLES WITH A SALMON BLANKET

PREPARATION: 15 MIN **COOKING:** 2-3 H **SERVINGS:** 4

INGREDIENTS

- 10 oz. salmon fillets
- Salt and pepper, to taste
- 1 package frozen Asian stir fry vegetable blend
- 2 tablespoons soy sauce
- 2 tablespoons honey
- 2 tablespoons lemon juice
- 1 teaspoon sesame seeds (optional)

DIRECTIONS

1. Season the salmon with salt and pepper. Mix the soy sauce, honey, and lemon juice in a separate bowl. Put the Asian vegetables in the bottom of a slow cooker.
2. Lay the fillets over the vegetables and then pour the soy sauce mixture over everything; if you're using the sesame seeds, sprinkle them on top now.
3. Cook everything on low for 2 to 3 hours. Transfer the vegetables and fish to a plate and cover with the sauce from the slow cooker.

Nutrition: *Calories: 110 Fat: 3g Carbs: 18g Protein: 3g*

392. SEAFOOD CHOWDER

PREPARATION: 15 MIN **COOKING:** 7 H **SERVINGS:** 4

INGREDIENTS

- 2 pounds frozen fish filets, thawed
- ¼ pound bacon or streaky salt pork, diced
- 1 medium onion, chopped
- 4 medium red-skinned potatoes, peeled, cubed
- 2 cups of water
- 1 to 1½ teaspoons kosher salt
- ¼ teaspoon pepper
- 1 can (12 oz.) evaporated milk

DIRECTIONS

1. Cut the fillets into bite-sized chunks and place them in the slow cooker. Sauté the bacon or pork over medium heat until golden brown. Add the onions and sauté some more.
2. Drain the oil and add the sautéed mixture to the slow cooker. Add the rest of the ingredients, except the milk, and cook everything on low for 5 to 6 hours.
3. Pour the milk into the cooker and continue cooking for another hour. Transfer everything to a bowl and serve.

Nutrition: *Calories: 174 Fat: 7g Carbs: 15g Protein: 8g*

393. SHRIMP FRA DIAVOLO

PREPARATION: 15 MIN **COOKING:** 3 H 25 MIN **SERVINGS:** 2

INGREDIENTS

- 1 tablespoon coconut oil
- 1 medium onion, diced
- 6 cloves garlic, minced
- 1 teaspoon red pepper flakes
- ¼ cup chicken or vegetable broth
- 3 large tomatoes, grilled, peeled, and diced
- 1 tablespoon minced parsley
- ½ teaspoon freshly ground black pepper
- ½ pound medium-size shrimp shelled
- Chopped Chives for serving

DIRECTIONS

1. Heat-up oil in a pan over medium heat. Add the onion, garlic, and pepper and sauté until the onions are translucent, for about 10 minutes.
2. Transfer to the slow cooker and add the broth, tomatoes, parsley, and black pepper. Cook for 2 to 3 hours on low.
3. Add the shrimp and cook for 15 minutes on high or until the shrimp has changed color and has become opaque. Put the chopped chives before serving, if desired.

Nutrition: *Calories: 278 Fat: 9.3g Carbs: 20.3g Protein: 26.3g*

394. WHITE BEANS WITH TUNA

PREPARATION: 15 MIN   **COOKING:** 10 H 30 MIN   **SERVINGS:** 4

INGREDIENTS

- 2 tablespoons garlic-infused oil
- 1-pound small white beans, soaked overnight and drained
- 6 cups of water
- 2 cups chopped tomatoes
- 2 6 ½ oz. can white tuna in water, drained and flaked
- 1 ½ teaspoon dried basil
- Salt and pepper, to taste

DIRECTIONS

1. Combine the garlic-infused oil with the beans and 6 cups water in the slow cooker. Cover and cook for 2 hours on high. Continue cooking 8 hours on low. Add remaining fixings and cook within 30 minutes on high. Serve.

Nutrition: *Calories: 238 Fat: 4.4 g Carbs: 20 g Protein: 27g*

395. COCONUT CLAMS

PREPARATION: 15 MIN   **COOKING:** 6 H   **SERVINGS:** 2

INGREDIENTS

- ¼ cup of coconut milk
- 2 eggs, whisked
- 1 tablespoon olive oil
- 10 oz. canned clams, chopped
- 1 green bell pepper, chopped
- 1 yellow onion, chopped
- Salt and black pepper to taste

DIRECTIONS

1. 1. Combine all the fixings in the slow cooker. Cover, and cook on low for 6 hours. Divide among serving bowls or plates and enjoy!

Nutrition: *Calories: 271 Fat: 4.2g Carbs: 16g Protein: 7.6g*

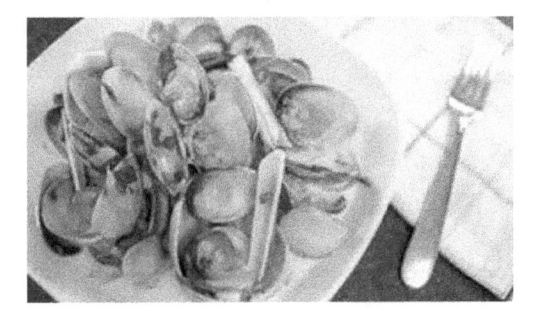

396. SEAFOOD GUMBO

PREPARATION: 15 MIN   **COOKING:** 5 H   **SERVINGS:** 4

INGREDIENTS

- 8-10 bacon strips, sliced
- 2 stalks celery, sliced
- 1 medium onion, sliced
- 1 green pepper, chopped
- 2 garlic cloves, minced
- 2 cups chicken broth
- 1 14-ounce can dice tomatoes, undrained
- 2 tablespoons Worcestershire sauce
- 2 teaspoons salt
- 1 teaspoon dried thyme leaves
- 1-pound large raw shrimp, peeled, deveined
- 1 pound fresh or frozen crabmeat
- 1 10-ounce box frozen okra, thawed and sliced into ½-inch pieces

DIRECTIONS

1. Cook the bacon in your skillet on medium heat. When crisp, drain and transfer to a slow cooker. Drain off drippings, leaving just enough to coat the skillet.
2. Sauté celery, onion, green pepper, and garlic until vegetables are tender, then transfer the sautéed vegetables to the slow cooker. Add the broth, tomatoes, Worcestershire sauce, salt, and thyme.
3. Cover and cook within 4 hours on low or for 2 hours on high. Add the shrimp, crabmeat, and okra. Cover and cook within 1 hour longer on low or 30 minutes longer on high.
4.
5. Cover and cook within 4 hours on low or for 2 hours on high. Add the shrimp, crabmeat, and okra. Cover and cook within 1 hour longer on low or 30 minutes longer on high.

Nutrition: *Calories: 273 Fat: 8g Carbs: 11g Protein: 4g*

397. JALAPEÑO SPICY TUNA

PREPARATION: 10 MIN   **COOKING:** 2H   **SERVINGS:** 4

INGREDIENTS

- 1 tablespoon olive oil
- 2-3 jalapeño peppers, membrane and seeds removed and finely diced
- 1 red bell peppers, trimmed and chopped
- 1 garlic clove, minced
- ¾ pound tuna loin, cubed
- Salt and black pepper

DIRECTIONS

1. Grease the inside cooking surface of the slow cooker with olive oil. In it, combine all the ingredients except the tuna. Cook on low for 3 hours and 45 minutes.
2. Season the tuna with salt and pepper. Open the lid and add the tuna, spooning some of the sauce over the fish—cook on high for 15 minutes. Serve hot.

Nutrition: *Calories: 202 Fat: 4.1g Carbs: 16.3g Protein: 4.5g*

398. SEASONED LARGE SHRIMP

PREPARATION: 15 MIN **COOKING:** 2 H 30 MIN **SERVINGS:** 4

INGREDIENTS

- ½ cup chicken broth
- ½ cup white wine (optional; if using white wine, reduce chicken broth to ¼ cup)
- 2 tablespoons olive oil
- 2 teaspoons garlic, chopped
- 2 teaspoons parsley, minced
- 1-pound large raw shrimp, thawed

DIRECTIONS

1. Place all the fixings except the shrimp in your slow cooker and mix. Place the shrimp into the mixture and cook everything on low for 2 hours and 30 minutes.
2. Remove the shrimp and place in a bowl. Stir the mixture one last time and then pour over the shrimp. Serve and enjoy.

Nutrition: *Calories: 130 Fat: 1 g Carbs: 15 g Protein: 4g*

399. MUSHROOMS SNAPPER

PREPARATION: 15 MIN **COOKING:** 6 H **SERVINGS:** 4

INGREDIENTS

- 1 cup sour cream
- 1 onion, diced
- ¼ cup almond milk
- 1 tsp salt
- 7 oz cremini mushrooms
- 1 tsp ground thyme
- 1 tbsp ground paprika
- 1 tsp ground coriander
- 1 tsp kosher salt
- 1 tbsp lemon juice
- 1 tsp butter
- 1 lb. snapper, chopped
- 1 tsp lemon zest

DIRECTIONS

1. Season the snapper with thyme, paprika, coriander, salt, lemon zest, and lemon juice in a bowl. Cover the snapper and marinate it for 10 minutes.
2. Grease the insert of the slow cooker with butter and add a snapper mixture. Add cremini mushrooms, onion, almond milk, and sour cream.
3. Put the cooker's lid on and set the cooking time to 6 hours on low. Serve warm.

Nutrition: *Calories: 248 Fat: 6.3g Carbs: 31.19g Protein: 20g*

400. ORANGE COD

PREPARATION: 15 MIN **COOKING:** 3 H **SERVINGS:** 4

INGREDIENTS

- 1-pound cod fillet, chopped
- 2 oranges, chopped
- 1 tablespoon maple syrup
- 1 cup of water
- 1 garlic clove, diced
- 1 teaspoon ground black pepper

DIRECTIONS

1. Mix cod with ground black pepper and transfer to the slow cooker. Add garlic, water, maple syrup, and oranges. Close the lid and cook the meal on high for 3 hours.

Nutrition: *Calories: 150 Protein: 21.2g Carbs: 4.8g Fat: 1.2g*

401. COD WITH SHRIMP SAUCE

PREPARATION: 15 MIN **COOKING:** 2 H **SERVINGS:** 4

INGREDIENTS

- 1 lb. cod fillets, cut into medium pieces
- 2 tbsp parsley, chopped
- 4 oz. breadcrumbs
- 2 tsp lemon juice
- 2 eggs, whisked
- 2 oz. butter, melted
- ½ pint milk
- ½ pint shrimp sauce
- Salt and black pepper to the taste

DIRECTIONS

1. 1. Toss fish with crumbs, parsley, salt, black pepper, and lemon juice in a suitable bowl. Add butter, milk, egg, and fish mixture to the insert of the slow cooker.
2. 2. Put the cooker's lid on and set the cooking time to 2 hours on high. Serve warm.

Nutrition: *Calories: 231 Fat: 3g Carbs: 10g Protein: 5g*

402. BAKED COD

PREPARATION: 15 MIN   **COOKING:** 3 H   **SERVINGS:** 2

INGREDIENTS

- 2 cod fillets
- 2 teaspoons cream cheese
- 2 tablespoons bread crumbs
- 1 teaspoon salt
- ½ teaspoon cayenne pepper
- 2 oz Mozzarella, shredded

DIRECTIONS

1. Sprinkle the cod fillets with cayenne pepper and salt. Put the fish in the slow cooker. Then top it with cream cheese, bread crumbs, and mozzarella. Close the lid and cook the meal for 5 hours on low. Serve.

Nutrition: *Calories: 210 Protein: 29.2g Carbs: 6.2g Fat: 7.6g*

403. COD STICKS

PREPARATION: 15 MIN   **COOKING:** 1 H 30 MIN   **SERVINGS:** 2

INGREDIENTS

- 2 cod fillets
- 1 teaspoon ground black pepper
- 1 egg, beaten
- 1/3 cup breadcrumbs
- 1 tablespoon coconut oil
- ¼ cup of water

DIRECTIONS

1. Cut the cod fillets into medium sticks and sprinkle with ground black pepper. Dip or soak the fish in the beaten egg, then coat in the breadcrumbs.
2. Pour water into the slow cooker. Add coconut oil and fish sticks. Cook the meal on high for 1 hour and 30 minutes. Serve.

Nutrition: *Calories: 254 Protein: 25.3g Carbs: 13.8g Fat: 11g*

404. HOT SALMON AND CARROTS

PREPARATION: 15 MIN   **COOKING:** 3 H   **SERVINGS:** 2

INGREDIENTS

- 2 tablespoons chili powder
- ½ teaspoon garlic powder
- 1-pound tilapia
- 2 tablespoons lemon juice
- 2 tablespoons olive oil

DIRECTIONS

1. Place all ingredients in a mixing bowl. Stir to combine everything. Marinate in the fridge within 15 minutes.
2. Get a foil and place the fish, including the marinade, in the middle of the foil. Fold the foil and crimp the edges to seal. Place inside the slow cooker—cook on high for 2 hours or on low for 4 hours.

Nutrition: *Calories: 193 Fat: 7g Carbs: 6g   Protein: 6g*

405. CHILI-RUBBED TILAPIA

PREPARATION: 15 MIN   **COOKING:** 4 H   **SERVINGS:** 4

INGREDIENTS

- 2 teaspoons olive oil
- 8 tomatoes, chopped
- 1 garlic clove, minced
- ¼ cup basil, chopped
- 4 Italian whole wheat bread slices, toasted
- 3 tablespoons low-sodium veggie stock
- Black pepper to the taste

DIRECTIONS

1. In your slow cooker, mix tomatoes with basil, garlic, oil, veggie stock, and black pepper, stir, cover, cook on high within 2 hours and then leave aside to cool down. Divide this mix on the toasted bread and serve as an appetizer.

Nutrition: *Calories: 183 Carbs: 2.9g Protein: 23.4g Fat: 11.3g*

406. FISH MIX

PREPARATION: 15 MIN **COOKING:** 2 H 30 MIN **SERVINGS:** 4

INGREDIENTS

- 4 white fish fillets, skinless and boneless
- ½ teaspoon mustard seeds
- Salt and black pepper to the taste
- 2 green chilies, chopped
- 1 teaspoon ginger, grated
- 1 teaspoon curry powder
- ¼ teaspoon cumin, ground
- 2 tablespoons olive oil
- 1 small red onion, chopped
- 1-inch turmeric root, grated
- ¼ cup cilantro, chopped
- 1 and ½ cups of coconut cream
- 3 garlic cloves, minced

DIRECTIONS

1. Heat a slow cooker with half of the oil over medium heat, add mustard seeds, ginger, onion, garlic, turmeric, chilies, curry powder, and cumin, stir and cook for 3-4 minutes.
2. Add the rest of the oil to your slow cooker, add spice mix, fish, coconut milk, salt, pepper, cover, and cook on High for 2 hours and 30 minutes. Divide into bowls and serve with the cilantro sprinkled on top.

Nutrition: *Calories: 500 Fat: 34g Carbs: 13g Protein: 44g*

407. CHILI BIGEYE JACK (TUNA)

PREPARATION: 15 MIN **COOKING:** 3 H 30 MIN **SERVINGS:** 4

INGREDIENTS

- 9 oz tuna fillet (bigeye jack), roughly chopped
- 1 teaspoon chili powder
- 1 teaspoon curry paste
- ½ cup of coconut milk
- 1 tablespoon sesame oil

Nutrition: *Calories: 341 Protein: 14.2g Carbs: 2.4g Fat: 31.2g*

DIRECTIONS

1. Mix curry paste plus coconut milk and pour the liquid into the slow cooker. Add tuna fillet and sesame oil. Then add chili powder. Cook the meal on high for 3 hours and 30 minutes. Serve.

408. COD AND BROCCOLI

PREPARATION: 15 MIN **COOKING:** 3 H **SERVINGS:** 2

INGREDIENTS

- 1-pound cod fillets, boneless
- 1 cup broccoli florets
- ½ cup veggie stock
- 2 tablespoons tomato paste
- 2 garlic cloves, minced
- 1 red onion, minced
- ½ teaspoon rosemary, dried
- A pinch of salt and black pepper
- 1 tablespoon chives, chopped

DIRECTIONS

1. In your slow cooker, mix the cod with the broccoli, stock, tomato paste, and the other ingredients, toss, put the lid on and cook on low for 3 hours. Divide the mix between plates and serve.

Nutrition: *Calories: 200 Fat: 13g Carbs: 6g Protein: 11g*

409. THYME MUSSELS

PREPARATION: 15 MIN **COOKING:** 2 H 30 MIN **SERVINGS:** 2

INGREDIENTS

- 1-pound mussels
- 1 teaspoon dried thyme
- 1 teaspoon ground black pepper
- ½ teaspoon salt
- 1 cup of water
- ½ cup sour cream

DIRECTIONS

1. In the mixing bowl, mix mussels, dried thyme, ground black pepper, and salt. Then pour water into the slow cooker.
2. Add sour cream and cook the liquid on High for 1 hour and 30 minutes. Add mussels and cook them for 1 hour on high or until the mussels are opened. Serve.

Nutrition: *Calories: 161 Protein: 14.5g Carbs: 5.9g Fat: 8.6g*

410. SEABASS BALLS

PREPARATION: 15 MIN **COOKING:** 2 H **SERVINGS:** 4

INGREDIENTS

- 1 teaspoon ground coriander
- ½ teaspoon salt
- 2 tablespoons flour
- ½ cup chicken stock
- 1 teaspoon dried dill
- 10 oz seabass fillet
- 1 tablespoon sesame oil

Nutrition: *Calories: 191 Protein: 16.6g Carbs: 3.2g Fat: 12.2g*

DIRECTIONS

1. Dice the seabass fillet into tiny pieces and mix with salt, ground coriander, flour, and dill. Make the medium size balls. Preheat the skillet well. Add sesame oil and heat it until hot.
2. Add the fish balls and roast them on high heat for 1 minute per side. Then transfer the fish balls to the slow cooker. Arrange them in one layer. Add water and close the lid. Cook the meal on high for 2 hours. Serve.

411. ASIAN SHRIMPS

PREPARATION: 15 MIN **COOKING:** 3 H **SERVINGS:** 2

INGREDIENTS

- ½ cup chicken stock
- 2 tablespoons soy sauce
- ½ teaspoon sliced ginger
- ½ pound shrimps, cleaned and deveined
- 2 tablespoons rice vinegar
- 2 tablespoons sesame oil
- 2 tablespoons toasted sesame seeds
- 2 tablespoons green onions, chopped

DIRECTIONS

1. Place the chicken stock, soy sauce, ginger, shrimps, and rice vinegar in the slow cooker. Give a good stir.
2. Cook on high within 2 hours or on low for hours. Sprinkle with sesame oil, sesame seeds, and chopped green onions before serving.

Nutrition: *Calories: 352 Carbs: 4.7g Protein: 30.2g Fat: 24.3g*

412. MASHED POTATO FISH CASSEROLE

PREPARATION: 15 MIN **COOKING:** 5 H **SERVINGS:** 4

INGREDIENTS

- 1 cup potatoes, cooked, mashed
- 1 egg, beaten
- ½ cup Monterey Jack cheese, shredded
- 1 cup of coconut milk
- 1 tablespoon avocado oil
- ½ teaspoon ground black pepper
- 7 oz cod fillet, chopped

DIRECTIONS

1. 1. Brush the slow cooker bottom with avocado oil. Then mix chopped fish with ground black pepper and put in the slow cooker in one layer.
2. 2.Top it with mashed potato and cheese. Add egg and coconut milk. Close the lid and cook the casserole on low for 5 hours. Serve.

Nutrition: *Calories: 283 Protein: 16.9g Carbs: 9.8g Fat: 20.7g*

413. CHILI CATFISH

PREPARATION: 15 MIN   **COOKING:** 6 H   **SERVINGS:** 4

INGREDIENTS

- 1 catfish, boneless and cut into 4 pieces
- 3 red chili peppers, chopped
- ½ cup of sugar
- ¼ cup of water
- 1 tablespoon soy sauce
- 1 shallot, minced
- A small ginger piece, grated
- 1 tablespoon coriander, chopped

Nutrition: *Calories: 200 Fat: 4g Carbs: 8g Protein: 10g*

DIRECTIONS

1. Put catfish pieces in your slow cooker. Heat a pan with the coconut sugar over medium-high heat and stir until it caramelizes.
2. Add soy sauce, shallot, ginger, water, and chili pepper, stir, pour over the fish, add coriander, cover and cook on low for 6 hours.
3. Divide fish between plates and serve with the sauce from the slow cooker drizzled on top.

414. ONION COD FILLETS

PREPARATION: 10 MIN   **COOKING:** 3 H   **SERVINGS:** 4

INGREDIENTS

- 1 onion, minced
- 4 cod fillets
- 1 teaspoon salt
- 1 teaspoon dried cilantro
- ½ cup of water
- 1 teaspoon butter, melted

DIRECTIONS

1. Sprinkle the cod fillets with salt, dried cilantro, and butter. Then place them in the slow cooker and top with minced onion. Add water and close the lid. Cook the fish on high for 3 hours. Serve.

Nutrition: *Calories: 109 Protein: 20.3g Carbs: 2.6g Fat: 2g*

415. TILAPIA IN CREAM SAUCE

PREPARATION: 10 MIN   **COOKING:** 5 H   **SERVINGS:** 4

INGREDIENTS

- 4 tilapia fillets
- ½ cup heavy cream
- 1 teaspoon garlic powder
- 1 teaspoon ground black pepper
- ½ teaspoon salt
- 1 teaspoon cornflour

DIRECTIONS

1. Mix cornflour with cream until smooth. Put the liquid into the slow cooker. Sprinkle the tilapia fillets with garlic powder, ground black pepper, and salt.
2. Place the fish fillets in the slow cooker and close the lid. Cook the fish on low for 5 hours.

Nutrition: *Calories: 151 Protein: 21.6g Carbs: 1.7g Fat: 6.6g*

416. HADDOCK CHOWDER

PREPARATION: 10 MIN   **COOKING:** 6 H   **SERVINGS:** 4

INGREDIENTS

- 1-pound haddock, chopped
- 2 bacon slices, chopped, cooked
- ½ cup potatoes, chopped
- 1 teaspoon ground coriander
- ½ cup heavy cream
- 4 cups of water
- 1 teaspoon salt

DIRECTIONS

1. 1. Put all fixings in the slow cooker and close the lid. Cook the chowder on low for 6 hours. Serve.

Nutrition: *Calories: 203 Protein: 27.1g Carbs: 2.8g Fat: 8.6g*

---

417. NUTMEG TROUT

PREPARATION: 10 MIN   **COOKING:** 3 H   **SERVINGS:** 4

INGREDIENTS

- 1 tablespoon ground nutmeg
- 1 tablespoon butter, softened
- 1 teaspoon dried cilantro
- 1 teaspoon dried oregano
- 1 teaspoon fish sauce
- 4 trout fillets
- ½ cup of water

DIRECTIONS

1. In the shallow bowl, mix butter with cilantro, dried oregano, and fish sauce. Add ground nutmeg and whisk the mixture.
2. Then grease the fish fillets with a nutmeg mixture and put in the slow cooker. Add the remaining butter mixture and water. Cook the fish on high for 3 hours. Serve.

Nutrition: *Calories: 154 Protein: 16.8g Carbs: 1.2g Fat: 8.8g*

---

418. CLAMS IN COCONUT SAUCE

PREPARATION: 10 MIN   **COOKING:** 2 H   **SERVINGS:** 2

INGREDIENTS

- 1 cup coconut cream
- 1 teaspoon minced garlic
- 1 teaspoon chili flakes
- 1 teaspoon salt
- 1 teaspoon ground coriander
- 8 oz clams

DIRECTIONS

1. Pour coconut cream into the slow cooker. Add minced garlic, chili flakes, salt, and ground coriander.
2. Cook the mixture on high for 1 hour. Then add clams and stir the meal well. Cook it for 1 hour on high more.

Nutrition: *Calories: 333 Protein: 3.5g Carbs: 19.6g Fat: 28.9g*

419. SWEET MILKFISH SAUTÉ

PREPARATION: 10 MIN **COOKING:** 3 H **SERVINGS:** 4

INGREDIENTS

- 2 mangos, pitted, peeled, chopped
- 12 oz milkfish fillet, chopped
- ½ cup tomatoes, chopped
- ½ cup of water
- 1 teaspoon ground cardamom

DIRECTIONS

1. Mix mangos with tomatoes and ground cardamom. Transfer the ingredients to the slow cooker. Then add milkfish fillet and water—cook on high for 3 hours. Carefully stir before serving.

Nutrition: *Calories: 268 Protein: 24g Carbs: 26.4g Fat: 8.1g*

420. CINNAMON CATFISH

PREPARATION: 10 MIN **COOKING:** 2 H 30 MIN **SERVINGS:** 2

INGREDIENTS

- 2 catfish fillets
- 1 teaspoon ground cinnamon
- 1 tablespoon lemon juice
- ½ teaspoon sesame oil
- 1/3 cup water

DIRECTIONS

1. Sprinkle the fish fillets with ground cinnamon, lemon juice, and sesame oil. Put the fillets in the slow cooker in one layer. Add water and close the lid. Cook the meal on high for 2 hours and 30 minutes.

Nutrition: *Calories: 231 Protein: 25g Carbs: 1.1g Fat: 13.3g*

CHAPTER 9.
VEGETABLES AND VEGETARIAN

421. CAULIFLOWER MASH

PREPARATION: 15 MIN **COOKING:** 3 H **SERVINGS:** 4

INGREDIENTS

- 1 head cauliflower, cut into bite-sized pieces
- 5 garlic cloves, smashed
- 4 cup vegetable broth
- 1/3 cup Greek yogurt
- 3 tbsp. butter, cut into cubes
- 2 tbsp. fresh chives, chopped
- 1 tbsp. fresh parsley, chopped
- 1 tbsp. fresh rosemary, chopped
- 1 tsp. garlic powder
- Salt
- ground black pepper, to taste

DIRECTIONS

1. In a slow cooker, place the cauliflower, garlic, and broth and stir to combine. Cook, covered for about 2 to 3 hours on high.
2. Uncover the slow cooker and through a strainer, drain the cauliflower and garlic, reserving ½ cup of the broth. Transfer the cauliflower into a bowl, and with a potato masher, mash the cauliflower slightly.
3. Add the yogurt, butter, and desired amount of reserved broth and mash until smooth. Add the herbs, garlic powder, salt, and black pepper and stir to combine. Serve warm.

Nutrition: *Calories: 105 Carbs: 5.4g Protein: 5.3g Fat: 7g*

422. MASHED POTATOES

PREPARATION: 15 MIN **COOKING:** 2 H 30 MIN **SERVINGS:** 4

INGREDIENTS

- 6 medium red potatoes, cut into ½-inch thick slices
- ½ cup scallions, chopped
- 1 tbsp. fresh oregano, chopped
- 2 tbsp. extra-virgin olive oil
- 2 tbsp. fresh lemon juice
- 2 oz. feta cheese, crumbled
- ½ cup half-and-half
- ¼ cup fresh parsley, chopped

DIRECTIONS

1. In a slow cooker, place the potatoes, scallions, oregano oil, and lemon juice and mix well. Cook, covered for about 2 hours and 30 minutes on high.
2. Uncover the slow cooker. Add the feta cheese and half-and-half and with a spoon until creamy. Serve warm with the garnishing of parsley.

Nutrition: *Calories: 148 Carbs: 21.9g Protein: 3.8g Fat: 5.7g*

423. MEAT-FREE MUSHROOM STROGANOFF

PREPARATION: 10 MIN **COOKING:** 5 H **SERVINGS:** 3

INGREDIENTS

- 1¼ lb. fresh mushrooms, halved
- 1 onion, sliced thinly
- 3 garlic cloves, minced
- 2 tsp. smoked paprika
- 1 cup vegetable broth
- 1 tbsp. sour cream
- Salt
- ground black pepper
- 4 tbsp. fresh parsley, chopped

DIRECTIONS

1. In a slow cooker, place the mushrooms, onion, garlic, paprika, and broth and stir to combine. Set the slow cooker on high and cook, covered for about 4 hours.
2. Uncover the slow cooker and stir in the sour cream, salt, and black pepper. Serve with the garnishing of parsley

Nutrition: *Calories: 87 Carbs: 12.2g Protein: 8.6g Fat:2.1g*

---

424. VEGGIES RATATOUILLE

PREPARATION: 15 MIN **COOKING:** 6 H **SERVINGS:** 4

INGREDIENTS

- 1 cup fresh basil
- 3 garlic cloves, minced
- 1/3 cup olive oil
- 2 tbsp. white wine vinegar
- 2 tbsp. fresh lemon juice
- 2 tbsp. tomato paste
- Salt, to taste
- 2 medium zucchinis, cut into small chunks
- 2 medium summer squash, cut into small chunks
- 1 small eggplant, cut into small chunks
- 1 large white onion, cut into small chunks
- 2 cup cherry tomatoes

DIRECTIONS

1. In a food processor, add the basil, garlic, oil, vinegar, lemon juice, tomato paste, salt, and pulse until smooth.
2. Put all the vegetables and top with the pureed mixture evenly in the bottom of a slow cooker. Cook, covered for about 5-6 hours on low. Serve hot.

Nutrition: *Calories: 125 Carbs: 11.5g Protein: 2.7g Fat: 8.9g*

425. COLORFUL VEGGIE COMBO

PREPARATION: 15 MIN   **COOKING:** 3 H   **SERVINGS:** 4

INGREDIENTS

- 1 tbsp. olive oil
- 1 lb. eggplant, peeled and cut into 1-inch cubes
- 1 small zucchini, chopped
- 1 small yellow squash, chopped
- 1 small orange bell pepper, seeded and chopped
- 1 small yellow bell pepper, seeded and chopped
- 1 large red onion, chopped
- 4 plum tomatoes, chopped
- 4 garlic cloves, minced
- 2 tsp. dried basil
- Salt
- ground black pepper, to taste
- 4 oz. feta cheese, crumbled

DIRECTIONS

1. In a slow cooker, place all the ingredients except for cheese and stir to combine. Cook, covered for about 3 hours on high. Serve hot with the topping of feta cheese.

Nutrition: Calories: 203 Carbs: 23.6g Protein: 8.1g Fat: 190.3

426. FRIDAY DINNER VEGGIE MEAL

PREPARATION: 15 MIN   **COOKING:** 4 H   **SERVINGS:** 4

INGREDIENTS

- 2 cans cannellini beans, rinsed and drained
- 1 can tomatoes (diced) with basil, garlic, and oregano
- 1 cup zucchini, chopped
- 1 cup red bell pepper, chopped
- ½ cup Kalamata olives pitted and halved
- 2 garlic cloves, minced
- ¼ cup fresh parsley, chopped
- Freshly ground black pepper, to taste
- 2 tbsp. balsamic vinegar
- 2 tbsp. fresh lemon juice
- 1 cup vegetable broth
- ¼ cup feta cheese, crumbled

DIRECTIONS

1. In a slow cooker, place all the ingredients except for cheese and stir to combine. Cook, covered for about 4 hours on low. Serve hot with the topping of feta cheese.

Nutrition: Calories: 181 Carbs: 27.1g Protein: 10.4g Fat: 3g

427. SPICY CHICKPEAS

PREPARATION: 15 MIN **COOKING:** 6 H **SERVINGS:** 4

INGREDIENTS

- 8 oz. dried chickpeas, soaked overnight and drained
- ½ cup extra-virgin olive oil
- 2 onions, chopped
- 1 (28-oz.) can crushed tomatoes
- 2 carrots, peeled and chopped
- 2 medium potatoes, chopped
- 3 garlic cloves, minced
- ½ bunch fresh cilantro stemmed and chopped
- ½ bunch fresh parsley stemmed and chopped
- ½ tsp. ground turmeric
- ½ tsp. paprika
- ½ tsp. ground cumin
- ¼ tsp. ground coriander
- ¼ tsp. ground cinnamon
- ¼ tsp. curry powder
- ¼ tsp. red pepper flakes, crushed
- Salt
- ground black pepper, to taste
- 1 tbsp. honey
- 3 cups of water

DIRECTIONS

1. In a bowl, mix butter with breadcrumbs and parsley, stir well, and leave aside. In your blender, mix basil with oil, parmesan, garlic, and lemon juice and pulse well.
2. Stuff mushrooms with this mix, pour the tomato sauce on top, sprinkle breadcrumbs mix at the end, and cook in the slow cooker on low for 5 hours. Arrange mushrooms on a platter and serve.

Nutrition: *Calories: 51 Fat: 1.1g Carbs: 9g Protein: 2.2g*

428. MEATLESS DINNER MEAL

PREPARATION: 15 MIN **COOKING:** 4 H 5 MIN **SERVINGS:** 4

INGREDIENTS

- 1 tbsp. olive oil
- 1 sweet onion, sliced thinly
- 3 garlic cloves, minced
- 30 oz. canned chickpeas, rinsed and drained
- 1 zucchini, chopped
- 1 cup roasted red peppers, chopped
- 1 cup olives, pitted
- 1 cup vegetable broth
- 1 tbsp. capers
- 1 tsp. dried rosemary
- 1 tsp. dried oregano
- 1 tsp. dried thyme
- 1 bay leaf
- Salt
- ground black pepper

DIRECTIONS

1. Heat-up oil over medium-high heat in a skillet and sauté the onions and garlic for about 4-5 minutes. Transfer the onion into the cooker with remaining ingredients and stir to combine.
2. Set the slow cooker on low and cook, covered for about 4 hours. Serve hot.

Nutrition: *Calories: 248 Carbs: 39.6g Protein: 9.3g Fat: 6.9g*

429. ITALIAN VEGGIE DINNER CASSEROLE

PREPARATION: 15 MIN **COOKING:** 8 H 20 MIN **SERVINGS:** 4

INGREDIENTS

- 1 can chickpeas, rinsed and drained
- 3 medium carrots, peeled and sliced
- 1 medium onion, chopped
- 1 can diced tomatoes with juice
- 2 garlic cloves, chopped finely
- 1 can Italian-style tomato paste
- 1 cup of water
- 2 tsp. sugar
- 1 tsp. Italian seasoning
- Salt
- ground black pepper, to taste
- 1½ cup frozen cut green beans, thawed
- 1 cup uncooked elbow macaroni
- ½ cup Parmesan cheese, shredded

DIRECTIONS

1. Put all the ingredients except for green beans, macaroni, and parmesan cheese and stir to combine in a slow cooker.
2. Set the slow cooker on low and cook, covered for about 6-8 hours. Uncover the slow cooker and stir in the green beans and macaroni.
3. Cook, covered for about 20 minutes on high. Top with cheese and serve hot.

Nutrition: *Calories: 506 Carbs: 87.1g Protein: 25.7g Fat: 8.4g*

430. FAMILIAR MEDITERRANEAN DISH

PREPARATION: 15 MIN **COOKING:** 4 H **SERVINGS:** 4

INGREDIENTS

- 2¼ cup unsalted vegetable broth
- 1½ cup uncooked quinoa, rinsed
- 1 (15½-oz.) can chickpeas, drained and rinsed
- 1 cup red onions, sliced
- 2 garlic cloves, minced
- 2½ tbsp. olive oil
- Salt, to taste
- 2 tsp. fresh lemon juice
- ½ cup roasted red bell peppers, drained and chopped
- 4 cup fresh baby arugula
- 12 kalamata olives, pitted and halved lengthwise
- 2 oz. feta cheese, crumbled
- 2 tbsp. fresh oregano, chopped

DIRECTIONS

1. In a slow cooker, place the broth, quinoa, chickpeas, onions, garlic, 1½ tsp. of the oil, and salt and stir to combine. Set the slow cooker on low and cook, covered for about 3-4 hours.
2. Meanwhile, in a bowl, add the lemon juice, remaining oil, and salt and mix well. Uncover the slow cooker and with a fork, fluff the quinoa mixture.
3. In the slow cooker, add the olive oil mixture, bell peppers, and arugula and gently combine. Over the pot for about 5 minutes before serving. Garnish with the olives, feta cheese, and oregano and serve.

Nutrition: *Calories: 536 Carbs: 78.5g Protein: 23.2g Fat: 16.1g*

431. ARTICHOKE PASTA

PREPARATION: 15 MIN **COOKING:** 8 H **SERVINGS:** 4

INGREDIENTS

- 3 cans diced tomatoes with basil, oregano, and garlic
- 2 cans artichoke hearts, drained and quartered
- 6 garlic cloves, minced
- ½ cup whipping cream
- 12 oz. dried fettuccine pasta
- ¼ cup pimiento-stuffed green olives
- ¼ cup feta cheese, crumbled

DIRECTIONS

1. Drain the juices from two of the cans of diced tomatoes. In a greased slow cooker, place the drained and undrained tomatoes alongside the artichoke hearts and garlic and mix well.
2. Set the slow cooker on low and cook, covered for about 6-8 hours. In a large pan of salted boiling water, cook the pasta for about 8-10 minutes or according to the package's directions.
3. Drain, then rinse under cold running water the pasta. Uncover the slow cooker and stir in the whipping cream.
4. Divide the pasta onto serving plates and top with artichoke sauce. Garnish with olives and cheese and serve.

Nutrition: *Calories: 479 Carbs: 82.2g Protein: 20.8g Fat: 10.4g*

432. VEGGIE LASAGNA

PREPARATION: 15 MIN **COOKING:** 2 H **SERVINGS:** 4

INGREDIENTS

- 1 package baby spinach, chopped roughly
- 3 large portobello mushroom caps, sliced thinly
- 1 small zucchini, sliced thinly
- 1 container part-skim ricotta cheese
- 1 large egg
- 1 can diced tomatoes
- 1 can of crushed tomatoes
- 3 garlic cloves, minced
- Pinch of red pepper flakes, crushed
- 15 uncooked whole-wheat lasagna noodles
- 3 cups part-skim mozzarella, shredded and divided

DIRECTIONS

1. Put the spinach, zucchini, ricotta cheese, and egg and mix well in a large bowl. In another bowl, add both cans of tomatoes with juice, garlic, and red pepper flakes and mix well.
2. In the bottom of a generously greased slow cooker, place about 1½ cup of the tomato mixture evenly. Place 5 lasagna noodles over the tomato mixture, overlapping them slightly and breaking them to fit in the pot.
3. Put half of the ricotta batter over the noodles. Now, place about 1½ cup of the tomato mixture and sprinkle with 1 cup of the mozzarella. Repeat the layers twice.
4. Cook, covered for about 2 hours on high. Uncover the slow cooker and sprinkle with the remaining mozzarella cheese. Immediately cover the cooker for about 10 minutes before serving.

Nutrition: *Calories: 289 Carbs: 37.1g Protein: 18.8g Fat: 8.2g*

433. HOMEMADE HUMMUS

PREPARATION: 15 MIN **COOKING:** 4 H **SERVINGS:** 4

INGREDIENTS

- 1½ cup dried chickpeas, rinsed
- 2-3 cups of water
- 2 garlic cloves, peeled
- ¼ cup olive oil
- 2 tbsp. fresh lemon juice
- ¼ cup tahini

DIRECTIONS

1. In a slow cooker, place the chickpeas and water. Set the slow cooker on high and cook, covered for about 4 hours.
2. Uncover the slow cooker, drain the chickpeas, reserve about 1/3 cup of the cooking liquid cooking and remaining ingredients, and pulse until smooth. Transfer the hummus into a bowl and refrigerator before serving.

Nutrition: *Calories: 190 Carbs: 19.7g Protein: 6.9g Fat: 10.1g*

434. BARBECUE KABOCHA SQUASH

PREPARATION: 15 MIN **COOKING:** 6-8 H **SERVINGS:** 2

INGREDIENTS

- 1 teaspoon extra-virgin olive oil
- ½ kabocha squash, seeded, peeled, and cut into 2-by-1-inch pieces
- 1 red onion, halved and sliced thin
- 1 small sweet potato, cut into 1-inch pieces
- 1 cup tomato sauce
- ½ cup low-sodium vegetable broth
- 1 teaspoon Dijon mustard
- 1 teaspoon smoked paprika
- 1 teaspoon garlic powder
- 1 teaspoon onion powder
- 1 teaspoon maple syrup or honey
- 1/8 teaspoon sea salt

DIRECTIONS

1. Oiled inside of the slow cooker with olive oil. Put the squash, red onion, and sweet potato into the slow cooker.
2. In a small bowl, whisk together the tomato sauce, vegetable broth, mustard, paprika, garlic powder, onion powder, maple syrup, and salt. Pour this mixture over the vegetables.
3. Cover and cook on low within 6 to 8 hours, or until the squash is very tender.

Nutrition: *Calories: 236 Fat: 0g Carbs: 48g Protein: 7g*

435. BRAISED QUINOA, KALE & SUMMER SQUASH

PREPARATION: 10 MIN   **COOKING:** 4 H   **SERVINGS:** 2

INGREDIENTS

- ½ cup quinoa
- ½ cup canned chickpeas drained and rinsed
- 1 cup diced summer squash
- 4 cups fresh kale
- 1 cup canned plum tomatoes, roughly chopped
- 2 cups low-sodium vegetable broth
- 1 tablespoon Italian herb blend
- 1/8 teaspoon sea salt

DIRECTIONS

1. Put all the fixings into the slow cooker, stirring to mix them thoroughly. Cover and cook on low within 4 hours.

Nutrition: *Calories: 342 Fat: 1g Carbs: 56g Protein: 19g*

---

436. ROSEMARY CAULIFLOWER & LENTILS

PREPARATION: 10 MIN   **COOKING:** 8 H   **SERVINGS:** 2

INGREDIENTS

- 1 cup cauliflower florets
- 1 cup lentils
- 1 tablespoon fresh rosemary
- 1 tablespoon roasted garlic
- Zest of 1 lemon
- 1 tablespoon extra-virgin olive oil
- 1/8 teaspoon sea salt
- Freshly ground black pepper
- 3 cups low-sodium vegetable broth
- Juice of 1 lemon
- ¼ cup roughly chopped fresh parsley

DIRECTIONS

1. Put the cauliflower, lentils, rosemary, garlic, lemon zest, and olive oil in the slow cooker. Season with salt and black pepper.
2. Pour the vegetable broth over the cauliflower and lentils. Cover and cook on low within 8 hours. Before serving, drizzle the cauliflower and lentils with lemon juice and sprinkle the parsley over the top.

Nutrition: *Calories: 484 Fat: 2g Carbs: 65g Protein: 34g*

437. MIXED BEAN CHILI

PREPARATION: 10 MIN   **COOKING:** 6-8 H   **SERVINGS:** 2

INGREDIENTS

- 1 (16-ounce) can mixed beans, drained and rinsed
- 1 cup frozen roasted corn kernels, thawed
- 1 cup canned fire-roasted diced tomatoes, undrained
- ½ cup diced onion
- 2 garlic cloves, minced
- 1 teaspoon ground cumin
- 1 teaspoon smoked paprika
- 1 teaspoon dried oregano
- 1/8 teaspoon sea salt

DIRECTIONS

1. Put all the ingredients in the slow cooker. Give them a quick stir to combine. Cover and cook on low within 6 to 8 hours. Serve.

Nutrition: *Calories: 257 Fat: 0g Carbs: 58g Protein: 13g*

---

438. CURRIED SWEET POTATOES WITH BROCCOLI & CASHEWS

PREPARATION: 15 MIN   **COOKING:** 6-8 H   **SERVINGS:** 2

INGREDIENTS

- 2 medium sweet potatoes, cut into 1-inch pieces
- 1 cup broccoli florets
- ½ cup diced onions
- 1 cup light coconut milk
- 1 teaspoon minced fresh ginger
- 1 teaspoon minced garlic
- Pinch red pepper flakes
- 1 tablespoon curry powder
- 1 teaspoon garam masala
- ¼ cup toasted cashews

DIRECTIONS

1. Put the sweet potatoes, broccoli, and onions into the slow cooker. Mix the coconut milk, ginger, garlic, red pepper flakes, curry powder, and garam masala in a small bowl. Pour this mixture over the vegetables.
2. Cover and cook on low within 6 to 8 hours until the vegetables are very tender but not falling apart. Just before serving, add the cashews and stir thoroughly.

Nutrition: *Calories: 582 Fat: 27g Carbs: 60g Protein: 10g*

439. MOROCCAN-STYLE CHICKPEAS WITH CHARD

PREPARATION: 15 MIN   **COOKING:** 8 H   **SERVINGS:** 2

INGREDIENTS

- ½ bunch Swiss chard stems diced and leaves roughly chopped
- 1 (16-ounce) can chickpeas, drained and rinsed
- ½ cup diced onion
- ½ cup diced carrots
- ¼ cup diced dried apricots
- 2 tablespoons roughly chopped preserved lemons (optional)
- 1 tablespoon tomato paste
- 1 teaspoon minced fresh ginger
- ¼ teaspoon red pepper flakes
- ½ teaspoon smoked paprika
- ½ teaspoon ground cinnamon
- ¼ teaspoon ground cumin
- 1/8 teaspoon sea salt

DIRECTIONS

1. Put all the fixings into the slow cooker. Stir everything together thoroughly. Cover and cook on low within 8 hours. Serve.

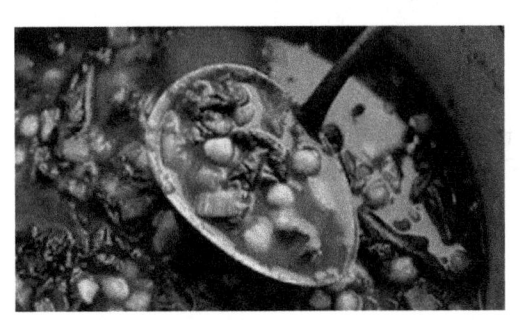

Nutrition: *Calories: 84 Fat: 0g Carbs: 17g Protein: 4g*

440. SPINACH & BLACK BEAN ENCHILADA PIE

PREPARATION: 15 MIN   **COOKING:** 6-8 H   **SERVINGS:** 2

INGREDIENTS

- 1 (15-ounce) can black beans, drained and rinsed
- ¼ cup low-fat cream cheese
- ¼ cup low-fat Cheddar cheese
- ½ cup minced onion
- 1 teaspoon minced garlic
- 1 teaspoon ground cumin
- 1 teaspoon smoked paprika
- 2 cups shredded fresh spinach
- 1 teaspoon extra-virgin olive oil
- 1 cup enchilada sauce, divided
- 4 corn tortillas
- ¼ cup fresh cilantro, for garnish

DIRECTIONS

1. Mix the beans, cream cheese, Cheddar cheese, onion, garlic, cumin, paprika, and spinach in a large bowl. Oiled inside of the slow cooker with olive oil.
2. Pour ¼ cup of enchilada sauce into the slow, spreading it across the bottom. Place one corn tortilla on top of the sauce, then top the tortilla with one-third of the black bean and spinach mixture.
3. Top this with a second corn tortilla, and then slather it with ¼ cup of enchilada sauce. Repeat this layering, finishing with a corn tortilla and the last ¼ cup of enchilada sauce.
4. Cover and cook on low within 6 to 8 hours. Garnish with the cilantro just before

Nutrition: *Calories: 373 Fat: 10g Carbs: 42g Protein: 13g*

441. SPINACH, MUSHROOM & SWISS CHEESE CRUSTLESS QUICHE

PREPARATION: 10 MIN   **COOKING:** 8 H   **SERVINGS:** 2

INGREDIENTS

- 1 teaspoon butter, at room temperature, or extra-virgin olive oil
- 4 eggs
- 1 teaspoon fresh thyme
- 1/8 teaspoon sea salt
- Freshly ground black pepper
- 2 slices whole-grain bread, crusts removed, cut into 1-inch cubes
- ½ cup diced button mushrooms
- 2 tablespoons minced onion
- 1 cup shredded spinach
- ½ cup shredded Swiss cheese

DIRECTIONS

1. Oiled inside of the slow cooker with the butter. In a small bowl, whisk together the eggs, thyme, salt, and a few black pepper grinds.
2. Put the bread, mushrooms, onions, spinach, and cheese in the slow cooker. Pour the egg mixture over the top and stir gently to combine. Cover and cook on low within 8 hours or overnight.

Nutrition: *Calories: 348 Saturated Fat: 9g Carbs: 21g Protein: 24g*

---

442. SEITAN TIKKA MASALA

PREPARATION: 10 MIN   **COOKING:** 6 H   **SERVINGS:** 2

INGREDIENTS

- 8 oz. seitan, cut into bite-size pieces
- 1 cup chopped green beans
- 1 cup diced onion
- 1 cup fire-roasted tomatoes, drained
- 1 teaspoon ground coriander
- 1 teaspoon ground cumin
- 1 teaspoon smoked paprika
- 1/8 teaspoon red pepper flakes
- 1 teaspoon minced fresh ginger
- 1 cup low-sodium vegetable broth
- 2 tablespoons coconut cream
- ¼ cup minced fresh cilantro, for garnish

DIRECTIONS

1. Put the seitan, green beans, onion, tomatoes, coriander, cumin, paprika, red pepper flakes, ginger, and vegetable broth in the slow cooker. Gently stir the ingredients together to combine.
2. Cover and cook on low within 6 hours. Allow the dish to rest, uncovered, for 10 minutes, then stir in the coconut cream and garnish the dish with the cilantro.

Nutrition: *Calories: 245 Fat: 3g Carbs: 24g Protein: 4g*

443. BUTTER SEITAN & CHICKPEAS

PREPARATION: 15 MIN **COOKING:** 6-8 H **SERVINGS:** 2

INGREDIENTS

- 1 teaspoon extra-virgin olive oil
- 8 oz. seitan, cut into bite-size pieces
- 1 (15-ounce) can chickpeas, drained and rinsed
- ½ cup minced onion
- 1 teaspoon minced garlic
- 2 tablespoons tomato paste
- 1 teaspoon minced fresh ginger
- ½ teaspoon garam masala
- 1 teaspoon curry powder
- Pinch red pepper flakes
- ½ teaspoon of sea salt
- 1 cup light coconut milk

Nutrition: *Calories: 302 Fat: 12g Carbs: 17g Protein: 4g*

DIRECTIONS

1. Oiled inside of the slow cooker with olive oil. Put all the fixings into the slow cooker and stir to mix thoroughly. Cover and cook on low within 6 to 8 hours.

444. TEMPEH SHEPHERD'S PIE

PREPARATION: 10 MIN **COOKING:** 8 H **SERVINGS:** 2

INGREDIENTS

- 1 cup frozen peas, thawed
- 1 cup diced carrots
- ½ cup minced onions
- 8 oz. tempeh
- 1/8 teaspoon sea salt
- Freshly ground black pepper
- 1½ cups prepared mashed potatoes
- 2 tablespoons shredded sharp Cheddar cheese

DIRECTIONS

1. Put the peas, carrots, onions, and tempeh in the slow cooker and gently stir to combine. Season the batter with the salt plus black pepper.
2. Spread the prepared mashed potatoes over the tempeh and vegetable mixture. Cover and cook on low within 8 hours. Sprinkle with the cheese just before serving.

Nutrition: *Calories: 476 Fat: 6g Carbs: 53g Protein: 32g*

445. TEMPEH-STUFFED BELL PEPPERS

PREPARATION: 10 MIN   **COOKING:** 6-8 H   **SERVINGS:** 2

INGREDIENTS

- 1 teaspoon extra-virgin olive oil
- 8 oz. tempeh, crumbled
- 1 cup frozen corn kernels, thawed
- ¼ cup minced onions
- 1 teaspoon minced garlic
- 1 teaspoon ground cumin
- 1 teaspoon smoked paprika
- 2 tablespoons pepper Jack cheese
- 1/8 teaspoon sea salt
- 4 narrow red bell peppers

DIRECTIONS

1. Oiled inside of the slow cooker with olive oil. In a medium bowl, combine the tempeh, corn, onions, garlic, cumin, paprika, cheese, and salt.
2. Cut the tops off each of the peppers and set the tops aside. Scoop out and discard the seeds and membranes from inside each pepper. Divide the tempeh filling among the peppers. Return the tops to each of the peppers.
3. Nestle the peppers into the slow cooker. Cover and cook on low within 6 to 8 hours, until the peppers are very tender.

Nutrition: *Calories: 422 Fat: 5g Carbs: 44g Protein: 28g*

446. TOFU RED CURRY WITH GREEN BEANS

PREPARATION: 10 MIN   **COOKING:** 6 H   **SERVINGS:** 2

INGREDIENTS

- 1 teaspoon extra-virgin olive oil
- 16 oz firm tofu, cut into 1-inch pieces
- 2 cups chopped green beans
- ½ red onion halved and sliced thin
- 1 plum tomato, diced
- 1 teaspoon minced fresh ginger
- 1 teaspoon minced garlic
- 2 teaspoons Thai red curry paste
- 1 cup of coconut milk
- 1 cup low-sodium vegetable broth

DIRECTIONS

1. 1. Oiled inside of the slow cooker with olive oil. Put all the ingredients into the slow cooker, and stir gently. Cover and cook on low within 6 hours.

Nutrition: *Calories: 538 Fat: 28g Carbs: 25g Protein: 25g*

447. TOFU STIR-FRY

PREPARATION: 10 MIN　　**COOKING:** 4-6 H　　**SERVINGS:** 2

INGREDIENTS

- 1 teaspoon extra-virgin olive oil
- ½ cup of brown rice
- 1 cup of water
- Pinch sea salt
- 1 (16-ounce) block tofu, drained and cut into 1-inch pieces
- 1 green bell pepper, cored and cut into long strips
- ½ onion halved and thinly sliced
- 1 cup chopped green beans, cut into 1-inch pieces
- 2 carrots, cut into ½-inch dice
- 2 tablespoons low-sodium soy sauce
- 1 tablespoon hoisin sauce
- 1 tablespoon freshly squeezed lime juice
- 1 teaspoon minced garlic
- Pinch red pepper flakes

DIRECTIONS

1. Oiled inside of the slow cooker with olive oil. Put the brown rice, water, and salt in the slow cooker and gently stir, so all the rice grains are submerged. Put the tofu, bell pepper, onion, green beans, and carrots over the rice.
2. In a measuring cup or glass jar, whisk together the soy sauce, hoisin sauce, lime juice, garlic, and red pepper flakes. Pour this batter over the tofu and vegetables.
3. Cover and cook on low for 4 to 6 hours, until the rice, has soaked up all the liquid and the vegetables are tender.

Nutrition: *Calories: 456 Fat: 3g Carbs: 63g Protein: 26g*

448. SPICY PEANUT RICE BAKE

PREPARATION: 10 MIN　　**COOKING:** 6-8 H　　**SERVINGS:** 2

INGREDIENTS

- 1 teaspoon extra-virgin olive oil
- ½ cup of brown rice
- 3 cups low-sodium vegetable broth, divided
- 4 collard leaves, ribs removed, chopped into thin ribbons
- ½ cup minced red onion
- 1 tablespoon minced ginger
- 2 tablespoons tomato paste
- ¼ cup unsalted creamy peanut butter
- 1 teaspoon Sriracha
- 1/8 teaspoon sea salt
- ¼ cup roughly chopped cilantro, for garnish
- Lime wedges, for garnish
- 2 tablespoons roasted peanuts, roughly chopped, for garnish

DIRECTIONS

1. 1. Oiled inside of the slow cooker with olive oil. Put the rice, 2 cups of broth, collard greens, and onion in the slow cooker.
2. 2.In a medium bowl, whisk together the remaining 1 cup of broth, ginger, tomato paste, peanut butter, Sriracha, and salt. Stir this mixture into the slow cooker.
3. 3.Cover and cook on low within 6 to 8 hours. Garnish each serving with fresh cilantro, a lime wedge, and the peanuts. Serve.

Nutrition: *Calories: 554 Fat: 13g Carbs: 59g Protein: 24g*

449. SQUASH AND ZUCCHINI CASSEROLE

PREPARATION: 10 MIN **COOKING:** 6 H **SERVINGS:** 4

INGREDIENTS

- 2 cups yellow squash, quartered and sliced
- 2 cups zucchini, quartered and sliced
- 1/4 cup Parmesan cheese, grated
- 1/4 cup butter, cut into pieces
- 1 tsp garlic powder
- 1 tsp Italian seasoning
- 1/4 tsp pepper
- 1/2 tsp sea salt

DIRECTIONS

1. Add sliced yellow squash and zucchini to a slow cooker. Sprinkle with garlic powder, Italian seasoning, pepper, and salt.
2. Top with grated cheese and butter. Cover with the lid and cook on low for 6 hours. Serve and enjoy.

Nutrition: *Calories: 107 Fat: 9.5g Carbs: 2.5g Protein: 2.6g*

---

450. ALMOND GREEN BEANS

PREPARATION: 10 MIN **COOKING:** 2H **SERVINGS:** 4

INGREDIENTS

- 1 lb. green beans, rinsed and trimmed
- 1/2 cup almonds, sliced and toasted
- 1 cup vegetable stock
- 1/4 cup butter, melted
- 6 oz onion, sliced
- 1 tbsp olive oil
- 1/4 tsp pepper
- 1/2 tsp salt

DIRECTIONS

1. Heat-up olive oil in a pan over medium heat. Add onion to the pan and sauté until softened. Transfer sautéed onion to a slow cooker.
2. Add remaining ingredients except for almonds to the slow cooker and stir well. Cover and cook on low within 3 hours. Top with toasted almonds and serve.

Nutrition: *Calories: 253 Fat: 21.6g Carbs: 14.5g Protein: 5.1g*

451. RANCH MUSHROOMS

PREPARATION: 10 MIN   **COOKING:** 3 H   **SERVINGS:** 4

INGREDIENTS

- 2 lb. mushrooms, rinsed, pat dry
- 2 packets ranch dressing mix
- 3/4 cup butter, melted
- 1/4 cup fresh parsley, chopped

DIRECTIONS

1. Add all ingredients except parsley to a slow cooker and stir well. Cover and cook on low within 3 hours. Garnish with parsley and serve.

Nutrition: *Calories: 237 Fat: 23.5g Carbs: 5.2g Protein: 5.1g*

---

452. ARTICHOKE SPINACH DIP

PREPARATION: 10 MIN   **COOKING:** 6 H   **SERVINGS:** 4

INGREDIENTS

- 8 oz cream cheese, softened
- 14 oz artichoke hearts, chopped
- 10 oz frozen spinach, thawed and drained
- 1/4 tsp garlic powder
- 2 tbsp water
- 2 cups of cottage cheese
- 1 tsp saltvv

DIRECTIONS

1. Add spinach, cream cheese, cottage cheese, water, and artichoke hearts to a slow cooker and stir well. Season with garlic powder and salt. Cover and cook on low within 6 hours. Stir well and serve.

Nutrition: *Calories: 230 Fat: 14.8g Carbs: 8.9g Protein: 15.7g*

453. TOMATO DIP

PREPARATION: 10 MIN **COOKING:** 1 H **SERVINGS:** 4

INGREDIENTS

- 8 oz cream cheese
- 1/4 cup sun-dried tomatoes
- 1 tbsp mayonnaise
- 3 garlic cloves
- 1/4 tsp white pepper
- 1 tsp pine nuts, toasted
- 3/4 oz fresh basil

DIRECTIONS

1. Add all fixings to a blender and blend until smooth. Pour mixture into a slow cooker. Cover and cook on low for 1 hour. Stir well and serve.

Nutrition: Calories: 47 Fat: 4.5g Carbs: 1g Protein: 1g

454. ITALIAN MUSHROOMS

PREPARATION: 10 MIN **COOKING:** 4 H **SERVINGS:** 4

INGREDIENTS

- 16 oz baby spinach
- 2 garlic cloves, minced
- 1 cup cheddar cheese, shredded
- 3 oz cream cheese

DIRECTIONS

1. Add all fixings to a slow cooker and stir well. Cover and cook on high within 1 hour. Stir well and serve.

Nutrition: Calories: 162 Fat: 15.6g Carbs: 4.8g Protein: 2.8g

455. GARLIC CHEESE SPINACH

PREPARATION: 10 MIN **COOKING:** 1 H **SERVINGS:** 4

INGREDIENTS

- 1 lb. mushrooms, cleaned
- 1 onion, sliced
- 1 packet Italian dressing mix
- 1/2 cup butter, melted

DIRECTIONS

1. Add onion and mushrooms to a slow cooker and mix well. Combine butter and Italian dressing mix and pour over the onion and mushrooms. Cover and cook on low for 4 hours. Serve and enjoy.

Nutrition: Calories: 216 Fat: 17.2g Carbs: 5.6g Protein: 12g

456. DILL CARROTS

PREPARATION: 10 MIN **COOKING:** 2 H **SERVINGS:** 4

INGREDIENTS

- 1 lb. carrots, peeled and cut into round pieces on the diagonal
- 1 tbsp butter
- 1 tbsp fresh dill, minced
- 3 tbsp water

DIRECTIONS

1. Add all fixings to a slow cooker and stir well. Cover and cook on low for 2 hours. Stir well and serve.

Nutrition: *Calories: 49 Fat: 1.9g Carbs: 7.7g Protein: 0.7g*

457. ROSEMARY GREEN BEANS

PREPARATION: 10 MIN **COOKING:** 1 H 30 MIN **SERVINGS:** 4

INGREDIENTS

- 1 lb. green beans, washed and trimmed
- 2 tbsp fresh lemon juice
- 1 tsp fresh thyme, minced
- 2 tbsp water
- 1 tbsp fresh rosemary, minced

DIRECTIONS

1. Add all fixings to a slow cooker and stir well. Cover and cook on low for 1 hour and 30 minutes. Stir well and serve.

Nutrition: *Calories: 40 Fat: 0.4g Carbs: 8.9g Protein: 2.2g*

458. VEGETABLE FAJITAS

PREPARATION: 10 MIN **COOKING:** 3 H 30 MIN **SERVINGS:** 4

INGREDIENTS

- 1 cup cherry tomatoes, halved
- 3 bell peppers, cut into strips
- 1 onion, sliced
- 1 tsp paprika
- 1 tbsp olive oil
- Pepper and salt

DIRECTIONS

1. Add onion, bell peppers, oil, smoked paprika, pepper, and salt to a slow cooker and stir well. Cover and cook on high within 1 hour and 30 minutes. Add cherry tomatoes and cook for 2 hours longer. Stir well and serve.

Nutrition: *Calories: 79 Fat: 3.9g Carbs: 11.4g Protein: 1.7g*

459. ROASTED BROCCOLI

PREPARATION: 10 MIN **COOKING:** 2 H **SERVINGS:** 4

INGREDIENTS

- 2 lb. broccoli florets
- 1 bell pepper, chopped
- 2 tsp olive oil
- Pepper and salt

DIRECTIONS

1. Add all fixings to a slow cooker and stir well to mix. Cover and cook on high for 2 hours. Stir well and serve.

Nutrition: *Calories: 89 Fat: 3.2g Carbs: 13.3g Protein: 7g*

460. TOMATOES, GARLIC AND OKRA

PREPARATION: 10 MIN **COOKING:** 2 H **SERVINGS:** 4

INGREDIENTS

- 1 1/2 cups okra, diced
- 1 small onion, diced
- 2 large tomatoes, diced
- 1 tsp hot sauce
- 2 garlic cloves, minced

DIRECTIONS

1. Add all fixings to a slow cooker and stir well. Cover and cook on low for 2 hours. Stir well and serve.

Nutrition: *Calories: 158 Fat: 4.1g Carbs: 26.3g Protein: 5.9g*

461. CAULIFLOWER RICE

PREPARATION: 10 MIN **COOKING:** 2 H **SERVINGS:** 4

INGREDIENTS

- 4 cups cauliflower, shredded
- 1 cup vegetable stock
- 1 cup of water
- 1 tablespoon cream cheese
- 1 teaspoon dried oregano

DIRECTIONS

1. Put all ingredients in the slow cooker. Close the lid and cook the cauliflower rice on high for 2 hours. Serve.

Nutrition: *Calories: 25 Protein: 0.8g Carbs: 3.9g Fat: 0.8g*

462. SQUASH NOODLES

PREPARATION: 15 MIN **COOKING:** 4 H **SERVINGS:** 4

INGREDIENTS

- 1-pound butternut squash, seeded, halved
- 1 tablespoon vegan butter
- 1 teaspoon salt
- ½ teaspoon garlic powder
- 3 cups of water

DIRECTIONS

1. Pour water into the slow cooker. Add butternut squash and close the lid. Cook the vegetable on high for 4 hours.
2. Then drain water and shred the squash flesh with the fork's help and transfer in the bowl. Add garlic powder, salt, and butter. Mix the squash noodles.

Nutrition: *Calories: 78 Protein: 1.2g Carbs: 13.5g Fat: 3g*

463. THYME TOMATOES

PREPARATION: 15 MIN   **COOKING:** 5 H   **SERVINGS:** 4

INGREDIENTS

- 1-pound tomatoes, sliced
- 1 tablespoon dried thyme
- 1 teaspoon salt
- 2 tablespoons olive oil
- 1 tablespoon apple cider vinegar
- ½ cup of water

DIRECTIONS

1. Put all fixings in the slow cooker and close the lid. Cook the tomatoes on low for 5 hours. Serve.

Nutrition: *Calories: 83 Protein: 1.1g Carbs: 4.9g Fat: 7.3g*

464. QUINOA DOLMA

PREPARATION: 15 MIN   **COOKING:** 4 H   **SERVINGS:** 4

INGREDIENTS

- 6 sweet peppers, seeded
- 1 cup quinoa, cooked
- ½ cup corn kernels, cooked
- 1 teaspoon chili flakes
- 1 cup of water
- ½ cup tomato juice

DIRECTIONS

1. Mix quinoa with corn kernels and chili flakes. Fill the sweet peppers with quinoa mixture and put them in the slow cooker. Add water and tomato juice. Close the lid and cook the peppers on high for 3 hours. Serve.

Nutrition: *Calories: 158 Fat: 4.1g Carbs: 26.3g Protein: 5.9g*

465. CREAMY PUREE

PREPARATION: 15 MIN **COOKING:** 2 H 30 MIN **SERVINGS:** 4

INGREDIENTS

- 3 cups cauliflower, roughly chopped
- ½ cup potato, chopped
- 3 oz Provolone, grated
- 2 tablespoons chives, chopped
- 1 cup milk
- ½ cup of water
- 1 teaspoon chili powder

DIRECTIONS

1. Pour water and milk into the slow cooker. Add cauliflower, potato, chives, and chili powder. Close the lid and cook the mixture on high for 2 hours. Then sprinkle the hash with provolone cheese and cook the meal on high for 30 minutes.

Nutrition: *Calories: 134 Protein: 9.3g Carbs: 9.5g Fat: 7.1g*

---

467. CHEESY CORN

PREPARATION: 5 MIN **COOKING:** 5 H **SERVINGS:** 4

INGREDIENTS

- 4 cups corn kernels
- ½ cup Cheddar cheese, shredded
- 1 tablespoon vegan butter
- 1 teaspoon ground black pepper
- 1 teaspoon salt
- 2 cups of water

DIRECTIONS

1. Mix corn kernels with ground black pepper, butter, salt, and cheese. Transfer the batter to your slow cooker and add water. Close the lid and cook the meal on low for 5 hours. Serve.

Nutrition: *Calories: 173 Protein: 6.9g Carbs: 23.6g Fat: 7.5g*

468. SHREDDED CABBAGE SAUTÉ

PREPARATION: 10 MIN **COOKING:** 6 H **SERVINGS:** 4

INGREDIENTS

- 3 cups white cabbage, shredded
- 1 cup tomato juice
- 1 teaspoon salt
- 1 teaspoon sugar
- 1 teaspoon dried oregano
- 3 tablespoons olive oil
- 1 cup of water

DIRECTIONS

1. Put all ingredients in the slow cooker. Carefully mix all ingredients with the help of the spoon and close the lid. Cook the cabbage sauté for 6 hours on low. Serve.

Nutrition: *Calories: 118 Protein: 1.2g Carbs: 6.9g Fat: 10.6g*

---

469. RANCH BROCCOLI

PREPARATION: 15 MIN **COOKING:** 1 H 30 **SERVINGS:** 4

INGREDIENTS

- 3 cups broccoli
- 1 teaspoon chili flakes
- 2 tablespoons ranch dressing
- 2 cups of water

DIRECTIONS

1. Put the broccoli in the slow cooker. Add water and close the lid. Cook the broccoli on high for 1 hour and 30 minutes.
2. Then drain water and transfer the broccoli to the bowl. Sprinkle it with chili flakes and ranch dressing. Shake the meal gently.

Nutrition: *Calories: 34 Protein: 2.7g Carbs: 6.6g Fat: 0.3g*

---

470. CHEDDAR MUSHROOMS

PREPARATION: 10 MIN **COOKING:** 6 H **SERVINGS:** 4

INGREDIENTS

- 4 cups cremini mushrooms, sliced
- 1 teaspoon dried oregano
- 1 teaspoon ground black pepper
- ½ teaspoon salt
- 1 cup Cheddar cheese, shredded
- 1 cup heavy cream
- 1 cup of water

DIRECTIONS

1. Pour water and heavy cream into the slow cooker. Add salt, ground black pepper, and dried oregano. Then add sliced mushrooms and cheddar cheese.
2. Cook the meal on low for 6 hours. When the mushrooms are cooked, gently stir them and transfer them to the serving plates.

Nutrition: *Calories: 239 Protein: 9.6g Carbs: 4.8g Fat: 20.6g*

471. PAPRIKA BABY CARROT

PREPARATION: 10 MIN **COOKING:** 2 H 30 MIN **SERVINGS:** 2

INGREDIENTS

- 1 tablespoon ground paprika
- 2 cups baby carrot
- 1 teaspoon cumin seeds
- 1 cup of water
- 1 teaspoon vegan butter

DIRECTIONS

1. Pour water into the slow cooker. Add baby carrot, cumin seeds, and ground paprika. Close the lid and cook the carrot on high for 2 hours and 30 minutes. Then drain water, add butter, and shake the vegetables. Serve.

Nutrition: *Calories: 60 Protein: 1.6g Carbs: 8.6g Fat: 2.7g*

472. BUTTER ASPARAGUS

PREPARATION: 15 MIN **COOKING:** 5 H **SERVINGS:** 4

INGREDIENTS

- 1-pound asparagus
- 2 tablespoons vegan butter
- 1 teaspoon ground black pepper
- 1 cup vegetable stock

DIRECTIONS

1. Pour the vegetable stock into the slow cooker. Chop the asparagus roughly and add to the slow cooker. Close the lid and cook the asparagus for 5 hours on low.
2. Then drain water and transfer the asparagus to the bowl. Sprinkle it with ground black pepper and butter.

Nutrition: *Calories: 77 Protein: 2.8g Carbs: 4.9g Fat: 6.1g*

473. JALAPENO CORN

PREPARATION: 10 MIN **COOKING:** 5 H **SERVINGS:** 4

INGREDIENTS

- 1 cup heavy cream
- ½ cup Monterey Jack cheese, shredded
- 1-pound corn kernels
- 3 jalapenos, minced
- 1 teaspoon vegan butter
- 1 tablespoon dried dill

DIRECTIONS

1. Pour heavy cream into the slow cooker. Add Monterey Jack cheese, corn kernels, minced jalapeno, butter, and dried dill. Cook the corn on low for 5 hours. Serve.

Nutrition: *Calories: 203 Protein: 5.6g Carbs: 9.3g Fat: 16.9g*

474. MASHED TURNIPS

PREPARATION: 10 MIN　　**COOKING:** 7 H　　**SERVINGS:** 4

INGREDIENTS

- 3-pounds turnip, chopped
- 3 cups of water
- 1 tablespoon vegan butter
- 1 tablespoon chives, chopped
- 2 oz Parmesan, grated

DIRECTIONS

1. Put turnips in the slow cooker. Add water and cook the vegetables on low for 7 hours. Then drain water and mash the turnips.
2. Add chives, butter, and parmesan. Carefully stir the mixture until butter and parmesan are melted. Then add chives. Remix the mashed turnips.

Nutrition: *Calories: 162 Protein: 8.6g Carbs: 15.1g Fat: 8.1g*

475. CRANBERRY, APPLE, AND SQUASH DISH

PREPARATION: 15 MIN　　**COOKING:** 4 H　　**SERVINGS:** 2

INGREDIENTS

- ¾ pound butternut squash, cubed and peeled
- 1 apple, cored, peeled, and chopped
- 2 tbsp. cranberries, dried
- ¼ diced onion
- ½ tsp. cinnamon
- ¼ tsp. nutmeg

DIRECTIONS

1. First, add the squash, apple, cranberries, onion, cinnamon, and nutmeg to the slow cooker. Stir well. Cook on high within 4 hours. Stir well, and serve warm.

Nutrition: *Calories: 72 Carbs: 17g Fat: 0g Protein: 0g*

476. VEGETARIAN CURRY WITH INDIAN SPICES

PREPARATION: 15 MIN **COOKING:** 5 H **SERVINGS:** 4

INGREDIENTS

- 2 potatoes, cubed
- 2 tbsp curry powder
- ½ red pepper, sliced
- 1 tbsp flour
- ½ ounce dried onion soup mix
- 1 tsp chili powder
- ¼ tsp red pepper flakes
- ¼ tsp cayenne pepper
- ½ sliced green pepper
- 7 oz. coconut cream, unsweetened
- 1 cup sliced carrots
- 2 tbsp fresh cilantro, chopped, for garnish

DIRECTIONS

1. Add the potatoes to the slow cooker. Stir together the flour, curry powder, chili powder, red pepper flakes, and cayenne pepper in a medium-sized bowl. Sprinkle this spice mixture over the potatoes. Stir well.
2. Add the peppers, onion soup mix, and coconut cream to the slow cooker. Stir well. Cover the slow cooker. Cook the mixture on low within 4 hours. As the mixture cooks, add water to keep the mix moist.
3. Add the carrots to the mixture—Cook for an additional 60 minutes. Add the cilantro for garnish, and serve the meal warm.

Nutrition: *Calories: 300 Carbs: 36g Fat: 6g Protein: 21g*

477. PARSNIP, TURNIP, AND CARROT TAGINE

PREPARATION: 15 MIN **COOKING:** 9 H **SERVINGS:** 4

INGREDIENTS

- ½ pound peeled and diced parsnips
- 1 diced onion
- ½ pound peeled and diced turnips
- ½ pound diced and peeled carrots
- 3 chopped apricots, dried
- ½ tsp. turmeric
- 2 chopped prunes
- ¼ tsp. ginger
- ¼ tsp. cinnamon
- 1 tsp. dried parsley
- 1 tsp. dried cilantro
- 7 oz. vegetable broth

DIRECTIONS

1. Add the parsnips, onion, turnips, carrots, apricots, turmeric, prunes, ginger, cinnamon, parsley, cilantro, and the broth to the slow cooker. Cook the mixture on low for 9 hours. Serve warm, and enjoy.

Nutrition: *Calories: 246 Carbs: 8g Fat: 2g Protein: 1g*

478. SPINACH AND PUMPKIN CHILI

PREPARATION: 15 MIN   **COOKING:** 4 H 30 MIN   **SERVINGS:** 4

INGREDIENTS

- 14 oz. diced tomatoes
- 7 oz. pure pumpkin puree
- 1/3 cup vegetable juice
- 1/3 cup chopped okra
- 1/3 cup chopped broccoli
- 1 tbsp. sugar
- ½ diced zucchini
- ½ diced onion
- 2 tsp. pumpkin pie spice
- ½ tsp. chili powder
- ½ tsp. salt
- 9 oz. fava beans
- 1 cup chopped spinach
- 2 tsp. white vinegar

DIRECTIONS

1. Add the tomatoes, pumpkin, okra, vegetable juice, sugar, broccoli, carrot, zucchini, onion, pumpkin pie spice, vinegar, chili powder, pepper, and salt the slow cooker.
2. Cook the chili on high within 4 hours. Stir in the spinach and the fava beans. Cook for another 30 minutes on high. Serve warm, and enjoy.

Nutrition: *Calories: 125 Carbs: 16g Fat: 6g Protein: 2g*

479. VEGGIE-FRIENDLY BUFFALO DIP

PREPARATION: 15 MIN   **COOKING:** 2 H   **SERVINGS:** 4

INGREDIENTS

- 8 oz. chicken-style vegetarian strips, diced
- 16 oz. low-fat ranch salad dressing
- 16 oz. cream cheese, softened
- 12 oz. hot sauce
- 1 cup Colby Jack cheese, shredded

DIRECTIONS

1. Add the fake chicken strips, cream cheese, hot sauce, and ranch dressing to the slow cooker. Stir well, and heat on low for 2 hours. Add the shredded cheese to the mixture. Stir well, and serve warm.

Nutrition: *Calories: 60 Carbs: 2g Fat: 5g Protein: 1g*

480. SPLIT BLACK LENTILS WITH CURRY

PREPARATION: 15 MIN   **COOKING:** 5 H   **SERVINGS:** 4

INGREDIENTS

- 3 cups of water
- 1 cup split black lentils
- 1 minced garlic clove
- ¼ chopped onion
- 1 tsp. sugar
- ½ tsp. turmeric powder
- 1 tsp. curry powder
- 1/3 cup heavy cream
- ½ inch of fresh ginger
- Salt to taste

DIRECTIONS

1. Add the water, onion, lentils, garlic, salt, sugar, curry powder, ginger root, and turmeric to the slow cooker. Stir well.
2. Cook on high within 5 hours. Put the cream in the slow cooker, stir until well combined, and serve warm.

Nutrition: *Calories: 51 Fat: 1.1g Carbs: 9g Protein: 2.2g*

CHAPTER 10.
BEVERAGES

481. MULLED WINE

PREPARATION: 5 MIN **COOKING:** 2 H **SERVINGS:** 8 GLASSES

INGREDIENTS

- 6 cups sweet red wine
- 1 cup apple cider
- 1/4 cup light brown sugar
- 1 small orange, sliced
- 1 cinnamon stick
- 4 whole cloves
- 2-star anise
- 4 cardamom pods, crushed

DIRECTIONS

1. Combine all the fixings in your slow cooker. Cover the pot and cook for 2 hours on high. The mulled wine is best served warm

Nutrition: *Calories: 227 Carbs: 29g Fat: 0g Protein: 0g*

482. CRANBERRY SPICED TEA

PREPARATION: 5 MIN **COOKING:** 2 H **SERVINGS:** 6 GLASSES

INGREDIENTS

- 4 cups of water
- 1 cup strong brewed black tea
- 1 cup cranberry juice
- 1/2 cup white sugar
- 2 cinnamon stick
- 2-star anise
- 2 cardamom pods, crushed
- 1 lemon, sliced

DIRECTIONS

1. Combine all the fixings in your slow cooker. Cook on high settings for 2 hours. Serve the drink warm.

Nutrition: *Calories: 80 Carbs: 22g Fat: 0g Protein: 0g*

483. ROSEMARY MULLED CIDER

PREPARATION: 15 MIN **COOKING:** 3 H **SERVINGS:** 6

INGREDIENTS

- 4 cups apple cider
- 2 cups rose wine
- 1 cup fresh or frozen cranberries
- 1 rosemary sprig
- 1/2 cup white sugar
- 1 cinnamon stick
- 2 whole cloves

DIRECTIONS

1. Combine all the fixings in your slow cooker. Cover and cook for 3 hours on low settings. Serve the beverage warm.

Nutrition: *Calories: 165 Carbs: 43g Fat: 0g Protein: 0g*

---

66. GARLIC AND TOMATO APPETIZER

PREPARATION: 10 MIN **COOKING:** 2H **SERVINGS:** 4

INGREDIENTS

- 2 teaspoons olive oil
- 8 tomatoes, chopped
- 1 garlic clove, minced
- ¼ cup basil, chopped
- 4 Italian whole wheat bread slices, toasted
- 3 tablespoons low-sodium veggie stock
- Black pepper to the taste

DIRECTIONS

1. In your slow cooker, mix tomatoes with basil, garlic, oil, veggie stock, and black pepper, stir, cover, cook on high within 2 hours and then leave aside to cool down. Divide this mix on the toasted bread and serve as an appetizer.

Nutrition: *Calories: 158 Fat: 4.1g Carbs: 26.3g Protein: 5.9g*

484. GINGERBREAD HOT CHOCOLATE

PREPARATION: 15 MIN   **COOKING:** 2 H   **SERVINGS:** 8 GLASSES

INGREDIENTS

- 6 cups whole milk
- 1 cup dark chocolate chips
- 1 cup sweetened condensed milk
- 2 tablespoons cocoa powder
- 1/2 teaspoon ground ginger
- 2 cinnamon stick
- 2 tablespoons maple syrup
- 1 pinch salt

DIRECTIONS

1. Combine all the fixings in your slow cooker. Cover the pot and cook for 2 hours on high settings. Serve the hot chocolate warm.

Nutrition: *Calories: 140 Carbs: 29g Fat: 3g Protein: 2g*

485. GINGERBREAD MOCHA DRINK

PREPARATION: 5 MIN   **COOKING:** 1 H 30 MIN   **SERVINGS:** 6

INGREDIENTS

- 3 cups whole milk
- 2 cups strongly brewed coffee
- 1/2 cup sweetened condensed milk
- 1/4 cup light brown sugar
- 1/2 teaspoon ground ginger
- 1/4 teaspoon cinnamon powder
- 1/4 teaspoon cardamom powder

DIRECTIONS

1. Combine all the fixings in a slow cooker. Cover the pot and cook for 1 1/2 hours on low settings. Serve the mocha drink warm.

Nutrition: *Calories: 270 Carbs: 40g Fat: 7g Protein: 12g*

486. SALTED CARAMEL MILK STEAMER

PREPARATION: 15 MIN   **COOKING:** 2 H   **SERVINGS:** 6 GLASSES

INGREDIENTS

- 4 cups whole milk
- 1 cup heavy cream
- 1 cup caramel sauce
- 1/4 teaspoon salt
- 1/4 teaspoon ground ginger
- 1 teaspoon vanilla extract

DIRECTIONS

1. Combine all the fixings in your slow cooker. Cook within 2 hours on low. Pour the steamer into glasses or mugs and serve right away.

Nutrition: *Calories: 150 Carbs: 28g Fat: 0g Protein: 10g*

487. APPLE CHAI TEA

PREPARATION: 15 MIN   **COOKING:** 4 H   **SERVINGS:** 8 GLASSES

INGREDIENTS

- 4 cups brewed black tea
- 4 cups fresh apple juice
- 1/3 cup white sugar
- 2 red apples, cored and diced
- 2 cinnamon stick
- 1-star anise
- 2 whole cloves
- 2 cardamom pods, crushed

DIRECTIONS

1. Combine all the fixings in your slow cooker. Cook the tea on low settings for 4 hours. Serve the tea warm.

Nutrition: *Calories: 170 Carbs: 0g Fat: 0g Protein: 0g*

488. GINGER PUMPKIN LATTE

PREPARATION: 15 MIN **COOKING:** 3 H **SERVINGS:** 6 GLASSES

INGREDIENTS

- 4 cups whole milk
- 1 cup pumpkin puree
- 1 cup brewed coffee
- 1/4 cup dark brown sugar
- 1 teaspoon ground ginger
- 1 cinnamon stick
- 1 pinch nutmeg

DIRECTIONS

1. Combine all the fixings in a slow cooker. Cover the pot and cook for 3 hours on low settings. Serve the latte warm.

Nutrition: *Calories: 422 Carbs: 57g Fat: 17g Protein: 10g*

489. HOT CARAMEL APPLE DRINK

PREPARATION: 15 MIN **COOKING:** 2 H **SERVINGS:** 8 GLASSES

INGREDIENTS

- 6 cups apple cider
- 1 cup apple liqueur
- 1 cup light rum
- 1/2 cup caramel syrup
- 2 red apples, cored and diced
- 2 cinnamon stick

DIRECTIONS

1. Mix all the ingredients in your slow cooker. Cover the pot and cook for 2 hours on low settings.

Nutrition: *Calories: 116 Carbs: 29g Fat: 0g Protein: 0g*

490. SPICED WHITE CHOCOLATE

PREPARATION: 15 MIN **COOKING:** 1 H 30 MIN **SERVINGS:** 6 GLASSES

INGREDIENTS

- 4 cups whole milk
- 1 cup sweetened condensed milk
- 1 cup white chocolate chips
- 1 cinnamon stick
- 1-star anise
- 1/2-inch piece of ginger, sliced
- 1 pinch nutmeg

DIRECTIONS

1. Combine all the fixings in your slow cooker. Cover it and cook for 1 1/2 hours on low settings. Serve the drink hot.

Nutrition: *Calories: 430 Carbs: 42g Fat: 24g Protein: 11g*

491. APPLE BOURBON PUNCH

PREPARATION: 15 MIN **COOKING:** 2H **SERVINGS:** 4 GLASSES

INGREDIENTS

- 3 cups apple cider
- 1 cup bourbon
- 1/2 cup fresh or frozen cranberries
- 2 cinnamon stick
- 2 whole cloves
- 1/4 cup light brown sugar

DIRECTIONS

1. Combine all the fixings in your slow cooker and cook for 2 hours on low settings. Serve the drink hot.

Nutrition: *Calories: 60 Carbs: 2g Fat: 0g Protein: 0g*

492. MAPLE BOURBON MULLED CIDER

PREPARATION: 10 MIN **COOKING:** 5 H **SERVINGS:** 6 GLASSES

INGREDIENTS

- 5 cups apple cider
- 1/2 cup bourbon
- 1/2 cup fresh apple juice
- 1/4 cup maple syrup
- 2-star anise

DIRECTIONS

1. Mix all the ingredients in your slow cooker. Cover the pot and cook for 1 1/2 hours on low settings. Serve hot.

Nutrition: *Calories: 120 Carbs: 28g Fat: 0g Protein: 0g*

493. AUTUMN PUNCH

PREPARATION: 15 MIN **COOKING:** 8 H **SERVINGS:** 4 GLASSES

INGREDIENTS

- 6 cups red wine
- 1 cup bourbon
- 1 cup cranberry juice
- 1 vanilla bean, split in half lengthwise
- 2 red apples, cored and diced
- 1 ripe pear, cored and sliced
- 1 cinnamon stick
- 2 whole cloves

DIRECTIONS

1. Combine all the fixings in your slow cooker. Cover and cook within 4 hours on low settings. The punch can be served both hot and chilled.

Nutrition: *Calories: 140 Carbs: 37g Fat: 0g Protein: 0g*

494. HOT SPICY APPLE CIDER

PREPARATION: 15 MIN **COOKING:** 3 H **SERVINGS:** 6 GLASSES

INGREDIENTS

- 5 cups apple cider
- 1 cup white rum
- 2 cinnamon stick
- 1/4 teaspoon chili powder
- 1-star anise
- 1 orange, sliced

DIRECTIONS

1. Combine all the fixings in your slow cooker. Cover the pot and cook for 3 hours on low settings. Serve the cider warm.

Nutrition: *Calories: 60 Carbs: 15g Fat: 0g Protein: 0g*

495. VANILLA LATTE

PREPARATION: 15 MIN **COOKING:** 2 H **SERVINGS:** 6 GLASSES

INGREDIENTS

- 4 cups whole milk
- 2 cups brewed coffee
- 1 vanilla pod, split in half lengthwise
- 1/4 cup sweetened condensed milk

DIRECTIONS

1. Combine all the fixings in your slow cooker. Cover and cook for 2 hours on low settings. Serve the latte warm.

Nutrition: *Calories: 73 Carbs: 13g Fat: 2g Protein: 2g*

CHAPTER 11.
SOUPS STEWS AND CHILIES

496. CHICKEN AND RICE STEW

PREPARATION: 15 MIN **COOKING:** 8 H **SERVINGS:** 4

INGREDIENTS

- 2 medium carrots
- 2 medium leeks
- 1 cup rice, uncooked
- 12 oz boneless chicken, without skin
- 1 tsp. thyme
- ½ tsp. rosemary
- 3 cans of chicken broth
- 1 can cream of mushroom soup
- ½ cup onion, chopped
- 1 clove garlic

DIRECTIONS

1. Place all the fixings in a slow cooker. Cover the slow cooker. Cook on low for 7 or 8 hours. or on high for 4 hours. Serve hot.

Nutrition: *Calories: 245.5 Fat: 6.2g Carbs: 21.2g Protein: 25.2g*

497. CHICKEN AND TORTILLA SOUP

PREPARATION: 15 MIN **COOKING:** 6-8 H **SERVINGS:** 4

INGREDIENTS

- 3 chicken breasts, boneless and skinless
- 15 oz. diced tomatoes
- 10 oz. enchilada sauce
- 1 chopped onion, medium
- 4 oz. chopped chili pepper, green
- 3 minced cloves garlic
- 2 cups of water
- 14.5-oz. chicken broth, fat-free
- 1 tbsp. cumin
- 1 tbs. chili powder
- 1 tsp. salt
- ¼ tsp. black pepper
- bay leaf
- 1 tbsp. cilantro, chopped
- 10 oz. of frozen corn
- 3 tortillas, cut into thin slices

DIRECTIONS

1. Place all the ingredients in the slow cooker. Stir well to mix. Cook on low heat for 8 hours or on high heat for 6 hours.
2. Transfer the chicken breasts to a plate and shred. Add chicken to other ingredients. Serve hot, garnished with tortilla slices.

Nutrition: *Calories: 93.4 Fat: 1.9g Carbs: 11.9g Protein: 8.3g*

498. STUFFED PEPPER SOUP

PREPARATION: 15 MIN   **COOKING:** 8 H   **SERVINGS:** 4

INGREDIENTS

- 1 lb. ground beef, drained
- 1 chopped onion, large
- 2 cups tomatoes, diced
- 2 chopped green peppers
- 2 cups tomato sauce
- 1 tbsp beef bouillon
- 3 cups of water
- pepper
- 1 tsp. of salt
- 1 cup of cooked rice, white

DIRECTIONS

1. Place all fixings in a slow cooker. Cook for 8 hours on low. Serve hot.

Nutrition: Calories: 216.1 Fat: 5.1g Carbs: 21.8mg Protein: 18.8g

499. HAM AND PEA SOUP

PREPARATION: 5 MIN   **COOKING:** 8 H   **SERVINGS:** 4

INGREDIENTS

- 1 lb. split peas, dried
- 1 cup sliced celery
- 1 cup sliced carrots
- 1 cup sliced onion
- 2 cups chopped ham, cooked
- 8 cups of water

DIRECTIONS

1. Place all the ingredients in the slow cooker. Cook on low for 8 hours. Serve hot.

Nutrition: Calories: 118.6 Fat: 1.9g Carbs: 14.5mg Protein: 11.1g

500. VEGETABLE STEW

PREPARATION: 15 MIN   **COOKING:** 8 H   **SERVINGS:** 4

INGREDIENTS

- 1 cup of corn
- 1 cup hominy
- 1 cup green beans
- 1 can peas, black-eyed
- 1 cup lima beans
- 1 cup chopped carrots
- 1 cup chopped celery
- 1 cup onion
- 1 can tomato sauce, small
- 2 cups vegetable broth
- 2 tbsp. Worcestershire sauce

DIRECTIONS

1. Place all the ingredients in the slow cooker. Cook on low for 8 hours. Serve hot.

Nutrition: *Calories: 186 Fat: 1.2g Carbs: 38.8mg Protein: 8.3g*

501. PEA SOUP

PREPARATION: 15 MIN   **COOKING:** 8 H   **SERVINGS:** 4

INGREDIENTS

- 16 oz. split peas, dried
- 1 cup chopped baby carrots
- 1 chopped onion, white
- 3 bay leaves
- 10 oz. cubed turkey ham
- 4 cubes chicken bouillon
- 7 cups of water

DIRECTIONS

1. Rinse and drain peas. Place all the ingredients in the slow cooker. Cook on low for 8 hrs. Serve hot.

Nutrition: *Calories: 122.7 Fat: 2g Carbs: 15mg Protein: 11.8g*

502. SOUP FOR THE DAY

PREPARATION: 15 MIN **COOKING:** 10 H **SERVINGS:** 4

INGREDIENTS

- 1 beefsteak, cubed
- 1 chopped onion, medium
- 1 tbsp. olive oil
- 5 thinly sliced medium carrots
- 4 cups cabbage
- 4 diced red potatoes
- 2 diced celery stalks
- 2 cans tomatoes, diced
- 2 cans beef broth
- 1 tsp. sugar
- 1 can tomato soup
- 1 tsp. parsley flakes, dried
- 2 tsp. Italian seasoning

DIRECTIONS

1. In a skillet, sauté onion and steak in oil. Transfer the sautéed mixture to the slow cooker. Put the rest of the fixings in the slow cooker. Cook on low for 10 hours. Serve hot.

Nutrition: Calories: 259.6 Fat: 6.7g Carbs: 31.6mg Protein: 18.9g

503. PORK AND FENNEL STEW

PREPARATION: 15 MIN **COOKING:** 8 H 10 MIN **SERVINGS:** 4

INGREDIENTS

- 8 cups of fennel, thinly sliced
- 1 onion, halved and sliced
- 2 ½ pounds pork shoulder, cubed
- 1 ½ tsp. kosher salt
- 1 ½ tsp. pepper, grounded
- 2 tbsp. olive oil, extra virgin
- ¾ cup white wine, dry
- 4 cloves minced garlic
- 1 tbsp. chopped rosemary
- 2 tsp. chopped oregano
- 28 ounce can tomato, whole

DIRECTIONS

1. Place onion and fennel on the bottom of the slow cooker. In another dish, sprinkle the pepper and salt on pork. In a skillet, pour in the oil.
2. Brown the pork that will fit in the skillet for 5 minutes. Transfer the pork to the slow cooker.
3. Put the wine into the pan, then scrape the brown pieces in the pan. Add the rest of the ingredients to the slow cooker. Cook on low for 8 hours. Serve hot.

Nutrition: Calories: 249 Fat: 13g Carbs: 9mg Protein: 20g

504. VEGETABLE GARBANZO STEW

PREPARATION: 15 MIN **COOKING:** 6 H 10 MIN **SERVINGS:** 2

INGREDIENTS

- 3 cups diced butternut squash
- 3 peeled and diced carrots
- 2 chopped onions
- 3 minced cloves of garlic
- 4 cups vegetable stock, low sodium
- 1 cup red lentils
- 2 tbsp. tomato paste, unsalted
- 2 tbsp. minced ginger
- 2 tsp. cumin, ground
- 1 tsp. turmeric
- ¼ tsp. saffron
- 1 tsp. pepper, ground
- ¼ cup lemon juice
- 16 oz. garbanzo beans
- ½ cup chopped peanuts, unsalted
- ½ cup chopped cilantro

DIRECTIONS

1. Sweat the vegetables in a Dutch oven. Brown the onion. Pour in the stock and scrape any pieces of vegetables sticking to the pan.
2. Now, add all the ingredients to the slow cooker. Cook on low for 6 hours. Stir the lemon juice into the slow cooker before serving. Garnish with peanuts and serve.

Nutrition: Calories: 287 Fat: 8g Carbs: 41mg Protein: 13g

505. CATALAN STEW

PREPARATION: 15 MIN **COOKING:** 8 H 13 MIN **SERVINGS:** 4

INGREDIENTS

- 2 chopped slices of pancetta
- 2 tbsp. olive oil, extra virgin
- 3 pounds chuck roast
- 1 cup red wine, dry
- 2 chopped onions
- 3 cups beef broth, low sodium
- 2 tbsp. tomato paste
- 4 minced cloves garlic
- 2 crushed cinnamon sticks
- 4 sprigs thyme
- 3 slices of peeled orange
- 1 ounce chopped dark chocolate
- 3 tbsp. chopped parsley

DIRECTIONS

1. Sauté pancetta in oil till crisp. Transfer it to the slow cooker. Using the same pan, sauté the beef. Transfer beef to the slow cooker as well.
2. Now, sauté onion for 3 minutes. Add wine, tomato paste, and vinegar to the sauté pan and stir to mix. Transfer this wine mixture to the slow cooker and sprinkle on the rest of the ingredients except parsley.
3. Cook on low for 8 hours. Stir when done. Add the chocolate and cook on high for 10 minutes. Remove cinnamon, orange peel, and thyme. Serve after garnishing with parsley.

Nutrition: *Calories: 421 Fat: 26g Carbs: 16mg Protein: 55g*

506. PORK STEW CARIBBEAN STYLE

PREPARATION: 15 MIN   **COOKING:** 7 H   **SERVINGS:** 4

INGREDIENTS

- 1 ½ pounds cubed pork loin
- 1 tbsp. thyme, dried
- ¼ tsp. allspice, ground
- white pepper, ground
- 1-pound Yukon potatoes, quartered
- 3 diced carrots
- 1-inch piece of ginger root, chopped
- 2 tsp. Worcestershire sauce
- 1 chopped clove garlic
- ½ cup sliced scallions
- 1 cup diced tomatoes

DIRECTIONS

1. Coat the pork with pepper, allspice, and thyme. Place remaining ingredients except for scallions in the slow cooker. Put in the pork along with the Worcestershire sauce.
2. Place the tomatoes on top. Cook on low for 7 hours. Serve the stew with scallions.

Nutrition: *Calories: 452 Fat: 27g Carbs: 25mg Protein: 50g*

507. KALE VERDE

PREPARATION: 15 MIN   **COOKING:** 6 H   **SERVINGS:** 4

INGREDIENTS

- ¼ cup olive oil, extra virgin
- 1 yellow onion, large
- 2 cloves garlic
- 2 oz. tomatoes, dried
- 2 cups yellow potatoes, diced
- 14-ounce tomatoes, diced
- 6 cups chicken broth
- white pepper, ground
- 1-pound o chopped kale

DIRECTIONS

1. Sauté onion for 5 minutes in oil. Add the garlic and sauté again for 1 minute. Transfer the sautéed mixture to the slow cooker.
2. Now, put the rest of the ingredients except pepper into the slow cooker. Cook on low for 6 hours. Season with white pepper to taste. Serve hot in heated bowls

Nutrition: *Calories: 257 Fat: 22g Carbs: 27mg Protein: 14g*

508. ESCAROLE WITH BEAN SOUP

PREPARATION: 15 MIN **COOKING:** 6 H **SERVINGS:** 4

INGREDIENTS

- 1 tbsp. olive oil
- 8 crushed cloves garlic
- 1 cup chopped onions
- 1 diced carrot
- 3 tsp. basil, dried
- 3 tsp. oregano, dried
- 4 cups chicken broth
- 3 cups chopped escarole
- 1 cup of northern beans, dried
- parmesan cheese, grated
- 14 oz. of tomatoes, diced

DIRECTIONS

1. Sauté garlic for 2 minutes in oil using a large soup pot. Except for the cheese, broth, and beans, add the rest of the ingredients and cook for 5 minutes.
2. Transfer the cooked ingredients to the slow cooker. Mix in the broth and beans. Cook on low for 6 hours. Garnish with cheese. Serve hot in heated bowls

Nutrition: *Calories: 98 Fat: 33g Carbs: 14mg Protein: 8g*

509. ITALIAN BEEF BARLEY SOUP

PREPARATION: 10 MIN **COOKING:** 5 H **SERVINGS:** 4

INGREDIENTS

- 2 pounds roasted beef roast
- 5 cups of water
- 4 cubes of beef broth, crumbled
- 1/2 onion, minced
- 1 can of tomato sauce
- 3/4 cup uncooked pearl barley
- salt and pepper to taste

DIRECTIONS

1. Combine beef, water, broth, onion, tomato sauce, barley, salt, and pepper in a slow cooker. Cover and cook on low within 5 hours.

Nutrition: *Calories: 512 Fat: 27.8g Carbs: 35.4g Protein: 29.7g*

510. CREAMY POTATO SOUP

PREPARATION: 15 MIN   **COOKING:** 6 H   **SERVINGS:** 4

INGREDIENTS

- 6 slices of bacon, cut into 1/2-inch pieces
- 1 onion, finely chopped
- 2 (10.5 oz.) condensed chicken broth
- 2 cups of water
- 5 large potatoes, diced
- 1/2 teaspoon of salt
- 1/2 teaspoon dried dill weed
- 1/2 teaspoon ground white pepper
- 1/2 cup all-purpose flour
- 2 cups half and half cream
- 1 (12 fluid ounce) can evaporate milk

DIRECTIONS

1. Put bacon and onion in a large, deep frying pan. Bake over medium heat until the bacon is evenly browned and the onions are soft. Drain excess fat.
2. Transfer the bacon and onion to a slow cooker and stir in the chicken stock, water, potatoes, salt, dill-weed, and white pepper. Cover and cook on the layer for 6 to 7 hours, stirring occasionally.
3. In a small bowl, beat the flour and half and half. Stir the soup together with the evaporated milk. Cover and cook another 30 minutes before serving.

Nutrition: *Calories: 553 Fat: 19.3g Carbs: 74.2g Protein: 22g*

511. SPLIT PEA SOUP WITH BACON & HASH BROWNS

PREPARATION: 15 MIN   **COOKING:** 8 H   **SERVINGS:** 4

INGREDIENTS

- 1/4-pound bacon, minced
- 1-pound split peas, rinsed
- 1/3 (20 oz.) package of frozen southern-style hash-brown potatoes
- 1 onion, minced
- 3 carrots, peeled and diced
- 3 ribs of celery, diced
- 2 cloves of garlic, finely chopped
- 1/8 teaspoon ground black pepper
- 1 pinch of red pepper flakes (optional)
- 8 cups chicken broth

DIRECTIONS

1. Put bacon in your large frying pan and cook over medium heat, occasionally turning, until light brown, about 5 minutes. Drain on kitchen paper.
2. Put bacon, split peas, baked potatoes, onion, carrots, celery, garlic, black pepper, red pepper flakes, and chicken broth in a slow cooker; stir to combine—Cook for 8 hours on low or high for 6 hours.

Nutrition: *Calories: 258 Fat: 2.9g Carbs: 43g Protein: 16.7g*

512. SOUTHWEST BLACK BEAN CHICKEN SOUP

PREPARATION: 15 MIN **COOKING:** 8 H **SERVINGS:** 4

INGREDIENTS

- 1 pound of cooked dark meat chicken
- 3 cans of black beans, rinsed
- 2 cans of chicken broth
- 2 cans tomatoes (diced) with green chili peppers
- 1 can of whole kernel corn
- ½ large onion, minced
- ½ cup chopped jalapeno peppers
- 2 cloves of garlic, minced
- 2 ½ teaspoons of chili powder
- 2 teaspoons of red pepper flakes
- 2 teaspoons of ground cumin
- 1 teaspoon ground coriander
- salt and ground black pepper to taste
- ½ cup sour cream, or to taste

Nutrition: *Calories: 389 Fat: 13.1g Carbs: 43.7g Protein: 26.6g*

DIRECTIONS

1. Put all fixing except for sour cream in a slow cooker; cook on low for 8 hours. Serve with about 1 tablespoon of sour cream on each serving.

513. ZUCCHINI SOUP

PREPARATION: 15 MIN **COOKING:** 4 H 17 MIN **SERVINGS:** 4

INGREDIENTS

- 1 & 1/2 pounds sweet Italian sausage
- 1/2-inch pieces of celery
- 2-pound zucchini, cut into 1/2-inch slices
- 2 cans of tomatoes in cubes
- 2 green peppers, cut into 1/2-inch slices
- 1 cup chopped onion
- 2 teaspoons of salt
- 1 teaspoon of white sugar
- 1 teaspoon dried oregano
- 1 teaspoon of Italian herbs
- 1 teaspoon dried basil
- 1/4 teaspoon garlic powder
- 6 tablespoons grated Parmesan cheese, or to taste

Nutrition: *Calories: 389 Fat: 23.6g Carbs: 25.8 Protein: 21.8g*

DIRECTIONS

1. Heat-up a large frying pan over medium heat. Cook and stir sausage in the hot frying pan until brown and crumbly, 5 to 7 minutes; drain and throw away fat. Mix celery with cooked sausage; cook and stir until the celery is soft, about 10 minutes.
2. Combine sausage mix, zucchini, tomatoes, bell pepper, onion, salt, sugar, oregano, Italian herbs, basil, and garlic powder in a slow cooker. Cook on low within 4 to 6 hours. Garnish each portion with 1 tablespoon of parmesan cheese.

514. GERMAN LENTIL SOUP

PREPARATION: 10 MIN   **COOKING:** 8 H 10 MIN   **SERVINGS:** 4

INGREDIENTS

- 2 cups of dried brown lentils, rinsed and drained
- 3 cups of chicken broth
- 1 bay leaf
- 1 cup chopped carrots
- 1 cup chopped celery
- 1 cup chopped onion
- 1 cup of cooked, diced ham
- 1 teaspoon Worcestershire sauce
- 1/2 teaspoon of garlic powder
- 1/4 teaspoon freshly grated nutmeg
- 5 drops of hot pepper sauce
- 1/4 teaspoon caraway seeds
- 1/2 teaspoon celery salt
- 1 tablespoon chopped fresh parsley
- 1/2 teaspoon ground black pepper

DIRECTIONS

1. Place lentils in a slow cooker. Add chicken broth, bay leaves, carrots, celery, onion, and ham. Season with Worcestershire sauce, garlic powder, nutmeg, hot pepper sauce, caraway seeds, celery salt, parsley, and pepper. Cover and cook on low within 8 to 10 hours. Remove laurel before serving.

Nutrition: *Calories: 221 Fat: 2.3 g Carbs: 34.2g Protein: 16g*

515. CHICKEN AND DUMPLINGS

PREPARATION: 15 MIN   **COOKING:** 6 H   **SERVINGS:** 4

INGREDIENTS

- 4 chicken fillets without skin, boneless
- 2 tablespoons butter
- 2 cans of condensed cream chicken soup
- 1 onion, finely chopped
- 2 packages of chilled biscuit dough, torn into pieces

DIRECTIONS

1. Place the chicken, butter, soup, and onion in a slow cooker and fill with enough water to cover.
2. Cover and cook on high within 5 to 6 hours. Place the cracked cookie dough in the slow cooker about 30 minutes before serving. Cook until the dough is no longer raw in the middle.

Nutrition: *Calories: 385 Fat: 18 g Carbs: 37 g Protein: 18.1 g*

516. CHICKEN TACO SOUP

PREPARATION: 15 MIN　　**COOKING:** 7 H　　**SERVINGS:** 4

INGREDIENTS

- 1 onion, minced
- 1 can of chili beans
- 1 can of black beans
- 1 can of whole kernel corn, drained
- 1 can of tomato sauce
- 1 can or bottle of beer
- 2 cans diced tomatoes with green peppers, undrained
- 1 taco herbs
- 3 whole chicken fillets without skin, without bones
- 8 oz grated cheddar cheese (optional)
- sour cream (optional)
- ground tortilla chips (optional)

DIRECTIONS

1. Put the onion, chili beans, black beans, corn, tomato sauce, beer, and diced tomatoes in a slow cooker. Add taco spices and stir to mix.
2. Place the chicken fillets on the mixture and press lightly until just covered with the other ingredients. Put the slow cooker on low heat, cover, and cook for 5 hours.
3. Remove the chicken fillets from the soup and let them cool for a long time to be handled. Stir the grated chicken back into the soup and continue to cook for 2 hours. Serve garnished with grated cheddar cheese, a dollop of sour cream, and possibly ground tortilla chips.

Nutrition: *Calories: 434 Fat: 17.7g Carbs: 42.3g Protein: 27.2g*

517. LENTIL AND HAM SOUP

PREPARATION: 15 MIN　　**COOKING:** 11 H　　**SERVINGS:** 4

INGREDIENTS

- 1 cup of dried lentils
- 1 cup chopped celery
- 1 cup chopped carrots
- 1 cup chopped onion
- 2 cloves of garlic, finely chopped
- 1 1/2 cups diced cooked ham
- 1/2 teaspoon dried basil
- 1/4 teaspoon dried thyme
- 1/2 teaspoon dried oregano
- 1 bay leaf
- 1/4 teaspoon of black pepper
- 32 grams of chicken broth
- 1 cup of water
- 8 teaspoons tomato sauce

DIRECTIONS

1. In a slow cooker, combine the lentils, celery, carrots, onion, garlic, and ham. Season with basil, thyme, oregano, bay leaf, and pepper.
2. Stir in the chicken stock, water, and tomato sauce—cover and cook on low for 11 hours. Discard the bay leaf before serving.

Nutrition: *Calories: 222 Fat: 6.1g Carbs: 26.3g Protein: 15.1g*

518. CABBAGE BEEF SOUP

PREPARATION: 5 MIN   **COOKING:** 8 H   **SERVINGS:** 4

INGREDIENTS

- 2 tablespoons vegetable oil
- 1-pound ground beef
- 1/2 large onion, minced
- 5 cups chopped cabbage
- 2 (16 oz.) cans of red kidney beans, drained
- 2 cups of water
- 24 grams of tomato sauce
- 4 beef broth cubes
- 1 1/2 teaspoon ground cumin
- 1 teaspoon of salt
- 1 teaspoon pepper

DIRECTIONS

1. Heat oil in a large soup pot over medium heat. Add minced meat and onion and fry until the beef is well browned and crumbled.
2. Drain the fat and move the meat to a slow cooker. Add cabbage, kidney beans, water, tomato sauce, broth, cumin, salt, and pepper. Stir to dissolve broth and cover.
3. Cook for 4 hours on a high or low for 6 to 8 hours. Stir occasionally. To enjoy!

Nutrition: *Calories: 211 Fat: 8.7g Carbs: 20.3g Protein: 14.1g*

519. SPLIT PEA SAUSAGE SOUP

PREPARATION: 15 MIN   **COOKING:** 5 H   **SERVINGS:** 4

INGREDIENTS

- 1 pound of dried split peas
- 10 cups of water
- 1 pound of smoked sausage of your choice, sliced
- 5 cubes of chicken broth
- 1 1/2 cups chopped carrot
- 1 cup chopped celery
- 2 potatoes, peeled and minced
- 1/2 teaspoon of garlic powder
- 1/2 teaspoon dried oregano
- 2 bay leaves
- 1 onion, minced

DIRECTIONS

1. In a slow cooker, combine the peas, water, sausage, broth, carrot, celery, potatoes, garlic powder, oregano, bay leaves, and onion. Cover and cook on high within 4 to 5 hours. Remove bay leaves before pouring them into bowls.

Nutrition: *Calories: 412 Fat: 13.1g Carbs: 50.8g Protein: 23.9g*

520. BEEF VEGETABLE SOUP

PREPARATION: 10 MIN **COOKING:** 6 H **SERVINGS:** 4

INGREDIENTS

- 1-pound diced beef
- 1 can of whole kernel corn, undrained
- 1 can of green beans
- 1 can of carrots with juice
- 1 can of sliced potatoes with juice
- 1 can of crushed tomatoes
- 1 package of beef with onion soup mix
- salt and pepper to taste

DIRECTIONS

1. Put meat, corn, green beans, carrots, potatoes, tomatoes, soup mix, and salt and pepper to taste in the slow cooker; stir to combine. Cook on low for at least 6 hours. Add water if necessary.

Nutrition: *Calories: 364 Fat: 16.2g Carbs: 38.8g Protein: 20g*

521. SPICY BLACK BEAN SOUP

PREPARATION: 5 MIN **COOKING:** 5 H **SERVINGS:** 4

INGREDIENTS

- 1 pound of dry black beans, soaked overnight, rinsed after
- 4 teaspoons diced jalapeno peppers
- 6 cups chicken broth
- 1/2 teaspoon of garlic powder
- 1 tbsp chili powder
- 1 tsp ground cumin
- 1 tsp cayenne pepper
- 3/4 tsp ground black pepper
- 1/2 tsp hot pepper sauce

DIRECTIONS

1. Mix beans, jalapenos, plus chicken broth in a slow cooker. Flavor it with garlic powder, chili powder, cumin, cayenne pepper, pepper, and hot pepper sauce.
2. Cook on high for 4 hours. Lower down the heat, then cook again within 2 hours or until you are ready to eat.

Nutrition: *Calories: 281 Fat: 2g Carbs: 49.7g Protein: 17.7g*

522. BEST ITALIAN SAUSAGE SOUP

PREPARATION: 15 MIN **COOKING:** 6 H **SERVINGS:** 4

INGREDIENTS

- & 1/2-pounds Italian sausage, sweet
- 2 cloves of garlic, finely chopped
- 2 small onions, finely chopped
- 2 cans of whole peeled tomatoes
- 1 1/4 cups of red wine, dry
- 5 cups of beef broth
- 1/2 teaspoon dried basil
- 1/2 teaspoon dried oregano
- 2 courgettes, sliced
- 1 green pepper, minced
- 3 tablespoons chopped fresh parsley
- 1 package of spinach fettuccine pasta
- salt and pepper to taste

Nutrition: *Calories: 436 Fat: 17.8g Carbs: 43.5g Protein: 21g*

DIRECTIONS

1. Cook the sausage in your large saucepan on medium heat until brown. Remove with a spoon with a slot and drain on kitchen paper. Pour fat from the pan and save 3 tablespoons.
2. Cook garlic and onion in reserved fat for 2 to 3 minutes. Stir in tomatoes, wine, broth, basil, and oregano. Transfer to a slow cooker and stir in sausage, zucchini, pepper, and parsley. Cover and cook on low within 4 to 6 hours.
3. Bring a pot of lightly salted water to a boil. Cook the pasta in boiling water until al dente, about 7 minutes.
4. Drain water and add pasta to the slow cooker. Let simmer for a few minutes and season with salt and pepper before serving.

523. HAM BONE SOUP

PREPARATION: 10 MIN **COOKING:** 2H **SERVINGS:** 4

INGREDIENTS

- 1 ham with some meat
- 1 onion, diced
- 1 can tomatoes with juice and diced
- 1 can of kidney beans
- 3 potatoes, diced
- 1 green pepper, without seeds and in cubes
- 4 cups of water
- 6 cubes of chicken broth

DIRECTIONS

1. Put the ham bone, onion, tomatoes, kidney beans, potatoes, plus green pepper in a slow cooker. Melt the bouillon cubes in water, then pour into the slow cooker. Cook on high until it is hot. Turn down the heat and cook for another 5 to 6 hours.

Nutrition: *Calories: 266 Fat: 1g Carbs: 53.3g Protein: 11.4g*

524. BRUSSELS SPROUTS SOUP

PREPARATION: 5 MIN **COOKING:** 8 H **SERVINGS:** 3

INGREDIENTS

- 1 lb. fresh brussels sprouts, halved
- 7 oz fresh baby spinach, torn
- 1 tsp of sea salt
- 1 cup of whole milk
- 3 tbsp of sour cream
- 1 tbsp of fresh celery, finely chopped
- 1 tsp of granulated sugar
- 2 cups of water
- 1 tbsp of butter

DIRECTIONS

1. Combine the ingredients in a slow cooker. Set the heat to low and cook for 8 hours. Open the cooker and transfer the soup to a food processor. Blend well to combine and serve.

Nutrition: *Calories: 194 Proteins 10g Carbs: 21.7g Fat: 9.8g*

525. CLASSIC RAGOUT SOUP

PREPARATION: 5 MIN   **COOKING:** 8 H   **SERVINGS:** 4

INGREDIENTS

- 1 lb. lamb chops, 1 inch thick
- 1 cup of peas, rinsed
- 4 medium-sized carrots, peeled and finely chopped
- 3 small onions, peeled and finely chopped
- 1 large potato, peeled and finely chopped
- 1 large tomato, peeled and roughly chopped
- 3 tbsp of extra virgin olive oil
- 1 tbsp of cayenne pepper
- 1 tsp of salt
- ½ tsp of freshly ground black pepper

DIRECTIONS

1. Cut meat into bite-sized pieces. Make the first layer in your slow cooker. Now add peas, finely chopped carrots, onions, potatoes, and roughly chopped tomato.
2. Add about three tablespoons of olive oil, cayenne pepper, salt, and pepper. Give it a good stir and close the lid. Set for 8 hours on low.

Tip: If you have some spare time, try this simple trick to give your ragout an extra flavor. Heat-up 2-3 tablespoons of olive oil in a large skillet. Add meat chops and briefly brown on both sides. Transfer to a slow cooker and follow the recipe. Frying the meat just before cooking doesn't take more than five minutes and will give you an extra crispy flavor you simply can't get by just cooking.

Nutrition: *Calories: 307 Proteins 24.9g Carbs: 23.3g Fat: 13g*

526. GORGONZOLA BROCCOLI SOUP

PREPARATION: 5 MIN   **COOKING:** 2 H   **SERVINGS:** 4

INGREDIENTS

- 10 oz of Gorgonzola cheese, crumbled
- 1 cup of broccoli, finely chopped
- 1 tbsp of olive oil
- ½ cup of full-fat milk
- ½ cup of vegetable broth
- 1 tbsp of parsley, finely chopped
- ½ tsp of salt
- ¼ tsp of black pepper, ground

DIRECTIONS

1. Grease the bottom of a slow cooker with olive oil. Add all ingredients and three cups of water. Mix well with a kitchen whisker until thoroughly combined.
2. Cover with a lid and cook for 2 hours on low settings. Remove from the heat and sprinkle with some fresh parsley for extra taste.

Nutrition: *Calories: 208 Proteins 11.8g Carbs: 7.6g Fat: 15.8g*

527. MOROCCAN CHICKPEA SOUP

PREPARATION: 15 MIN **COOKING:** 7 H **SERVINGS:** 4

INGREDIENTS

- 14 oz chickpeas, soaked
- 2 large carrots, finely chopped
- 2 small onions, peeled and finely chopped
- 2 large tomatoes, peeled and finely chopped
- 3 tbsp of tomato paste
- A handful of fresh parsley, finely chopped
- 2 cups of vegetable broth
- 3 tbsp of extra virgin olive oil
- 1 tsp of salt

DIRECTIONS

1. Soak the chickpeas overnight. Rinse and drain. Set aside. Oiled bottom of your slow cooker with three tablespoons of olive oil. Place the rinsed chickpeas, chopped onions, carrots, and finely chopped tomatoes.
2. Pour the vegetable broth and season with salt. Stir in tomato paste and securely lock the lid. Set the heat to low and cook for 7 hours. Sprinkle with fresh parsley and serve.

Nutrition: *Calories: 420 Proteins 18.9g Carbs: 58.6g Fat: 14g*

528. PUMPKIN SOUP

PREPARATION: 5 MIN **COOKING:** 4 H **SERVINGS:** 2

INGREDIENTS

- 2 lb. pumpkin, pureed
- 1 large onion, peeled and finely chopped
- 3 cups of vegetable broth
- 1 tbsp of ground turmeric
- ½ cup of double cream
- ½ tsp of salt
- A handful of fresh parsley
- 3 tbsp of extra virgin olive oil

DIRECTIONS

1. Place finely chopped onion, pureed pumpkin, turmeric, salt, and olive oil in your slow cooker. Add vegetable broth and stir well. Cover and set the heat to low. Cook for 4 hours.
2. Remove the lid, then stir in the double cream. Top with chopped parsley, then serve.

Nutrition: *Calories: 215 Proteins 5.6g Carbs: 19.2g Fat: 14.3g*

529. SPRING SPINACH SOUP

PREPARATION: 15 MIN **COOKING:** 8 H **SERVINGS:** 4

INGREDIENTS

- 1 lb. of lamb shoulder, cut into bite-sized pieces
- 12 oz fresh spinach leaves, torn
- 3 eggs, beaten
- 4 cups of vegetable broth
- 3 tbsp of extra virgin olive oil
- 1 tsp of salt

DIRECTIONS

1. Rinse and drain each spinach leaf. Cut into bite-sized pieces. Place in a slow cooker.
2. Sprinkle the meat generously with salt and transfer to a cooker, then put the other ingredients and whisk in three beaten eggs. Close the lid and cook for 8 hours on low.

Nutrition: *Calories: 325 Proteins 34.6g Carbs: 3.4g Fat: 19g*

530. THE SULTAN'S SOUP

PREPARATION: 10 MIN **COOKING:** 8 H **SERVINGS:** 4

INGREDIENTS

- 3 1/2 oz of carrots, finely chopped
- 3 ½ oz of celery root, finely chopped
- A handful of green peas, soaked
- A handful of fresh okra
- 2 tbsp of butter
- 2 tbsp of fresh parsley, finely chopped
- 1 egg yolk
- 2 tbsp of cheese
- ¼ cup of freshly squeezed lemon juice
- 1 bay leaf
- 1 tsp of salt
- ½ tsp of pepper
- 4 cups of beef broth plus one cup of water

DIRECTIONS

1. Preparing this lovely soup in a slow cooker is very easy. Combine the ingredients in a slow cooker and close the lid. Set the heat to low and cook for 8 hours. Serve warm and enjoy!

Nutrition: *Calories: 161 Proteins 2.8g Carbs: 9.1g Fat: 13g*

531. BACON CHILI

PREPARATION: 15 MIN   **COOKING:** 5 H   **SERVINGS:** 4

INGREDIENTS

- ½ tsp. pepper
- ¾ white onion
- 1 green bell pepper
- 1 Roma tomato
- 1 tbsp. chili powder
- 1 tsp. Worcestershire sauce
- 1 tsp. oregano
- 1 tsp. salt
- 2 cups chicken stock
- 2 jalapeno peppers
- 2 tsp. cumin
- 3 garlic cloves
- 30-oz. lean ground beef
- 5 slices of bacon

DIRECTIONS

1. Chop-up bacon, then adds to the pan. Cook until fat renders out, then the bacon is almost cooked. Then add beef to the pan, cooking till some color forms.
2. Chop up jalapeno peppers and garlic finely. Roughly chop up an onion, bell pepper, and tomato. Add 2 cups of stock to the slow cooker along with all other ingredients. Combine well.
3. Cook for 2 ½ hours on high or low for 5 hours. Serve.

Nutrition: *Calories: 527 Carbs: 7g Fat: 37g Protein: 51g*

532. STEAK LOVER'S CHILI

PREPARATION: 15 MIN   **COOKING:** 6 H   **SERVINGS:** 4

INGREDIENTS

- ¼ tsp cayenne pepper
- ½ cup sliced leeks
- ½ tsp cumin
- ½ tsp salt
- 1 cup chicken stock
- 1 tbsp chili powder
- 1/8 tsp pepper
- 2 ½ pounds steak, sliced into 1-inch cubes
- 2 cups canned tomatoes

Optional Toppings:
- ¼ cup shredded cheddar cheese
- ½ sliced avocado
- 1 tsp. cilantro
- 2 tbsp. sour cream

DIRECTIONS

1. Pour all ingredients into your slow cooker, except topping components. Stir well to incorporate. Set to cook on high 6 hours. Shred cubes of steak and break up tomatoes. Serve topped with desired toppings.

Nutrition: *Calories: 198 Carbs: 6g Fat: 19g Protein: 11g*

533. BUFFALO CHICKEN CHILI

PREPARATION: 15 MIN   **COOKING:** 8 H   **SERVINGS:** 4

INGREDIENTS

- ¼ - ½ cup buffalo wing sauce
- ¼ tsp. salt
- ½ tsp. celery salt
- ½ tsp. dried cilantro
- ½ tsp. garlic powder
- ½ tsp. onion powder
- 1 cup of frozen corn
- 1 package of ranch dressing mix
- 1-pound ground chicken
- 14 ½ ounce can fire-roasted tomatoes
- 15-ounce can white navy beans
- 2 cup chicken broth
- 8-oz. cream cheese

DIRECTIONS

1. Brown chicken in skillet till cooked. Place into the slow cooker. Mix in all remaining ingredients to chicken, mixing well to incorporate.
2. Cook within 4 hours on high or 8 hours on low. Stir well to incorporate cream cheese and wing sauce throughout the chili mixture.

Nutrition: *Calories: 277 Carbs: 11g Fat: 14g Protein: 17g*

534. NO BEAN CHILI

PREPARATION: 15 MIN   **COOKING:** 6-7 H   **SERVINGS:** 4

INGREDIENTS

- 1 cup of water
- 1 packet of chili seasoning
- 1 can dice tomatoes
- 1 can tomato sauce
- 2 pounds lean ground beef

DIRECTIONS

1. Cook ground beef and then add to slow cooker. Add the rest of your ingredients, stirring thoroughly to combine well.
2. Cook on low heat 6-7 hours. Serve topped with favorite toppings such as sour cream, cheese, diced onion, etc. Serve.

Nutrition: *Calories: 201 Carbs: 2g Fat: 19g Protein: 21g*

535. KICKIN' CHILI

PREPARATION: 15 MIN **COOKING:** 6-8 H **SERVINGS:** 4

INGREDIENTS

- ¼ cup pickled jalapeno slices
- ½ tsp. cayenne pepper
- 1 bay leaf
- 1 chopped red onion
- 1 tsp. garlic powder
- 1 tsp. onion powder
- 1 tsp. oregano
- 1 tsp. pepper
- 14 ½ oz can stew tomatoes
- 14 ½ oz can tomato with green chilies
- 2 ½ pounds ground beef
- 2 tbsp. cumin
- 2 tbsp. Worcestershire sauce
- 2 tsp. salt
- 3 diced celery ribs
- 4 tbsp. chili powder
- 4 tbsp. minced garlic
- 6-ounce can tomato paste

DIRECTIONS

1. Turn the slow cooker to low. Brown beef in skillet along with pepper, salt, and 2 tablespoons of minced garlic. Drain excess grease.
2. Pour beef into the slow cooker. Add remaining recipe components and mix well. Cook 6-8 hours on low. Serve.

Nutrition: *Calories: 137 Carbs: 5g Fat: 15g Protein: 16g*

536. CREAMY WHITE CHICKEN CHILI

PREPARATION: 15 MIN **COOKING:** 7 H **SERVINGS:** 4

INGREDIENTS

- ½ cup chicken stock
- ½ cup heavy cream
- ½ cup sour cream
- 1 tsp. cumin
- 1 tsp. garlic powder
- 2 pounds of chicken
- 2 tsp. chili powder
- 3 tbsp. butter
- 4-oz. cream cheese
- 9-oz. chopped green chilies
- Toppings:
- 1 cup shredded pepper jack cheese
- 1/3 cup peeled and chopped red onion
- 1/3 cup chopped cilantro

DIRECTIONS

1. Place chicken in the slow cooker. Add green chilies, chicken stock, garlic powder, cumin, and chili powder to chicken.
2. Set to cook on low 7 hours. Before you plan to eat, heat sour cream, cream cheese, heavy cream, and butter together in a pan, stirring till smooth. Shred chicken.
3. Pour cream cheese mixture over chicken, combining well to incorporate. Sprinkle with pepper jack, red onion, and cilantro.

Nutrition: *Calories: 486 Carbs: 6g Fat: 33g Protein: 39g*

537. OLD-FASHIONED LOW-CARB CHILI

PREPARATION: 15 MIN   **COOKING:** 3 H   **SERVINGS:** 4

INGREDIENTS

- 1 ½ cup diced celery
- 1 cup beef broth
- 1 chopped yellow onion
- 1 tbsp. cumin
- 1 tsp. garlic powder
- 1 tsp. Italian seasoning
- 1 tsp. pepper
- 1 tsp. salt
- 14 ½ oz crush tomatoes
- 14 ½ oz dice tomatoes with green chilies
- 2-pounds lean ground beef
- 2 tbsp. crushed red pepper flakes
- 3 tbsp. chili powder
- 3 tbsp. minced garlic
- 6-oz. tomato paste

DIRECTIONS

1. Cook beef in a pan until browned and drain grease. Add garlic to the pan and sauté 60 seconds.
2. Place beef in the slow cooker. Add remaining ingredients to beef. Stir to combine well— Cook within 6 hours on low or 3 hours on high. Serve.

Nutrition: *Calories: 318 Carbs: 4g Fat: 24g Protein: 17g*

538. SECRET CHOCOLATE CHILI

PREPARATION: 15 MIN   **COOKING:** 4 H   **SERVINGS:** 4

INGREDIENTS

- ½ onion
- 1 cup beef broth
- 1 cup black coffee
- 1 tbsp. chili powder
- 1 tbsp. cocoa powder
- 1 tbsp. soy sauce
- 1 tsp. cayenne pepper
- 1 tsp. cumin
- 10 drops liquid stevia
- 2 cans whole tomatoes
- 2-pounds ground beef
- 2 tbsp. butter
- 2 tbsp. Worcestershire sauce
- 2 tsp. garlic
- 2 tsp. paprika
- 6 slices of bacon
- 8-oz. kielbasa

DIRECTIONS

1. Puree both cans of tomatoes in a food processor and add to the slow cooker. Add spices and all liquid ingredients minus garlic and butter to sauce in the slow cooker.
2. Add stevia—brown beef in a pan. Drain and put to the side. Chop onion, then sauté it in a pan until softened.
3. Add bacon and kielbasa to the pan with the onion, cooking till bacon is crispy. Add sausage and bacon mixture along with garlic powder to slow cooker. Add beef to the slow cooker. Set to cook on high 4 hours.

Nutrition: *Calories: 492 Carbs: 7g Fat: 25g Protein: 17g*

539. NOT YOUR CAVEMAN'S CHILI

PREPARATION: 15 MIN **COOKING:** 4 H **SERVINGS:** 4

INGREDIENTS

- 1 ½ tsp cumin
- 1 cup beef broth
- 1 green pepper
- 1 onion
- 1 tsp. cayenne pepper
- 1 tsp. oregano
- 1 tsp. pepper
- 1 tsp. salt
- 1 tsp. Worcestershire sauce
- 1/3 cup tomato paste
- 2 ½ tbsp. chili powder
- 2-pounds stew meat
- 2 tbsp. olive oil
- 2 tbsp. soy sauce
- 2 tsp. fish sauce
- 2 tsp. minced garlic
- 2 tsp. paprika

DIRECTIONS

1. Chop up half of your meat into bite-sized pieces. Place the other half of your meat into your food processor, blending until ground.
2. Cut up onion and pepper into tiny pieces. Mix all your spices. Sauté beef in the pan along with ground beef.
3. Sauté veggies in meat grease until fragrant Add all ingredients into your slow cooker. Simmer on high for 2 ½ hours. Stir and simmer 20-30 more minutes.

Nutrition: *Calories: 390 Carbs: 5g Fat: 16g Protein: 27g*

540. 5-INGREDIENT CHILI

PREPARATION: 15 MIN **COOKING:** 2-3 H **SERVINGS:** 4

INGREDIENTS

- 15-oz. tomato sauce
- 2 diced onions
- Cumin and other spices to achieve desired taste, such as cilantro, garlic, salt, chili powder, etc.
- 3-4 cans diced tomatoes
- 3-4 pounds meat of choice (ground turkey, bison, sausage, venison, beef, etc.)

DIRECTIONS

1. Pour all ingredients into your slow cooker. Stir well to incorporate. Cook 2-3 hours on high or 5-6 hours on low.

Nutrition: *Calories: 503 Carbs: 6g Fat: 41g Protein: 29g*

CHAPTER 12.
SWEETS AND DESSERTS

541. BLUEBERRY LEMON CUSTARD CAKE

PREPARATION: 15 MIN **COOKING:** 3 H **SERVINGS:** 4 SLICES

INGREDIENTS

- 6 eggs separated
- 1/2 cup Coconut Flour
- 2 tsp lemon zest
- 1/3 cup lemon juice
- 1 tsp lemon liquid stevia
- 1/2 cup Swerve sweetener
- 1/2 tsp salt
- 2 cups heavy cream
- 1/2 cup fresh blueberries

DIRECTIONS

1. Put the egg whites into your stand mixer and whip until stiff peaks form. Set aside. Mix the yolks and remaining fixings except for blueberries in another bowl.
2. Fold the egg whites into the batter until just combined. Oiled slow cooker and pour the mixture into it.
3. Sprinkle the blueberries over the batter—cover and cook on low within 3 hours or until a toothpick comes out clean.
4. Allow cooling with the cover off for 1 hour, then place in the refrigerator to chill for 2 hours or overnight. Serve cold with a little sugar-free whipped cream if desired.

Nutrition: *Calories: 191 Fat: 17g Protein: 4g Carbs: 4g*

542. KETO FUDGE

PREPARATION: 5 MIN **COOKING:** 2 H **SERVINGS:** 4

INGREDIENTS

- 2 1/2 cups sugar-free chocolate chips
- 1/3 cup coconut milk
- 1 tsp. pure vanilla extract
- a dash of salt
- 2 teaspoons vanilla liquid stevia (optional)

DIRECTIONS

1. Mix coconut milk, chocolate chips, vanilla, stevia, plus salt in a slow cooker. Cover and cook on low within 2 hours.
2. Let it sit for 30 minutes to 1 hour. Stir well for 5 minutes until smooth.
3. Line a one-quart casserole dish with parchment paper and spread mixture. Chill 30 minutes or until firm. Serve and enjoy!

Nutrition: *Calories: 65 Fat: 5g Protein: 1g Carbs: 2g*

543. DARK CHOCOLATE CAKE

PREPARATION: 10 MIN **COOKING:** 3 H **SERVINGS:** 10 SLICES

INGREDIENTS

- Slow cooker size: 6-quart
- 1 cup plus 2 tbsp almond flour
- 1/2 cup Swerve Granular
- 1/2 cup cocoa powder
- 3 tbsp unflavored whey protein powder
- 1 1/2 tsp baking powder
- 1/4 tsp salt
- 6 tbsp butter melted
- 3 large eggs
- 2/3 cup unsweetened almond milk
- 3/4 tsp vanilla extract
- 1/3 cup sugar-free chocolate chips optional

DIRECTIONS

1. Oiled a 6-quart slow cooker. Mix almond flour, sweetener, cocoa powder, whey protein powder, baking powder, and salt in a medium bowl.
2. Mix in butter, eggs, almond milk plus vanilla extract, then mixes in chocolate chips, if using.
3. Put into the prepared slow cooker and cook on low within 2 to 2 1/2 hours. Turn the slow cooker off, let cold 20 to 30 minutes, and then cut into pieces and serve warm. Serve with lightly sweetened whipped cream.

Nutrition: *Calories: 205 Fat: 17g Protein: 7.4g Carbs: 8.4g*

544. PUMPKIN PECAN SPICE CAKE

PREPARATION: 10MIN **COOKING:** 3 H **SERVINGS:** 4

INGREDIENTS

- Slow cooker size: 6-quart
- 1 1/2 cups raw pecans
- 3/4 cup Swerve Sweetener
- 1/3 cup coconut flour
- 1/4 cup unflavored whey protein powder
- 2 tsp baking powder
- 1 1/2 tsp ground cinnamon
- 1 tsp ground ginger
- 1/4 tsp ground cloves
- 1/4 tsp salt
- 1 cup pumpkin puree
- 4 large eggs
- 1/4 cup butter melted
- 1 tsp vanilla extract

DIRECTIONS

1. Grease the ceramic liner of the 6-quart slow cooker or line with parchment paper.
2. Grind pecans using a food processor or high-powered blender. Transfer to a bowl and whisk in sweetener, coconut flour, whey protein powder, baking powder, cinnamon, ginger, cloves, and salt.
3. Stir in pumpkin puree, eggs, butter, and vanilla until well combined. Spread into the prepared slow cooker and set to low. Cook 2 1/2 to 3 hours, or until set and top is barely firm to the touch. Serve and enjoy!

Nutrition: *Calories: 344 Fat: 30.4g Protein: 8.3g Carbs: 10g*

545. GLAZED WALNUTS

PREPARATION: 5 MIN **COOKING:** 2 H **SERVINGS:** 4

INGREDIENTS

- 16 oz. walnuts
- ½ cup butter
- ½ cup maple syrup
- 1 tsp. vanilla extract

DIRECTIONS

1. Put the walnuts, butter, maple syrup, and vanilla extract into the slow cooker. Cook for 2 hours on low.
2. Stir every 25 minutes to be sure all the walnuts are covered and not burned. After the time is over, take the walnuts off and cool on parchment paper. Serve.

Nutrition: *Calories: 205 Fat: 17g Protein: 7.4g Carbs: 8.4g*

546. KETO GRANOLA

PREPARATION: 10 MIN **COOKING:** 2 H **SERVINGS:** 4

INGREDIENTS

- 1/3 cup coconut oil
- 1 tsp vanilla extract
- 1 tsp vanilla stevia
- 1/2 cup almonds
- 1/2 cup walnuts
- 1/2 cup pecans
- 1/2 cup hazelnuts
- 1 cup sunflower seeds
- 1 cup pumpkin seeds
- 1 cup unsweetened shredded coconut
- 1/2 cup sweetener
- 1 tsp ground cinnamon
- 1 tsp salt

DIRECTIONS

1. Set your slow cooker to low, then put coconut oil, and allow it to melt. Once melted, add vanilla extract and stevia. Stir well before adding nuts, seeds, and coconut.
2. Stir the granola mixture well to make sure all is coated. Whisk the sweetener, cinnamon, and salt together, then sprinkle over the nut and seed mixture.
3. Cover and cook on low within 2 hours or until you can smell them and they appear browned and toasted. Stir every 30 minutes.
4. Pour and spread out onto a baking pan to cool and refrigerate. Keep stored in a covered container.

Nutrition: *Calories: 327 Fat: 31g Protein: 7g Carbs: 8g*

547. MAPLE CUSTARD

PREPARATION: 15 MIN **COOKING:** 2 H **SERVINGS:** 4

INGREDIENTS

- 2 egg yolks
- 2 eggs
- 1 cup heavy cream
- 1/2 cup whole milk
- 1/4 cup brown sugar
- 1 tsp maple extract
- 1/4 tsp salt
- 1/2 tsp cinnamon

DIRECTIONS

1. Combine all the fixings into a stand mixer and blend on medium-high. Oiled six 4-ounce capacity ramekins, then put the batter into each, filling each only 3/4 way.
2. Put 4 ramekins on the bottom of the slow cooker. Arrange the other 2 on top of the bottom ramekins.
3. Cook within 2 hours on high. Remove from the slow cooker and cool to room temperature for 1 hour, then place in the fridge to chill for 2 hours. Enjoy with some sugar-free whipped cream and a sprinkle of cinnamon!

Nutrition: *Calories: 190 Fat: 18g Protein: 4g Carbs: 2g*

548. RASPBERRY CREAM CHEESE COFFEE CAKE

PREPARATION: 15 MIN **COOKING:** 4 H **SERVINGS:** 4

INGREDIENTS

Cake Batter:
- 1 1/4 almond flour
- 1/2 cup swerve sweetener
- 1/4 cup coconut flour
- 1/4 cup protein powder
- 1 1/2 tsp baking powder
- 1/4 tsp salt
- 3 large eggs
- 6 tbsp butter melted
- 2/3 cup water
- 1/2 tsp vanilla extract

Filling:
- 8 oz. cream cheese
- 1/3 cup powdered Swerve Sweetener
- 1 large egg
- 2 tbsp whipping cream
- 1 1/2 cup fresh raspberries

DIRECTIONS

1. Oiled a 6-quart slow cooker.
2. For the cake batter, mix the almond flour, sweetener, coconut flour, protein powder, baking powder, plus salt in a medium bowl. Mix in the eggs, melted butter, plus water, then set aside.
3. For the filling, beat the cream cheese plus sweetener until smooth. Mix in the egg, whipping cream, plus vanilla extract.
4. Put about 2/3 of the batter in the prepared slow cooker. Put the cream cheese batter over the batter in the pan and spread evenly. Put the raspberries.
5. Put the rest of the batter over the filling in a small spoonful. Bake on low within 3 to 4 hours. Allow cooling completely before serving. Serve and enjoy!

Nutrition: *Calories: 239 Fat: 19.2g Protein: 7.5g Carbs: 7g*

549. PUMPKIN PIE BARS

PREPARATION: 15 MIN   **COOKING:** 3 H   **SERVINGS:** 16

INGREDIENTS

Crust:
- 3/4 cup shredded coconut, unsweetened
- 1/4 cup cocoa powder, unsweetened
- 1/2 cup raw sunflower seeds, unsalted or sunflower seed flour
- 1/4 teaspoon salt
- 1/4 cup sweetener
- 4 tablespoons butter softened

Filling:
- 1 29 oz. can make pumpkin puree
- 1 cup heavy cream
- 6 eggs
- 1/2 teaspoon salt
- 1 tablespoon vanilla extract
- 1 tablespoon pumpkin pie spice
- 1 teaspoon cinnamon liquid stevia
- 1 teaspoon pure stevia extract
- Optional: 1/2 cup sugar-free chocolate chips

DIRECTIONS

1. Process all the fixings for the crust in a food processor. Oiled bottom of a slow cooker.
2. Press the crust batter onto the bottom of the slow cooker as evenly as possible. Put the filling fixings to a stand mixer and blend.
3. Mix in or top filling using the optional chocolate chips if desired. Pour batter onto the crust. Cover and cook on low within 3 hours.
4. Uncover, then let it cool 30 minutes, then refrigerate for at least 3 hours. Slice and serve!

Nutrition: *Calories: 151 Fat: 12.4g Protein: 5.4g Carbs: 6.2g*

550. LEMON CUSTARD

PREPARATION: 15 MIN   **COOKING:** 3 H   **SERVINGS:** 4

INGREDIENTS

- 5 large egg yolks
- 1/4 cup freshly squeezed lemon juice
- 1 tbsp lemon zest
- 1 tsp vanilla extract
- 1/2 tsp liquid stevia
- 2 cups whipping cream or coconut cream
- lightly sweetened whipped cream or whipped coconut

DIRECTIONS

1. Mix the egg yolks, lemon juice, lemon zest, vanilla, and liquid stevia in a medium bowl. Mix in the heavy cream and divide the batter among 4 small ramekins or jars.
2. Put a rack in the bottom of the slow cooker, then put the ramekins on the rack. Put enough water to reach half of the ramekins. Cover and cook on low within 3 hours.
3. Remove, then let cool at room temperature, then chill thoroughly in the refrigerator (about 3 hours). Top with whipped cream and serve.

Nutrition: *Calories: 319 Fat: 30g Protein: 7g Carbs: 3g*

551. APPLE BROWN

PREPARATION: 10 MIN **COOKING:** 4 H **SERVINGS:** 4

INGREDIENTS

- 3 lbs. cooking apples, cored and in 2-inch pieces
- 10 slices of bread, broken into small pieces
- ¾ cup brown sugar
- ¼ teaspoon nutmeg, ground
- ½ teaspoon cinnamon, ground
- ½ cup butter, melted
- 1/8 teaspoon salt

DIRECTIONS

1. Put the apples in the slow cooker. In a bowl, assemble and mix bread cubes and all other ingredients and spread them on top of the apples. Cook within 2 ½ to 4 hours on low.

Nutrition: *Calories: 142 Carbs: 29g Fat: 2g Protein: 1g*

552. BAKED CUSTARD

PREPARATION: 15 MIN **COOKING:** 3 H **SERVINGS:** 4

INGREDIENTS

- 3 eggs, beaten lightly
- 1/3 cup sugar, granulated
- 1 teaspoon vanilla
- ¼ teaspoon ground nutmeg
- 2 cups of milk

DIRECTIONS

1. Assemble and mix milk, eggs, vanilla, and sugar in a bowl. Grease a small baking dish, pour the mixture, and drizzle some nutmeg.
2. Add 1 ½ or 2 cups of water to the baking dish, cover it in an aluminum foil, and place on a rack in the slow cooker—Cook for 2 ½ 3 hours on high. Serve.

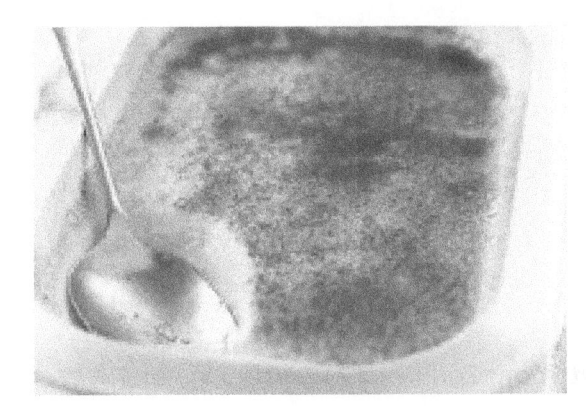

Nutrition: *Calories: 102 Carbs: 14g Fat: 3g Protein: 0g*

553. CARAMEL RUM FONDUE

PREPARATION: 15 MIN **COOKING:** 2 H **SERVINGS:** 4

INGREDIENTS

- 1 bag (14 oz.) oz. caramels
- 2/3 cup whipping cream
- ½ cup miniature marshmallows
- 2 to 3 teaspoons rum

DIRECTIONS

1. Assemble and cook the whipping cream and caramels in a slow cooker. Cook within 1 hour and 30 minutes on low and make sure the caramels have melted. Add and mix the rum and marshmallows and cook for 30 minutes longer. Serve.

Nutrition: *Calories: 125 Carbs: 25g Fat: 2g Protein: 1g*

554. TRIPLE CHOCOLATE MESS

PREPARATION: 10 MIN **COOKING:** 6 H **SERVINGS:** 4

INGREDIENTS

- 20 oz. chocolate cake mix
- 6 oz. chocolate chips
- 4 eggs
- 4 oz. instant chocolate pudding mix
- 1 cup of water
- 1-pint sour cream
- ¾ cup oil

DIRECTIONS

1. Grease the slow cooker. Assemble all ingredients and coon for 5-6 hours on low. It comes out better if you do not lift the lid while cooking. Best served with ice cream.

Nutrition: *Calories: 190 Carbs: 21g Fat: 11g Protein: 2g*

555. RICE PUDDING

PREPARATION: 10 MIN **COOKING:** 5 H **SERVINGS:** 4

INGREDIENTS

- ¾ cup short-grain rice
- 15 oz. evaporated milk
- 2 cups of water
- 1/3 cup white sugar
- ½ cup raisins
- 1 ½ teaspoons vanilla
- ¾ teaspoon salt
- 3-inch cinnamons stick

DIRECTIONS

1. Assemble all the ingredients and stir well in a slow cooker. Cook on low for 2 to 2 ½ hours on high. Stir a few times in between. Serve.

Nutrition: *Calories: 232 Carbs: 52g Fat: 2g Protein: 4g*

556. CARAMEL PIE

PREPARATION: 10 MIN **COOKING:** 7 H **SERVINGS:** 4

INGREDIENTS

- 15 oz. sweetened milk, condensed
- 1 9-inch graham cracker crust
- 8 oz. frozen whipped topping, thawed
- 1 ½ oz. English toffee-flavored candy bars, coarsely ground

DIRECTIONS

1. Cook condensed milk in a slow cooker for 6-7 hours, whisking every 30 minutes. Pour into the cracker crust and let cool.
2. Sprinkle the whipped topping and on top of that, sprinkle the ground candy bar. Cover and refrigerate. Serve.

Nutrition: *Calories: 125 Carbs: 25g Fat: 2g Protein: 1g*

557. BERRY COBBLER

PREPARATION: 15 MIN **COOKING:** 2 H 30 MIN **SERVINGS:** 4

INGREDIENTS

- 1 ¼ cups all-purpose flour
- 2 tablespoons sugar
- 1 cup of sugar
- 1 teaspoon baking powder
- ¼ teaspoon cinnamon, ground
- 1 egg, lightly beaten
- ¼ cup non-fat milk
- 2 tablespoons canola oil
- 1/8 teaspoon salt
- 2 cups raspberries, unsweetened
- 2 cups blueberries, unsweetened
- 2 cups reduced-fat vanilla frozen yogurt

DIRECTIONS

1. Assemble 1 cup flour, baking powder, 2 tablespoon sugar, and cinnamon in a bowl. Assemble the egg, oil, milk, and mix both the bowls' contents to make them into a batter.
2. Grease a slow cooker and spread the batter evenly. In a bowl, assemble the salt, the rest of the flour, and sugar. Toss in the berries and coat them—Cook for 2 and 30 minutes on low. Serve.

Nutrition: *Calories: 153 Carbs: 25g Fat: 5g Protein: 1g*

558. MINTY HOT FUDGE SUNDAE CAKE

PREPARATION: 15 MIN **COOKING:** 4 H 30 MIN **SERVINGS:** 4

INGREDIENTS

- 5 tablespoons baking cocoa
- 1 cup packed brown sugar
- 1 cup all-purpose flour
- 2 teaspoons baking powder
- 1/8 teaspoon almond extract
- ½ teaspoon vanilla extract
- 2 tablespoons melted butter
- ½ cup evaporated milk
- 5 oz. mint Andes candies
- 1 cup boiling water
- ½ teaspoon salt
- 4 teaspoons instant coffee granules
- Whipped cream, vanilla ice cream, and maraschino cherries

DIRECTIONS

1. Assemble the flour, brown sugar, 3 tablespoons cocoa, salt, and baking powder in a bowl. In another bowl, assemble the extracts, butter, and milk.
2. Mix the contents of the two bowls and place them in a greased slow cooker. Crush and drizzle the candies on top.
3. Assemble the coffee, water, and the rest of the brown sugar and cocoa. Pour this mixture over the slow cooker. Remember not to stir.
4. Cook for 4 hours and 30 minutes on high. Serve with whipped cream, vanilla ice cream, and maraschino cherries.

Nutrition: *Calories: 280 Carbs: 0g Fat: 13g Protein: 5g*

559. CRANBERRY STUFFED APPLES

PREPARATION: 15 MIN **COOKING:** 4-5 H **SERVINGS:** 4

INGREDIENTS

- 5 medium apples
- ¼ cup brown sugar
- 1/3 cup cranberries, chopped
- 2 tablespoons walnuts, chopped
- 1/8 teaspoon nutmeg, ground
- ¼ teaspoon cinnamon, ground
- Either whipped cream or vanilla ice cream.

DIRECTIONS

1. Peal out the core of the apples, leaving the bottom intact. In a bowl, assemble the brown sugar, walnuts, cranberries, and nutmeg and stuff the apples with this mix. Cook for 4-5 hours on low. Serve either with whipped cream or with vanilla ice cream.

Nutrition: *Calories: 136 Carbs: 31g Fat: 2g Protein: 1g*

---

560. MOLTEN MOCHA CAKE

PREPARATION: 15 MIN **COOKING:** 3 H **SERVINGS:** 4

INGREDIENTS

- 4 eggs
- 1 cup of sugar
- 3 teaspoons vanilla extract
- ½ cup butter, melted
- 1 cup all-purpose flour
- 1 tablespoon instant coffee granules
- ½ cup baking cocoa
- ¼ teaspoon salt

DIRECTIONS

1. Assemble the eggs, butter, sugar, and vanilla in a bowl and beat until blended. In a separate bowl, assemble the cocoa, flour, coffee, and salt and whisk. Add this to the egg mixture and place in a slow cooker. Cook for 2 ½ to 3 hours on low. Serve.

Nutrition: *Calories: 250 Carbs: 32g Fat: 13g Protein: 6g*

561. PUMPKIN PIE PUDDING

PREPARATION: 15 MIN   **COOKING:** 6-7 H   **SERVINGS:** 4

INGREDIENTS

- 15 oz. Pumpkin puree
- 2 ½ teaspoons pumpkin pie spice
- 2 teaspoons vanilla extract
- 12 oz. evaporated milk
- 2 large eggs, beaten
- 2 tablespoons butter, melted
- ½ cup biscuit or baking mix
- ¾ cup of sugar
- Whipped topping, optional

DIRECTIONS

1. Assemble and mix all the ingredients except the topping in a greased slow cooker. Cook for 6-7 hours on low. Spread topping before serving.

Nutrition: *Calories: 168 Carbs: 30g Fat: 3g Protein: 5g*

562. NUTTY APPLE STREUSEL

PREPARATION: 15 MIN   **COOKING:** 6-8 H   **SERVINGS:** 4

INGREDIENTS

- 6 cups tart apples, peeled and sliced
- ¼ teaspoon ground allspice
- 1 ¼ teaspoon ground cinnamon
- ¼ teaspoon ground nutmeg
- 2 tablespoons softened butter
- ¾ cup 2% milk
- ¾ cup of sugar
- 1 teaspoon vanilla extract
- ½ cup biscuit or baking mix
- 2 eggs

Topping:
- 3 tablespoons cold butter
- 1/3 cup packed brown sugar
- 1 cup biscuit crumbs
- ½ cup sliced almonds

DIRECTIONS

1. Assemble the apples, allspice, cinnamon, and nutmeg in a medium-slow cooker. Assemble in a small bowl the eggs, butter, sugar, milk, vanilla, and the baking mix.
2. Spoon the mixture over the apples. Cook for 6-8 hours on low. Mix all toppings and spread over the dessert, and serve.

Nutrition: *Calories: 100 Carbs: 12g Fat: 5g Protein: 1g*

563. PRUNE DESSERT

PREPARATION: 15 MIN **COOKING:** 3 H **SERVINGS:** 4

INGREDIENTS

- 2 cups dried and pitted prunes, soaked overnight in water
- Lemon or orange peel, from half an orange
- ¼ cup almonds or walnuts, chopped
- ½ cup of sugar
- 2/3 cup boiling water
- Whipped cream or some whipped topping

DIRECTIONS

1. Assemble all ingredients in a slow cooker and cook for 3 hours on high. Discard the rest and serve the prunes topped with whipped cream or some whipped topping

Nutrition: *Calories: 80 Carbs: 20g Fat: 0g Protein: 0g*

564. PEACH BUTTER

PREPARATION: 15 MIN **COOKING:** 8-11 H **SERVINGS:** 1 JAR

INGREDIENTS

- 6 cups peaches, unsweetened
- 1 and ½ cup apricot nectar
- 3 cups white sugar
- 1 teaspoon vanilla
- 2 tablespoons orange or lemon juice

DIRECTIONS

1. Puree the peaches and assemble all the ingredients in a slow cooker. Cook for 3 hours on low, stirring every hour.
2. Uncover and cook till the excess liquid evaporates, or 5-8 hours, depending on your cooker. Store or serve.

Nutrition: *Calories: 30 Carbs: 8g Fat: 0g Protein: 0g*

565. FRUIT COBBLER

PREPARATION: 15 MIN   **COOKING:** 5 H 30 MIN   **SERVINGS:** 4

INGREDIENTS

- 2 cups frozen peach, sliced
- 2 cups mixed frozen berries
- ½ teaspoon nutmeg
- 2 tablespoons cornstarch
- 1 teaspoon vanilla extract
- ½ teaspoon cinnamon, ground
- ½ cup brown sugar
- 20 oz. white cake mix
- ½ cup melted butter

DIRECTIONS

1. Grease the slow cooker. Mix the berries and peaches. Add cornstarch and coat well. Stir in the nutmeg, vanilla, cinnamon, and brown sugar.
2. Pour the white cake mix and sprinkle it with melted butter. Cook for 3 to 3 ½ hours on high. Serve.

Nutrition: *Calories: 235 Carbs: 43g Fat: 65g*

566. CHERRY ALMOND DESSERT OATMEAL

PREPARATION: 15 MIN   **COOKING:** 7 H   **SERVINGS:** 4

INGREDIENTS

- 2 cups vanilla almond milk
- 1 ½ cups water
- 1 cup steel-cut oats
- ¾ cup dried tart cherries
- ½ cup unsweetened organic applesauce
- 1 tablespoon ground flax seed
- ½ teaspoon pure almond extract
- Pinch of salt
- A drizzle of organic honey

DIRECTIONS

1. Grease your slow cooker with a coconut-oil based spray. Add everything to the cooker except honey and cover. Cook on low for 7 hours. When time is up, divide into bowls, drizzle each with honey, and serve!

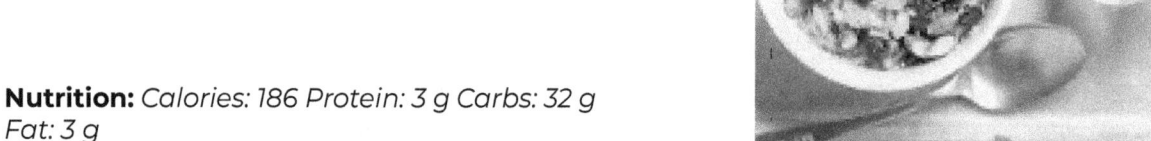

Nutrition: *Calories: 186 Protein: 3 g Carbs: 32 g Fat: 3 g*

567. MOLTEN LAVA CAKE

PREPARATION: 15 MIN **COOKING:** 2 H **SERVINGS:** 4

INGREDIENTS

Cake:
- 2 cups oat flour
- 1 ½ cups organic coconut sugar
- 1 cup unsweetened coconut milk
- 6 tablespoons organic cocoa powder
- 4 tablespoons grass-fed melted butter
- 1 tablespoon baking powder
- 2 teaspoons vanilla
- 1 teaspoon salt

Sauce:
- 2 cups boiling water
- ¾ cup of organic coconut sugar
- ½ cup organic cocoa powder
- ¼ cup of organic honey

DIRECTIONS

1. Grease a slow cooker with a coconut-oil based cooker. In a bowl, mix flour, cocoa, sugar, salt, and baking powder.
2. Add in melted butter, vanilla, and coconut milk until smooth. Pour into the slow cooker. In another bowl, looking to the sauce list, mix cocoa powder and sugar. Sprinkle over cake batter. In a third bowl, mix honey and boiling water.
3. Pour over the cake without mixing, and cover the lid. Cook on high for 1 ½-2 hour. You can tell the cake is done when it's puffed up and firm on top, with the sauce having sunk to the bottom. Serve warm!

Nutrition: *Calories: 317 Protein: 5 g Carbs: 65 g Fat: 7 g*

568. MAPLE CRÉME BRÛLÉE

PREPARATION: 15 MIN **COOKING:** 2 H 30 MIN **SERVINGS:** 3

INGREDIENTS

- Créme:
- Boiling water
- 1 1/3 cups heavy whipping cream
- 3 egg yolks
- ½ cup of coconut sugar
- ½ teaspoon pure organic maple extract
- ¼ teaspoon cinnamon
- Topping:
- 3 teaspoons coconut sugar

DIRECTIONS

1. In a saucepan, heat cream until the sides begin to bubble on the sides gently. While that is getting hot, whisk eggs, yolks, sugar, and cinnamon together.
2. When the cream is forming bubbles on the side, then remove it from heat. Stir a little of this hot cream into the yolks.
3. Pour yolks into the pan and constantly whisk to integrate, then put the maple. Move créme into 6-oz. ramekins.
4. Put in your slow cooker and pour in one inch's worth of boiling water. Cook on high for 2 hours and 30 minutes hours until the ramekins jiggle, but the center is set.
5. Cool for 10 minutes outside of the cooker before wrapping in saran wrap and refrigerating for 4 hours.
6. When you're ready to eat, add 1 teaspoon of sugar per ramekin on top, and Brulee with a torch. Enjoy!

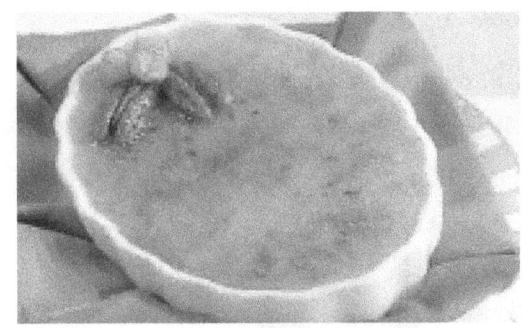

Nutrition: *Calories: 578 Protein: 5g Carbs: 44g Fat: 44g*

569. LEMON PUDDING CAKE

PREPARATION: 15 MIN **COOKING:** 2 H **SERVINGS:** 4

INGREDIENTS

- 2/3 cup plain Greek yogurt
- 2 egg yolks
- 2 egg whites
- ½ cup of coconut sugar
- ¼ cup flour
- 1 lemon's worth of juice and zest
- ¼ teaspoon salt
- Water

DIRECTIONS

1. Grease four 6-ounce ramekins. In a bowl, whisk flour, salt, and sugar. In another bowl, mix egg yolks, yogurt, lemon juice, and lemon zest.
2. When smooth, add dry ingredients into wet until just mixed. In another bowl, beat the egg whites until you get stiff peaks.
3. Fold whites into the batter. Divide batter into the ramekins and set in your slow cooker. Put in just enough water to reach the halfway mark.
4. Close lid and cook on low for 2 hours. Cool for 10 minutes before serving!

Nutrition: Calories: 216 Protein: 6g Carbs: 35g Fat: 6g

570. CHAI-SPICED PEARS

PREPARATION: 15 MIN **COOKING:** 3-4 H **SERVINGS:** 4

INGREDIENTS

- 4 pears
- 2 cups fresh orange juice
- 5 whole cardamom pods
- ¼ cup pure maple syrup
- 1-inch piece of sliced peeled ginger
- 1 halved cinnamon stick

DIRECTIONS

1. Peel pears and cut off the bottom so it stands up in the slow cooker. Carefully remove the cores without destroying the fruit.
2. Put pears in the slow cooker, standing up. Add the rest of the ingredients, spooning some juice over the top of the pears.
3. Cook on low for 3-4 hours, basting again with liquid every hour. When the pears are soft, they're done!

Nutrition: *Calories: 253 Protein: 2g Carbs: 61g Fat: 1g*

571. CRANBERRY WALNUT BREAD PUDDING

PREPARATION: 15 MIN **COOKING:** 4 H **SERVINGS:** 4

INGREDIENTS

- 5 cups cubed whole-wheat (or whole-grain) bread
- 2 ½ cups whole organic milk
- 3 beaten organic eggs
- ½ cup unsweetened dried cranberries
- ½ cup chopped walnuts
- ½ cup pure maple syrup
- ½ cup grass-fed butter
- 1 teaspoon pure vanilla extract
- Dash of cinnamon

DIRECTIONS

1. In a bowl, whisk milk, eggs, syrup, cinnamon, and vanilla together. Add bread and press it down so it's submerged. Soak for 10 minutes.
2. In the meantime, grease your slow cooker with a coconut-oil based spray. When 10 minutes have passed, add nuts and cranberries to the pudding.
3. Pour into the slow cooker—Cook for 4 hours on low.
4. Add butter to a saucepan. Cook on medium, stirring every once and a while, to get brown butter. The butter will become aromatic, like a caramel, and get an amber color. Serve.

Nutrition: *Calories: 488 Protein: 8g Carbs: 35g Fat: 26g*

572. ALMOND BANANA BREAD

PREPARATION: 15 MIN **COOKING:** 4 H **SERVINGS:** 4

INGREDIENTS

- 3 mashed bananas
- 2 cups whole-wheat flour
- 2 organic eggs
- 1 cup of organic coconut sugar
- ¾ cup sliced almonds
- ½ cup grass-fed softened butter
- 1 teaspoon baking powder
- 1 teaspoon pure almond extract
- ½ teaspoon baking soda
- ½ teaspoon salt
- ¼ teaspoon cinnamon
- 1/8 teaspoon nutmeg

DIRECTIONS

1. Grease your slow cooker with a coconut-oil based spray. In a large bowl, mix sugar, eggs, butter, and almond extract.
2. Add in baking soda, baking powder, salt, nutmeg, and cinnamon. Stir in flour. Stir in your mashed bananas and almonds.
3. Move batter to your slow cooker and cover with 3 paper towels—Cook for 4 hours on low.
4. When time is up, carefully turning the slow cooker pot upside down on a plate to remove the bread. Serve at room temperature or cold!

Nutrition: *Calories: 570 Protein: 11g Carbs: 85g Fat: 23g*

573. MAPLE ROASTED PEAR CRUMBLE

PREPARATION: 15 MIN   **COOKING:** 4 H 30 MIN   **SERVINGS:** 4

INGREDIENTS

- 6 firm pears, cut in half
- ½ cup of water
- ¼ cup pure maple syrup
- 1 teaspoon pure vanilla extract
- 1 teaspoon cinnamon
- ½ teaspoon ginger
- ¼ teaspoon nutmeg
- Crumble:
- 2/3 cups rolled oats
- 2 tablespoons organic coconut sugar
- 1 tablespoon pure maple syrup
- 1 tablespoon coconut oil

DIRECTIONS

1. Put all the fixings in the first list in the slow cooker. Cook on high within 1 hour, and then switch to low for 4 hours. When done, put pears and some cooking liquid in an 8x8 baking dish.
2. For the crumble, pulse the ingredients in the second list in a food processor until oats are sticky. Sprinkle topping on pears and bake in a 350-degree oven for 30 minutes. Serve!

Nutrition: *Calories: 260 Protein: 2g Carbs: 57g Fat: 3g*

574. SUGARY MANDARIN & ALMOND PUDDING

PREPARATION: 10 MIN   **COOKING:** 2 H 30 MIN   **SERVINGS:** 2

INGREDIENTS

- ½ mandarin, sliced
- Juice of 1 mandarin
- 1 tablespoon sugar
- 2 oz. butter, soft
- 1 egg
- ½ cup of sugar
- ½ cup flour
- ½ teaspoon baking powder
- ½ cup almonds, ground
- Cooking spray

DIRECTIONS

1. Grease your slow cooker with cooking spray, sprinkle half of the sugar on the bottom, and arrange mandarin slices.
2. In a bowl, mix butter with the rest of the sugar, egg, almonds, flour, baking powder, and the mandarin juice and whisk well
3. Spread this over mandarin slices, cover, cook on high for 2 hours and 30 minutes, transfer to a platter, and serve cold. Enjoy!

Nutrition: *Calories: 200 Fat: 4g Carbs: 8g Protein: 6g*

575. SUGARY PLUMS

PREPARATION: 10 MIN **COOKING:** 3 H **SERVINGS:** 2

INGREDIENTS

- 6 plums, halved and pitted
- ½ cup of sugar
- 1 teaspoon cinnamon, ground
- ¼ cup of water
- 1 tablespoon cornstarch

DIRECTIONS

1. Put plums in your slow cooker, add sugar, cinnamon, water, and cornstarch, stir, cover, and cook on low for 3 hours. Serve as a dessert.

Nutrition: *Calories: 180 Fat: 2g Carbs: 8g Protein: 8g*

576. CARDAMOM PLUM CREAM

PREPARATION: 10 MIN **COOKING:** 7 H **SERVINGS:** 2

INGREDIENTS

- 1 and ½ pounds plums, pitted and halved
- ½ cup of water
- ¼ teaspoon cinnamon, ground
- ¼ teaspoon cardamom, ground
- ¼ cup of sugar

DIRECTIONS

1. Put plums and water in your slow cooker, cover, and cook on low for 1 hour. Add cinnamon, sugar, and cardamom, stir, cover, cook on low for 6 hours more, divide into jars and serve. Enjoy!

Nutrition: *Calories: 280 Fat: 2g Carbs: 10g Protein: 6g*

577. VANILLA RHUBARB MIX

PREPARATION: 10 MIN **COOKING:** 6 H **SERVINGS:** 4

INGREDIENTS

- 2 cups rhubarb, chopped
- 1 tablespoon butter, melted
- ¼ cup of water
- ½ cup of sugar
- ½ teaspoon vanilla extract

DIRECTIONS

1. Put rhubarb in your slow cooker, add water and sugar, stir gently, cover, and cook on low for 6 hours. Add butter and vanilla, stir and keep in the fridge until it's cold. Enjoy!

Nutrition: *Calories: 200 Fat: 2g Carbs: 6g Protein: 1g*

578. PEACHES AND WHISKEY SAUCE

PREPARATION: 10 MIN **COOKING:** 2 H **SERVINGS:** 2

INGREDIENTS

- ½ cup brown sugar
- 1 and ½ cups peaches, pitted and cut into wedges
- 3 tablespoons whiskey
- ½ cup white sugar
- 1 teaspoon lemon zest, grated

DIRECTIONS

1. In your slow cooker, mix peaches with brown and white sugar, whiskey, and lemon zest, stir, cover, and cook on high for 2 hours. Divide into bowls and serve warm.

Nutrition: *Calories: 200 Fat: 4g Carbs: 9g Protein: 4g*

579. COCONUT CHOCOLATE CREAM

PREPARATION: 10 MIN **COOKING:** 1 H **SERVINGS:** 2

INGREDIENTS

- 2 oz. coconut cream
- 2 oz. dark chocolate, cut into chunks
- ½ teaspoon sugar

DIRECTIONS

1. In a bowl, mix coconut cream with chocolate and sugar, whisk well, pour into your slow cooker, cover, cook on high for 1 hour, divide into bowls and serve cold. Enjoy!

Nutrition: *Calories: 242 Fat: 12g Carbs: 9g Protein: 4g*

580. MAPLE CHERRY & COCOA COMPOTE

PREPARATION: 10 MIN   **COOKING:** 2 H   **SERVINGS:** 2

INGREDIENTS

- ¼ cup of cocoa powder
- ½ cup red cherry juice
- 2 tablespoons maple syrup
- ½ pound cherries pitted and halved
- 1 tablespoon sugar
- 1 cups of water

DIRECTIONS

1. In your slow cooker, mix cocoa with cherry juice, maple syrup, cherries, water, and sugar, stir, cover, cook on high for 2 hours, divide into bowls and serve cold. Enjoy!

Nutrition: *Calories: 200 Fat: 1g Carbs: 5g Protein: 2g*

---

581. DATES CASHEW CAKE

PREPARATION: 10 MIN   **COOKING:** 2 H   **SERVINGS:** 2

INGREDIENTS

For the base:
- ¼ cup dates pitted
- ½ tablespoon water
- ¼ teaspoon vanilla
- ¼ cup almonds

For the cake:
- 1 and ½ cups cashews, soaked for 8 hours
- ½ cup blueberries
- ½ cup maple syrup
- ½ tablespoon vegetable oil

DIRECTIONS

1. In your food processor, mix dates with water, vanilla, and almonds, pulse well, transfer it to a working surface, flatten and arrange it on the bottom of your slow cooker.
2. In your blender, mix maple syrup with coconut oil, cashews, and blueberries, blend well, spread over crust, cover, and cook on high for 2 hours. Leave the cake to cool down, slice, and serve.

Nutrition: Calories: 200 Fat: 3g Carbs: 12g Protein: 3g

THE SLOW COOKER COOKBOOK

581. DATES CASHEW CAKE

PREPARATION: 10 MIN   **COOKING:** 5 H   **SERVINGS:** 4

INGREDIENTS

- 20 mushrooms, stems removed
- 2 cups basil, chopped
- 1 cup tomato sauce, no-salt-added
- 2 tablespoons parsley, chopped
- ¼ cup low-fat parmesan, grated
- 1 and ½ cups whole wheat breadcrumbs
- 1 tablespoon garlic, minced
- ¼ cup low-fat butter, melted
- 2 teaspoons lemon juice
- 1 tablespoon olive oil

DIRECTIONS

1. In a bowl, mix butter with breadcrumbs and parsley, stir well, and leave aside. In your blender, mix basil with oil, parmesan, garlic, and lemon juice and pulse well.
2. Stuff mushrooms with this mix, pour the tomato sauce on top, sprinkle breadcrumbs mix at the end, and cook in the slow cooker on low for 5 hours. Arrange mushrooms on a platter and serve.

Nutrition: *Calories: 51 Fat: 1.1g Carbs: 9g Protein: 2.2g*

582. NUTMEG APPLES

PREPARATION: 10 MIN   **COOKING:** 1 H   **SERVINGS:** 2

INGREDIENTS

- ½ teaspoon cinnamon powder
- 3 oz. apples, cored and chopped
- 1 egg, whisked
- ¼ cup whipping cream
- 1 tablespoon sugar
- ½ teaspoon nutmeg, ground
- 1 teaspoon vanilla extract
- 2 tablespoons pecans, chopped

DIRECTIONS

1. In your slow cooker, mix cream, vanilla, nutmeg, sugar, apples, egg, and cinnamon, stir, cover, cook on high for 1 hour, divide into bowls, sprinkle pecans on top, and serve cold. Enjoy!

Nutrition: *Calories: 260 Fat: 3g Carbs: 14g Protein: 3g*

583. APPLE VANILLA CAKE

PREPARATION: 10 MIN **COOKING:** 2 H 30 MIN **SERVINGS:** 2

INGREDIENTS

- 1 and ½ cups apples, cored and cubed
- 1 and ½ tablespoons sugar
- 1 tablespoon vanilla extract
- 1 egg
- ½ tablespoon apple pie spice
- 1 cup white flour
- ½ tablespoon baking powder
- ½ tablespoon butter, melted

DIRECTIONS

1. In a bowl, mix eggs with butter, pie spice, vanilla, apples, and sugar and stir using your mixer. In another bowl, mix baking powder with flour, stir, add to apple mix, stir again well, transfer to your slow cooker, cover, cook on high for 2 hours and 30 minutes, leave cake aside to cool down, slice, and serve.

Nutrition: *Calories: 200 Fat: 2g Carbs: 5g Protein: 4g*

584. PEACH CRACKERS COBBLER

PREPARATION: 10 MIN **COOKING:** 4 H **SERVINGS:** 2

INGREDIENTS

- 2 cups peaches, peeled and sliced
- 3 tablespoons sugar
- ½ teaspoon cinnamon powder
- 1 cup sweet crackers, crushed
- ¼ teaspoon nutmeg, ground
- ¼ cup milk
- 1 teaspoon vanilla extract
- Cooking spray

DIRECTIONS

1. In a bowl, mix peaches with half of the sugar and cinnamon and stir. In another bowl, combine crackers with the rest of the sugar, nutmeg, almond milk, and vanilla extract and stir.
2. Oiled your slow cooker with cooking spray, spread peaches on the bottom, add crackers mix, spread, cover, and cook on low for 4 hours. Divide cobbler between plates and serve.

Nutrition: *Calories: 212 Fat: 4g Carbs: 7g Protein: 3g*

585. MILKY BLUEBERRY & ALMOND CAKE

PREPARATION: 10 MIN **COOKING:** 1 H **SERVINGS:** 2

INGREDIENTS

- ¼ cup flour
- ¼ teaspoon baking powder
- ¼ teaspoon sugar
- ¼ cup blueberries
- ½ cup milk
- 1 teaspoon olive oil
- ½ teaspoon lemon zest, grated
- ¼ teaspoon vanilla extract
- ¼ teaspoon lemon extract
- Cooking spray

DIRECTIONS

1. In a bowl, mix flour with baking powder and sugar and stir. Add blueberries, milk, oil, lemon zest, vanilla extract, and lemon extract and whisk well.
2. Spray your slow cooker with cooking spray, line it with parchment paper, pour cake batter, cover pot, and cook on high for 1 hour. Leave the cake to cool down, slice, and serve.

Nutrition: *Calories: 200 Fat: 4g Carbs: 10g Protein: 4g*

586. PEARS & ORANGE SAUCE

PREPARATION: 10 MIN **COOKING:** 4 H **SERVINGS:** 2

INGREDIENTS

- 2 pears, peeled and cored
- 1 cup of orange juice
- 2 tablespoons maple syrup
- 1 teaspoon cinnamon powder
- ½ tablespoon ginger, grated

DIRECTIONS

1. In your slow cooker, mix pears with orange juice, maple syrup, cinnamon, ginger, cover, and cook on low for 4 hours. Divide pears and sauce between plates and serve warm.

Nutrition: *Calories: 250 Fat: 1g Carbs: 12g Protein: 4g*

587. SUGARY ALMOND COOKIES

PREPARATION: 10 MIN **COOKING:** 2 H 30 MIN **SERVINGS:** 2

INGREDIENTS

- 1 tablespoon vegetable oil
- 2 eggs
- ¼ cup of sugar
- ¼ teaspoon vanilla extract
- ¼ teaspoon baking powder
- 1 cup flour
- ¼ cup almonds, chopped

DIRECTIONS

1. In a bowl, mix oil with sugar, vanilla extract, and eggs and whisk. Add baking powder, almond meal, and almonds and stir well.
2. Line your slow cooker with parchment paper, spread cookie mix on the bottom of the pot, cover, cook on low for 2 hours and 30 minutes, leave aside to cool down, cut into medium pieces and serve.

Nutrition: *Calories: 220 Fat: 2g Carbs: 6g Protein: 6g*

588. ZESTY STRAWBERRIES MARMALADE

PREPARATION: 10 MIN **COOKING:** 4 H **SERVINGS:** 2

INGREDIENTS

- 5 oz. strawberries, chopped
- ¼ pound sugar
- Zest of ½ lemon, grated
- 1-ounce raisins
- 1 1/2 oz. water

DIRECTIONS

1. In your slow cooker, mix strawberries with sugar, lemon zest, raisins, water, stir, cover, and cook on high for 4 hours. Divide into small jars and serve cold.

Nutrition: *Calories: 250 Fat: 3g Carbs: 6g Protein: 1g*

589. CHERRY COLA CAKE

PREPARATION: 15 MIN **COOKING:** 4 H **SERVINGS:** 4

INGREDIENTS

- ¼ cup of cocoa powder
- ¼ cup light brown sugar
- ¼ teaspoon salt
- ½ cup butter, melted
- ½ cup whole milk
- ½ teaspoon baking powder
- ½ teaspoon baking soda
- 1 ½ cups all-purpose flour
- 1 cup cola
- 1 teaspoon vanilla extract
- 2 cups cherries, pitted

DIRECTIONS

1. Combine the cola, sugar, butter, vanilla, and milk in a container. Put in the flour, cocoa powder, salt, baking powder, and baking soda and stir to mix.
2. Fold in the cherries. Spoon the batter in your slow cooker, switch your slow cooker to low, and cook for about 4 hours. Let the cake cool in the pot before you slice and serve.

Nutrition: *Calories: 440 Carbs: 62g Fat: 21g Protein: 3g*

---

590. AMARETTI CHEESECAKE

PREPARATION: 15 MIN **COOKING:** 6 H **SERVINGS:** 4

INGREDIENTS

- Crust:
- ¼ cup butter, melted
- 6 oz. Amaretti cookies, crushed
- Filling:
- ½ cup sour cream
- ½ cup white sugar
- 1 tablespoon Amaretto liqueur
- 1 tablespoon vanilla extract
- 24 oz. cream cheese
- 4 eggs

DIRECTIONS

1. Combine the crushed cookies with butter, then move the mixture to your slow cooker and press it well on the bottom of the pot.
2. For the filling, combine the cream cheese, sour cream, eggs, sugar, vanilla, and liqueur and stir to mix.
3. Pour the filling over the crust and cook for about six hours on low settings. Let the cheesecake cool before you slice and serve.

Nutrition: *Calories: 232 Carbs: 32g Fat: 24g Protein: 11g*

591. APPLE CINNAMON BRIOCHE PUDDING

PREPARATION: 15 MIN   **COOKING:** 6 H   **SERVINGS:** 4

INGREDIENTS

- ½ teaspoon ground ginger
- 1 cup evaporated milk
- 1 cup sweetened condensed milk
- 1 cup whole milk
- 1 teaspoon cinnamon powder
- 1 teaspoon vanilla extract
- 16 oz. brioche bread, cubed
- 2 tablespoons white sugar
- 4 eggs
- 4 Granny Smith apples, peeled and cubed

DIRECTIONS

1. Combine the brioche bread, apples, cinnamon, ginger, and sugar in your slow cooker. Mix the 3 types of milk in a container. Put in the eggs and vanilla and mix thoroughly.
2. Pour this mix over the bread, then cover the pot and cook for about 6 hours on low settings. The pudding tastes best when slightly warm.

Nutrition: *Calories: 176 Carbs: 22g Fat: 7g Protein: 6g*

---

592. BANANA WALNUT CAKE

PREPARATION: 15 MIN   **COOKING:** 4 H   **SERVINGS:** 4

INGREDIENTS

- ¼ teaspoon salt
- ½ cup canola oil
- 1 ¼ cups all-purpose flour
- 1 cup chopped walnuts
- 1 cup white sugar
- 1 teaspoon baking powder
- 1 teaspoon vanilla extract
- 2 eggs
- 4 small ripe bananas, mashed

DIRECTIONS

1. Mix the sugar plus oil in a container for about two minutes, then add the eggs and continue mixing for a few minutes until fluffy.
2. Put in the vanilla and bananas, fold in the flour, baking powder and salt, and walnuts. Pour the batter into your slow cooker and bake for about 4 hours on low. Slice and serve.

Nutrition: *Calories: 120 Carbs: 24g Fat: 3g Protein: 1g*

593. BLACK FOREST CAKE

PREPARATION: 15 MIN **COOKING:** 4 H **SERVINGS:** 4

INGREDIENTS

- ½ cup butter softened
- ½ cup of cocoa powder
- ½ teaspoon salt
- ¾ cup white sugar
- 1 cup all-purpose flour
- 1-pound pitted cherries
- 1 tablespoon cornstarch
- 1 teaspoon baking powder
- 1 teaspoon vanilla extract
- 2 tablespoons kirsch
- 3 eggs
- Whipped cream for serving

DIRECTIONS

1. Combine the cherries, kirsch, and cornstarch in the slow cooker. For the batter, combine the butter, sugar, and vanilla in a container until creamy.
2. Put in the eggs, fold in the rest of the ingredients, and not over-mix the batter. Spoon the batter over the cherries and cook for about 4 hours on low. Serve the cake chilled, with the topping of whipped cream.

Nutrition: *Calories: 295 Carbs: 30g Fat: 18g Protein: 4g*

594. BLUEBERRY DUMPLING PIE

PREPARATION: 15 MIN **COOKING:** 5 H **SERVINGS:** 4

INGREDIENTS

- ¼ cup light brown sugar
- ½ cup butter, chilled and cubed
- ½ teaspoon salt
- 1 ½ cups all-purpose flour
- 1 ½ pound fresh blueberries
- 1 tablespoon lemon zest
- 1 teaspoon baking powder
- 2 tablespoons cornstarch
- 2 tablespoons white sugar
- 2/3 cup buttermilk, chilled

DIRECTIONS

1. Combine the blueberries, cornstarch, brown sugar, and lemon zest in the slow cooker. For the dumpling topping, combine the flour, salt, baking powder, sugar, and butter in a container and mix until sandy.
2. Mix in the buttermilk and stir to mix. Drop a spoonful of batter over the blueberries, switch your slow cooker to a low setting, and cook for about 5 hours. Allow the dessert to cool before you serve.

Nutrition: *Calories: 320 Carbs: 41g Fat: 16g Protein: 3g*

595. BROWNED BUTTER PUMPKIN CHEESECAKE

PREPARATION: 15 MIN   **COOKING:** 6 H   **SERVINGS:** 4

INGREDIENTS

Crust:
- ½ cup butter
- 1 ¼ cups crushed graham crackers

Filling:
- ¼ cup butter
- ½ cup light brown sugar
- ½ teaspoon cardamom powder
- 1 cup pumpkin puree
- 1 pinch salt
- 1 teaspoon cinnamon powder
- 1 teaspoon ground ginger
- 24 oz. cream cheese
- 4 eggs

DIRECTIONS

1. For the crust, start by browning the butter. Put the butter in a saucepan and cook for a few minutes until it starts to look golden. Let cool slightly.
2. Combine the browned butter with crushed crackers, then move the mixture in your slow cooker and press it well on the bottom of the pot.
3. For the filling, brown ¼ cup butter as described above, mix in the pumpkin puree, cream cheese, eggs, sugar, salt, cinnamon, ginger, and cardamom.
4. Pour the mixture over the crust, switch your slow cooker to low, and cook for about 6 hours. Let the cheesecake cool down before you slice and serve.

Nutrition: *Calories: 142 Carbs: 23g Fat: 2g Protein: 11g*

---

596. BUTTER LIME CAKE

PREPARATION: 15 MIN   **COOKING:** 2 H   **SERVINGS:** 4

INGREDIENTS

- ¼ teaspoon salt
- 1 ¼ cups white sugar
- 1 ½ cups all-purpose flour
- 1 cup butter, softened
- 1 cup buttermilk
- 1 lime, zested and juiced
- 1 teaspoon baking powder
- 1 teaspoon vanilla extract
- 3 eggs

DIRECTIONS

1. Combine the butter and sugar in a container until creamy, for about 2 minutes. Put in the eggs, one by one, then mix in the vanilla, buttermilk, lime zest, and lime juice.
2. Fold in the rest of the ingredients, then pour the batter into a greased slow cooker. Secure the lid, switch the slow cooker to high, and cook for about 2 hours. Let the cake cool in the pot before you serve.

Nutrition: *Calories: 286 Carbs: 63g Fat: 2g Protein: 5g*

597. BUTTERSCOTCH CAKE

PREPARATION: 15 MIN   **COOKING:** 4 H   **SERVINGS:** 4

INGREDIENTS

- ½ cup butter softened
- ½ cup white sugar
- ½ cup whole milk
- ½ teaspoon salt
- 1 ½ cups all-purpose flour
- 1 cup butterscotch chocolate chips, melted
- 1 cup hot water
- 1 teaspoon baking powder

DIRECTIONS

1. Combine the butter and sugar in a container until creamy, at least 5 minutes. Put in the melted butterscotch chips, then mix in the milk and hot water.
2. Fold in the flour, salt, and baking powder, then pour the batter into your slow cooker—Bake for about 4 hours on low. Let cool completely before you serve.

Nutrition: *Calories: 211 Carbs: 42g Fat: 4g Protein: 2g*

598. CARAMEL APPLE CRISP

PREPARATION: 15 MIN   **COOKING:** 6 H   **SERVINGS:** 4

INGREDIENTS

- ¼ cup butter, chilled
- ½ cup caramel sauce
- ½ cup rolled oats
- ½ teaspoon cinnamon powder
- 1 cup all-purpose flour
- 1 pinch salt
- 1 tablespoon cornstarch
- 6 Granny Smith apples, peeled, cored, and sliced

DIRECTIONS

1. Combine the apples, caramel sauce, cinnamon, and cornstarch in the slow cooker. For the topping, combine the flour, oats, butter, and salt in a container until grainy.
2. Spread the topping over the apples, switch your slow cooker to a low setting and cook for about six hours. Allow the crisp to cool in the pot before you serve.

Nutrition: *Calories: 160 Carbs: 31g Fat: 1g Protein: 5g*

599. CARAMEL PEAR PUDDING CAKE

PREPARATION: 15 MIN **COOKING:** 4 H **SERVINGS:** 4

INGREDIENTS

- ¼ cup butter, melted
- ¼ cup whole milk
- ¼ teaspoon salt
- ½ cup of sugar
- ½ teaspoon cinnamon powder
- ¾ cup caramel sauce
- 1 teaspoon baking powder
- 2/3 cup all-purpose flour
- 4 ripe pears, cored and sliced

DIRECTIONS

1. Mix the flour, baking powder, sugar, salt, plus cinnamon in a container. Put in the butter and milk and stir to mix.
2. Put the pears in your slow cooker and top with the batter. Drizzle the batter with caramel sauce, switch your slow cooker to low, and cook for about 4 hours. Let the cake cool before you serve.

Nutrition: *Calories: 223 Carbs: 42g Fat: 6g Protein: 2g*

600. COCONUT CONDENSED MILK CUSTARD

PREPARATION: 15 MIN **COOKING:** 5 H **SERVINGS:** 4

INGREDIENTS

- 1 ¼ cups sweetened condensed milk
- 1 can (15 oz.) coconut milk
- 1 cup evaporated milk
- 1 tablespoon vanilla extract
- 1 teaspoon lime zest
- 6 eggs

DIRECTIONS

1. Combine the eggs, coconut milk, condensed milk, vanilla, lime zest, and evaporated milk in a container. Pour the mixture in the slow.
2. Secure the lid, switch your slow cooker to low, and cook for about 5 hours. Let cool before you serve.

Nutrition: *Calories: 154 Carbs: 26g Fat: 5g Protein: 0g*

CONCLUSION

So, congratulations on making it this far on your slow cooking journey! Where slow cookers really shine is when it comes to helping you live your regular busy life and eat healthily. They allow you to get home after a long day of work and let the slow cooker do all of the work. Or, let you throw your ingredients in, set the slow cooker, and take a shower or have a peaceful evening together with your family and friends.

While you may not always be able to use your slow cooker every single day, it will certainly make your meal preparation a whole lot easier. You'll be able to throw everything in while you finish up the dishes and clean up the house. Then, you can enjoy a hot meal with your friends or family once you're done! When you have a good slow cooker recipe in your repertoire, it can be effortless to eat healthy while still caring for your family's needs.

Some slow cooker meals are even relatively healthy already. You'll never have to worry about additional salt, fat, or sugar because the slow cooker does all of the work. You'll never be able to make something taste better than your slow cooker will! There are no shortcuts for having a good meal, so they're the perfect vessel for a healthy meal.

At the same time, slow cooker meals also have plenty of room for variations to change things up. There are many different kinds of dishes that can be made in a slow cooker. Whether you love meat dishes or you're a vegetarian, there are recipes out there for you. Every member of your family will be surprised and can enjoy a delicious, healthy meal.

I hope you have enjoyed these slow cooker recipes. I wish you success in taking another step towards improving your health, controlling your food intake and gaining more time to be yourself in your busy schedules.

So, let's wrap this cookbook up with one last tip. Always read the instructions before using! The best way to use any appliance, especially the slow cooker, is to read the instructions and keep them handy when you are slow cooking. They may be a little dense to read at first, but the instructions will tell you the exact instructions to follow each step.

So, have happy slow cooking and enjoy good healthy food!

THE SLOW COOKER COOKBOOK

RECIPE INDEX

INTRODUCTION	4
CHAPTER 1. HOW TO USE THE SLOW COOKER, TIPS AND TRICKS	6
CHAPTER 2. BREAKFAST	9
1. ZUCCHINI & SPINACH WITH BACON	10
2. PEPPERONI PIZZA WITH MEAT CRUST	10
3. SPINACH & SAUSAGE PIZZA	11
4. GREEK-STYLE FRITTATA WITH SPINACH AND FETA CHEESE	11
5. NUT & ZUCCHINI BREAD	12
6. CHEESE & CAULIFLOWER BAKE	12
7. HAM & CHEESE BROCCOLI BRUNCH BOWL	13
8. EGGPLANT & SAUSAGE BAKE	13
9. THREE-CHEESE ARTICHOKE HEARTS BAKE	14
10. SWEET HAM MAPLE BREAKFAST	14
11. SAUSAGE CASSEROLE BREAKFAST	15
12. MUSHROOM BACON BREAKFAST	15
13. ZUCCHINI CINNAMON NUT BREAD	16
14. HAM AND SPINACH FRITTATA	16
15. CHEESE GRITS	17
16. PINEAPPLE CAKE WITH PECANS	17
17. POTATO CASSEROLE FOR BREAKFAST	18
18. CINNAMON ROLLS	18
19. QUINOA PIE	19
20. QUINOA MUFFINS WITH PEANUT BUTTER	19
21. VEGGIE OMELETS	20
22. APPLE PIE WITH OATMEAL	20
23. VANILLA FRENCH TOAST	21
24. GREEK EGGS CASSEROLE	21
25. BANANA BREAD	22
26. TREACLE SPONGE WITH HONEY	22
27. STICKY PECAN BUNS WITH MAPLE	23
28. VEGETARIAN POT PIE	23
29. BLUEBERRY PORRIDGE	24
30. CAULIFLOWER AND EGGS BOWLS	24
31. MILK OATMEAL	25
32. ASPARAGUS EGG CASSEROLE	25
33. VANILLA MAPLE OATS	26
34. RASPBERRY OATMEAL	26
35. PORK AND EGGPLANT CASSEROLE	27
36. BABY SPINACH RICE MIX	27
37. BABY CARROTS IN SYRUP	28
38. GREEN MUFFINS	28
39. SCALLIONS AND BACON OMELET	29
40. COWBOY BREAKFAST CASSEROLE	29
41. MAPLE BANANA OATMEAL	30
42. POTATO MUFFINS	30
43. EGGS AND SWEET POTATO MIX	31
44. VEGGIE HASH BROWN MIX	31
45. COCONUT CRANBERRY QUINOA	32
46. SCRAMBLED EGGS IN RAMEKINS	32
47. ENCHILADA BREAKFAST CASSEROLE	33
48. WHITE CHOCOLATE OATMEAL	33
49. BACON-WRAPPED HOTDOGS	34
50. APPLE GRANOLA CRUMBLE	34
51. BANANA AND COCONUT MILK STEEL-CUT OATS	35
52. SPINACH AND MOZZARELLA FRITTATA	35
53. QUINOA ENERGY BARS	36
54. OVERNIGHT APPLE OATMEAL	36
55. APPLE WALNUT STRATA	36
56. NUTTY OATMEAL	37
57. BACON AND WAFFLE STRATA	37
58. HONEY APPLE BREAD PUDDING	38
59. SAUSAGE ROLLS	38

60. BREAKFAST PITAS	39	95. BBQ CHICKEN DIP	56
CHAPTER 3.SNACKS & APPETIZERS	**40**	96. LEMON SHRIMP DIP	57
61. OREGANO SALSA	41	97. ZUCCHINI STICKS	57
62. SMOKED PAPRIKA CAULIFLOWER SPREAD	41	98. CHICKEN CORDON BLEU DIP	57
63. FRENCH STYLE SALAD	42	99. EGGPLANT ZUCCHINI DIP	58
64. STEVIA AND BULGUR SALAD	42	100. CALAMARI RINGS BOWLS	58
65. PARMESAN STUFFED MUSHROOMS	43	101. CHICKEN BITES	59
66. GARLIC AND TOMATO APPETIZER	43	102. MAPLE GLAZED TURKEY STRIPS	59
67. TAHINI DIP	44	103. LENTILS ROLLS	60
68. LIME JUICE SNACK	44	104. CAULIFLOWER BITES	60
69. CUMIN HUMMUS	45	105. LEMON PEEL SNACK	60
70. PEPPERCORNS ASPARAGUS	45	106. CANDIED PECANS	61
71. LIGHT SHRIMP SALAD	46	107. DILL POTATO SALAD	61
72. MUSHROOM SALSA WITH PUMPKIN SEEDS	46	108. STUFFED PEPPERS PLATTER	62
73. ONION CHICKPEAS DIP	46	109. PEANUT SNACK	62
74. GARLIC AND BEANS SPREAD	47	110. CORN DIP	63
75. SOUR CREAM DIP	47	111. APPLE DIP	63
76. SIMPLE MEATBALLS	47	112. BEEF AND CHIPOTLE DIP	64
77. TASTY CHICKEN WINGS	48	113. PINEAPPLE AND TOFU SALSA	64
78. CHICKEN SPREAD	48	114. BUFFALO MEATBALLS	65
79. DIFFERENT CHICKEN DIP	49	115. GLAZED SAUSAGES	65
80. CARROT DIP	49	116. BULGUR AND BEANS SALSA	66
81. PEPPERONI DIP	50	117. CHEESY MIX	66
82. EGGPLANT SPREAD	50	118. BEETS SALAD	66
83. JALAPENO POPPERS	51	119. LENTILS SALSA	67
84. FISH STICKS	51	120. TACOS	67
85. SPICY PECANS	52	**CHAPTER 4.RICE, GRAINS & BEANS**	**68**
86. SAUSAGE APPETIZER	52	121. THREE BEAN MEDITERRANEAN CHILI	69
87. ASPARAGUS SPREAD	53	122. BEANS AND BARLEY STEW	69
88. BROCCOLI DIP	53	123. MEDITERRANEAN LENTILS AND RICE	70
89. CRAB AND ONION DIP	53	124. ITALIAN-MEDITERRANEAN MULTI-BEAN SOUP	70
90. SPINACH AND BACON DIP	54	125. SLOW COOKED GREEN BEANS	71
91. BEAN PESTO DIP	54	126. SPANISH RICE	71
92. CHEESY CHILI PEPPER DIP	55	127. WHOLE WHEAT LASAGNA	72
93. CREAMY MUSHROOM SPREAD	55	128. HOMINY CHILI	72
94. PORK TOSTADAS	56	129. SANTA FE BLACK BEANS	73

#	Recipe	Page
130.	CHICKEN AND CHICKPEA TAGINE	73
131.	WHITE BEAN AND SMOKED HAM SOUP	74
132.	CINCINNATI CHILI	74
133.	BLACK BEAN AND SWEET POTATO CHILI	75
134.	WHITE LIME TOFU CHILI	75
135.	BAKED BEANS	75
136.	BBQ BEANS	76
137.	SWEET & TANGY COWBOY BEANS	76
138.	JALAPENO PINTO BEANS	77
139.	HAWAIIAN BEANS	77
140.	HEALTHY WILD RICE	78
141.	HERBED BROWN RICE	78
142.	RED BEANS & RICE	79
143.	PUMPKIN RISOTTO	79
144.	PARMESAN RISOTTO	80
145.	MEXICAN RICE	80
146.	MEXICAN QUINOA	80
147.	APPLE CINNAMON QUINOA	81
148.	SPINACH BARLEY RISOTTO	81
149.	CUBAN BLACK BEANS	81
150.	TOMATILLO RICE	82
151.	VEGETABLE FRIED RICE	82
152.	PAELLA	83
153.	PORTOBELLO BARLEY	83
154.	WILD RICE WITH MIXED VEGETABLES	84
155.	SAFFRON RICE	84
156.	BULGUR WITH BROCCOLI AND CARROT	85
157.	RED BEANS AND RICE	85
158.	SPINACH RICE	85
159.	BROWN RICE AND VEGETABLES	86
160.	CURRIED RICE	86
161.	CHIPOTLE BLACK BEAN SALAD	87
162.	MEDITERRANEAN CHICKPEAS	87
163.	CURRIED LENTILS	88
164.	BOURBON BAKED BEANS	88
165.	ITALIAN CHICKPEAS	89
166.	SWEET AND SPICY CHICKPEAS	89
167.	MEDITERRANEAN CHICKPEAS AND BROWN RICE	90
168.	RICE PILAF	90
169.	WILD RICE AND MUSHROOM CASSEROLE	91
170.	RICE WITH CHICKEN AND ASPARAGUS	91
171.	CILANTRO-LIME CHICKEN AND RICE	92
172.	INDIAN SPICED BROWN RICE WITH GROUND LAMB	92
173.	BARLEY AND CHICKPEA RISOTTO	93
174.	COCONUT QUINOA CURRY	93
175.	SWEET AND SOUR BEANS	94
176.	NAVY BEAN SOUP WITH HAM	94
177.	COCONUT RED BEANS AND RICE	95
178.	RANCH STYLE PINTO BEANS	95
179.	GARLIC VEGGIE LENTILS	95
180.	VEGETARIAN CALICO BEANS	96
CHAPTER 5. SIDE DISHES		**97**
181.	SUMMER SQUASH MIX	98
182.	HOT ZUCCHINI MIX	98
183.	CREAMY BUTTER PARSNIPS	98
184.	BUTTERNUT SQUASH AND EGGPLANT MIX	99
185.	CLASSIC VEGGIES MIX	99
186.	SPINACH AND SQUASH SIDE SALAD	100
187.	CHEDDAR POTATOES MIX	100
188.	OKRA AND CORN	101
189.	ROASTED BEETS	101
190.	CAULIFLOWER PILAF	102
191.	MARJORAM RICE MIX	102
192.	CINNAMON SQUASH	102
193.	BROCCOLI FILLING	103
194.	THYME BEETS	103
195.	KALE AND HAM MIX	103
196.	BALSAMIC CAULIFLOWER	104
197.	BLACK BEANS MIX	104

198. BUTTER GREEN BEANS	105	
199. CORN SAUTÉ	105	
200. SAGE PEAS	105	
201. TOMATO AND CORN	106	
202. DILL MUSHROOM SAUTÉ	106	
203. CARROTS AND SPINACH MIX	107	
204. COCONUT POTATOES	107	
205. SAGE SWEET POTATOES	108	
206. CAULIFLOWER AND ALMONDS	108	
207. ROSEMARY LEEKS	108	
208. SPICY BRUSSELS SPROUTS	109	
209. POTATOES AND LEEKS MIX	109	
210. ORANGE CARROTS MIX	109	
211. BAKED APPLES	110	
212. BAKED POTATOES	110	
213. PUMPKIN PUREE	111	
214. GARLIC PARSLEY POTATOES	111	
215. CRANBERRY-ORANGE CHUTNEY	112	
216. CREAMY CORN	112	
217. SWEET POTATOES WITH MARSHMALLOWS	113	
218. GREEN BEANS AND BACON	113	
219. CHUNKY APPLESAUCE	114	
220. PARMESAN GARLIC POTATOES	114	
221. COCONUT-PECAN SWEET POTATOES	115	
222. SUGAR CARROTS WITH GINGER	115	
223. SWEET ACORN SQUASH	116	
224. SWEET POTATOES WITH ORANGE	116	
225. VEGGIE AND GARBANZO MIX	116	
226. MUSHROOMS AND SAUSAGE MIX	117	
227. GLAZED BABY CARROTS	117	
228. BUTTERY MUSHROOMS	118	
229. CAULIFLOWER RICE AND SPINACH	118	
230. MAPLE SWEET POTATOES	119	
231. SWEET POTATO MASH	119	
232. DILL CAULIFLOWER MASH	120	
233. EGGPLANT AND KALE MIX	120	
234. THAI SIDE SALAD	120	
235. MINT FARRO PILAF	121	
236. PARMESAN RICE	121	
237. LEMON ARTICHOKES	122	
238. ITALIAN EGGPLANT	122	
239. CABBAGE AND ONION MIX	122	
240. BALSAMIC OKRA MIX	123	

CHAPTER 6. POULTRY — **124**

241. CHICKEN CURRY	125	
242. STUFFED CHICKEN BREASTS	125	
243. CHICKEN HEARTS	126	
244. HONEY CHICKEN DRUMSTICKS	126	
245. ROSEMARY LEMON CHICKEN	127	
246. ROTISSERIE CHICKEN	127	
247. SALSA CHICKEN	128	
248. TURMERIC CHICKEN	128	
249. MARINARA CHICKEN	129	
250. CHOCOLATE CHICKEN	129	
251. COCONUT CURRIED CHICKEN	130	
252. BUFFALO CHICKEN	130	
253. TERIYAKI CHICKEN	130	
254. PULLED BBQ CHICKEN	131	
255. LEMON THYME CHICKEN	131	
256. CHICKEN AND GRAVY	132	
257. CILANTRO LIME CHICKEN	132	
258. GARLIC CHICKEN	133	
259. CARIBBEAN JERK CHICKEN	133	
260. BALSAMIC CHICKEN	134	
261. CAESAR CHICKEN	134	
262. CHEESY CHEDDAR CHICKEN	135	
263. LEMON BUTTER CHICKEN	135	
264. TAHINI CHICKEN	135	
265. SHREDDED MEXICAN CHICKEN	136	
266. PARMESAN CHICKEN DRUMSTICKS	136	
267. MEDITERRANEAN CHICKEN	137	
268. LEMON GARLIC CHICKEN	137	
269. SWEET & SMOKY PULLED CHICKEN	138	

270. MEXICAN CHICKEN FAJITA SOUP	138	304. MEATBALLS & GREEN BEANS	156
271. CREAMY TUSCAN GARLIC CHICKEN	139	305. BEEF IN BALSAMIC VINEGAR	157
272. CHICKEN STEW	139	306. MEDITERRANEAN PORK TENDERLOIN	157
273. CURRIED CHICKEN TACOS	140	307. MEDITERRANEAN PORK ROAST	158
274. RANCH CHICKEN	140	308. PORK CHOPS & COUSCOUS	158
275. CHICKEN AND SAUSAGE	141	309. CREAMY PORK CHOPS WITH POTATOES	159
276. CRACK CHICKEN	141	310. MEDITERRANEAN PORK CHOPS	159
277. CHEESY ADOBO CHICKEN	142	311. GREEK SHREDDED BEEF	160
278. GREEN BEANS & CHICKEN THIGHS	142	312. PORK WITH SWEET POTATOES & MUSHROOMS	160
279. PIZZA CHICKEN	143	313. MOROCCAN LAMB	161
280. CHICKEN WITH BACON GRAVY	143	314. MEDITERRANEAN LAMB CHOPS	161
281. CHICKEN LO MEIN	144	315. GREEK LEG OF LAMB	162
282. CHICKEN BACON CHOWDER	144	316. BEEF TENDERLOIN WITH ROSEMARY	162
283. SESAME GINGER CHICKEN	145	317. BRAISED ROUND STEAK WITH ROSEMARY	163
284. COCO LOCO CHICKEN CURRY	145	318. BRAISED BEEF TENDERLOIN WITH BROCCOLI AND SESAME	163
285. RANCH CHICKEN WITH BROCCOLI	146	319. OLD RANCH PORK CHOPS	164
286. GARLIC PARMESAN CHICKEN WINGS	146	320. LAMB SHANKS WITH CELERY ROOT	164
287. LUAU CHICKEN	147	321. BACON OMELET	165
288. SOUTHWEST CHICKEN	147	322. GREEK BEEF STEW WITH PAPRIKA	165
289. CAROLINA-STYLE VINEGAR CHICKEN	148	323. CREAMY LAMB LEGS	166
290. CHICKEN CACCIATORE WITH ZOODLES	148	324. GRILLED AROMATIC BEEF-PORK PATTIES	166
291. BOK CHOY CHICKEN	149	325. MARINATED CURRY-SPICED GOAT	167
292. CHICKEN TIKKA MASALA	149	326. MUSTARD OLIVES WITH PORK LOIN	167
293. CHILI LIME CHICKEN WINGS	150	327. PORK FILLETS WITH MUSTARD-MUSHROOMS SAUCE	168
294. GARLIC CHICKEN & MUSHROOM CHOWDER	150	328. PORK TENDERLOIN WITH CREAMY MUSHROOMS SAUCE	168
295. SAUCY DUCK	151	329. SIRLOIN STEAK WITH BROCCOLI	169
296. CHICKEN ROUX GUMBO	151	330. SUCCULENT LAMB	169
297. CIDER-BRAISED CHICKEN	152	331. LAMB WITH MINT AND GREEN BEANS	170
298. CHUNKY CHICKEN SALSA	152	332 BRAISED LAMB STEW	170
299. DIJON CHICKEN	153	333. KERALA LAMB STEW	171
300. CHICKEN DIPPED IN TOMATILLO SAUCE	153	334. FALL-OFF-THE-BONE LAMB SHANKS	171
CHAPTER 7. MEAT	**154**	335. LAMB CHOPS	171
301. MEDITERRANEAN BEEF BRISKET	155	336. GARLIC LAMB ROAST	172
302. SPANISH BEEF	155		
303. BEEF WITH ARTICHOKES & OLIVES	156		

#	Recipe	Page
337.	LAMB SHANKS WITH TOMATOES	172
338.	LAMB CURRY	172
339.	LAMB STROGANOFF	173
340.	GROUND LAMB CASSEROLE	173
341.	LAMB HOTPOT	173
342.	BALSAMIC BEEF POT ROAST	174
343.	BEEF BOURGUIGNON WITH CARROT NOODLES	174
344.	BEEF & BROCCOLI	175
345.	BEEF CURRY	175
346.	BEEF DIJON	176
347.	BEEF RIBS	176
348.	BEEF STROGANOFF	177
349.	CABBAGE & CORNED BEEF	177
350.	CHIPOTLE BARBACOA – MEXICAN BARBECUE	178
351.	CORNED BEEF CABBAGE ROLLS	178
352.	CUBE STEAK	179
353.	ITALIAN MEATBALLS & ZOODLES	179
354.	LONDON BROIL	180
355.	MACHACA - MEXICAN POT ROAST	180
356.	CRANBERRY PORK ROAST	181
357.	PULLED PORK	181
358.	BALSAMIC PORK TENDERLOIN	182
359.	HONEY MUSTARD BARBECUE PORK RIBS	182
360.	PORK CHOPS WITH BROCCOLI	183
CHAPTER 8. FISH AND SEAFOOD		**184**
361.	POACHED SALMON	185
362.	APRICOT SALSA SALMON	185
363.	ORANGE FISH FILLETS	186
364.	FISH WITH TOMATOES	186
365.	SHRIMP SCAMPI	187
366.	CLAM CHOWDER	187
367.	LEMON PEPPER TILAPIA WITH ASPARAGUS	188
368.	PESTO SALMON WITH VEGETABLES	188
369.	MUSTARD GARLIC SHRIMPS	189
370.	MUSTARD CRUSTED SALMON	189
371.	FIVE-SPICE TILAPIA	190
372.	PROSCIUTTO-WRAPPED SCALLOPS	190
373.	SHRIMPS AND SAUSAGE JAMBALAYA STEW	191
374.	SPICY BASIL SHRIMP	191
375.	SCALLOPS WITH SOUR CREAM AND DILL	192
376.	SALMON WITH LIME BUTTER	192
377.	SPICY CURRIED SHRIMPS	192
378.	SMOKED TROUT	193
379.	SALMON WITH GREEN PEPPERCORN SAUCE	193
380.	COCONUT CURRY COD	193
381.	ALMOND CRUSTED TILAPIA	194
382.	BUTTERED BACON AND SCALLOPS	194
383.	LEMONY SHRIMPS IN HOISIN SAUCE	194
384.	GARLIC BUTTER TILAPIA	195
385.	BUTTERY SALMON WITH ONIONS AND CARROTS	195
386.	CALLOPED POTATOES WITH SALMON	196
387.	LEMON-HERB SALMON	196
388.	ORANGE VINEGAR SALMON	197
389.	COD STEW	197
390.	FISH AND BEANS	198
391.	ASIAN VEGETABLES WITH A SALMON BLANKET	198
392.	SEAFOOD CHOWDER	199
393.	SHRIMP FRA DIAVOLO	199
394.	WHITE BEANS WITH TUNA	200
395.	COCONUT CLAMS	200
396.	SEAFOOD GUMBO	201
397.	JALAPEÑO SPICY TUNA	201
398.	SEASONED LARGE SHRIMP	202
399.	MUSHROOMS SNAPPER	202
400.	ORANGE COD	203
401.	COD WITH SHRIMP SAUCE	203
402.	BAKED COD	204
403.	COD STICKS	204
404.	HOT SALMON AND CARROTS	205

405. CHILI-RUBBED TILAPIA	205
406. FISH MIX	206
407. CHILI BIGEYE JACK (TUNA)	206
408. COD AND BROCCOLI	207
409. THYME MUSSELS	207
410. SEABASS BALLS	208
411. ASIAN SHRIMPS	208
412. MASHED POTATO FISH CASSEROLE	208
413. CHILI CATFISH	209
414. ONION COD FILLETS	209
415. TILAPIA IN CREAM SAUCE	209
416. HADDOCK CHOWDER	210
417. NUTMEG TROUT	210
418. CLAMS IN COCONUT SAUCE	210
419. SWEET MILKFISH SAUTÉ	211
420. CINNAMON CATFISH	211

CHAPTER 9. VEGETABLES AND VEGETARIAN — 212

421. CAULIFLOWER MASH	213
422. MASHED POTATOES	213
423. MEAT-FREE MUSHROOM STROGANOFF	214
424. VEGGIES RATATOUILLE	214
425. COLORFUL VEGGIE COMBO	215
426. FRIDAY DINNER VEGGIE MEAL	215
427. SPICY CHICKPEAS	216
428. MEATLESS DINNER MEAL	216
429. ITALIAN VEGGIE DINNER CASSEROLE	217
430. FAMILIAR MEDITERRANEAN DISH	217
431. ARTICHOKE PASTA	218
432. VEGGIE LASAGNA	218
433. HOMEMADE HUMMUS	219
434. BARBECUE KABOCHA SQUASH	219
435. BRAISED QUINOA, KALE & SUMMER SQUASH	220
436. ROSEMARY CAULIFLOWER & LENTILS	220
437. MIXED BEAN CHILI	221
438. CURRIED SWEET POTATOES WITH BROCCOLI & CASHEWS	221
439. MOROCCAN-STYLE CHICKPEAS WITH CHARD	222
440. SPINACH & BLACK BEAN ENCHILADA PIE	222
441. SPINACH, MUSHROOM & SWISS CHEESE CRUSTLESS QUICHE	223
442. SEITAN TIKKA MASALA	223
443. BUTTER SEITAN & CHICKPEAS	224
444. TEMPEH SHEPHERD'S PIE	224
445. TEMPEH-STUFFED BELL PEPPERS	225
446. TOFU RED CURRY WITH GREEN BEANS	225
447. TOFU STIR-FRY	226
448. SPICY PEANUT RICE BAKE	226
449. SQUASH AND ZUCCHINI CASSEROLE	227
450. ALMOND GREEN BEANS	227
451. RANCH MUSHROOMS	228
452. ARTICHOKE SPINACH DIP	228
453. TOMATO DIP	229
454. ITALIAN MUSHROOMS	229
455. GARLIC CHEESE SPINACH	229
456. DILL CARROTS	230
457. ROSEMARY GREEN BEANS	230
458. VEGETABLE FAJITAS	230
459. ROASTED BROCCOLI	231
460. TOMATOES, GARLIC AND OKRA	231
461. CAULIFLOWER RICE	232
462. SQUASH NOODLES	232
463. THYME TOMATOES	233
464. QUINOA DOLMA	233
465. CREAMY PUREE	234
467. CHEESY CORN	234
468. SHREDDED CABBAGE SAUTÉ	235
469. RANCH BROCCOLI	235
470. CHEDDAR MUSHROOMS	235
471. PAPRIKA BABY CARROT	236
472. BUTTER ASPARAGUS	236
473. JALAPENO CORN	236
474. MASHED TURNIPS	237

475. CRANBERRY, APPLE, AND SQUASH DISH	237
476. VEGETARIAN CURRY WITH INDIAN SPICES	238
477. PARSNIP, TURNIP, AND CARROT TAGINE	238
478. SPINACH AND PUMPKIN CHILI	239
479. VEGGIE-FRIENDLY BUFFALO DIP	239
480. SPLIT BLACK LENTILS WITH CURRY	240

CHAPTER 10. BEVERAGES — 241

481. MULLED WINE	242
482. CRANBERRY SPICED TEA	242
483. ROSEMARY MULLED CIDER	243
66. GARLIC AND TOMATO APPETIZER	243
484. GINGERBREAD HOT CHOCOLATE	244
485. GINGERBREAD MOCHA DRINK	244
486. SALTED CARAMEL MILK STEAMER	245
487. APPLE CHAI TEA	245
488. GINGER PUMPKIN LATTE	246
489. HOT CARAMEL APPLE DRINK	246
490. SPICED WHITE CHOCOLATE	247
491. APPLE BOURBON PUNCH	247
492. MAPLE BOURBON MULLED CIDER	247
493. AUTUMN PUNCH	248
494. HOT SPICY APPLE CIDER	248
495. VANILLA LATTE	248

CHAPTER 11. SOUPS STEWS AND CHILIES — 249

496. CHICKEN AND RICE STEW	250
497. CHICKEN AND TORTILLA SOUP	250
498. STUFFED PEPPER SOUP	251
499. HAM AND PEA SOUP	251
500. VEGETABLE STEW	252
501. PEA SOUP	252
502. SOUP FOR THE DAY	253
503. PORK AND FENNEL STEW	253
504. VEGETABLE GARBANZO STEW	254
505. CATALAN STEW	254
506. PORK STEW CARIBBEAN STYLE	255

507. KALE VERDE	255
508. ESCAROLE WITH BEAN SOUP	256
509. ITALIAN BEEF BARLEY SOUP	256
510. CREAMY POTATO SOUP	257
511. SPLIT PEA SOUP WITH BACON & HASH BROWNS	257
512. SOUTHWEST BLACK BEAN CHICKEN SOUP	258
513. ZUCCHINI SOUP	258
514. GERMAN LENTIL SOUP	259
515. CHICKEN AND DUMPLINGS	259
516. CHICKEN TACO SOUP	260
517. LENTIL AND HAM SOUP	260
518. CABBAGE BEEF SOUP	261
519. SPLIT PEA SAUSAGE SOUP	261
520. BEEF VEGETABLE SOUP	262
521. SPICY BLACK BEAN SOUP	262
522. BEST ITALIAN SAUSAGE SOUP	263
523. HAM BONE SOUP	263
524. BRUSSELS SPROUTS SOUP	263
525. CLASSIC RAGOUT SOUP	264
526. GORGONZOLA BROCCOLI SOUP	264
527. MOROCCAN CHICKPEA SOUP	265
528. PUMPKIN SOUP	265
529. SPRING SPINACH SOUP	266
530. THE SULTAN'S SOUP	266
531. BACON CHILI	267
532. STEAK LOVER'S CHILI	267
533. BUFFALO CHICKEN CHILI	268
534. NO BEAN CHILI	268
535. KICKIN' CHILI	269
536. CREAMY WHITE CHICKEN CHILI	269
537. OLD-FASHIONED LOW-CARB CHILI	270
538. SECRET CHOCOLATE CHILI	270
539. NOT YOUR CAVEMAN'S CHILI	271
540. 5-INGREDIENT CHILI	271

CHAPTER 12. SWEETS AND DESSERTS — 272

- 541. BLUEBERRY LEMON CUSTARD CAKE — 273
- 544. PUMPKIN PECAN SPICE CAKE — 274
- 545. GLAZED WALNUTS — 275
- 546. KETO GRANOLA — 275
- 547. MAPLE CUSTARD — 276
- 548. RASPBERRY CREAM CHEESE COFFEE CAKE — 276
- 549. PUMPKIN PIE BARS — 277
- 550. LEMON CUSTARD — 277
- 551. APPLE BROWN — 278
- 552. BAKED CUSTARD — 278
- 553. CARAMEL RUM FONDUE — 279
- 554. TRIPLE CHOCOLATE MESS — 279
- 555. RICE PUDDING — 280
- 556. CARAMEL PIE — 280
- 557. BERRY COBBLER — 281
- 558. MINTY HOT FUDGE SUNDAE CAKE — 281
- 559. CRANBERRY STUFFED APPLES — 282
- 560. MOLTEN MOCHA CAKE — 282
- 561. PUMPKIN PIE PUDDING — 283
- 562. NUTTY APPLE STREUSEL — 283
- 563. PRUNE DESSERT — 284
- 564. PEACH BUTTER — 284
- 565. FRUIT COBBLER — 285
- 566. CHERRY ALMOND DESSERT OATMEAL — 285
- 567. MOLTEN LAVA CAKE — 286
- 568. MAPLE CRÉME BRÛLÉE — 286
- 569. LEMON PUDDING CAKE — 287
- 570. CHAI-SPICED PEARS — 287
- 571. CRANBERRY WALNUT BREAD PUDDING — 288
- 572. ALMOND BANANA BREAD — 288
- 573. MAPLE ROASTED PEAR CRUMBLE — 289
- 574. SUGARY MANDARIN & ALMOND PUDDING — 289
- 575. SUGARY PLUMS — 290
- 576. CARDAMOM PLUM CREAM — 290
- 577. VANILLA RHUBARB MIX — 290
- 578. PEACHES AND WHISKEY SAUCE — 291
- 579. COCONUT CHOCOLATE CREAM — 291
- 580. MAPLE CHERRY & COCOA COMPOTE — 292
- 581. DATES CASHEW CAKE — 292
- 581. DATES CASHEW CAKE — 293
- 582. NUTMEG APPLES — 293
- 583. APPLE VANILLA CAKE — 294
- 584. PEACH CRACKERS COBBLER — 294
- 585. MILKY BLUEBERRY & ALMOND CAKE — 295
- 586. PEARS & ORANGE SAUCE — 295
- 587. SUGARY ALMOND COOKIES — 296
- 588. ZESTY STRAWBERRIES MARMALADE — 296
- 589. CHERRY COLA CAKE — 297
- 590. AMARETTI CHEESECAKE — 297
- 591. APPLE CINNAMON BRIOCHE PUDDING — 298
- 592. BANANA WALNUT CAKE — 298
- 593. BLACK FOREST CAKE — 299
- 594. BLUEBERRY DUMPLING PIE — 299
- 595. BROWNED BUTTER PUMPKIN CHEESECAKE — 300
- 596. BUTTER LIME CAKE — 300
- 597. BUTTERSCOTCH CAKE — 301
- 598. CARAMEL APPLE CRISP — 301
- 599. CARAMEL PEAR PUDDING CAKE — 302
- 600. COCONUT CONDENSED MILK CUSTARD — 302

CONCLUSION — 304

CPSIA information can be obtained
at www.ICGtesting.com
Printed in the USA
BVHW011041130121
597717BV00008B/213